# THE 388 TATTOOS OF CAPTAIN GEORGE

## AND THE 389 TALES OF HOW HE GOT THEM

Cover Image: Folies Bergère poster, 1874 (Bibliothèque Nationale de France, Department of Prints and Photography)

Cover Background Image and Endpapers (Ingram edition): Detail of drawing of George Costentenus's tattoos, from *Atlas der Hautkrankheiten*, 1872. (Image provided courtesy of the University of Illinois Chicago Library, Special Collections and University Archives)

Back Cover Image: Color image of Costentenus's torso from *Atlas der Hautkrankheiten*, 1872. (Image provided courtesy of the University of Illinois Chicago Library, Special Collections and University Archives)

ISBN: 978-1-958604-32-8 (print) 978-1-958604-33-5 (ebook)
Library of Congress: 2025922079

By Amelia Klem Osterud with Fritz Grobe
Edited by Thom Wall
Cover by Fritz Grobe
Illustrations by Thayer Slichter
Cover Typography by Jon Bartels

Modern Vaudeville Press
113 E Mayland St
Philadelphia, PA 19144
United States of America

www.ModernVaudevillePress.com

Ordering Information: Quantity sales. Special discounts are available on quantity purchases by corporations, associations, and others. For details, contact the "Special Sales Department" at the address above.

# THE 388 TATTOOS
# OF CAPTAIN GEORGE

## AND THE 389 TALES
## OF HOW HE GOT THEM

*Being the Allegedly True Story of the World's Most Famous Tattooed Man*
*As Researched and Told by Amelia Klem Osterud with Fritz Grobe*

Modern Vaudeville Press
Philadelphia, PA USA

I can only say that truth is frequently much stranger than fiction.

*— The Life and Adventures of Captain Costentenus*, 1881[1]


It is always the best policy to speak the truth—
unless, of course, you are an exceptionally good liar.

*— Jerome K. Jerome, The Idler*, 1892[2]

1 *The True Life and Adventures of Capt. Costentenus, The Tattooed Greek Prince,* (New York Popular Publishing Co, 1881), 3.

2 Jerome K. Jerome, "The Idler's Club," *Idler*, February 1892, 118.

# CONTENTS

## CHAPTER ONE

# CAPTAIN GEORGE

### The *Suevia*, 1876

On May 10, 1876, the steamship *Suevia* left Hamburg, Germany for its regularly-scheduled voyage to New York. At 360 feet long and 41 feet wide, with four decks, she was one of Germany's largest passenger vessels—and one of the newest of the Hamburg America Line.[3] Six hundred third-class passengers were packed into small cabins below decks, but for the 170 passengers able to afford a first- or second-class cabin, the *Suevia* was a comfortable floating hotel.

Up in one of the second-class cabins was a man traveling under the name Georg Constantinos, described on the ship's manifest as a 46-year-old merchant from Vienna. This was not his first ocean voyage, but it was one of the most important of his life.

On the 15-day voyage across the Atlantic, it is most likely that Constantinos kept to his stateroom as much as he could. He was a

3 "Germany's Largest Steamship," *New York Tribune*, November 20, 1874.

distinctive man who often attracted unwanted attention. At five feet, nine inches tall and often described as well-fed, he was tall and stout in a time when poor nutrition kept many people short and lean. He had a thick, bushy beard, and his long, dark hair was often braided and wound around the top of his head. But his hair and beard didn't quite hide the fact that his face was covered in blue and red tattoos. His cheeks, his forehead, and even his scalp had been inked with elaborate designs.

And it wasn't just that. Constantinos was covered from head to foot in tattoos. A reporter once described his skin as looking like a velvety fabric stretched tight around his body.[4] Almost every inch was spectacularly covered in exotic animals and mysterious symbols.

Over the years, he had been known by many names: Georg Konstaninos, Djorji Costentenus, Yolos Constantinos, and more. Although he could neither read nor write, he spoke at least five languages. And he told so many tales about himself—including the origin of his tattoos—that the truth has been hard to find.

He said he was a Greek patriot who had fought against his Ottoman oppressors. He claimed he had been a pirate in the Mediterranean. He told of traveling across Asia as a bodyguard and being cruelly tortured by an Eastern despot. In his 1881 "autobiographical" pamphlet, *The Life and Adventures of Captain Costentenus*, he spun stories of hiding in an Egyptian harem disguised as a girl, being sold into slavery in Persia, and making daring escapes from mortal danger with mysterious and beautiful women.

Which of these were true and which were just good stories?

Before traveling to America, Constantinos had already caused a minor sensation in Europe. Over the past five years, he'd appeared before mid-sized crowds throughout the continent, from medical theaters in Vienna filled with fascinated university students to street festivals as far east as Ukraine. Now, he was trying something new.

It had been over a generation since the last well-known

---

4 "Local Matters," *Bangor Daily Whig & Courier*, July 25, 1876.

tattooed men had performed in Europe and America, and memories of these men had faded like old tattoos. This newcomer was not only about to step into the vacancy, he was going to surpass their successes. His predecessors—men such as Joseph Kabris (a Frenchman tattooed on the Pacific island of Nuku Hiva) and James O'Connell (the tattooed Irish jig dancer)—could never have dreamed of such international fame within their lifetimes.

The *Suevia* was bringing Constantinos to the United States to join famed showman Phineas Taylor Barnum's *Greatest Show on Earth*. In a few short months, he would be known around the world as "Captain George Costentenus, the Tattooed Greek." He would go on to cross paths with many of the most important and interesting figures in the golden age of American circus: wirewalker and promoter William Hunt a.k.a. the Great Farini; clown and presidential candidate Dan Rice; Zazel, the original "human cannonball"; and circus innovators William Coup and Dan Castello—to name a few. With the backing of Barnum's publicity machine and the seemingly inexhaustible American appetite for the unusual, this tattooed man was on his way to becoming one of the most famous performers in American circus history.

●

I've been chasing the ghost of Captain George Costentenus for years now.

In 2012, I met my friend Anna at the University of Chicago's Library of the Health Sciences' Special Collections and Archives Department. I've been fascinated by tattoos for as long as I can remember, and Anna was excited to show me a rare book that had images of a tattooed man in it. I gamely went, not really knowing what to expect, and honestly, not that excited. That was about to change.

The book was the 1872 *Atlas der Hautkrankheiten* (Atlas of Skin Diseases), written by Dr. Ferdinand Hebra. Hebra was the founder of the Vienna School of Dermatology, and the *Atlas* was one of the most influential books in the development of modern dermatology. At 23 inches tall and 19 inches wide, it was enormous. The library staff brought the combined Volumes 7 and 8 to our table and Anna and I slowly flipped through the pages together. It was fascinating and unsettling.

*Images of Costentenus in* Atlas der Hautkrankheiten, *1872*
*(National Library of Medicine)*

The paper was stiff and crumbling at the edges, filled with beautifully rendered color drawings of some really horrible-looking skin conditions. There were lots of nasty and uncomfortable facial warts, hands covered with lesions, and a woman with a blue face—conditions that you really hope there's a cure for now. Surprisingly, among these images of skin diseases were illustrations of several people who did not fit: a pair of white-haired children with albinism, a young boy with so much hair it completely covered his face—and "Georg Constantin," covered in blue and red tattoos.

The image is spectacular—and much nicer to look at than the facial warts. His large brown eyes seem bright and intelligent. Blue cats surrounded by red blobs face off across his forehead, dozens of blue dots creep out from his beard, and the skin under his eyes has stars on it. Only his nipples, ears, lips, and lightly freckled nose are not tattooed. Everything else is decorated. I was instantly taken with him.

This was not the first time I'd come across the Captain. I'd previously encountered him in a few tattoo history books while doing research for my book *The Tattooed Lady: A History*.[5] I found him again at Harvard's Houghton Library in 2014, though I was less impressed. They brought me several boxes of cardboard-mounted photos of late 19th century circus and sideshow performers—and a set of white cotton gloves to wear while I sorted through them. There were a few faded photographs of the Captain, looking grumpy and not particularly approachable. Compared to many of the photos of tattooed women and men from a decade or two later, his images are not very impressive. They make him look more like someone with a weird rash than a tattooed man. Whether the photos never really showed the tattoos clearly or if the details have faded over time, I don't know.

It was the striking images in *Atlas der Hautkrankheiten* that stuck with me. In 20 years of research on tattooing, I've looked at a lot of historical portraits of tattooed people. Costentenus's tattoos are in a league of their own. In the West, only eight tattooed people were exhibited (or exhibited themselves) before Captain George. All eight had traditional Inuit or Pacific Islander tattoos with geometric designs—all quite different from Captain George's.

The first two were Inuit women with facial tattoos who were kidnapped in the 1500s. The first, whose name is unknown, was kidnapped by French whalers with her young daughter in 1566

---

5 Amelia Klem Osterud, *The Tattooed Lady: A History*, (Speck Press, 2009.)

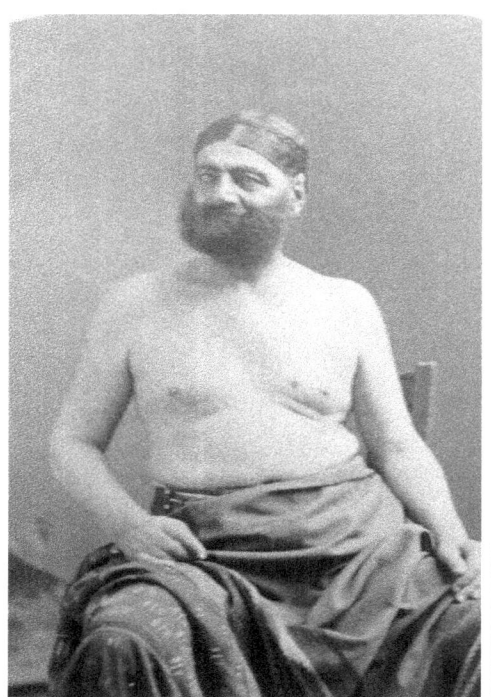
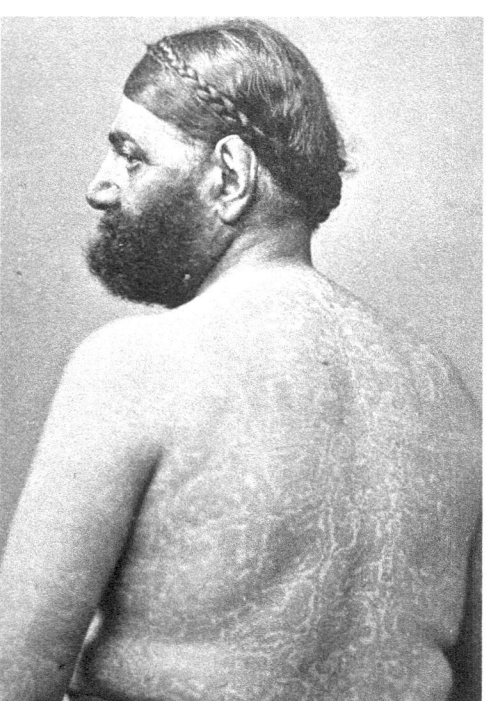

*Photographs of Costentenus, front (1876) and back (undated) (TCS 7. Harvard Theatre Collection, Houghton Library, Harvard University, and courtesy of Nick Vaccaro's collection of American Circus Photography)*

and exhibited in Antwerp for eight months. Their subsequent fate is unknown. The second, a woman known as "Ignorth" (most likely a corruption of the Inuit word arnaq, meaning woman), was kidnapped by British explorer Martin Frobisher in 1577. "Ignorth" was "painted about the eyes and balls of the cheek with a blue colour like the ancient Britains [sic]."[6] Frobisher forced her to England to exhibit her with her infant son and another, unrelated Inuit man. All three died shortly after their arrival.

In the late 1600s, a man from the Pacific Islands named Jeoly was sold in slavery in the Philippines to a British naturalist and pirate named William Dampier.[7] Jeoly had Micronesian geometric patterns

6 Neil Cheshire, et al, "Frobisher's Eskimos in England," *Archivaria* 10 (1980): 29.

7 Diana and Michael Preston, *A Pirate of Exquisite Mind: Explorer, Naturalist, and Buccaneer, The Life of William Dampier,* (Walker and Co.,2004): 204; Lars Krutak, "Myth Busting Tattoo (Art) History," Lars Krutak: Tattoo Anthropologist, August 22, 2013 https://www.larskrutak.com/myth-busting-tattoo-art-history/.

tattooed on his torso, arms, and legs. He was sold once again, renamed "Prince Giolo," and exhibited as "a wonder of the age."[8] A piece of his tattooed skin was preserved and stored at the Anatomy School collections at Oxford University. By the early 20th century, it had been lost.

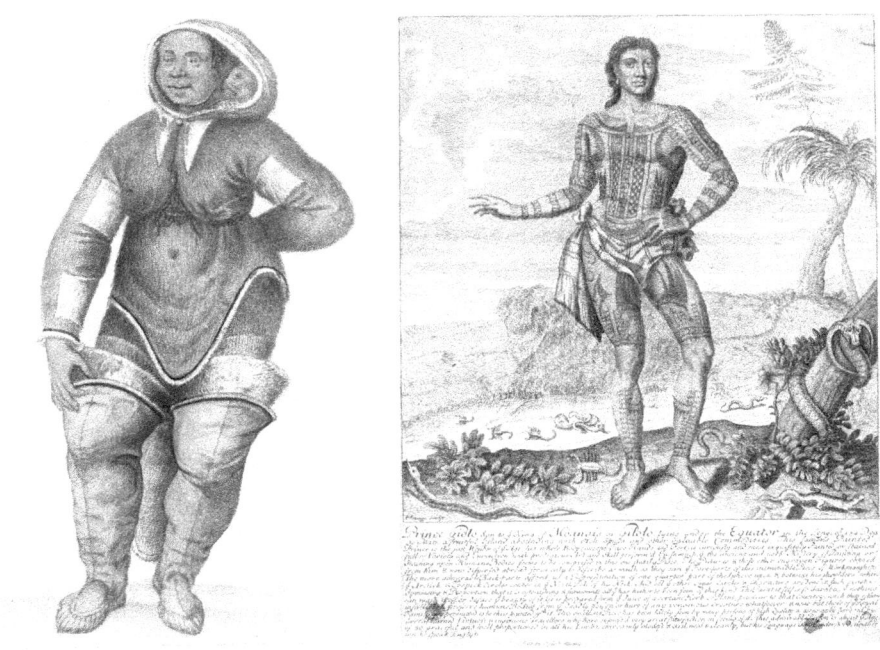

*Portraits of "Ignorth" (left) and Jeoly (right)*
*(© The Trustees of the British Museum and Mitchell Library, State Library of NSW)*

About a hundred years after Jeoly, a man from the Pacific island of Ra'iatea named Mai (sometimes called Omai) was brought to England by Captain James Cook. (Cook's first voyage to the South Seas had brought back the word "tattoo" from the Polynesian language.) The surviving portraits of Mai show only thin lines and dots on the backs of his hands. But his Tahitian tattoos likely included curved lines covering his buttocks and small designs on the inside of each arm. Mai somehow had more control of his own life than his predecessors and returned home after two years in England.

---

8 Preston, *A Pirate of Exquisite Mind*, 218.

*Portraits of Joseph Kabris (top left) and John Rutherford (top right) and Barnet Burns (bottom left), (Images courtesy of Alexander Turnbull Library, Wellington, New Zealand)*

The final four tattooed performers who preceded Captain George were all Western men who had been tattooed in the South Pacific in the early 1800s. Frenchman Joseph Kabris had sparse Polynesian geometric patterns on his face and body. Englishmen John Rutherford and Barnet Burns had traditional Māori facial tattoos (and probably more on other parts of their bodies). And Irishman James O'Connell had Micronesian patterns on his arms, chest, and legs.

Most other tattooed Europeans of this time had typical Western imagery: ships, flags, military insignia, crudely drawn faces, and even cruder women. These designs were invariably scattered across the person's body with spaces in between, making the tattoos look as if they were dropped here and there haphazardly.

In the lithograph from Volume 8 of the *Atlas der Hautkrankheiten*, you can see immediately that Costentenus's tattoos were anything but typical for a 19th century Westerner—and unlike any of his exhibited predecessors. His were of a style practiced by the Shan people of southeastern Burma (now Myanmar). The Shan designs were tightly packed together on his skin. The lithograph shows blue elephants, birds, snakes, and cats, as well as unusual creatures that look as if they're straight out of fantasy. The animals are surrounded by red and blue scribbles, which I later learned were text. (The artist trying to depict the tattoos couldn't read the Burmese language and just did his best to represent the symbols.)

Sir James George Scott, a journalist and British administrator of the Shan States in Burma after Britain took control in 1886, published a book under the pseudonym Shway Yoe called *The Burman: His Life and Notions*. This book contains a chapter on Shan tattooing, describing how men were tattooed from the belly button to the knee.[9] While Costentenus's tattoos extended to cover his whole body, Scott's description of Shan designs matches up with what we can see of Costentenus's: "all kind of animals, tigers, cats, monkeys, and elephants being the commonest... Each representation is surrounded by a roughly oval tracery of a variety of letters of the alphabet, which form a curious and remarkably effective frame. Thus each animal has a setting of its own."[10]

The *Atlas der Hautkrankheiten* also includes an extraordinary diagram on the page opposite the vibrant color lithograph of Costentenus that meticulously labels the different animals and symbols on his face and chest. Many of the animals on his chest were identified with callout letters such as (h) for tigers, (i) for lions, and (k) for elephants. Numerous small star-shaped designs, (b), were noted

9. Andrew Dalby, "Sir George Scott, 1851-1935, Explorer of Burma's Eastern Borders, in *Explorers of South-East Asia: Six Lives*, Kuala Lumpur/New York: Oxford University Press, 1995, p. 108-157.

10. Yoe, Shway (Sir George Scott), *The Burman: His Life and Notions*, London: McMillan and Co., 1896, p. 40-41.

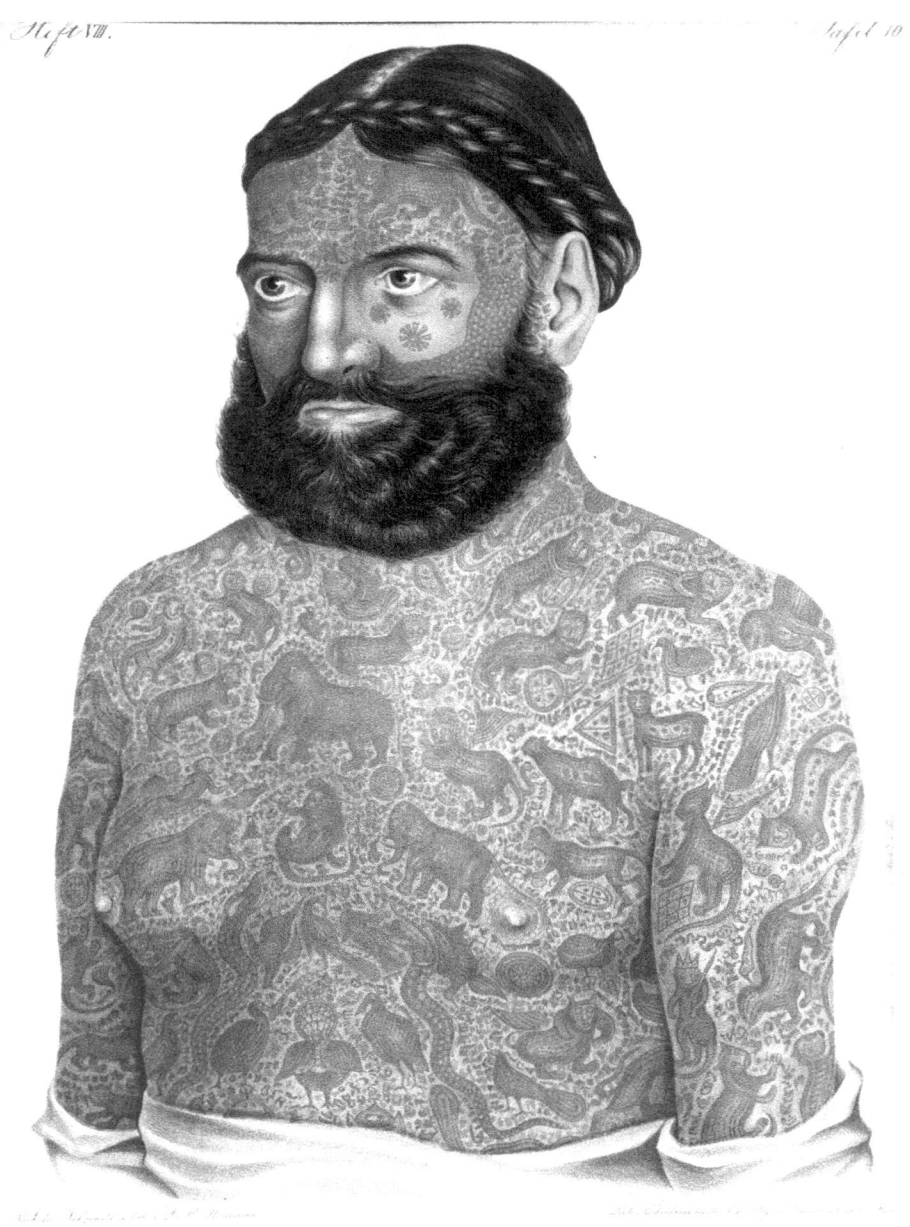

*Color image of Costentenus's torso from* Atlas der Hautkrankheiten, *1872, (Image provided courtesy of the University of Illinois Chicago Library, Special Collections and University Archives)*

*Line drawing of Costentenus's torso from* Atlas der Hautkrankheiten, *1872, (Image provided courtesy of the University of Illinois Chicago Library, Special Collections and University Archives)*

on his scalp as well as on his face. Oddly, his ear, (f), was labeled, even though it was not tattooed at all.[11]

When Anna and I returned the *Atlas* to the library staff, something had clicked. Seeing this guy and his spectacular body suit of tattoos, I wanted to get to know him. I wanted to ask him questions about his wild tattoos, about his travels, about what it was like to be under the scrutiny of a bunch of Austrian scientists who decided to put him in a book about skin diseases, of all things.

I've now spent the past several years getting to know Captain George Costentenus. Thanks to countless hours combing through archives and online databases, I have been able to document his extensive career in circus sideshows, dime museums, and other eclectic venues throughout the United States and Europe. It's been a fascinating challenge. Circus people were not the best of record keepers, and most employees worked for one show in one season and a different show the next. Performers may have worked for any number of dime museums in the off season, traveling from city to city depending on the week or month. And over the years, Captain George went by various names—with consistently inconsistent spellings. All this has made tracking his career a long and intensive process.

Even some of the most basic questions about his life have been hard to pin down. When was he born? I've found three different birth dates. Where was he born? He gave many different answers and I can find no definitive records. Was he really a captain—or did P. T. Barnum simply make that up? When and where did he die? Can we even find out?

He came from a part of the world that has had so much upheaval that even when there were records, many of them have been lost. But I love a good research challenge. Digging into old records, deciphering documents, figuring out what details are right and what details are wrong, trying to see when someone in the past made a mistake or when they were intentionally obscuring the truth—all of

---

11 Hebra, Ferdinand, "Ein tättowirter Mann: Homo Notis Compunctus," *Atlas der Hautkrankheiten, Lfg. 8. Albinismus, Leucoderma, Lentigo, Chloasma, Argyria, Naevus Verrucosus, Homo Notis Compunctus*, Kaiserl.-Königl. Hof- und Staatsdruckerei, Wien, 1872, p. 94.

that is fun for me. It's a complicated jumble of dates and places, and there is very little documentation to verify anything Costentenus said. We've got to sort through all his claims and try to decide what is true and what is humbug!

In *The Life and Adventures of Captain Costentenus*, he said that he was born in 1836 in Albania (which was then part of the vast Ottoman Empire), in a village that "no longer exists even in name, save for the mouldering ruins of a few cottages." But on his first U.S. passport application, he gave a birthdate of March 15, 1833, saying he was born in Athens. Later, he said he'd been born in Souli, Greece, as well as Souli, Albania (improbably on the Fourth of July). In earlier accounts, he was referred to as a Souliote, a group of Christians who lived in the mountains on the Greek/Albanian border. The Souliotes had an almost mythic reputation as fierce fighters during the Greek War of Independence against the Ottomans in the 1820s. Yet another article said that he was from a neighborhood of Constantinople called Tatavla. Nicknamed "Little Athens," Tatavla was home to at least 20,000 Ottoman Greeks.

One newspaper article claimed that Costentenus was not Greek at all. In 1877, the *Lowell Daily Citizen* in Massachusetts wrote that James Cooley Fletcher, a Presbyterian minister and missionary for the American Tract Society, had met Costentenus while traveling in Italy and that "the captain said that he had himself tattooed expressly for the show business. Mr. Fletcher says that the man is not a Greek, but an Italian."[12] This is probably humbug. It's remotely possible that Fletcher did meet the tattooed man in Italy in the 1870s, but the missionary was hardly a man with no agenda. Many ministers of the time saw the circus—and popular entertainment in general—as morally corrupt. Painting Costentenus as opportunistic and deceptive would fit with this view.

Costentenus did speak fluent Greek, and throughout his career, he reliably referred to himself as Greek, so I think we can take him at his word on that. And honestly, he might not have known his own birthdate. This was not uncommon at the time, especially among people who were illiterate. His last U.S. passport application in 1894

---

12 "Various Items," *Lowell Daily Citizen*, August 24, 1877.

was probably the most truthful, giving no specific birthdate, just the year 1833.

I have no idea what his childhood was like or where he spent it, since he never talked about it outside of some unlikely tales of adventure. There are a few clues we can follow. He spoke not only Greek but Arabic and Persian fluently, and he knew at least enough French, Spanish, Italian, German, and English to get by. But he was also illiterate, unable to sign his name with anything more than an X. So he must have traveled far and wide enough to acquire a variety of spoken languages, but his childhood was not fortunate enough to include learning to read and write. We can deduce that he originally came from a Greek community somewhere within the Ottoman Empire, and then his life became nomadic. He probably spent more time away from his Greek community than within it. He may have been raised as a servant or a slave—or spent his childhood trying to get by on the streets of Constantinople. He may have grown up working for another Souliote family in the mountains or spent it aboard a ship as a cabin boy, essentially raised by sailors. Here, all we can do is speculate.

While many details about Costentenus's origins will never be known, once he returned to Europe as a tattooed man, newspapers tracked his every move. I have gathered these reports to reconstruct his story.

The first definitive evidence puts him in Vienna in October of 1870.

•

## Vienna, 1870

He was most likely in his late 30s, freshly arrived from the East, and covered in tattoos. In Vienna, then the capital city of the Austro-Hungarian Empire, he would have had a chance of making it big. The bustling city was expanding rapidly, quickly transforming itself into a modern showpiece in preparation for the 1873 World's Fair. Perhaps Costentenus saw the upcoming fair as an opportunity to catapult himself into a successful career in show business. Certainly, the city was full of possibilities. His immediate tattooed predecessors in Europe—Kabris, Rutherford, and Burns—had set the model decades before. They had displayed themselves at small offices and halls, tried to obtain patronage (either from royalty or the scientific world), and invented adventure stories to further entertain their audiences.

So Costentenus started putting out the word that there was a new act in Vienna, available for hire. Most likely, he first appeared in smaller venues, and before long, he came to the attention of a group of medical men.

Medical communities across Europe were fascinated with "curiosities" (literally rare or novel people or things) in the second half of the 19th century. After Charles Darwin published *On the Origin of Species* in 1859, academics were practically falling over one another to explain and categorize the odd and the exotic. They invited people with unusual medical conditions out of the realm of traveling fairs and royal patronage and into more scientific settings. Physicians would invite performers like the "Aztec Children" (two individuals born with microcephaly, where the head is smaller than expected) and "Krao, the Ape Girl" (a very hairy young lady, most likely from Laos) to their surgical theaters or professional associations. To be clear, these were not respectful medical examinations, but rather exhibitions before select academic audiences. And they were every bit as problematic as they seem.

The audience members would ask probing questions while visually—and sometimes physically—examining the curiosities. This could be quite invasive and the subjects had little control of the limits of these inspections. The academics would publish their conclusions (often furthering racist ideas of Western superiority) in scholarly journals. Newspapers would reprint portions of these articles for the public. The performers could then use their "scientific" status in their advertising, making sure the public knew they were real. It was, in the end, beneficial for the performers' careers, and it helped the doctors make names for themselves.

This is exactly the path Costentenus followed to launch his career in Europe. On October 25, 1870, he met with members of Vienna's medical community. The audience included Dr. Ferdinand Hebra (author of the aforementioned *Atlas der Hautkrankheiten*, with its illustrations of Costentenus) and Dr. Moritz Kaposi (who is remembered for identifying the skin cancer that bears his name, Kaposi's sarcoma). They wondered how Costentenus had even survived the process of getting so many tattoos. Did he have an unusually high tolerance for pain? What were the effects on his body of so many needle punctures? Wild speculation began on just how many punctures had been involved—and how many gallons of blood he had lost.

Two days later, Kaposi brought the tattooed man to a special meeting of the Gesellschaft der Ärzte (the Society of Physicians) so they could examine him further. The group in the room that day included university faculty and students, as well as members of the Association of Artists and the Anthropological Society. The man they called Georg Constantin would not have been the first person with a tattoo who they had seen, as members of the working class throughout Europe had tattoos. But Costentenus had many more than anyone else they'd come across.

Kaposi described Costentenus as "beautifully and powerfully built" as he undressed and stood on a platform before the audience.[13] While it's not clear how they distinguished one tattoo from another, they somehow arrived at a total of 388 designs covering him from head to toe.

The doctors were surprised that his skin was "fine and smooth," and that his glands were not swollen.[14] Costentenus's palms, Kaposi and Hebra noted, were filled with line drawings that looked as if they were drawn with hard chalk pastels in red and blue. The joints of his fingers also had markings on them, as did his feet, toes, and penis (ouch). That, they noted, was marked with blue lines and stars. What was not tattooed? They listed only his ears, his nose, his lips,

13 Moritz Kaposi, "Der Tätowirte von Birma," *Wiener Medizinische Wochenschrift*, Nr 2 (1872): 41.

14 Kaposi, "Der Tätowirte von Birma," 42.

the backs of his hands, the soles of his feet, and his scrotum.

He said he was 43 years old and from Albania—but a native Greek speaker. Kaposi noted that he also spoke several other languages, including a little German. When asked about the origin of his tattoos, Costentenus told them two conflicting stories. In one tale, he had been mining for gold in China, got involved in the losing side of a local dispute, and had been tattooed as punishment. In another tale, he had been a mercenary soldier fighting for the French, before he was captured by the Chinese and tattooed by four men who threatened him with death.[15] It seems that Costentenus was trying out different origin stories with the group to see what would stick. Kaposi was, unsurprisingly, skeptical of both versions. But the doctors did comment that, after several conversations with the tattooed man, they had no doubt that he had been to Southeast Asia.

One of the observant audience members was a Dr. Müller, an "Orientalist" who was vocal that Costentenus's stories of being tattooed by the Chinese were not true. The Dr. Müller in question was most likely Dr. Friedrich Müller, who was a professor of Sanskrit and comparative linguistics at the University of Vienna. He was the founder of linguistic ethnography, which is the study of how language and culture are connected. Dr. Müller recognized the language woven through Costentenus's tattoos as a form of Burmese. Having studied the languages and cultures of the region, he may have also recognized the particular style of tattooing as coming from the Shan States in Burma. But for whatever reason, Hebra and Kaposi weren't willing to accept outright that the tattoos were Burmese. Despite Müller's insistence, they only went so far as to say that the blue and red lettering was "allegedly Burmese... and partly hieroglyphic... the whole picture a peculiar harmonious whole."[16]

Also in the audience on that day in Vienna was one of the region's best known photographers, Ludwig Angerer. Hired by Kaposi and Hebra to take a full-length portrait of the tattooed man, Angerer was a Hungarian-born former pharmacist who had opened the first photographic studio in Vienna in 1858. He had introduced small,

15 Kaposi, "Der Tätowirte von Birma," 41.

16 Hebra, *Atlas der Hautkrankheiten*, 95.

inexpensive photographic prints to the masses in Vienna, but Angerer was also known for his large-format formal portraits, including the first of the entire Austro-Hungarian royal family.[17]

It was the larger format that Angerer took of Costentenus that day, creating the first known photograph of the Tattooed Greek. He's nude, as he would have appeared before the Viennese audience. He stands tall, with one arm resting on a draped cabinet, the other on his hip. He's looking off to the side, and it's hard not to wonder what he's thinking about.

As with the other photographs of Costentenus, it's impossible to know if his tattoos were faded and blurry in real life or if it's just

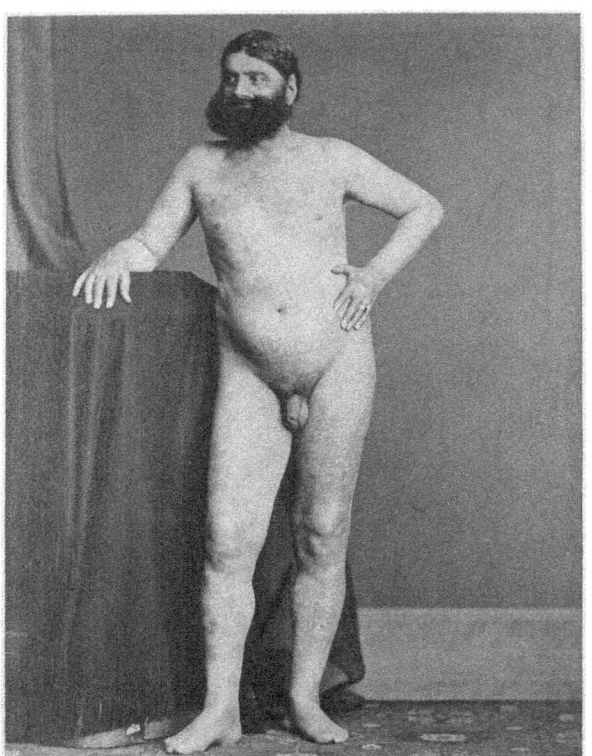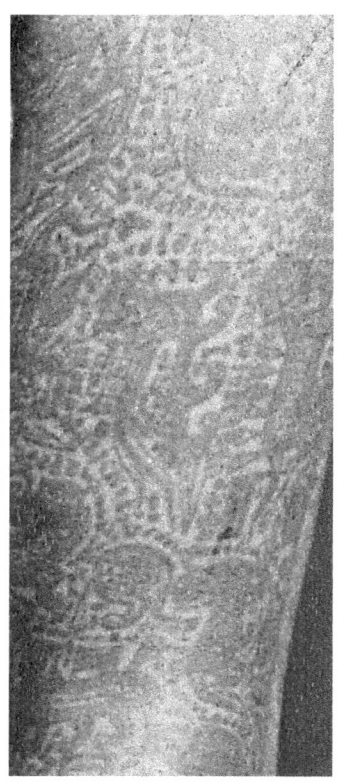

*Nude photograph of Costentenus taken by Ludwig Angerer, Vienna, 1870, and an enhanced detail of his left leg from the same photograph (Wellcome Collection)*

17 "Ludwig Angerer," *Monoskop*, August 2019: https://monoskop.org/Ludwig_Angerer. Accessed Sept. 23, 2021.

the poor image quality. Most of Costentenus's tattoos are washed out, with the exception of the areas in shadow: his stomach and left leg. These look like what Scott described in *The Burman* as the "old style" of Shan tattooing, still seen in Burma at that time. This old style "was to cover every available piece of skin with tracery, so that the figures became blurred and indistinct, and on a dark skin grown old were practically not visible without careful examination."[18]

•

## Across Europe, 1872 - 1876

The first account of Costentenus's appearance in Vienna actually appeared in the *British Medical Journal* in November 1871, beating Hebra and Kaposi to print by a few months.[19] Their article in *Wiener Medizinische Wochenschrift* (Viennese Medical Weekly) was finally published in 1872. But by then, Costentenus had moved on and was slowly working his way across the continent. Perhaps he grew impatient waiting for the World's Fair to begin or new opportunities sprang up elsewhere. Kaposi and Hebra's article did provide the Tattooed Greek with the international notoriety that he sought. Their German-language article was translated and republished in various other medical journals over the next few years in Great Britain, Germany, and Denmark.[20] Sections of the article even popped up in several American newspapers like the *Chicago Inter Ocean*: "As the Albanian acknowledges to have been in the region of this country [Burma], the Burmese are entitled to whatever credit may belong to the performance of this operation."[21]

18 Yoe, *The Burman*, 41.

19 "Tattooed From Head To Foot," *British Medical Journal*, No. 566 (Nov. 4, 1871): 532.

20 "Tattooed" British Medical Journal; Rudolf Virchow, "Uber den Tattowirten Sulioten Costanti," *Zeitschrift für Ethnologie*, (1872): 201; "Sektionen for Anatomi og Fysiologi," Forhandlinger ved de Skandinaviske Naturforskeres 11 (1873): 497.

21 "Tattooing: An Interesting Review Suggested by the Tichborne Case," *The Inter Ocean*, April 20, 1872.

While the academics wrote about Costentenus in their journals, the man himself caused a stampede of spectators at a Hungarian newspaper office in January of 1872.[22] Dionys von Pazmandy, the editor of a paper called *Delejm* in the city of Pest (which merged with the city of Buda to become Budapest the following year) saw an opportunity to earn a little extra cash. He offered Sunday showings of the tattooed man—but he got more than he bargained for.

The red posters that appeared throughout Buda and Pest invited "an audience of educated gentlemen" to visit his newspaper's offices to see the "tattooist Konstantin."[23] Certainly, this was no display suited for women, children, or the uneducated, since the tattooed man most likely displayed himself in the nude. It would be far too scandalous for the fairer sex and clearly, the uneducated classes would take it completely the wrong way.

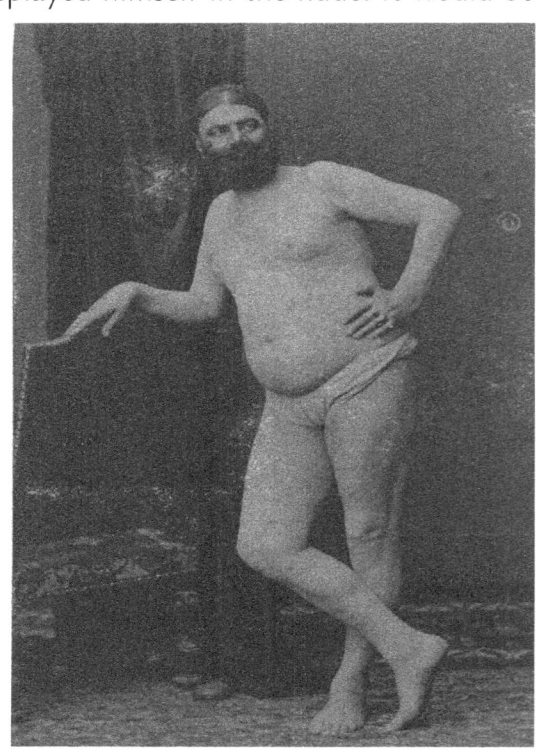

A German-language newspaper *Neue Freie Presse* commented that "Georg Konstantin" didn't really understand how to book and exhibit himself yet. It seems von Pazmandy didn't know what he was doing either. Spectators of all ages, genders, and classes mobbed the performance. The *Presse* reported that the crowd included apprentices, Sunday strollers, and schoolchildren—as well as men so coarse that they didn't remove their hats

*Photograph of Costentenus taken by the studio of Emile Tourtin, Paris, 1874 (P. T. Barnum Museum, Bridgeport, Connecticut)*

22 "Eine Redaction als Schaubude," *Neue Freie Presse*, January 29, 1872.

23 "Eine Redaction als Schaubude."

from their heads.[24] They "crowded, pushed, cursed..." and broke the doors that got in their way. Von Pazmandy's landlord "was happy to get away with just a few injured ribs and not to see his apartment completely demolished."[25]

Throughout 1872, the news of the tattooed man spread widely. He was sighted in Berlin several times, but he canceled all of his performances there, supposedly due to a lingering, unnamed illness he had brought back from Asia.[26] He popped up in Teplice, a city on the German/Czech border. Despite the extreme heat, he was seen wrapped up in a fine fur collar, leaning against a pillar, watching a parade.[27] And he made it to Copenhagen in mid-1873, appearing at another medical gathering. He told the local paper that he planned to stay for a few weeks, probably earning additional money at other, less scientific venues.[28]

By 1874, Costentenus was in Paris, appearing at the now-legendary Folies Bergère. The Folies, which had opened in 1869 as Folies Trévise, had been built as an opera house but quickly expanded its offerings to include other performances, such as acrobats, dancers, and nude women. When Costentenus appeared there in 1874, it featured a large indoor garden at the entrance with spiral staircases leading up to second story galleries.[29] On their main stage, he was introduced as "Yolos Constantinos," and it was said that he'd "already sold his skin to a patient collector, who wants to make a beautiful cushion."[30]

The tattooed man had upgraded his act since the near-riot in Hungary two years before. Here, the curtain rose to show him

---

24 "Eine Redaction als Schaubude."

25 "Eine Redaction als Schaubude."

26 Virchow, *Zeitshcrift für Ethnologie*, 201.

27 "Aus den Wünschen Andern und Wäldern," *Neuen Fremden Blatt*, Sept. 18, 1872.

28 "Georgios Konstantinos," *Dagens Nyheder*, July 14, 1873.

29 Shane Peacock, *The Great Farini: The High-Wire Life of William Hunt*, (Viking/Penguin Books, 1995): 221.

30 "Théatre des Folies-Bergére, L'Homme Tatoué," *L'Album Theatral*, Sept. 22, 1874. The first name "Yolos" is a generic Greek first name in French, a name that is short-hand for denoting where the person is from.

standing, flanked by two men. He slowly shrugged out of a red coat and handed it to one of the two men before starting to turn around, "raising his arms, stretching out his chest and taking poses."[31] After his striptease on stage, he walked down into the room, and strolled along the paths of the theater's floor. The spectators climbed onto their benches to see him up close and cheer.[32]

All this was just the beginning. Back in 1872, Costentenus's first appearance in the American press had predicted that "Barnum will undoubtedly secure him."[33] This proved prophetic. After five years of making headlines across Europe, Costentenus looked west to the United States, where P. T. Barnum and the *Greatest Show on Earth* were waiting to make him a household name.

---

31 "L'Homme Tatoue," *L'Album Theatral.*

32 "L'Homme Tatoue," *L'Album Theatral.*

33 "Tattooing: An Interesting Review," *Inter Ocean.*

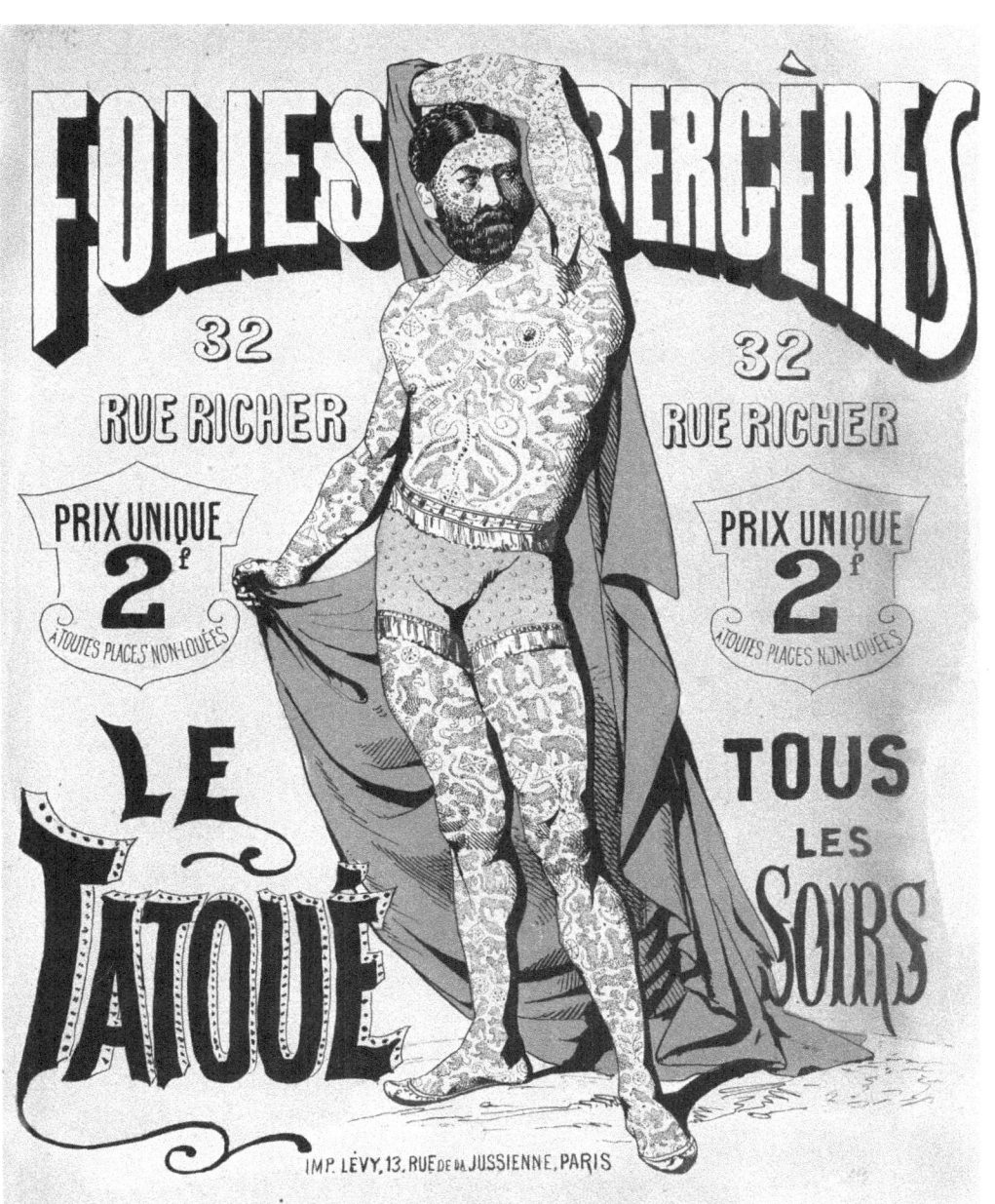

*Folies Bergère poster, 1874*
*(Bibliothèque Nationale de France, Department of Prints and Photography)*

## CHAPTER TWO

# BARNUM*

*and a few of the people whose work he took credit for, like William Coup and Dan Castello*

In Europe, Georg Kostantinus had appeared in a mishmash of offices, fairs, and medical venues. In the United States, Captain George Costentenus would break into a world of circus sideshows and dime museums. But surprisingly, the man who would make him famous, Phineas Taylor Barnum, had only recently stepped into the circus world in a serious way. Although Barnum's name is now synonymous with the American circus, it wasn't until 1871, at the age of 60, that the infamous showman found massive success under the big top tent. That was when he started working with William Coup and Dan Castello—and the golden age of American circus began. It would be even later, when he was 70, that Barnum would meet James A. Bailey and they would launch what would become the *Barnum and Bailey Circus*. And it wasn't until well after Barnum's death that the Ringling Brothers bought the show and combined it with their own. Today, *Ringling Brothers and Barnum & Bailey Circus* is still touring— and is still known as the *Greatest Show on Earth*. But Barnum's first forays into the traveling show as a young man were a far cry from the successful show that still carries his name.

The image of Barnum we have today was heavily influenced by his own formidable promotional skills. He not only sold people on his shows and museums, he sold them on himself. Advertisements for his shows included not just images of circus and sideshow acts, but prominently featured his portrait. Barnum updated and republished his autobiography almost annually, packing the pages with accomplishments that were slanted in his favor. In reality, Barnum was a (mostly) successful businessman, a mediocre politician, a masterful promoter, and a shrewd salesman. He was also a huckster who frequently took advantage of the gullibility of his audiences, a trickster who made the ordinary seem to be something extraordinary, and a braggart who often took credit for the work of his business partners. He both exploited the people he promoted and gave them employment and independence. He became an abolitionist, but he had also exhibited enslaved people. His morals and ethics were complicated, to say the least.

Most of all, Barnum had an instinct for understanding what intrigued people and a drive to find ways to profit from that. He gambled on an endless stream of businesses, from a lottery to a newspaper to a museum—making and losing huge amounts of money many times. He even declared bankruptcy once, after an investment in a clock company went bad. He was both a clever entrepreneur and a ruthless opportunist. He was a man who had "a flair for entertaining people and an instinct for promotion," ready to try anything that would simultaneously entertain crowds, make him money, and heighten his own fame.[34]

Barnum was 65, at the end of his partnership with William Coup and Dan Castello, when he turned Captain George Costentenus into the world's most famous tattooed man. But he had honed his talents for finding and exhibiting unique humans over many decades.

•

---

34 Philip B. Kunhardt, Jr., Philip B. Kunhardt III, Peter W. Kunhardt, *P. T. Barnum, America's Greatest Showman,* (Alfred A. Knopf, 1995): 27.

## Before the *Greatest Show on Earth*: 1810 - 1870

Even as a child in Connecticut in the early 1800s, Barnum had been a salesman. He had worked in a variety of small stores before settling on selling lottery tickets as a teenager, developing his skills in fast talking and scheming.[35] By 1835, young Barnum had bought a share in a grocery store in New York City. That's when he stumbled on the first of the many people he would promote and profit from: Joice Heth. An enslaved woman, Heth was being exhibited in Philadelphia by a man claiming that she had been George Washington's nanny—and was 161 years old. This was, unsurprisingly, not true. But Barnum saw the opportunity to make serious cash. He leased the act—and the woman—from her enslaver.[36]

At first, the act was very successful, but when Heth's popularity began to wane, Barnum began a campaign that would

*Broadside promoting Joice Heth, 1835, (Courtesy Somers Historical Society)* "THE GREATEST Natural & National CURIOSITY IN THE WORLD. JOICE HETH, Nurse to GEN. GEORGE WASHINGTON, (the Father of our Country,)..."

---

35 Kunhardt, *P. T. Barnum*, 4-10.

36 Benjamin Reiss, *The Showman and the Slave: Race, Death, and Memory in Barnum's America*, (Harvard University Press, 2001): 25-26.

inform his relationship with the press for the rest of his life. He wrote anonymous letters to several papers claiming that Heth was a fake. The letters didn't question Heth's age or history. Instead, they questioned her humanity. The letters alleged she was made of rubber, bone, and springs. Barnum's trick worked. Crowds hurried back to see if she was a real woman or an automaton. Barnum had learned the power of both lying to the public and manipulating the press.

Very little is known of Joice Heth, but she was probably no more than 80 years old, not 161.[37] That determination was made by Dr. David L. Rogers, a surgeon and anatomist associated with the New York College of Physicians and Surgeons. Prior to Heth's death, Rogers had expressed interest in performing a postmortem. So when she died in 1836, Barnum staged a public autopsy. This was, at the time, a popular—if gruesome—form of educational entertainment.[38] Rogers, for example, had performed a public dissection of James D. Jeffers, a.k.a. Charles Gibbs, one of the last active pirates in the Caribbean who had been captured on Long Island in 1830 and hanged in 1831.[39] For Heth's autopsy, Barnum—being Barnum—charged admission. Rogers did his examination in front of an audience of 1,500 paying spectators.[40] In examining Heth's organs, coronary arteries, cardiac valves, and brain, Rogers did not find "ossification" that would have indicated to him such advanced age.[41]

Exhibiting Joice Heth introduced Barnum to the flourishing world of itinerant performers. In the early 19th century, this included everything from fire-eaters and magicians to lecturers like the author Washington Irving.[42] This was a world that would develop along with Barnum, allowing him to try promoting a variety of acts on rented stages in the early years of his career. He signed one of the acts, a juggler and plate spinner, to Aaron Turner's successful *Old Columbian*

---

37 Kunhardt, *P. T. Barnum*, 20-23.

38 James R. Wright, Jr., "How the Public Autopsy of a Slave Joice Heth Launched P.T. Barnum's Career as the Greatest Showman on Earth," *Clinical Anatomy*, Oct. 2018 (7): p. 960, doi: 10.1002/ca.23276.

39 Wright, "How the Public Autopsy of a Slave," 961.

40 Wright, "How the Public Autopsy of a Slave," 961.

41 Wright, "How the Public Autopsy of a Slave," 962.

42 Reiss, *The Showman and the Slave*, 28-29.

*Circus* in 1836.[43] Barnum himself worked as the show's secretary, treasurer, and ticket seller—learning the ropes of the trade. When the contract was up, Barnum put his earnings into making his own show, which toured the south through 1837 as *Barnum's Grand Scientific and Musical Theater*.[44] He also tried a steamship show on the Mississippi and a wagon show that traveled from Canada to New Orleans. None of these were particularly successful.[45]

In 1841, at the age of 31, he was back in New York and still looking for his surefire ticket to fame and fortune. His latest scheme: purchasing "Scudder's American Museum" on Broadway, near City Hall Park, and transforming it into a spectacular exhibition space. Museums like Scudder's were not highbrow attractions for the upper class. They were cheap and popular. Admission was typically a dime (less than four dollars in today's money), and a whole circuit of what came to be called "dime museums" sprang up in cities across the country.[46] While the earliest museums in the U.S., like Peale's in Philadelphia, had been created with education and moral improvement in mind, dime museums met the need for affordable entertainment for the working class. In everything from small storefronts to massive halls, dime museums combined exhibits with live entertainment under one roof. They had dioramas, panoramas, fine art, waxworks, taxidermied specimens, theater—and live curiosities.

Was Barnum thinking that a museum would be his big break or was he simply jumping into an available opportunity? Either way, "Barnum's American Museum" was to be his most successful enterprise thus far. He expanded it from a collection of taxidermied specimens to include live acts of all types. He brought in ventriloquists, trained birds, flea circuses, the country's first Punch and Judy puppet show, and James O'Connell—the tattooed jig dancer.[47]

Barnum's first tattooed man—and the first performing in

43 Kunhardt, *P. T. Barnum*, 24.

44 Kunhardt, *P. T. Barnum*, 25.

45 Kunhardt, *P. T. Barnum*, 18-30.

46 "Purchasing Power Today of a US Dollar Transaction in the Past," MeasuringWorth, 2025, https://www.measuringworth.com/calculators/ppowerus/.

47 Kunhardt, *P. T. Barnum*, 36-40.

the United States—O'Connell had been working steadily in dime museums and circuses since 1836. Born in Ireland, he claimed he had survived two shipwrecks in the Pacific before being stranded—and tattooed—on the island of Pohnpei in Micronesia. The only surviving image depicting O'Connell's tattoos is a rough line drawing included in a pamphlet he sold at his performances. He reportedly had tattoos on his left hand and both arms, as well as his thighs, back and abdomen.

*Drawing of James O'Connell showing tattooed designs on his forearms, from* The Life and Adventures of James F. O'Connell, The Tattooed Man, *1846, (Collection of the Library of Congress)*

He apparently added chest and facial tattoos later in life. Newspapers said that "on the streets, women and children screamed in horror when they met him."[48] At Barnum's museum, he danced Irish jigs and gave an unlikely and melodramatic "historical account of his sufferings for eleven years, while a prisoner in the hands of barbarous savages in the North Pacific Ocean."[49] Decades later, Barnum would help craft similarly sensational and racist stories for Costentenus.

Barnum's museum also showcased wax figures of famous people, artworks, models, artifacts, and antiques. He added a lush rooftop garden with great views of the city and fireworks at night. And he advertised like crazy. He draped the exterior of the museum with banners, projected illusions on the building, bought newspaper ads and traveling advertising carts—anything to get the museum before the eyes of potential paying guests.

Three years after purchasing the museum, Barnum claimed to have 30,000 exhibits.[50] He expanded the lecture room and created a theater where he staged morality plays. He put on flower shows, dog shows, and even baby shows, where infants would vie for prizes like "reddest hair." He also gave space to a growing number of unusual acts: rope dancers, snake charmers, ventriloquists, jugglers, and fortune tellers.

Always trying to make more money, Barnum sent some of his most popular performers and exhibits on tours throughout the country. These traveling shows varied in focus—from the Swedish soprano Jenny Lind to little person Charles Stratton, a talented performer who Barnum had transformed into "General Tom Thumb." He sent out automatons like clockwork singing birds and mechanical human figures, as well as unusual animals like the "Woolly Horse" and curiosities like the infamous "Fejee Mermaid." The "mermaid" was advertised with images of beautiful women with fish tails. In reality, it was a preserved specimen that combined body parts from two dead

---

48 Saul Riesenberg, "The Tattooed Irishman," *Smithsonian Journal of History* (1968) 3, No. 1, 15.

49 "Barnum's American Museum," *New York Herald*, November 15, 1842.

50 Andrea Stulman Dennett, *Weird and Wonderful: The Dime Museum in America*, (New York University Press, 1997): 26.

monkeys and a salmon.[51]

In 1849, he tried creating an entire traveling tent show out of the museum. Over its four year run, the show had two names: *Barnum's Asiatic Caravan, Museum and Menagerie* and *P. T. Barnum's Grand Colossal Museum and Menagerie*. While Barnum did well financially, the reviews were bad nearly everywhere the show went. It was called "a most disreputable and shabby affair." The display of wax figures was "nothing but a charnel house and putrid carcasses," and the animals in the menagerie were "old, worn-out lazy lions."[52] Big success on the road continued to elude him, and the museum remained his biggest triumph.

Like many showmen, Barnum's fortunes rose and fell throughout the years. At the museum's peak, Barnum claimed it was the most popular attraction in the country, with more than 15,000 visitors a day.[53] Although he continued to recruit and exhibit human oddities through the Civil War, his luck was about to change.[54] On July 13, 1865, a fire broke out. It was just past noon, and the museum was crowded with paying customers. The water tanks and pumps that Barnum had installed on the roof for just this type of emergency were put into action, but they weren't enough.[55] All the people were successfully evacuated, but the museum and all its contents, including most of the animals, were destroyed. Ned, the Learned Seal, was one of the lucky few to survive the blaze, supposedly dragged out of the fire by a Brooklyn fireman and taken by cart to a fishtank in the Fulton Fish Market.[56]

Barnum's losses were staggering. He valued the collections at

---

51 Yunte Huang, *Inseparable: The Original Siamese Twins and Their Rendezvous with American History*, (Liveright Publishing, 2018): 264—term "Barnumize" defined as the process by which Barnum acquired, prepped, and controlled oddities.

52 Stuart Thayer, "Bad Press, Bad Crowds, Circus Historical Society, https://classic. circushistory.org/Thayer/Thayer.htm.

53 Tina Kelley, "A Museum Visit From an Armchair, *New York Times*, July 1, 2005, https://www.nytimes.com/2000/07/01/nyregion/a-museum-to-visit-from-an-armchair.html.

54 Kunhardt, *P. T. Barnum*, 102.

55 Kunhardt, *P. T. Barnum*, 193.

56 Kunhardt, *P. T. Barnum*, 193.

more than $400,000 (eight million dollars in today's money), but he had only insured them for a tenth of that.[57] Amazingly, he reopened just four months later in a rented building about a mile farther up Broadway. He packed the new museum full of recently acquired objects and newly hired curiosities. But less than three years later, he lost the new museum as well. In the early hours of March 3, 1868, a fire started in a defective chimney and swept through the building. Unfortunately, the fire department was out battling another fire at the time. It took them an hour to get through the snow-covered streets to the museum. By then it was too late. By the morning, the ruined building was covered in a shining layer of ice, and crowds braved the cold weather for weeks to come and gawk at the museum.

Barnum would not reopen the American Museum after the second fire. He was 58 years old and had been running the museum for almost half his life. He decided to direct his energy and remaining money into politics and—eventually—the circus.

*Stereoscopic photograph, "Barnum's Museum in ice. Fire 1868"*
*(From The New York Public Library)*

---

57 Neil Harris, *Humbug: The Art of P.T. Barnum*, (Little, Brown & Co., 1973): 169; MeasuringWorth.

# The Golden Age of American Circus Begins: 1870 - 1872

Even though the museum was gone, it had made Barnum spectacularly rich and equally famous. So it was no wonder that, in the fall of 1870, he was approached by two young showmen from Wisconsin looking for a partnership. William Coup and Dan Castello wanted Barnum to invest in a show that they'd created and toured with for the past year, *Dan Castello's Circus and Egyptian Caravan*. Barnum said no.

Now 60 years old, he had recently retired from his first foray into politics after a term in the Connecticut Legislature. He was taking it easy. But Coup persisted, saying "the old showman could stay in retirement, all they wanted was his name" (and money).[58] Coup and Castello proposed that they would handle the day-to-day operations, and Barnum would get two-thirds of the profits. On its face, that sounds like it was an incredible deal for Barnum and not so good for Coup and Castello. However, when Barnum finally said yes, his financial infusion into their modest show would transform it into one worth more than three times what it had been.[59] The partnership would be everything Coup and Castello had hoped for, but also more than they had bargained for.

William Coup, born in Indiana in 1837, had joined none other than *Barnum's Asiatic Caravan* as a roustabout at age 16. Roustabouts were general laborers for the circus, setting up tents, moving wagons, hauling water for animals, and handling anything else that needed doing behind the scenes. It became apparent that Coup's talents lay in management and logistics, as he worked his way up to assistant manager of several circuses in the 1850s and 1860s.[60] Sometime in late 1869 or early 1870, he supposedly bumped into Dan Castello on the streets of Chicago, and the two started working together.

---

58 Stuart Thayer and William L. Slout, *Grand Entrée: The Birth of the Greatest Show on Earth 1870-1875*, Clipper Studies in Theatre No. 17 (The Borgo Press: 1998): 15.

59 Thayer and Slout, *Grand Entrée*, 1-14.

60 Sverre O. and Faye O. Braathen. "Circus Monarchs: Wm. Cameron Coup," *Bandwagon*, March-April 1970, 4-5.

Dan Castello, the more well-known of the two, was born in Ontario around 1832 and had also begun his circus career as a teenager. Over the years, he worked as an acrobat, a clown, and an animal trainer.[61] He was the first performer to do a double somersault over eight horses—but a disastrous attempt at bison training ended with him tossed head over heels out of the ring. He, too, moved into a management role in the 1860s, running his own circuses in the United States and Europe.[62]

It's likely that Coup, the logistics expert, approached Castello with an idea: building a show that would travel by steamship. So for the first part of the 1870 season, they used Lake Michigan as the show's highway. They transitioned to wagons in Wisconsin and eventually made their way to Minnesota that October.[63]

Eager to expand the following season, they kept pushing Barnum to invest, and he finally agreed. Barnum decided—against his family's wishes—that he needed a new project. It was time to go back to work. But Barnum would be a handful. He wrote to Coup on October 8, 1870, agreeing to invest in the show and lend it his famous name. And he ominously added: "I will spare time to cook up the show in New York when you come."[64] Barnum would clearly not be satisfied to be just a figurehead.

Over their next five seasons of successes and struggles, Barnum was the idea man and the promoter, while Coup and Castello made the ideas happen. Barnum even admitted to a newspaper, "I get men who know what they are about... I'd burst up in a year if I undertook to manage a circus. I don't know anything about the details of the business."[65] Another newspaper commented that, "hereafter,

---

61 W. Gordon Yadon, "Dan Castello," *The Banner Line*, March 15, 1968, 3-4, Circus World Museum Library, Wisconsin Historical Society.

62 Stuart Thayer. "Prelude to Barnum: The Coup and Castello Circus of 1870," *Bandwagon*, July-August 1970, 18; Fred Dahlinger, Jr., and Stuart Thayer, *Badger State Showmen: A History of Wisconsin's Circus Heritage*, (Grote Publishing): 29-30.

63 Thayer and Slout, *Grand Entrée*, 13-14.

64 William C. Coup, *Sawdust and Spangles: Stories & Secrets of the Circus*, (H.S. Stone and Co., 1901), https://www.gutenberg.org/files/36219/36219-h/36219-h.htm.

65 "A Chat With Barnum," *London Era*, July 29, 1877.

when the great Barnum show is mentioned, much of its success will be attributed to its able manager, Billy Coup."[66] That's not what happened. Over the years, Barnum's talent for publicity and his iron control over his legacy all but erased the roles Coup and Castello played in his massive success.

Their first season together featured a large menagerie that combined newly purchased animals with those of Coup and Castello's previous show. And Barnum recruited several people from his American Museum days. The show now featured a French giant; a teenager with dwarfism named Leopold Kahn who Barnum billed as "Admiral Dot"; Anne Leak, "the young lady born without arms"; and five-year-old Annie Jones, billed as "the Infant Esau, or Bearded Child".[67] Due to the addition of so many animals, acts, and oddities, this was the first time that a performance ring, menagerie, and museum were housed in separate tents on a circus lot. This necessity launched the era of the sideshow, literally, an extra show on the side.

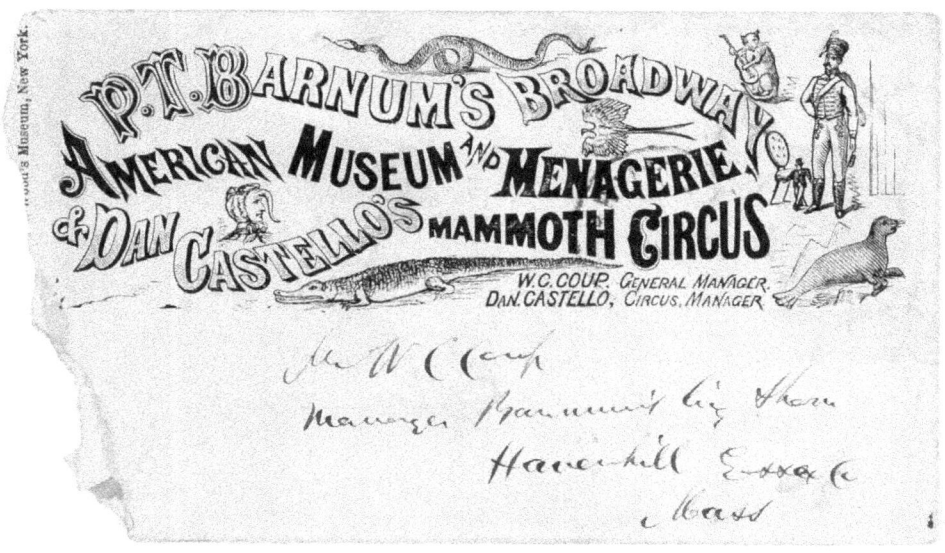

*Letter envelope from P. T. Barnum to William C. Coup, June 28, 1871, (Collection of The John and Mable Ringling Museum of Art, Tibbals Circus Collection)*

---

66 Kit Clarke, "Among the Showmen: Successful Managers, Tricks of the Profession, Etc." *New York Clipper*, November 25, 1871.

67 "Circuses: The Tenting Season of '71," *New York Clipper*, April 8, 1871.

*P. T. Barnum's Great Traveling Museum, Menagerie, Caravan, and Hippodrome* opened in Brooklyn on April 10, 1871, and from there hit most of the states in the northeast. Receipts were good. Reviews were ecstatic. In Rochester, New York, the *Democrat and Chronicle* proclaimed that "the show... is beyond anything we had reason to anticipate."[68] In Montpelier, Vermont, like many cities, the show sold out quickly and "conquered the town."[69] The three partners were pleased and started making plans for 1872. How could they get to more places? How could they pack more people into the tents? How could they make even more money?!

Coup and Castello's two largest contributions to the partnership—and to circus history in general—occurred here: they moved the massive show by train and they introduced a second ring to the big top (the largest, main tent). Of course, Barnum, ever the self-promoter, would later take credit for both innovations.

Moving by horse-drawn wagon from town to town was slow. And Coup noticed how widely the daily receipts had varied in 1871. In the larger cities, the show generally brought in two to three times what it made in the small towns.[70] If they moved the show by train, he suggested, they could go efficiently from big city to big city. They could even travel by night.

A few smaller shows had traveled by rail for parts of seasons—Castello, for instance, had put his circus on the train for some of the 1868 and 1869 seasons—but they still had to use wagons wherever there was no rail.[71] Between 1868 and 1873, however, more than 30,000 miles of new track was laid.[72] Now the railroad went where they wanted to go.

It was a fight to get Barnum to agree to the plan. "I was... mentally fatigued by my partner's opposition and his requests to

---

68 "Barnum's Show," *The Rochester Democrat and Chronicle*, Sep 19, 1871, p. 4.

69 "Barnum's Great Show," *Vermont Watchman and State Journal*, Aug. 9, 1871, p. 3.

70 Braathen, "Circus Monarchs," 6.

71 W. Gordon Yadon, "Dan Castello," p. 6.

72 Richard White, *Railroaded: The Transcontinentals and the Making of Modern America*. (Norton, 2011): 50.

45

abandon the scheme," Coup later wrote in his autobiography.[73] Coup finally wore Barnum down and negotiated agreements with various railroad companies. The 1872 show would be the largest circus put on rails at this time—and it would be designed to travel that way. Coup adapted all the set-up and take-down procedures to manage transporting such a large show on railroad cars. He created systems with metal planks and hooks to get the circus wagons on and off the train safely and efficiently.[74]

As Coup had hoped, this moved them farther and faster than ever before. The show opened in New York City in April of 1872 and worked its way south and west to Kansas by August. From there, it traveled north into Iowa, Illinois, and Wisconsin, ending in Detroit in October.[75]

The new method of sticking to larger cities worked, but it also meant considerably larger crowds at each show. Newspapers regularly reported that huge numbers of people had to be turned away. So now the tent needed to be bigger. But Castello said that "Barnum came to me and asked what were we going to do, as the canvas was getting so big that the people could not see." Castello's solution changed everything: "I told him that we would have to put in two rings."[76] Essentially, the show was duplicated so that more people could see. The performances were more or less the same in each ring, with Castello sitting between them, ringing a bell to keep the acts in sync.[77]

All these improvements worked. While nearly 1 in 4 circuses closed early that year due to low attendance, Barnum, Coup, and Castello's 1872 show grossed a million dollars, with the profits exceeding $200,000.[78] This powerhouse team had found a winning formula.

---

73 *Sawdust and Spangles,* Coup, 66.

74 Coup, *Sawdust and Spangles*, 7.

75 Thayer & Slout, *Grand Entrée*, 165-169.

76 Thayer & Slout, *Grand Entrée*, 38.

77 Thayer & Slout, *Grand Entrée*, 38.

78 Thayer & Slout, *Grand Entrée*, 43; $1 million is $27 million in 2025, $200,000 is $5.4 million in 2025, per Williamson, Measuring Worth.

Their rapid expansion in these years foreshadowed what the American circus would become in the next two decades: the largest entertainment juggernaut the country had ever seen. Multiple massive shows would fight for supremacy. Not only would these shows go by rail, so would the audiences: special excursion trains would bring people from outlying areas into the big cities just for a day at the circus. Shows would also continue to expand their tents to hold larger and larger audiences. They would add yet another ring, and the three-ring circus would become the standard. The golden age of American circus had begun. When he arrived in New York in 1876, George Costentenus would be a large part of its success, drawing huge crowds to shows for the five years he worked for Barnum.

Unfortunately for Barnum, Coup, and Castello, there were still some serious bumps in the road ahead. Some of the problems were out of their control—and some were of Barnum's own making. The three seasons before Captain George arrived would leave Barnum scrambling to recover and desperate for renewed success.

•

## Financial Struggles and Personal Conflicts: 1872 - 1875

First, the show's winter headquarters, the Hippotheatron in New York City, burned to the ground on Christmas Eve, 1872. Several performing dogs and all of the exotic menagerie animals were trapped in their cages and died. The fire also destroyed a number of props and costumes, including Admiral Dot's wardrobe.[79] Coup and Barnum argued over the expenses of rebuilding, but in March of 1873, the show reopened even bigger than the year before.[80]

Their formula still worked. The recreated Barnum, Coup, and Castello show rolled out from Brooklyn on a special train, traveling

---

79 "Burning of Barnum's," *New York Herald*, December 25, 1872, 14.

80 Thayer & Slout, *Grand Entrée*, 48

through New England, across New York, and into the Midwest as far as Chicago. From there, they turned east, returning to Brooklyn via Philadelphia.[81] Reviews of the show were good, with one newspaper commenting that "Barnum's has come... he has conquered."[82] Once again, they increased seating capacity. With more seats, more tickets were sold, but the cost of the fire put a dent in the season's profits.

*Photograph of P. T. Barnum's Great Traveling Exposition and World's Fair, 1873, (Robert L. Parkinson Circus World Library, Baraboo, Wisconsin)*

That fall, financial trouble hit the entire country: the Panic of 1873. Triggered in part by huge speculative investments in railroads, the panic led to six years of economic depression. Banks failed, thousands of businesses closed, and unemployment soared. Within a year, more than 100 railroads were bankrupt. Across the country, people had less money to spend on entertainments like the circus. For decades, this was called the Great Depression—until it was surpassed by the crash of 1929.

On top of that, Barnum himself caused trouble. Despite all the success he had had with Coup and Castello, Barnum insisted on

81 Thayer & Slout, *Grand Entrée*, 58.

82 "Barnum's Great Show," *Rutland Daily Herald*, 16 Jun 1873, 3.

changing the show for 1874 and 1875. He switched from a traditional circus format to that of a hippodrome, an oval track for horse racing inspired by those of ancient Greece. He then dashed off to Europe to visit the World's Fair in Vienna, leaving the actual creation of the traveling racetrack to his partners.[83]

He complicated things even further when he decided to duplicate an extravagant British pageant called *The Congress of Monarchs*. At great expense, the chariots, wagons, and other equipment were all shipped back to New York and modified for American audiences to become *The Congress of Nations*. Putting all this together into the hippodrome show was a painful tug of war. Barnum bought props and animals and hired performers in Europe, while Coup fought to control the costs.[84] They pushed on, leased land at the site of a former railroad depot, and started construction on the racetrack.

*Stereoscopic photograph of the interior of Barnum's Roman Hippodrome, E. & H. T. Anthony Stereoscope, 1874, (From The New York Public Library)*

The new show opened in New York in April of 1874, boasting horse races, chariot races, races between men standing on two

---

83 P. T. Barnum, *Struggles and Triumphs*, (Alfred A. Knopf: 1927): p. 691; Thayer and Slout, *Grand Entrée*, 69.

84 Thayer and Slout, *Grand Entrée*, 69; A. H. Saxon, *PT Barnum: The Legend and the Man*, (Columbia University Press, 1989): 239-240.

horses, and even "elephant, monkey, and ostrich racing."[85] But unlike the previous years of ceaseless travel, this show barely moved. Parts of the show went under canvas to Boston, Philadelphia, Baltimore, Pittsburgh, and Cincinnati. But the menagerie was too expensive to move, so most of the animals stayed behind.

While there are no available receipts for 1874, independent accounts say that the show was successful. But this was the beginning of the end for Barnum's partnership with Coup and Castello. Nineteenth century circus agent John Dingess, in an unpublished memoir, said that building the hippodrome destroyed Coup's health. He went to Europe to recuperate, but he continued to argue with Barnum via transatlantic messages. Barnum insisted that the *Congress of Nations* would continue through the winter, while Coup contended that audiences wanted a fresh show. Worn out, Coup gave Barnum an ultimatum: unless they could come to an agreement, Coup would quit the partnership "as soon as convenient to him."[86]

Coup, ultimately, was right about the winter season. Audiences had already seen the *Congress* and stayed away. Then, when the show hit the road in the spring, the 1875 season "ended up being one of the worst in the history of traveling amusements."[87] Many would-be ticket buyers were still suffering from the effects of the Panic of 1873—and the weather was terrible. First, there was snow, snow, and more snow, forcing the cancellation of many performances. When things finally warmed up, rain replaced the snow. Half of the traveling shows that went out for the season didn't finish the summer. While Barnum's show made it through, it racked up substantial debt.

Either Coup had decided that now was the time to stick to his ultimatum or the bad finances were the last straw. Coup and Castello paid off their portion of the debt and sold their stake in the show to another established group of circus managers. Known as the Flatfoots, this group had started in the menagerie business in

---

85 Thayer & Slout, *Grand Entrée*, 86.

86 John A. Dingess, Dingess Manuscript (unpublished manuscript, 1901): 373-374. Typescript copy at the Robert L. Parkinson Library and Research Center, Circus World Museum.

87 Thayer & Slout, *Grand Entree*, 154

New York around 1835 and was massively successful. Their nickname supposedly came from an incident where they threatened to crush a rival company, saying that, "we put our foot down flat."[88] By 1876, the Flatfoots consisted of one original member, John J. Nathans, and the sons of three others. This illustrious group came to an arrangement with Barnum that was similar to Coup and Castello's: Barnum got half of the profits and the Flatfoots split the rest.[89] This partnership would have similar longevity—and similar arguments.

While Coup may have blamed Barnum privately for over-the-top spending, publicly, he was polite and professional. "I have only to say that I WANTED to sell and the new firm bought, and, as they will have a good show, I wish them success."[90]

Coup turned his attention to opening the New York Aquarium, while Castello went off to start a new traveling show. The hippodrome materials were auctioned off in November. The hippodrome building itself, on property owned by Cornelius Vanderbilt, was leased to a composer and bandleader named Patrick Gilmore. During the Civil War, Gilmore had written the lyrics to the wildly popular song "When Johnny Comes Marching Home." He renamed the hippodrome building "Gilmore's Garden," and hosted concerts, flower shows, beauty contests, and dog shows.[91] In 1879, Vanderbilt's grandson took over the property and renamed it Madison Square Garden. The original Garden was demolished in 1889, and was relocated three times, but it has remained a home to the circus to this day.

•

88 Stuart Thayer, "The Flatfoot Party and the Zoological Institute," Circus Historical Society, https://classic.circushistory.org/Thayer/Thayer2c.htm.

89 Kunhardt, P.T. Barnum, 250.

90 "Card," New York Clipper, April 1, 1876, 3.

91 Madison Square Garden I, Ticket Dogs, http://hockey.ballparks.com/NHL/NewYorkRangers/1stoldindex.htm.

After finding huge success (and stumbling) with Coup and Castello, Barnum was at a pivotal point in his circus career. He needed a comeback after the disaster that was the 1875 season. And he got one. Capitalizing on the excitement surrounding the nation's 100th birthday, Barnum and the Flatfoots created a huge, patriotic spectacle.

Barnum described the show in a letter to Mark Twain as "a real old-fashioned Yankee-Doodle, Hail-Columbia Fourth-of-July celebration every day."[92] The circus ring was filled with star performers. The sideshow, now called "The Centennial Palace of Wonders," was stacked with curiosities. But this year's show also had fireworks, patriotic songs, a marching group of fife and drum players in Revolutionary costume, and a platform wagon carrying costumed figures of George Washington and General Lafayette—with a live American bald eagle. According to leaks courtesy of Barnum's own publicity machine, he'd borrowed nearly a million dollars "to make a Centennial show... that will eclipse all his former efforts."[93]

And for the first time, the show was called *P. T. Barnum's Greatest Show on Earth.*

With more than 70 performers and a crew of over 100, they started in April in New York at the American Institute Hall on Third Avenue, before hitting the road to New England—where they would pick up their newest star.

---

92 *Selected Letters of PT Barnum*, edited by A. H. Saxon, New York: Columbia Press, 1983; 197.

93 "Multiple News Items," *Idaho Weekly Avalanche* (Silver City, Idaho), Saturday, January 01, 1876; Issue 19; $31,000,000 in 2025, per Williamson, Measuring Worth.

# CHAPTER THREE

# THE CENTENNIAL

When the *Suevia* landed in New York harbor on May 25, 1876, the traveling merchant calling himself Georg Constantinos was treated just like millions of other immigrants. He was processed through Castle Garden (the predecessor to Ellis Island) and turned out onto the teeming streets of New York City. From there, he made his way up the East Coast to Rhode Island, where he joined the Barnum Centennial Show in Providence on June 6.

There's no way to know exactly how Costentenus had come to Barnum's attention. Given how quickly he joined the show, it is likely that Barnum or one of his many agents had made contact with Costentenus in Europe. An agent looking for new acts in Europe could not have missed the widespread publicity for the tattooed man— or the excitement that followed him everywhere he went. Barnum himself may have heard about Costentenus when he was in Vienna visiting the World's Fair in 1873.

However he came to Barnum's attention, Costentenus's

transformation was swift. No longer was he "Georg Konstantin, der Tätowirte [sic] von Birma"—the tattooed man of Burma.[94] He was now "Captain George Costentenus, the Tattooed Greek Albanian."[95] The name change was classic Barnum. He gave the tattooed man fictional military credentials just like he had with the giant Colonel Goshen and little people Major Atom, Commodore Nutt, and General Tom Thumb.

Even before Costentenus caught up with the tour in progress, Barnum's publicity experts were churning out press to promote his newest act. Less than a week after Costentenus landed in New York, newspapers across the country had his name. *The Inter Ocean* in Chicago reported that "Barnum has secured a Greek Albanian, who is to travel with the show. His name is Captain George Costentenus. He is tattooed from head to foot."[96] A Utica, New York paper reported on a press appearance that Barnum scheduled with his new curiosity: "The first impression on looking upon this man is that of a finely-modeled statue covered with hieroglyphics... it is still difficult to realize that he is not robed a la Harlequin, until, the warm flesh is touched and found soft and moist as that of an infant..."[97]

Several papers announced that "Mr. Barnum is to pay Captain George $100 a day."[98] This made Costentenus sound very important (which would be what Barnum wanted), but it's definitely an exaggeration. Because so few financial records exist from the 1870s, it's impossible to say exactly what Barnum really did pay Costentenus, but $100 a day would amount to Captain George getting paid about 20% of the show's profits for the season. He was a big draw, but he wasn't that big.

As they had in Europe, newspaper advertisements proclaimed that leading members of the medical community had authenticated

---

94 *Wiener Medizinische Wochenschrift*, 1872

95 "A Man with a Private Picture Gallery," *Cincinnati Enquirer*, June 6, 1876.

96 "People and Things," *Inter Ocean*, June 03, 1876; 4.

97 "A Novel Picture Gallery," *Utica Morning Herald and Daily Gazette*, June 2, 1876; "People and Things" *Inter Ocean*, June 3, 1876.

98 "People and Things," *Inter Ocean*, June 3, 1876, 4; $3,000 in 2025, per Measuring Worth.

this new curiosity. Here, they claimed that he had been examined by a group of Harvard-educated doctors: Oliver Wendell Holmes, Sr. (also a well-known writer and father of future Supreme Court Justice Oliver Wendell Holmes, Jr.), R.M. Hodges, Samuel A. Green (a future mayor of Boston), Joseph S. Jones, and S.J. McDougall. This distinguished group had supposedly declared that Costentenus was "proof of how much suffering man... can bear."[99]

Had these doctors actually examined Costentenus? There are no surviving records noting an examination of a tattooed man by any of these men. It's particularly suspicious that R. M. Hodges made no mention of such an event in his meticulous daily diary. He recorded the weather, whom he called on, where he walked to, and what verses he prayed. How could he overlook something as momentous as viewing a tattooed man?

A letter from Barnum to Holmes on June 19, 1876—just after the tattooed man joined the show—suggests that the idea for the "authentication" was Holmes's:

"Gratitude for your kindness inspires me to assure you that I should never have presumed to *think* of placing your name on one of my 'posters,' as you laughingly suggested today. I simply desire the public to be assured by a gentleman so widely known and honored that my tattooed man is *genuine*. If I can in any manner reciprocate your great courtesy, pray command me."[100]

Whether or not the distinguished doctors ever laid eyes on Captain George, Holmes's "laughingly suggested" endorsement appeared in newspaper advertisements throughout the country that season.

After the Captain's debut in Providence, the show traveled north to New Hampshire and then Maine. Costentenus got acquainted with American audiences in smaller towns before a two-week stand in Boston. As the Fourth of July approached, the nation's citizens

---

99 "P. T. Barnum and the Glorious Centennial Fourth of July in Lowell," *Lowell Daily Citizen*, June 24, 1876.

100 *Selected Letters of PT Barnum*, 200.

prepared to celebrate the country's 100th anniversary with red, white, and blue bunting, parades, fireworks, and the circus.

•

*Photographs of Captain George, by renowned photographer José María Mora, New York, December 1876, (TCS 7. Harvard Theatre Collection and Collection of The John and Mable Ringling Museum of Art, Tibbals Circus Collection)*

*Advertisement for Barnum's Greatest Show on Earth, 1876 (Robert L. Parkinson Library and Archives, Circus World Museum)*

"THE MOST MEMORABLE OF MORTAL MARVELS, CAPT. COSTENTENUS

A noble Greek Albanian, who suffered, and was the only one to survive, the awful three months' agony of being literally Tattooed from Head to Foot! / In Chinese Tartary, as punishment for engaging in rebellion against the king. He is the amazement of the Medical Faculty, and the Press pronounce him wonderful, far beyond description."

# The Fourth of July

On July 4, 1876—the day of the Centennial itself—Barnum's show was in Lowell, Massachusetts. A rapidly-growing industrial city, Lowell was bustling with people seeking jobs in its huge mills and factories. The city would have ballooned even more on the Centennial, with visitors from surrounding farms and villages coming to celebrate—and see the circus. A reporter commented that "it would take a visitor all day to see all that is to be seen at this splendid show... Its appointments are perfect; its menagerie the most varied ever seen in a traveling show." Importantly, he added that "the performances are as entertaining and meritable as they are unexceptionable."[101] In other words, the show was not only great fun, there was nothing morally upstanding people of the day would have disapproved of.

Barnum occasionally traveled with the show that season, talking to reporters and addressing crowds of spectators. But on this particular day he was home in Bridgeport, Connecticut, entertaining guests.[102] Barnum's unwillingness to travel more extensively with the show became a point of contention with the Flatfoots, and there is some irony in Barnum not being at his Centennial Show on the Centennial itself.

The celebrations started at dawn, waking up residents with a ringing of the city's bells and a military salute. A massive parade started lining up at five o'clock in the morning. Marchers represented the "Continentals of '76" and the "Antiques and Horribles"—a tradition first seen in Lowell in 1851, where a mock military company donned wacky uniforms as a satire of politicians and other public figures.[103] Thrown into this motley mix were groups of local tradespeople—including a group of weavers pulling a miniature weaving room complete with working looms—and members of Barnum's show. Traditionally, the circus announced its arrival in a new town with

101 "Barnum's Great Show: First Day's Performance," *Richmond Dispatch*, Sept. 19, 1876.

102 "Brief Mention," *Hartford Courant*, July 6, 1876, p. 2.

103 Ben Zimmer, "Where Did the Supreme Court Get Its Parade of Horribles?" *Boston Globe*, July 1, 2012.

its own parade, sending beautifully decorated wagons, costumed performers, and fantastic animals through the streets. But here, the Barnum show simply expanded the spectacle of Lowell's Centennial parade.

Cash prizes were awarded to the best parade displays, but the committee refused to award the $75 first prize to members of Company Q or the Lowell Bleachery for their "impudent and gratuitous insult" to the mayor over a liquor license dispute.[104] Nevertheless, the festivities continued, with speeches, a baseball game, a band concert on the South Common, a regatta, and horse racing at the fairgrounds.

With Barnum's elephants, lions, and giraffes nearby, the smells of the animals, both exotic and mundane, mingled with the smells of food from local vendors and the sweat of the crowds in the intense midday heat. People pushed their way through the dust and the noise into the tent city that Barnum's workers had set up after rolling into town early that morning. The massive main tent in the center was large enough to hold 8,000 paying customers. It was surrounded by smaller tents for the sideshow and menagerie, as well as dressing rooms, stables, and the cookhouse—"moons, as it were, to the great planet."[105] Flapping overhead, gigantic canvas banners painted in vibrant colors advertised giants and little people, ventriloquists and comedians, and, most likely, the Tattooed Greek. The crowds would have jammed around the ticket wagon, where admission was 50 cents for adults and 25 cents for children.[106] For a typical worker at one of the local mills, tickets for the whole family would have cost more than two days' wages.

There was no escaping the excitement of the circus, even on a national holiday that offered many other distractions. Performers stood on platforms outside the sideshow tents with snakes wrapped

104 "The Centennial Fourth," *Lowell Daily Citizen*, July 5, 1876, p. 2; $2,300 in 2025, per Measuring Worth.

105 Fred Dahlinger, Jr., "The American Circus Tent," *The American Circus*, (Yale University Press, 2012): 208.

106 "Menagerie, Museum and Circus," *Brooklyn Eagle*, Oct. 28, 1876; *Twenty-Eighth Annual Report of the Bureau of Statistics of Labor*, (Wright and Potter Printing Co., 1898): 6, https://babel.hathitrust.org/cgi/pt?id=chi.35711510&view=1up&seq=8; $15.10 for adults, $7.70 for children in 2025, per Measuring Worth.

around their bodies or with lions on leashes. Barnum's "talkers" were yelling continuously above the hum of the crowd, enticing people to buy an extra ticket for the museum of curiosities, stop for a lemonade, or see the animals captured in faraway lands. It was bright and loud, turbulent and wildly colored—a cacophony of sound and music and chaos. Even if you had been to a circus before, Barnum's enormous Centennial Show would have been a sight to behold.

The sideshow was its own small kingdom of three tents. Once your eyes adjusted to the relative darkness inside the first tent, you would have seen a stage with curtains, "like a regular theatre" for singing and dancing performances.[107] The sideshow managers had advertised earlier in the year that they wanted the "best looking male and female performers" for this troupe.[108] Then you would have made your way to the "black tent," a darkened space with historical dioramas and "moving figures illustrating... Dante's dream of the infernal regions."[109]

The third tent housed the museum of curiosities, where performers stood on platforms around the sides. You would have seen Admiral Dot, "the Cupid of the Dwarfs," in his uniform, answering questions from the crowd about his height and weight. Sword swallowers would have demonstrated their skills about three feet away from you. And "Zuruby Hannum, the Circassian Lady," would have told you about her daring (and fictional) escape from the Ottoman slave trade and her time in the harems of the Far East.

Barnum had presented his first "Circassian lady" at the American Museum in 1864—a woman with the unlikely stage name Zaluma Agra.[110] Women from Circassia (a real place between the Black Sea and the Caspian Sea in what is now the North Caucasus region of Russia) had long been stereotyped as ideal beauties. They were

107 "Circuses," *The New York Clipper*, March 4, 1876.

108 "Wanted," *The New York Clipper*, February 19, 1876.

109 "Circuses," *The New York Clipper*, March 4, 1876.

110 Rosemarie Garland-Thomson, *Freakery: Cultural Spectacles of the Extraordinary Body*, (New York University Press, 1996): 249–50; Betsy Golden Kellem, "Circassian Beauty in the American Sideshow," Public Domain Review, Sept. 16, 2021, https://publicdomainreview.org/essay/circassian-beauties.

symbols of a racist notion of "white racial purity."[111] The sideshow act drew on myths about white women being kept as sexual slaves in the Ottoman Empire, as well as racist and now-discounted ideas about humanity's origins in the Caucasus Mountains.

Barnum's Circassian women were, unsurprisingly, not from Circassia. Rather, they were local women who adopted an afro-like hairstyle, reportedly by soaking their hair in beer and teasing it out to maximize both hair volume and dramatic effect. The act would evolve into a tamer version as the century concluded: the Moss Haired Girl, who kept the hairdo, but took a step away from the racism.

Back in Barnum's Centennial Palace of Wonders, Zuruby Hannum, Admiral Dot, and the sword swallowers were joined by dozens of other sideshow performers, including a German giantess, a famous clog dancer, a Parisian ballet troupe, a team of glass blowers,

a group of musicians—and Captain George Costentenus, "Tattooed from Head to Foot!"

After wandering around the sideshow tents, looking at and listening to some of these performers, you would have taken a seat by the stage for the main sideshow. The master of ceremonies was Professor Samuel S. Smith, "Expositor of Natural History and Human Curiosities." Smith was a noted ringmaster and sideshow lecturer for Barnum—and "one of the best talkers who ever

*Photograph of Zuruby Hannum, circa 1865, (National Portrait Gallery, Smithsonian Institution; Frederick Hill Meserve Collection)*

---

111 Kellem, "Circassian Beauty ."

ZALUMA AGRA.
"THE STAR OF THE EAST."

*Photograph of Barnum's original Circassian Lady, Zaluma Agra, "The Star of the East," undated cabinet card, (collection of the author)*

entered the arena."[112] When Captain George stepped up onto the stage to show off his tattoos, Professor Smith would have launched into his own wild version of the Tattooed Greek's life. That story had evolved over Costentenus's five years of performing throughout Europe, and it had become quite the tall tale.

The crowd in Lowell that day would have heard that Costentenus was "a descendant of a noble Greek family, from the province of Albania." In 1867—so the story went—he had been mining in Chinese Tartary (northern and western China) with an American and a Spaniard. The three men joined a local rebellion, but unfortunately, they chose the losing side.[113] The rebellion was crushed and the three were taken prisoner. Instead of being beheaded (that would have been too simple), they were tortured. By being tattooed. For three months. The tattooing was so painful that "it required six men to hold him while one man performed the operation."[114] After the tattooing covered their entire bodies, the three men managed to escape. Six months later, the American was dead and the Spaniard had gone blind (and then he also died). Costentenus, being the strongest

---

112 "Charles H. Day," *New York Clipper*, 22 Oct 1892, 522.

113 "The Tattooed Nobleman: A Full Description of the Wonder," *Bangor Daily Whig & Courier*, July 25, 1876.

114 "The Tattooed Nobleman," *Bangor Daily*.

of the group, survived "and is in good health."[115]

The story, of course, was total fiction.

American audiences, frankly, never seemed to care. There has always been debate about how much audiences believed the outrageous sideshow pitch stories. Certainly some attendees did not. However, many did, or simply didn't care to question their outlandishness. Either way, the appeal was undeniable. Sideshow pitch stories connected the audience with the performer, often had an educational angle to mollify moralists, and usually reflected the news of the day or popular storylines from literature. Much of Captain George's story was lifted by Barnum's press agents from Kaposi's article in *Wiener Medizinische Wochenschrift*. They seem to have used the best parts, skipped the boring stuff, and made up the rest.

Like most pitch stories, it doesn't stand up to scrutiny. In Vienna, Costentenus had said that he was one of 11 people who joined the French in fighting against the Chinese. Now, he was one of three swept up in a local revolt. Why would their captors go to such lengths to torture the three men, rather than simply executing them? How would the tattooing have killed the American and the Spaniard months later? Are we talking about massive infection from the tattoos? Were they killed by shock after seeing themselves completely transformed into "one of the greatest human curiosities ever seen"?[116] And how does blindness come into this? (Oddly, this is not the only mention of a performer going blind from tattooing. Nora Hildebrandt, who would become famous in 1882 as one of the first two tattooed women to appear on sideshow and museum stages, claimed to have gone blind from tattooing, but somehow, her sight had been restored.)

However ridiculous the details of Captain George's story may sound today, they would follow him for the rest of his career. The story would be added to and embellished, but here, in 1876, all the key elements were in place for Barnum to promote the Tattooed Greek.

Costentenus's story was not the only wild tale in the museum

---

115 "The Tattooed Nobleman," *Bangor Daily*.

116 "The Tattooed Nobleman," *Bangor Daily*.

tent. The museum tent that Fourth of July day in Lowell teemed with "educational" nonsense, from Costentenus's travel narrative to the German giant Madame Kathinka overestimating her height, followed by the antics of Yeppo, the "Wild Boy," who was a regular boy with a "savage"-inspired costume and theatrical antics. Sideshows and museums were filled with all varieties of strange stories and exaggerated claims, from people billed as "Missing Links" (the supposed evolutionary links between man and ape), "Happy Families" (different predatory animals all living together in one enclosure), and "cannibals" (regular Americans in costume), along with people of all heights and sizes, projection tricks, and more. Exaggeration was the currency of the sideshow, using storytelling to turn the ordinary into the extraordinary and the unusual into the fantastic— an entertainment impulse as old as humanity. Under the big top, you could see amazing feats of human strength and skill, but the museum tent was more about presentation and, often, outright lies. These lies, however, were the entertainment—a reassurance to audiences of their own normality. And they were as popular as the skilled performers, with many curiosities going on to become celebrities, as Captain George would.

After touring the museum tent and listening to tales of adventure, you could make your way to the menagerie, which was packed with more than 60 cages of exotic animals. In 1876, most Americans had never seen anything more exotic than raccoons and house cats. While a few public zoos and menageries had opened in large cities in the 1860s and 1870s, their offerings were fairly tame. But here in Barnum's menagerie, there were elephants, exotic birds, strange lizards, and the featured attraction: a baby hippopotamus. Barnum claimed it had cost him more than $25,000 to acquire "the only living hippopotamus in America,—all others advertised being base frauds."[117]

The animals shared the menagerie tent with a series of presidential portraits (capitalizing on the patriotism surrounding the country's 100th birthday) and a collection of automatons (early clockwork robots) belonging to Wesley Jukes, a skilled mechanic and

---

117 "P. T. Barnum's Greatest Show on Earth," *Bangor Daily Whig and Courier*, July 27, 1876; "Barnum's Latest: The New and Greatest Show on Earth," Boston Daily Advertiser, June 20, 1876; $77,000 in 2025, per Measuring Worth.

the museum's superintendent. The automatons in 1876 included miniature circus performers, musicians, and magicians, all operated by a steam engine.[118]

When a bugle blast sounded, you would hurry to take your seat in the massive main tent. Rows of bleacher-style planks surrounded a single ring under "a 150 foot round top with one 50 foot middle piece."[119]

The big show started with a parade of camels, elephants, horses, and costumed performers dressed as lords and ladies, before the curiosities filed in.[120] The baby hippopotamus followed, walking behind his trainer, and then various national anthems were sung. There was an act of trained doves, a team of oxen, and a horse and a stag bounding over gates. You gazed up at "the most grand... performance ever given."[121] Other star attractions were the Japanese acrobatic duo Satsuma and Little All Right, William Carlo's trick ponies, and Martin Lowande and Jeanette Watson's exciting bareback riding.[122]

This show, like other contemporary circus shows, depended on skilled human and animal acts for the main entertainment. Later circuses would develop massive spectacles with intricately costumed theatrical performances in the ring, but this was still the era when the trick rider and acrobat reigned supreme.

All this action—from the museum tent to the menagerie and the big top—was recreated by the Barnum organization twice daily, at 1 PM and 7 PM. From the outside it looked like chaos, but in reality,

118 "P. T. Barnum's New and Greatest Show on Earth is Coming on Three Monster Special Trains," *Aurora*, May 19, 1876.

119 Frank A. Robbins, "The Barnum Show in 1876," *Billboard* 22, No. 12, March 19, 1910, 23; William Slout, *A Royal Coupling: The Historic Marriage of Barnum and Bailey,* (Emeritus Enterprise: California, 2000): 139.

120 "Barnum's Latest: The New and Greatest Show on Earth," *Boston Daily Advertiser*, June 20, 1876.

121 Barnum's Great Show: First Day's Performance," *Richmond Dispatch*, September 19, 1876.

122 "Barnum's Latest," *Boston Daily Advertiser*; "Barnum's Great Show," *Richmond Dispatch*; "Barnum's Latest," Boston Daily Advertiser.

the circus was a well-oiled machine. Barnum's team rolled up the show after the evening performance, loaded everything onto the train, and moved on to the next city on the route during the night. Performers bunked on trains when shows were on the move, and in hotels when the show was in town for a few days.

*Photograph of bareback rider Martin Lowande and two of his sons, undated, (Collection of the author)*

The show only spent one day in Lowell. They packed up the entire operation that night and rolled down the tracks to Nashua, New Hampshire for the next day's stand. Today, this would be a quick 20-mile drive down the highway. Back then, it was a slow overnight trip on the local railroads, with performers trying to get some sleep while the train lumbered through the dark countryside. Most performers slept in cars that had multiple bunks. Sometimes performers even shared a bunk. It was not a cushy existence, but for many performers, it was a better living than working the family farm or toiling away in an urban factory. And circus life allowed for travel in a time when many never strayed very far from their birthplaces.

As the train pulled up across the state line into Nashua early that morning, the show would have awakened and started setting up the tents once again for another show in another town. All that season, the Barnum train crisscrossed the Northeast, bringing the animals, the automatons, the acrobats, and the Tattooed Greek to towns and cities in Maine, Vermont, New Hampshire, Massachusetts, New York, Pennsylvania, Maryland, and New Jersey, before ending back where they had started, in New York City. All season long, most of the advertisements prominently featured Captain Costentenus, with a portrait modeled on the illustration from the *Atlas der Hautkrankheiten*.[123]

There are no remaining records about how financially well the Centennial Show performed that season, but the reviews were very good. In article after article, newspaper after newspaper, reviewers were stunned by Costentenus's red and blue tattooing: "There is not a single point on his body which is not covered... so that it is impossible to discover what was the natural color of his skin."[124] One attendee thought that the Tattooed Greek looked as if he was wearing a "dark blue coat" and was amazed that this was the man's skin.[125] Yet another reporter called him "a statue covered with hieroglyphics."[126]

123 "In All Its Great Entirety: P. T. Barnum's New and Greatest Show on Earth," *Fitchburg Daily Sentinel*, August 17, 1876.

124 "Barnum's Great Show" *Richmond Dispatch*.

125 "City and Vicinity: Locals in Brief," *Lowell Daily Citizen*, June 24, 1876 p. 2

126 "A Novel Picture Gallery," *Utica Morning Herald and Daily Gazette*, June 2, 1876.

Throughout 1876, the newspapers from the East Coast to the Midwest practically shouted with excitement about Costentenus, "The Most Memorable of Mortal Marvels."[127] For both Barnum and Captain George, this was the beginning of years of raging success.

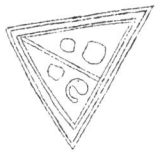

127 "In All Its Great Entirety!" *Fitchburg Daily Sentinel* August 14, 1876.

CHAPTER FOUR

# WITH THE *GREATEST SHOW ON EARTH*

When the Centennial season came to a close, all the equipment was hauled back to New England. The performers either went home for the winter or found work in dime museums around the country. Captain George made his way to New York City to work for the Bunnell brothers, George and John. This would have been an easy leap for Costentenus, since the brothers had also been working for Barnum that season.

The Bunnells had been managing Barnum's museum tent since 1872. They were so good at what they did that Barnum himself invested in their permanent museum. According to a contract dated November 2, 1876, Barnum fronted the brothers money to start Bunnell's New American Museum in New York City.[128]

---

128 *Salmagundi Ledger*, Manuscripts, PT Barnum Research Collection, Bridgeport History Center, https://archives.lib.uconn.edu/node/24215.

This is where Costentenus went after his first season with Barnum. No doubt the Bunnells knew the Tattooed Greek would be a guaranteed money maker. They quickly snapped him up and he opened at their museum on November 27, 1876—even before Barnum's Centennial show had officially closed.[129]

Costentenus worked at Bunnell's until the new year, when he departed for Philadelphia's Concert Hall. There, he worked alongside a group of "Australian Bushmen" for the month of January. At this point, it should come as no surprise that these "Bushmen" were of questionable origin. There were a variety of people advertised as "Bushmen" during this time period. Some were Aboriginals forced to travel and perform, while others were hustlers who transformed themselves into something they were not. Either way, the acts were problematic—to say the least.

As the winter marched on, Costentenus went to Boston for the month of February, appearing at the Liberty Tree Building. The *Boston Globe* commented that he was "certainly a wonderful illustration of how much humanity is capable of enduring."[130] By March, he was back in New York City with Barnum, the Flatfoots, and the Bunnells, preparing for his second season with the *Greatest Show on Earth*.

It began with four weeks at Gilmore's Garden from April 9 to May 5, 1877, before setting out on an ambitious tour that introduced the Tattooed Greek to the Midwest.[131] The show was massive in comparison with 1876. According to that season's route book (a detailed report on that year's tour—and an invaluable historical record) there were 50 railroad cars hauling 317 employees, 117 horses, four elephants, four camels, and much more.[132] They headed north through New England, crossed into Ontario in late May, and made their way to Wisconsin at the beginning of July. They went as far west as Kansas before turning back across Missouri, Indiana, and Kentucky

129 George C. D. Odell, *Annals of the New York Stage Volume 10*, (AMS Press, 1970): 294.

130 "Various Entertainments," *Boston Globe*, Feb. 12, 1877, p. 3.

131 "P. T. Barnum's Show," *New York Clipper*, April 21, 1877.

132 *Route Book, Season of 1877, P. T. Barnum's New and Greatest Show on Earth*, Circus Historical Society, https://classic.circushistory.org/History/PTB1877.htm .

as the fall deepened.

Once again, the publicity trumpeted that a group of trusted medical men had found the tattooed man to be 100% genuine. But last season's group of East Coast doctors wouldn't convince people

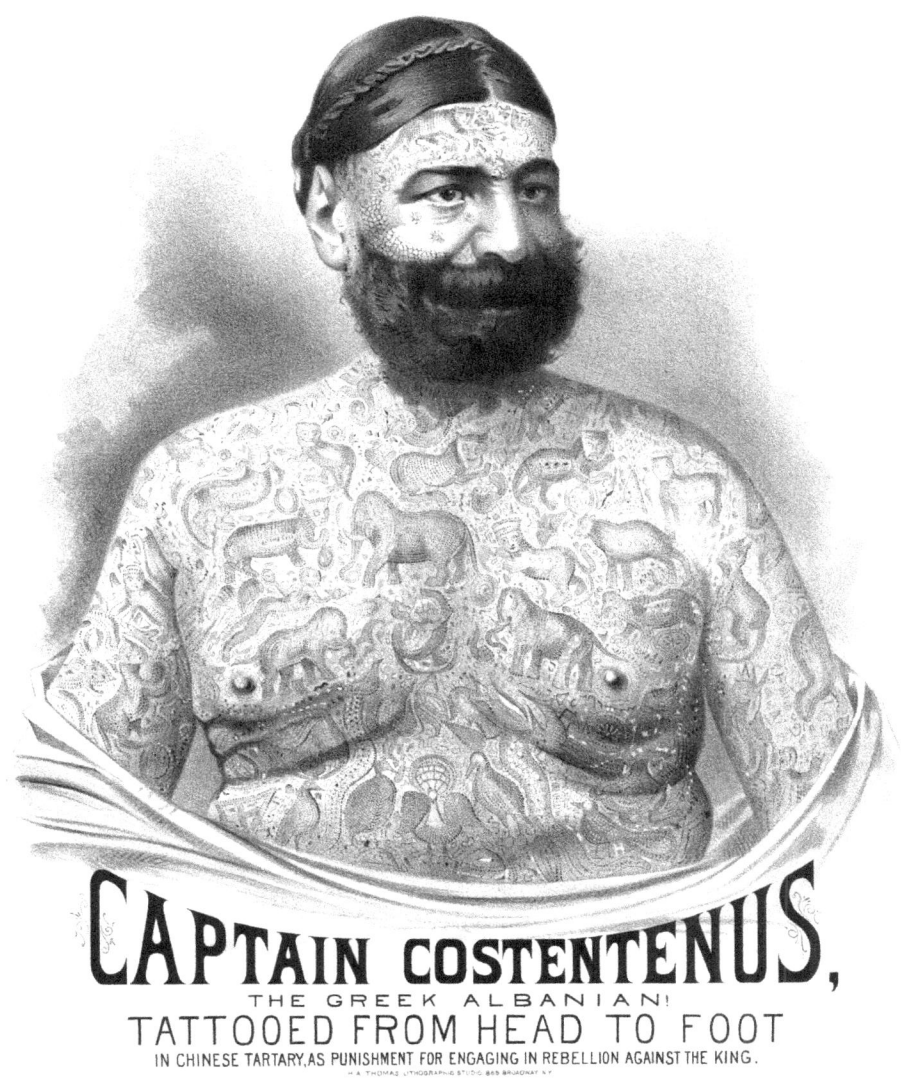

*Half sheet poster for Captain Costentenus, 1877*
*(Robert L. Parkinson Library & Archives, Circus World Museum, Baraboo, Wisconsin)*

in the Midwest. So this time, it was St. Louis doctors William Porter and William S. Edgar who had supposedly examined Costentenus. They apparently recognized him from Hebra's description as the man exhibited in Vienna and attested to his authenticity.[133] Barnum, as always, worked to counter the public's general skepticism of sideshow acts—a skepticism fueled by his own history of dubious exhibits.

The show crossed the Appalachian mountains in October before heading north through Virginia, stopping in the nation's capital on October 27. According to the route book, even President Rutherford B. Hayes wanted to see the tattooed man: "Prof. S. S. Smith and Capt. George Costentenus were before President by special request, and Captain Costentenus is to receive a fine gold medal as a present from the President of the United States, R. B. Hayes."[134] After such a highlight, the season ended a few days later in Philadelphia, having traveled an astonishing 8,300 miles.

For the next three seasons, Costentenus, Barnum, the Flatfoots, and the Bunnells would continue on in much the same way. Several handwritten ledger pages in a scrapbook at the Bridgeport Public Library show that the annual receipts were quite good, ranging from $429,000 to $573,000.[135] The numbers weren't as good as the peak years of 1872 and 1873 ($1 million and $1.5 million, respectively), but still, these were good years for the show.[136]

Barnum took half the profits and the Flatfoots split the rest, which was one of several sources of friction between the partners. When one of the Flatfoots died, Barnum thought he should get the dead man's share. Quite reasonably, the remaining Flatfoots thought this was ridiculous.[137] They also fought over how little Barnum was traveling with the show and how he was diluting the power of his name by licensing it to other, less reputable shows.

133 "The Tattooed Man: Barnum's Great Contribution to History and Ethnology," *St. Louis Globe-Democrat*, August 24, 1877.

134 *Route Book, Season of 1877.*

135 $13 million to $19 million in 2025, per Measuring Worth.

136 *Salmagundi Ledger*; $37 million to $41 million in 2025, per Measuring Worth.

137 Saxon, *PT Barnum*, 266-277.

Despite these disagreements, when it came time for Barnum and the Flatfoots to renegotiate their contract, they struck up a new agreement that was good until 1880. It appeared that Barnum had won most of the arguments. The agreement was remarkably similar to the previous one, but with stipulations that Barnum didn't have to visit the show as often and that he could speculate on other entertainment ventures.[138]

•

Meanwhile, Captain George continued to draw huge crowds—and developed a reputation for being cranky and confrontational. He got into altercations with pushy audience members, would-be robbers, and even fellow performers.

In 1877, the *Chicago Daily Tribune* reported that the Captain cut open his own leg with a knife after an audience member accused him of being a fraud.[139] At a show in Hartford in 1880, he supposedly "slapped an elderly man sharply in the face" after the man pinched him to see if he was real.[140] Costentenus stormed out of a dime museum in Troy, New York, that same year and tried to get the train back to New York City after being pinched, once again. He "went wild with rage, and for a while terror reigned."[141] Yet another newspaper reported that he left the platform during a show in Connecticut because a woman tried to rub his tattoos off with her handkerchief.[142] While most performers didn't complain publicly about being touched, it must have been both unpleasant and relentless. Clearly, some audience members thought that buying a ticket entitled them to poke and prod the performers.

Offstage, Costentenus was a target for thieves. Banks of this era were small and local, so travelers like Costentenus had to carry

---

138 Saxon, *PT Barnum,* 267.

139 "Capt. Costentenus," *Chicago Daily Tribune*, March 1, 1877, 3.

140 "Hartford and Vicinity," *Hartford Daily Courant*, March 11, 1880.

141 "Fact and Fancy Focused," *New York Clipper*, February 7, 1880.

142 "Where Clocks and Watches are Made," *Evening Star* July 22, 1879.

much of their wealth with them. Costentenus no doubt attracted attention not just for his tattoos, but also because he wore "very handsome diamond rings and other jewelry, valued... at... $3,000."[143] A week before the 1878 season opener at Gilmore's Garden in New York City, Costentenus walked across Madison Square to a bar in the Albemarle Hotel, one of the largest and grandest hotels on Broadway. Unfortunately for Costentenus, on the way in, he was punched in the side by "Cathcart, a well-known [troublemaker], and a man known as 'The Doctor'." The ensuing fight left the tattooed man dazed on the floor—but still in possession of his valuables.[144]

A year later, Captain George was tipped off by Mademoiselle Clark, the show's "fat lady," that she had overheard a group of men talking about his diamonds. On the way back to his hotel, three men stopped him and asked what time it was. Forewarned, the Captain promptly knocked one of them down and they fled. At the local police station, Costentenus asked for permission to carry a weapon, which would have been one way to take care of the problem.[145]

During the 1878 season, conflict also broke out backstage. Costentenus got into a brawl with Colonel Routh Goshen, "the Palestine Giant." Goshen, whose real name was Arthur James Caley, stood about 7 feet 5 inches tall and weighed in at around 400 pounds. Caley was not born in Jerusalem, as his publicity claimed, but on the Isle of Man in 1824. He started performing in England around 1851 as "the Manx Giant." By the 1860s, Caley had faked his own death in Paris, possibly to cash in on a life insurance policy, and moved to the United States. There, he took on a new name and rank, courtesy of P. T. Barnum.[146]

Captain Costentenus and Colonel Goshen had not been getting along all season. In June of 1878, when the show was in Toronto, the two fake military men came to blows in the dressing room. The Colonel

143 "Capt. Costentenus Beaten," *New York Times*, March 31, 1878; $100,000 in 2025, per Measuring Worth.

144 "Capt. Costentenus Beaten," *New York Times*.

145 "The Troubles of the Tattooed Greek," *Cincinnati Star* 19 Dec 1879, 6.

146 John Quirk, *The Manx Giant: The Amazing Story of Arthur Caley*, (Manx Heritage Foundation, 2009.)

# COL. GOSHEN

## THE PALESTINE

# GIANT!

## 7 Feet 6 Inches High.

He is the Tallest, the Largest and the Strongest Man of modern times. In every sense of the word, he is a Giant, and stands, like the towering Alps, above

## TEN THOUSAND

### MARVELOUS

# CURIOSITIES

#### WHICH I HAVE NOT THE SPACE TO DESCRIBE.

The Temperate and the Intemperate Family ;

### AUTOMATON

## MUSICIANS,

&c. &c

*Advertisement with a drawing of Colonel Goshen, 1878, (Used with permission from Illinois State University's Special Collections, Milner Library)*

"COL. GOSHEN, THE PALESTINE GIANT! 7 Feet 6 Inches High. He is the Tallest, the Largest and the Strongest Man of modern times. In every sense of the word, he is a Giant, and stands, like the towering Alps, above TEN THOUSAND MARVELOUS CURIOSITIES WHICH I HAVE NOT THE SPACE TO DESCRIBE."

reportedly picked up Captain George and threw him. So Costentenus, "scorning the assistance of the clowns," threw a "tent stake-pin" at the giant. Circus tent stakes are typically about three to four feet long, one or one and a half inches in diameter, and made of wood or iron. It would have been hard to throw such a heavy object. While it was an aggressive move, it didn't really help the situation. Goshen punched the Tattooed Greek and knocked him flat.[147]

147 "Worth More Alive Than When Stuffed," *Cincinnati Enquirer,* June 8, 1878.

Assistant Manager Ad Nathans, younger brother of one of the Flatfoots, stepped in. He insisted that if the two men were going to continue the fight, they needed to take it into the arena and finish it in front of the audience. (Like all the Flatfoots, Ad Nathans tried to seize every opportunity to make a buck.) Goshen declined, and Costentenus sulked off to nurse his injuries—swearing to get Goshen back. Colonel Goshen claimed, "I could have killed him, but I thought he was worth more alive than stuffed, so for Barnum's sake I only bruised him a little."[148] The Captain spent several days out of the public eye, recuperating from his injuries. He doesn't seem to have followed up on his threats of revenge, which was smart, given Goshen's size. Costentenus did, however, start talking about leaving the show.

When they came to Chicago about a month after the fight, Barnum mentioned in an interview that Costentenus was planning on returning to Vienna that next winter. Was Barnum sending a veiled hint to the Captain to shape up, or was Costentenus really looking to quit? Either way, the Tattooed Greek stayed with the show and didn't go back to Europe for several more years. "He is a strange man," Barnum said. "He gave us great trouble till the giant thrashed him... He came to me and said... 'I'm not a coward, but he is a great man, too big.'"[149]

It's worth noting that there's no way to prove or disprove that any of these conflicts and controversies actually happened. It would have been classic Barnum to invent such stories for publicity. Costentenus was, after all, a red-hot celebrity, and Barnum would have fanned the flames in any way possible. However, given the consistency with which reports surfaced about Costentenus's fights and bad moods, it seems likely that there was some truth to the stories.

The reports of Costentenus's actions in 1877 and 1878 paint a picture of a surly loner with few friends. A reporter saw him sitting quietly at a hotel on a rainy day, noting that "Barnum's tattooed warrior was holding service by himself"—sitting alone while other

148 "Worth More Alive," *Cincinnati Enquirer*.

149 "Phineas T. Barnum, An Interesting Chat with the Proprietor of 'The Greatest Show on Earth'," *Inter Ocean*, July 30, 1878.

performers chatted and got ready for the evening train ride.[150] Was he lonely? Newspaper articles never mentioned Costentenus's personal life. There were no marriages to other performers for publicity. There were no jovial discussions of friendships with promoters or managers. Either he guarded his privacy well or he wasn't a very social man.

There were a few men who might have been his friends or companions. Over the course of his years with Barnum, Costentenus had three different agents or attendants working with him—though it's not clear exactly what they did. His first year with the *Greatest Show on Earth*, he had an "attendant," a Mr. Conklin.[151] The next year, he had an "agent," named William J. Dalrymple, and for his last two years, a different agent named John Hannigan.[152]

•

There are so few traces left of who this man was, outside of how he was marketed to the world. Barnum even confessed to not really knowing much about him: "If you should find out he was a pirate I should not be surprised."[153] But what Barnum did or didn't know about Costentenus didn't stop him from making even wilder claims about his origins. Newspaper ads in 1877 introduced a spectacular new drawing of Costentenus stretched out and tied to the ground, while an exotic-looking woman tattooed him. The accompanying text added a shocking new number: "7,000,000 blood producing punctures."[154]

---

150 "At the Hotels," *St. Louis Globe-Democrat*, August 25, 1879.

151 "Barnum's Latest," *New York Times*, October. 7, 1876.

152 *Route Book, Season of 1877; Route Book, Season of 1879, P. T. Barnum's New and Greatest Show on Earth*, Circus Historical Society, https://classic.circushistory.org/History/PTB1879.htm; *Route Book, Season of 1880, P. T. Barnum's Greatest Show on Earth*, Circus Historical Society, https://classic.circushistory.org/History/PTB1880.htm.

153 "Phineas T. Barnum, An Interesting Chat with the Proprietor of 'The Greatest Show on Earth'," *Inter Ocean*, July 30, 1878.

154 "P. T. Barnum's New and Only Greatest Show on Earth," *Evening Herald*, May 14, 1877.

# P. T. BARNUM'S
# New and Only Greatest Show on Earth.

### IN WATER-PROOF TENTS, COVERING SEVERAL ACRES. $1,000,000 INVESTED.
### A GREAT AND AMUSING ACADEMY OF OBJECT TEACHING.

# Museum, Menagerie, Circus, and Hippodrome.

Will travel by rail, on 100 Steel Cars of its own, passing through New York, the Canadas, Michigan, Illinois, Minnesota, Wisconsin, Indiana, Iowa, Missouri, and Texas. The Museum contains 100,000 rare and startling curiosities, including the most remarkable Captain COSTENTENUS, a Greek nobleman, who was

## TATTOED FROM HEAD TO FOOT

in Chinese Tartary, as punishment for engaging in rebellion against the King.

The **MENAGERIE** consists of by far the largest collection of living wild animals that ever travelled, among which are the $25,000 Hippopotamus from the river Nile, Sea Lions from Alaska, Giraffes, the African Lioness and her little royal Cubs, no larger than cats, a picture of which occupies a full page in HARPER'S WEEKLY of April 28th. The six beautiful jet-black $30,000 Trakene Stallions, from Paris, present amazing and ENTIRELY NOVEL performances, which have been witnessed with delight by over 200,000 ladies, gentlemen, and children this spring at Barnum's great Hippodrome Building in New York. This picture shows them

*Advertisement with a drawing of Costentenus being tattooed, Harper's Weekly, May 26, 1877, (Collection of the author) "The Museum contains 100,000 rare and startling curiosities, including the most remarkable Captain COSTENTENUS, a Greek nobleman, who was TATTOOED FROM HEAD TO FOOT in Chinese Tartary, as punishment for engaging in rebellion against the King."*

This ridiculous made-up number was repeated in many news articles, quantifying the suffering that Costentenus had endured.

Barnum pushed the envelope as far as he could with these salacious details. Circuses were often the target of clergymen and town leaders who disapproved of such entertainment: "One circus in a community will do more harm, leave more low, vulgar sayings behind it after one performance, than almost anything that could be brought into it; and yet everybody, almost, patronizes them."[155] "We hope our people will keep away from it. No institution of the EVIL ONE is in our judgment, more demoralizing, corrupting, destructive of the best interests of society than a circus. Do not go; we entreat both young and old not to go to the circus."[156]

With Costentenus and his tattoos, there was blood, there was nudity, there was torture! There was plenty to draw people in—and offend the anti-circus crowd. Barnum tried to shock 19th century sensibilities in promoting the Tattooed Greek without crossing the line. Previous tattooed men had not been presented in this way. In the 1830s and 40s, James O'Connell had been described in the press as a talented dancer—a tattooed man who was pleasant and fun. But 19th century audiences, despite what the moralists would have preferred, loved the tales of blood and torture. As they do today, sex and violence sold tickets. Barnum would not have used graphic imagery of Costentenus being tortured by an exotic, scantily-clad woman if it hadn't worked.

Outside of these advertisements, there had never been a reference to Costentenus being tattooed by a woman in any stories or printed literature. And while Costentenus supposedly had been tattooed in China, the woman in the illustration isn't depicted as Chinese. The image is just more humbug.[157]

The 1878 season's ads featured the same image of Costentenus's

---

155 Linda A. Fisher, Carrie Bowers, *Agnes Lake Hickok: Queen of the Circus, Wife of a Legend,* (University of Oklahoma Press: 2009): 136.

156 Fisher, Bowers, *Agnes Lake Hickok*, 136.

157 "P.T. Barnum's New and Only Greatest Show on Earth," *Harper's Weekly*, May 26, 1877.

torture, but Barnum's ad men swapped out the adjacent images. Old line drawings of hippos and leaping horses were replaced by a portrait of Barnum himself, with giant lettering declaring *P. T. Barnum's Own and Only Greatest Show on Earth*. Another large image featured a ringmaster surrounded by at least eight trained horses with plumed harnesses, promoting that season's "Troupe of Foreign Stallions."[158] Below Costentenus's image was a drawing of his nemesis Colonel Goshen. The giant was shown towering over a small woman and holding a tiny child in one hand. His sword was as tall as the woman standing next to him, which could have been true to scale. Some of the 1878 advertisements skipped the images of horses and amazing curiosities altogether. Those had just one image: Barnum himself.[159]

Newspaper reports from these years swung back and forth between imagining the barbarity of the tattooing Costentenus had endured and detailing the prurient spectacle of seeing him in person. *The City Times* of Janesville, Wisconsin, reported that inking each tattoo had drawn a tear and a drop of blood. "We had been thinking up to that time that it must have been fun to let a female slave write her sentiments on a fellow, but the thought of a barrel of brine and another barrel of blood effectively drowned out what romance we had associated with the proceeding."[160] *The Daily Whig & Courier* of Bangor, Maine, said, "Upon a close inspection... it is seen that he is entirely naked... it has so much the appearance of being clothed that he might walk through the public streets without any one suspecting that he was not dressed in tights."[161]

•

---

158 "PT Barnum's Own and Only Greatest Show on Earth," *Fayette County Herald*, August 15, 1878.

159 "'Time Cannot Wither...'" *The Portland Daily Press*, June 8, 1878.

160 "Barnum's Behemoth," *City Times*, June 19, 1877, CWM Mss 68 Barnum Circus Papers 1967-1918, Box 1 Folder 4, P.T. Barnum Clippings 1876-1880, Circus World Museum Library, Wisconsin Historical Society.

161 "Local Matters," *Bangor Daily Whig & Courier*, July 25, 1876.

*Barnum poster, mentioning Col. Goshen, Little Queen Mab, and Capt. Costentenus, 1879, (Robert L. Parkinson Library & Archives, Circus World Museum, Baraboo. Wisconsin)*

Despite his headliner status with Barnum's show, Costentenus was unhappy. After the 1878 season, he was still talking about going back to Europe, this time to Paris.[162] Perhaps he did. There was no sign of him that winter in any of the East Coast dime museums—or anywhere else, for that matter. Maybe his encounter with Colonel Goshen had shaken him enough that he needed time away from the public eye to nurse his wounded pride. Or maybe he was just tired and took some time off. But when Barnum's 1879 show opened in New York's American Institute building on April 12, Costentenus was back.

By then, Barnum's profits had started to slip. The receipts for 1879 decreased almost 7% from the year before, and the ads were more subdued. The images were those of more standard acts, such as the trained horses and his two equestrienne stars, Madame Elise Dockrill and Emma Lake.

Elise Dockrill, "The Empress of the Arena," was the first woman to ride and drive four horses as well as perform handstands on the back of a horse while it leapt over hurdles. She had worked for Barnum since 1872, and by 1877, she was such a star that she traveled in half of Barnum's private railroad car.

Emma Lake, "America's Side Saddle Queen," was the adopted daughter of American circus royalty. Her mother Agnes Lake was an equestrienne who became the first female circus owner in the United States—after her husband Bill was murdered by a man who had been thrown out of a show for not paying. (Bill Lake was Agnes's *first* husband named Bill to be murdered. She married folk hero Wild Bill Hickock in March 1876, and he was shot in the back a few months later while playing poker in a saloon in Deadwood, South Dakota. Thankfully, Agnes's third husband was not named Bill and was not shot to death.)

It's not clear why Barnum's 1879 advertisements changed focus from curiosities to Dockrill and Lake. With ticket sales down, perhaps Barnum chose to emphasize the foundation of the circus: talent and horses—or more specifically, talent on horses. The curiosities were limited to a small line of text: "A museum of 50,000 curiosities, Capt.

---

162 "Evening Echoes," *New Journal*, October 14, 1878, 4.

Costentenus, the Tattooed Greek, Col. Goshen, the Palestine Giant, Little Queen Mab, the Smallest and Prettiest Dwarf ever seen, a sight worth coming 100 miles to see."[163] While Captain George remained a big draw for Barnum, he was no longer the biggest.

In 1880, the ads were wildly varied. Some were text only, some were the portrait of Barnum, some had the image of Costentenus getting tattooed, and some featured performing horses. The only constant was the hype of that season's new star: Zazel, the first human cannonball.[164] Her "cannon," powered by rubber springs, was the invention of her manager, William Hunt, a.k.a. the Great Farini. In future years, Farini would be instrumental in finally bringing the Tattooed Greek back to perform in Europe once again.

The 1880 season took the show further west, introducing Costentenus to Colorado, Nebraska, Texas, and Arkansas. This was the last time he would be part of the *Greatest Show on Earth*. At this point, he was a veteran American showman, greeted at one stop in the Midwest "by his old newspaper friends."[165] One reporter mused that "anybody in the country who has not seen him must live far in the backwoods."[166]

But his status as one of Barnum's top acts had slipped. Emma Lake, Zazel, and Madame Nelson (with her flock of trained doves) had taken over the top spots.[167] Increasingly, when Captain George was mentioned, he was just a part of the museum of 50,000 curiosities, not a top-billed star.[168]

It's unclear if Barnum didn't renew Costentenus's contract

---

163 PT Barnum's Own and Only Greatest Show on Earth, *Daily Republican*, October 8, 1879.

164 "The Sensation of the Day," *Rock Island Argus*, June 9, 1880; "When Barnum Comes," *Weekly Oskaloosa Herald*, July 8, 1880; "Barnum's Day: The People's Holiday," Omaha Daily Bee, July 30, 1880; "Coming, Entire and Undivided," *Mexico Weekly Ledger*, August 26, 1880.

165 "Amusements," *St. Louis Globe-Democrat*, September 1, 1880.

166 "The Dwarves and Giants: Who Some of Them Are, and How They Live," *Evening Star*, October 29, 1881.

167 "When Barnum Comes," *Galveston News*, October 24, 1880.

168 "Barnum's Day, The People's Holiday," *Omaha Daily Bee*, July 30, 1880.

or if Captain George finally followed through on his threats to leave the show. Either way, he returned to New York after the *Greatest Show on Earth* wrapped up in Missouri in November 1880. He lined up bookings with several dime museums that kept him occupied and employed for several months. But he was ready for some time off.

•

## Off the Stage and In the Papers

Costentenus had been working almost nonstop since his debut in Vienna in 1870. If he managed his money well, he should have been able to afford some time off. It appears that he started taking well-deserved summer breaks in 1880. The Captain wasn't the first successful curiosity to take a vacation. For the equestrians, acrobats, and most other big top performers, working summers was a necessity. That was when most shows went out touring. But sideshow performers, who were more likely to be working winters in dime museums as well, could sometimes manage a summer vacation.

For curiosities like Captain George, however, it could be hard to enjoy some quiet time—and keep a low profile.

In July of 1831, for example, Chang and Eng Bunker, the so-called Siamese twins (famous conjoined twins who were actually ethnic Chinese but born in Siam), took a break from their grueling schedule of performances. It ended up not being very relaxing. They went to Lynnfield, Massachusetts, for "a little relaxation and amusement... going out occasionally for the purpose of fishing, shooting, etc."[169] Unfortunately for the brothers, they were hounded and harassed by the townspeople. A mob followed them when they went hunting, and Chang and Eng ended up firing their weapons at the crowd in self-defense. They were arrested, hauled before a judge, and fined $200

---

169 Huang, *Inseparable,* 112.

for assault and disturbing the peace.[170] How do you take a vacation when your mere presence draws such attention?

The Tattooed Greek clearly found someplace more private than the twins had, since he managed to stay out of the newspapers (and out of jail) on his breaks. For the most part. He showed up in a few articles in 1881—but they seem to have been made up stories. At this point in his career, the Tattooed Greek had become part of the American consciousness, so his name showed up in a number of fictionalized and humorous articles.

The *Boston Globe* published the first of these articles about Costentenus in early May of 1881. In "Loving a Curiosity," a nameless, wealthy, and beautiful young woman started visiting the Captain at Bunnell's Museum on the Bowery. She was initially "spellbound... of his almost perfect physique... and the tattooing of his nude body."[171] The two conversed in French, "growing more affectionate." But the Tattooed Greek grew uncomfortable with the young woman's attention to his nudity, so he began to wear a robe when she visited. "From that day the young lady's fervor began to wane."

This article gets right to the heart of the concern many Americans had about circuses, sideshows, theaters, and ballets—anywhere the human body was less-than-fully covered. What harm would that "nudity" cause to the impressionable? What sin and scandal would creep into what they viewed as a God-fearing, Christian nation? This article is likely a cautionary tale, not a true story of a young lady consumed by a "mysterious but uncontrollable infatuation" with the mostly-nude tattooed man.

Also appearing that summer in a number of newspapers was a humorous article about two young boys from Orange, Pennsylvania. After the boys saw the Tattooed Greek, they decided to emulate him—with oil paints.[172] One boy painted the other with numerous "tattoos." But after a shirtless exhibition in a breezy shed, he then got pneumonia. Did this really happen? Probably not. Especially because being shirtless in a breezy shed does not cause pneumonia.

---

170 Huang, *Inseparable*, 114-115; $7,600 in 2025, per Measuring Worth.

171 "Loving a Curiosity," *Boston Globe*, May 1, 1881.

172 "From Our Exchanges," *The Perry County Democrat*, May 11, 1881.

Two articles claimed that Costentenus appeared at Coney Island, but these seem to be humbug. *The New York Times* claimed he was spotted at "a very small opera-house in the lively precincts of West Brighton" when he was actually out west in Nebraska with Barnum's show.[173] And the *New York Clipper* ran an article on the development of Coney Island saying that the Tattooed Greek was appearing at "the Great and Only Ten-Cent Museum." This was described as a "rough shanty" near "the incomplete new iron pier."[174] The Captain was "dressed in a fur cap and overcoat and refuses to strip because the crowd is too small."[175] Was Costentenus really there? If he was, other newspapers didn't take note—which is highly unlikely.

Another interesting item appeared in the *Brooklyn Union-Argus* in 1880. This one was neither made up nor salacious. While working at Allen's Dime Museum in Brooklyn that November, George Costentenus made a trip across the East River to the Superior Court of the City of New York. After five years of touring throughout the country, he had decided to become a citizen of the United States. He swore before clerk Thomas Boese that he renounced "forever all allegiance and fidelity to... the King of Greece."[176] This Declaration of Intent was, in the latter part of the 19th century, the first step towards becoming an American citizen.

All these stories show just how famous Captain George had become. These tales of romance, young imitators, and new citizenship assumed that readers were already familiar with him. No newspaper would make references to the Tattooed Greek like these if they weren't confident everyone knew who he was.

---

173 "Incidents at the Island: Lightings Playing Among the Clouds," *New York Times*, Aug. 8, 1880.

174 "Shows and Showmen of Coney Island," *New York Clipper*, July 23, 1881, 281.

175 "Shows and Showmen," *New York Clipper.*

176 George C. D. Odell, *Annals of the New York Stage Volume 11,* (AMS Press, 1970): 401; "Amusements," Brooklyn Union-Argus November 13, 1880; National Archives at New York City; New York, New York; NAI Title: *Petitions for Naturalization, 1793-1906*; NAI Number: 5324244; Record Group Title: Records of the Immigration and Naturalization Service, 1787-2004; Record Group Number: 85.

•

After all this, Costentenus moved on from the *Greatest Show on Earth*. He would not return to the show that had made him so famous. He wasn't the only one. First, the Flatfoots pulled out, ending their five-year partnership with Barnum in November of 1880.[177] Barnum had invited them to continue their arrangement into 1881, but for a smaller percentage of the profits. Barnum was squeezing the Flatfoots to make room for his new partners, James A. Bailey and James L. Hutchinson.[178] Of course, Barnum hadn't told the Flatfoots he had signed with these two new partners. Bailey and Hutchinson's existing show, *Cooper, Bailey and Co.'s Great London Circus*, had been providing the *Greatest Show on Earth* with stiff competition since its return from a lengthy Australian tour in 1877-1878. This new partnership would go on to become the famed *Barnum and Bailey Circus* that would carry Barnum's name long after his death. But the Flatfoots, facing a pay cut, unsurprisingly declined to be folded into this new agreement.

Barnum, for his part, thought the split with the Flatfoots was amicable, commenting that "I hope you… will all come up and see how things are fixed here… I feel grateful that we have got along together so pleasantly and profitable for five years."[179] It's unclear if the Flatfoots felt the same way. Judging from the earlier difficulties they'd had—and the issues that Coup and Castello had also had with Barnum—perhaps five years of working with Barnum was enough. Or perhaps they didn't appreciate having another partnership contract signed behind their backs while they were out on the road with the circus.

The Bunnell brothers also departed, after nine years running Barnum's sideshows. It's not clear if they were pushed out to make room for Bailey's museum manager or if they left of their own accord. There's no evidence either way. The Bunnells' New American Museum in New York City, with Barnum's silent financing, was going

177 Saxon, *P.T. Barnum*, 273.

178 Saxon, *P. T. Barnum*, 283; Kunhardt, *P. T. Barnum*, 272.

179 Saxon, *P.T. Barnum*, 400.

well. Their museum, like Barnum's back in the 1840s and 1850s, had become a successful New York institution. After their partnership with Barnum dissolved, the Bunnells moved the museum to a new location, opening in early December 1879. There, they employed many of the sideshow performers they had promoted for Barnum— including Captain George.[180]

The Bunnells hired both Costentenus and his former adversary Colonel Goshen, as well as a few new performers to fill out their new space.[181] The Tattooed Greek settled into a year of steady work with the Bunnells. He appeared at their museum (now nicknamed "The Hub"), as well as at their Brooklyn location and a few other temporary museum spaces they leased in other cities. Costentenus and the Bunnells' traveling museum company spent the month of April in Buffalo at St. James Hall, and May in Baltimore at The Masonic Hall. They entertained large crowds at each stop that spring.[182]

In these new circumstances, Costentenus was now talking to the audiences for himself—though apparently in French. And his story continued to evolve. He now claimed that he had been captured in a revolution in Turkistan (which was another way to say Central Asia/ Western China). He also said he had been tattooed by a princess while bound at full length on the ground. At long last, he appeared to be referencing the image that Barnum had used in his advertisements. But a reporter who spoke with him in Buffalo had his doubts, wondering if the tattooist was really "some other female, but for show purposes a princess is most effective."[183]

Costentenus had left Barnum behind, but he had picked up a talent for overstatement from his former employer. The Captain laid it on thicker than ever, claiming that he had "suffered more than

180 "Introductory," *New York Clipper*, December 4, 1880; "G.B. Bunnell's Great Show," *New York Clipper* November 27, 1880.

181 "A Chinese Fair," *New York Clipper*, January 15, 1881; *Route Book, Season of 1880*.

182 "How He Suffered," Buffalo Evening News, April 19, 1881; "Unterhaltungen," *Der Deutsche Correspondent*, May 4, 1881; "Two Days," *Poughkeepsie Eagle-News*, May 23, 1881.

183 "How He Suffered," *Buffalo Evening News*.

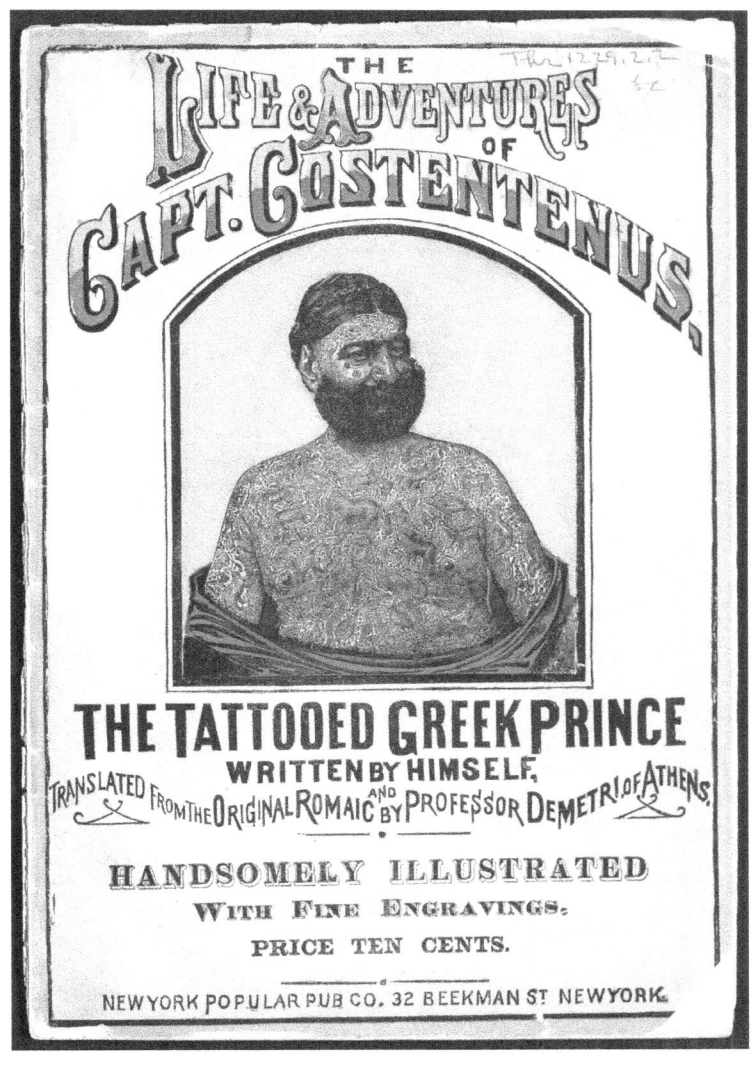

The cover of Costentenus's 1881 "autobiography," (THR 1229.2.10*, Harvard Theatre Collection, Houghton Library, Harvard University)

"THE LIFE & ADVENTURES OF CAPT. COSTENTENUS, THE TATTOOED GREEK PRINCE, WRITTEN BY HIMSELF, TRANSLATED FROM THE ORIGINAL ROMAIC BY PROFESSOR DEMETRI OF ATHENS. HANDSOMELY ILLUSTRATED WITH FINE ENGRAVINGS. PRICE TEN CENTS*."

*($3 in 2025, per Measuring Worth.)

Jesus Christ."[184] And for the first time, his entire life story was written down, in all its questionable glory, in an epic 1881 "autobiographical" pamphlet, *The Life and Adventures of Captain Costentenus.*

184 "How He Suffered" *Buffalo Evening News* April 19, 1881.

# CHAPTER FIVE

# THE LIFE AND ADVENTURES OF CAPTAIN COSTENTENUS, THE TATTOOED GREEK PRINCE

The Captain's pamphlet begins:

## INTRODUCTORY.

Urged by the importunities of many thousands of people in all parts of the civilized globe, and in a spirit of gratitude to the great American people to who I owe, under Providence, the preservation of my life and liberty from the oppressions of barbarian tyranny, I have consented, with much reluctance, to give to the world the particulars of my strange and most eventful life. I have hitherto refrained from the task, because I am aware that many of my adventures are so much out of the common course that they will be deemed incredible.

On this head I can only say that truth is frequently much stranger than fiction. The very fact of my now being alive and in good health is so extraordinary, that many eminent surgeons and doctors have refused to believe in the indelible nature of the patterns which cover my body from the very crown of my head–beneath the hair–to the tips of my fingers and toes, till convinced by ocular examination and the strictest tests of which science is capable.

Before my appearance settled the question it was asserted to be IMPOSSIBLE for any living man to survive the operation of tattooing when extended over the whole surface of the skin. The inflammation well known to accompany it is so severe, that its continuance for a period of three months was deemed necessarily fatal to the most powerful constitution.

Yet the *facts remain*, and, as they exist in me, they are a living contradiction to all the doctors of Europe and America. I *was* tattooed in one operation, as is proven by the unity of the pattern which covers my body; and yet I live, as thousands–nay, millions–can witness, a hale man, without one square inch of my skin from which blood has not flowed under the torturing points of the tattooing-needles.

I am myself alone a living contradiction of all humanity. No man ever suffered as I have suffered, and it need excite no wonder that no man ever had such a strange life as mine. With this brief explanation let me proceed to my task.

DJORDGI KONSTANTINUS.

••

While many sideshow performers had promotional pamphlets, *The Life and Adventures of Captain Costentenus* is something special. It takes the reader on an epic journey across multiple continents with exotic harems, loathsome pirates, daring escapes, passionate love stories (complete with beautiful princesses), and finally, captivity and torture by tattooing. Costentenus (and Barnum) had been expanding and refining his story since his debut in Vienna 11 years previously. But here, ghostwriters at the New York Popular Publishing Company took the Tattooed Greek's story to a new level. It's as if they had a checklist of plot points guaranteed to appeal to American audiences.

Performers would often sell pamphlets and photographs at their shows to pick up a bit of extra income. There are few records of what the profits were, but financial ledger pages in a Barnum scrapbook at the Bridgeport Public Library in Connecticut show that Costentenus's photographs brought in $325 in 1877 (about $10,000 in today's money).

Souvenir pamphlets were an extension of the acts in written form, molded by contemporary agendas.[185] While never written by the performer (the two leading publishers, the New York Popular Publishing Company and Merchant's Gargling Oil, hired writers to churn out these stories), the booklets did "provide the protagonists with a voice and some determination over their legacy."[186] They are worth looking at in detail, but with a skeptical eye.

The standard curiosity pamphlet had a simple formula: a wild story that purported to be the performer's biography, a physical description that stretched the truth, and testimonials by famous people vouching for the act's authenticity. Often, the pamphlet presented the performer as a positive moral example—a good person despite the differences that made them a curiosity.[187] If the performer was from a foreign land (or just pretending to be), there would also be historical and geographical information about the performer's supposed homeland.[188]

For example, an 1831 pamphlet, *An Historical Account of the Siamese Twin Brothers, From Actual Observations* ("For sale only at the exhibition room. Price 12 ½ cents.") presented the story of Chang and Eng Bunker.[189] It begins with a testimonial from the president of

185 John Woolf, *The Wonders: The Extraordinary Performers Who Transformed the Victorian Age*, (Pegasus Books, 2019): 46, 56.

186 Woolf, *The Wonders*, 46.

187 Woolf, *The Wonders*, 56.

188 The Circassian Girl: Zalumma Agra "Star of the East" Now on Exhibition at Barnum's Museum (Jas. B. Rodgers Co, 1873), P.T. Barnum Research Collection, Bridgeport History Center Archives, http://hdl.handle.net/11134/110002:2330; History of Rudolph Lucasie, a Native of Lenabon, Madagascar... On Exhibition at Barnum's American Museum (New York, 1860), Circus World Museum Library, Wisconsin Historical Society.

189 James W. Hale, *An Historical Account of the Siamese Twin Brothers, From Actual Observations,* (Elliot and Palmer, 1831), https://archive.org/details/historicalaccoun01hale_0/page/12/mode/2up; $5 in 2025 per Measuring Worth.

the Royal College of Surgeons: "…the public may be assured that the projected exhibition of these remarkable and interesting youths is in no respect deceptive; and further that there is nothing whatever, offensive to delicacy in the said exhibition."[190]

Purportedly written by their manager, this pamphlet describes Chang and Eng's childhood in Siam (now Thailand) and their voyage to America. It provides a portrait and physical descriptions, along with reassurances of the twins' good health and acute intellects. Their "shrewdness and keenness of remark" are detailed in stories of their interactions with the public, such as: "A visitor once came in the room, who had but one eye; upon which they observed to the door-keeper that the gentleman should have paid only half price for admission, as he had only half the chance to see which others had." There is also a geography lesson on the land of the twins' birth, as many readers would have had no idea where Siam was. Then, for a dose of racist sensationalism (disguised as educational information), the booklet throws in a graphic description of the prince of Laos poisoning himself to escape a gruesome execution. It concludes with a medical discussion of the twins' condition, including how doctors did not recommend surgical separation. The twins themselves, it said, "have no reason to wish for a change."

Chang and Eng's pamphlet was sensational—and successful, just like their act. By 1834, their dramatic booklet was in its 10th edition of 2,000 copies.

All four of Costentenus's tattooed predecessors in the 1800s also had their own "autobiographical" pamphlets:

• Joseph Kabris's *Précis Historique et Véritable du Séjour de Joseph Kabris* was published in the early 19th century,
• John Rutherford's *An Account of the Capture of the Ship Agnes* was first published in 1829,
• Barnet Burns's *A Brief Narrative of the Remarkable History of Barnet Burns* appeared in 1835,
• and James O'Connell's *The Life and Adventures of James F.*

---

190 Hale, *An Historical Account of the Siamese Twin Brothers*, 1.

*O'Connell* was published in 1842.[191]

All of these booklets incorporated a popular trope of the time: the captivity narrative. Each man had been traveling somewhere

Tattooing of O'Connell and Keenan.

"With a sudden blow from a stick she drove the thorns into my flesh; one needs must when the devil drives, so I summoned all my fortitude, set my teeth, and bore it like a martyr."—Page 38

*Drawing of bare-breasted native women painfully tattooing O'Connell and Keenan, from Henry Howe's* Life and Death on the Ocean: A Collection of Extraordinary Adventures, *1855, (Library of Congress), "With a sudden blow from a stick she drove the thorns into my flesh; one needs must when the devil drives, so I summoned all my fortitude, set my teeth, and bore it like a martyr."*

---

191 Joseph Kabris, *Précis Historique et Véritable du Séjour de Joseph Kabris, Natif de Bordeaux, Dans les Isles Mendoça, Situées dans l'Océan Pacifique, Sous le 10e Degré de Latitude Sud, 240e Degré de Longitude*, (F. Mari, not dated); John Rutherford, *An Account of the Capture of the Ship Agnes, Commanded by Capt. Coffin; The Murder of The Captain and Eight of Her Crew by the Natives of New Zealand in 1816*, (C. Malley, Horse Market, 1829); Barnet Burns, *A Brief Narrative of the Remarkable History of Barnet Burns, an English Sailor, Who Has Lately Been Exhibiting at the 'Surrey Zoological Gardens,' and Other Place of Amusement*, (E. Justins and Son, Printers, 1835); James F. O'Connell, *The Life and Adventures of James F. O'Connell, The Tattooed Man: During a Residence of Eleven Years in New Holland and the Caroline Islands.*

exotic and was captured by "savages." They tattooed him against his will, and after this excruciating torture, he was rescued or managed to escape. This trope continued to be used by later performers, including tattooed women, whose gender added a prurient element to the pamphlets.

Besides being a thrilling framework for each performer's story, the captivity narrative provided an easy explanation of why they had so many tattoos. They hadn't made the scandalous choice to get covered in ink. It had been forced upon them! Now they had no choice but to earn their living by standing on a stage, mostly nude, because they were too "freakish" to be gainfully employed elsewhere.

These captivity narratives were grounded in the racist idea that Westerners were "civilized" and everyone else was "savage." Attitudes toward people from other cultures were (and still are) often based on prejudice, suspicion, and a sense of superiority. The pamphlets mirrored that. American audiences were eager to believe in their own importance. "The ability to assign primitiveness to other people affirmed the sense of belonging... and enjoying the ability to do this as an audience member was a popular form of entertainment."[192]

Sideshow acts and the pamphlets they sold reinforced these attitudes. The tales that sideshow talkers used to pull in audiences were never just about the performers themselves. The narratives were built around themes in popular books and prominent news stories of the day. They often threw in cameos by real, well-known people, to add exciting brushes with fame—or infamy—with little regard for the truth. In the sideshow business, giving the audience a fantastic story was always part of the game of making more money.[193]

Looking at it in this context, *The Life and Adventures of Captain Costentenus* is both a work of delight and loaded with problematic narratives. At 23 pages, this "autobiography" is one of the longest of the genre. While it claims to be "written by himself, and translated from the original Romaic by Professor Demetri of Athens," the Captain

---

192 Linda Frost, *Never One Nation: Freaks, Savages, and Whiteness in US Popular Culture, 1850-1877*, (University of Minnesota Press, 2005): 4-5.

193 Robert Bogdan, *Freak Show: Presenting Human Oddities for Amusement and Profit*, (Chicago, 1988): 95-96.

was illiterate. The ghostwriter who undoubtedly crafted this lengthy booklet recast Captain George Costentenus, surly tattooed performer, as a man of action and adventure. The cover features a crude, two-color lithographic version of the *Atlas of Hautkrankheiten*'s image of Costentenus, and brags that it is "handsomely illustrated with fine engravings."[194] The story begins much as many other performer pamphlets did, with background on Costentenus's childhood. The writer assures the reader that, while they won't believe much of what is on the following pages, it is true and accurate. We are in for a wild ride, spun out in 18 short chapters.

••

## CHAPTER I.
## MY CHILDHOOD.

I was born in the Turkish province of Albania, in Turkey, in the year 1836. The village in which I first saw the light no longer exists even in name, save for the mouldering ruins of a few cottages, from which forty years' rains have removed the black smoke-stains which once told of the torch of the incendiary.

Marked almost from my birth for misfortune and vicissitude, my after life fulfilled the promise only too well.

••

The first chapter dives right in with exaggerated and questionable claims. As usual, Costentenus's birth year might be right—or it might not be. His later passport documents contradict the narrative and give his birth year as 1833 and his birthplace as Athens.[195] But the decade and his Greek heritage are at least consistent.

The pamphlet introduces his parents, Constantine Constantinus, whose name was "corrupted by the Turks into its present

---

194 Djordgi Konstantinus, *The Life and Adventures of Capt. Costentenus, The Tattooed Greek Prince*, (New York Popular Publishing Co., 1881), Harvard Theatre Collection, Thr 1229.2.10. Houghton Library, Harvard University, Cambridge,. Mass.

195 National Archives and Records Administration (NARA); Washington D.C.; NARA Series: *Passport Applications, 1795-1905; Roll #: 260; Volume #: Roll 260 - 01 Nov 1883-31 Dec 1883*; Konstantinus, *Life and Adventures*, 3.

form, Costentenus,"[196] and Maryam, who "had the misfortune to be too beautiful to escape the eye of the tyrannical Pasha of Yanina."

His hometown "was the sole remnant of a once flourishing colony of Greek nobles... who had fled Constantinople when it was taken by the Turks"[197] in 1455. These former nobles "reared their flocks in peace... and trained up their children to love Greece and to hate their infidel invaders."[198] His family, "as direct descendents of Constantine the Great, had been considered the heads of our little band from time immemorial."

The pamphlet is setting Costentenus up for greatness here. He was descended from nobility, backing up the claims made in newspapers and on the cover of the pamphlet that he was a prince. While Christianity isn't mentioned, American readers of the time would have understood the implied subtext: these Greeks were holding the line of Western Civilization in both culture and religion, fleeing their Muslim oppressors, and keeping their sacred culture safe.

> The pasha smiled; and men used to say that the smile of Ali Tebelen was more dangerous than his frown.

Now the plot thickens, and a historical figure joins the story: "It was under Ali Tebelen [sic], the bloody Pasha of Yanina, that the woes of my native village came to their culmination a few years after my birth."[199] Ali Pasha of Tepelena was indeed a real man, born sometime around 1740 in Albania. He rose to prominence as the leader of a band of brigands. Through murder, threats, and military force, he expanded his wealth and power to become an important Ottoman governor. Ali ruled over the Pashalik of Yanina (parts of Albania, Greece, and Macedonia), and for a time, he was largely independent from the Ottomans. Eventually, the sultan sent troops to reign in Ali's unchecked power, and Ali was killed in the ensuing conflict.

---

196 Konstantinus, *Life and Adventures*, 3.

197 Konstantinus, *Life and Adventures*, 3.

198 Konstantinus, *Life and Adventures*, 3.

199 Konstantinus, *Life and Adventures*, 3.

Lord Byron, who met Ali in 1809, described him as "very fat and not tall, but with a fine face... He has the appearance of any thing but his real character, for he is... guilty of the most horrible cruelties."[200] Byron's description of Ali to the Western world was one of many that introduced this minor Ottoman despot to the world, making him "the inspiration for a host of more or less fanciful books, articles, and dramas, becoming in Western Europe the best-known figure in the Ottoman Empire."[201] It's not surprising, then, that Ali would appear in a sideshow pamphlet nearly 60 years after his death. He had been made into the prototypical Ottoman villain, and his name still conjured images of death and terror.

*Portrait of Ali Pasha by Charles Robert Cockerell, from* Travels in Sicily, Greece and Albania, Volume 1, *by Thomas Smart Hughes, 1820, (American Geographical Society Library, University of Wisconsin-Milwaukee)*

Unfortunately, there's a problem with Ali Pasha's presence in Costentenus's narrative: he died in 1822, long before any of Captain George's alleged birthdates. The author was playing fast and loose with dates, knowing that the average reader wasn't likely to know such details.

One of the most well-known stories of Ali Pasha's cruelty appeared in poetry and an opera. A young Greek woman was kidnapped from her home by Ali's soldiers and imprisoned with a number of prostitutes. The next night, so the story went, Ali had all of the women tied up in sacks, taken out to the middle of a lake, and

---

200 David Brewer, *The Greek War of Independence: The Struggle for Freedom from Ottoman Oppression*, (Abrams Press, 2022): 36.

201 Brewer, *The Greek War of Independence*, 36.

dumped into the water to drown.[202] In Costentenus's story, he was with his mother at the market to sell silk when she was noticed by Ali Pasha. Both Costentenus and his mother were kidnapped by Ali's men and taken to his harem. Would they, too, meet a grisly end?

'Kill me!' she cried. 'Kill me! I am the wife of Constantine Costentenus, and you are a coward.'

The narrative does not spell out Costentenus's mother's rape, but the undercurrent is there. "I can dimly remember my mother... always in tears, all that day..." But suddenly, the women of the harem were shrieking and Costentenus's mother stood holding a dagger dripping with blood. She had resisted Ali's advances and stabbed him.[203] In an instant, there was a flash and a bang and "my mother fell dead before my eyes, shot through the heart."

Years later, the pamphlet says, he finally learned what had really happened that fateful night: Costentenus's father, upon hearing of the abduction of his wife and son, followed their trail, broke into the harem, and saw his wife struggling with Ali. In that moment, he decided that he needed to spare her further degradation, so (plot twist!) he was the one who shot her! This quick death had saved his wife from a crueler fate, presumably a slow death by drowning, tied up in a sack. Then, in a final act of defiance, Constantine Costentenus took his own life. In retribution, Ali Pasha destroyed the Costentenuses' village and drove their remaining family out of Albania. But he would take in the boy as his own. Young Costentenus would be raised by the women of Ali Pasha's harem, growing up ignorant of his name, his family's origin, and their fate.

The melodrama is high, and this is only the end of the first chapter.

••

CHAPTER II.
MY BOYHOOD.

---

202 Brewer, *The Greek War of Independence*, 37.

203 Konstantinus, *Life and Adventures*, 4.

As a child, after the memory of these terrible events had died away, I was as happy as a spoiled child could be. The women of the harem petted and indulged me to my heart's content, and I grew up in the enjoyment of every sort of luxury.

••

Ali Pasha died within the year (never mind that he actually died many years earlier), and his entire harem was sent to Cairo to "the care of his friend and fellow Albanian Mehemet Ali, Viceroy of Egypt."[204]

Here we have another real Ottoman ruler who readers would have recognized. Mehemet (or Muhammad) Ali was born in 1769 in what is now Greece and rose through the ranks of the Ottoman military to become the governor of Egypt.[205] He consolidated his power by murdering thousands of members of the military class in Egypt—and anyone else who got in his way.[206] His family would rule Egypt until 1952, and today, he is thought of by many as the founder of modern Egypt. At least here we have a historical figure whose life span did actually overlap that of Costentenus.

Under Mehemet Ali's roof, so the pamphlet says, Costentenus was raised like a young Muslim prince, "taught to read the Koran, to ride and handle arms." He "was considered—and I say it without any vanity—a beautiful child."[207] As a result of his rather feminine beauty, "the women of the harem were fond of dressing me up as a girl and passing me off as such." Although he "rebelled stoutly against this," he was even introduced to Mehemet Ali as a girl named Fatima. Princess Zuleika, the viceroy's favorite, pretended that Fatima was her new maid. No one outside the harem ever suspected that Fatima was really young Costentenus.

---

204 Konstantinus, *Life and Adventures*, 4.

205 Helene Anne B. Rivlin, "Muḥammad Alī." *Encyclopedia Britannica*, https://www.britannica.com/biography/Muhammad-Ali-pasha-and-viceroy-of-Egypt, accessed December 2, 2021.

206 Caroline Finkel, *Osman's Dream: The History of the Ottoman Empire*, (Basic Books, 2005) 426-428.

207 Konstantinus, *Life and Adventures*, 4.

Mehemet Ali became seriously ill in 1848 and died in the following year (a rare instance of the pamphlet actually sticking to facts). His son Ibrahim took over and sent Princess Zuleika to the sultan in Constantinople as a gift. Zuleika was able to choose two others to accompany her. So Costentenus, as Fatima, found himself "in the company of my mistress and the black slave Saad on board a brig bound for Constantinople."[208]

Once on the ship, Zuleika revealed to the boy that (big plot twist!) his true name was Djorji Costentenus, son of the "King of the Mountains," and she was actually his cousin, Aspasia![209] They were both Greek Christians. Not only that, they weren't Ottoman subjects at all, but British! According to Aspasia, they'd both been born on the Greek island of Corfu, which, as part of the Ionian Islands, was British. Here, the pamphlet further dignifies this tattooed man to

*Mehemet Ali in his palace, lithograph by Louis Haghe after David Roberts, from* The Holy Land, Syria, Idumea, Arabia, Egypt, and Nubia, Volume 6, *1849, (American Geographical Society Library, University of Wisconsin-Milwaukee)*

---

208 Konstantinus, *Life and Adventures*, 5.

209 Konstantinus, *Life and Adventures*, 5.

Western readers of the time. He was not only a Greek prince, he was also a Christian and a British subject.

The name Aspasia is plucked from ancient Greek history. A contemporary of Socrates and Plato, Aspasia was a philosopher, romantically attached to the legendary Athenian politician Pericles.[210] Several 19th century authors used Aspasia and Pericles as characters in romantic novels and poems. For many readers, her name would have conjured beauty and sensitivity, as well as intelligence.

Costentenus's Aspasia, shedding her disguise as Zuleika, told the young man that she had been engineering their escape from the harem for years. She had stolen the viceroy's state jewels and arranged for a British frigate to rescue them before they reached Constantinople. But (brace yourself), it was just then that "the deep sullen doom of a distant gun came rolling over the sea."

••

CHAPTERS III - VIII:
THE CHASE, THE PIRATES,
THE PIRATE'S DEN, THE EXPLOSION,
OUR SECOND ESCAPE, WRECKED.

Aspasia looked at me with a new expression. She, who had been the leader and protector up to that time, had become the helpless one. She looked up to me in admiration, and whispered:

"Oh... how brave you are! But what can a boy like you do?"

••

It's clear at this point that *The Life and Adventures of Captain Costentenus* is more of a dime novel than an autobiography. Chang and Eng Bunker's pamphlet was a traditional sideshow biography, sticking close-ish to the facts of their lives. The Captain's story is pure, sensational fiction.

---

210 Rosie Tanabe, "Aspasia," New World Encyclopedia, https://www.newworldencyclopedia.org/p/index.php?title=Aspasia&oldid=1060004, accessed December 16, 2021.

The pamphlet rolls on.

The viceroy had discovered the theft of his jewels, and an Egyptian steamship was in hot pursuit. Aspasia and young Djorji bribed the captain of their ship with one of the gems to help them get away, but (there's always a but), "Little did we know the trap into which we had fallen. Better had the Egyptian steamer caught us than to suffer what we afterward did."[211]

The ship's captain was greedy, and he wanted all the jewels—and Aspasia—for himself. Young Costentenus tried to defend her, but "in a trice, [the captain] had me by the throat." They thought all was lost. But... just then, the ship was attacked by pirates! (What's a seafaring story without pirates?)

Djorji ran up on deck to join the fight. But the cowardly captain and his men were on their knees, hopeless as Greek pirate ships surrounded them. Costentenus's bravery and harsh words shamed the crew into fighting, but the pirates soon won the day. Knocked unconscious during the battle, Costentenus awoke on the pirate ship. But he was not killed, for Aspasia had caught the eye of the pirate captain.[212]

The pirate captain was named Perikles (of course), in reference to the ancient Aspasia's romantic partner. In keeping with history, this Perikles was "entirely infatuated" with Aspasia. She was to be his pirate queen and Costentenus was allowed to join his crew. But in this version, Aspasia did not return Perikles's affections. She kept him at arm's length, stalling their marriage. While young Djorji learned looting and pillaging, the cousins secretly plotted their escape.

> "Perikles shall never have you," I answered, grinding my teeth. "I will kill him first..."

After a year with the pirates, Aspasia and Djorji had fallen in love.

The idea of cousins falling in love and planning to marry used

211 Konstantinus, *Life and Adventures*, 6.

212 Konstantinus, *Life and Adventures*, 6.

to be common. In 1881, when the pamphlet was published, it was widespread and considered normal, so this relationship would not have scandalized readers of the late 19th century.

The day before Aspasia would finally have to marry Perikles, the cousins agreed that the time had come. They must seize their moment to escape.[213]

That night, the pirates got drunk in their den, toasting their captain and his bride-to-be. Costentenus distracted them with a speech while Aspasia snuck off to a waiting rowboat. When Aspasia gave the signal, Djorji shot Perikles and ran to the boat. With a "howl of fury," the pirates gave chase. But the cousins had sabotaged all the other rowboats—and they had rigged the pirates' den and their ship to explode. With one shot from his pistol, Costentenus ignited the pitch and powder they had laid down. "The effect of my shot was all that I could have desired."

> We were alone on the sea, floating on the ebb tide further away every moment from the pirates' island, amid a chaos of floating spars and fragments of wreck.

"Not a pirate had survived," and the two young lovers sailed on, "neither knowing nor caring whither we went, so long as we were together in our love."

But things just can't be that easy for our two doomed lovers.

Two columns of smoke appeared on the horizon. At first, they thought these were English steamships looking for pirates. Soon, the number of steamers increased. And they started shooting. One ship closed in to take them captive and raised its flag. It was Egyptian! Would Costentenus and Aspasia be recognized and executed for stealing the viceroy's jewels?

> I knew that my death was certain if I reached Egypt, but I felt sure that something would happen to avert it at the last moment.

---

213 Konstantinus, *Life and Adventures*, 7.

The steamship's captain turned out to be someone they knew from their time in the harem. While he was suspicious of the pair, he didn't fully recognize them. He called for a slave, Seyd Hamet, who had been chief of the eunuchs in the harem. The old slave recognized Aspasia at once. Aspasia was locked up below and Costentenus was tied up in the rigging as the ship made its way back to Egypt. Once there, the captain informed him, Costentenus would probably be "flayed alive and impaled."

The next night, Seyd Hamet, the same slave who had betrayed their identities to the captain, came up to Costentenus and, for some reason, cut him free, slipping a knife in his hand. Costentenus found Aspasia (accidentally killing Seyd Hamet in the process) and they escaped yet again. Desperately, the two sailed away from the steamship in the night.

But...

The wind grew fiercer than ever, and the waves came rolling after us as if to devour our little boat...

*Costentenus kills Perikles, with Aspasia ready in their boat, from* The Life and Adventures of Captain Costentenus, *(The 1229.2.10\*, Houghton Library, Harvard University)*

A dangerous storm sprang up and battered the young lovers' boat. But when the storm broke, Mount Carmel and the shores of what is now Israel appeared on the horizon. Djorji and Aspasia saw three other ships dashed on the dangerous rocks ahead, but they kept their course toward shore. Mount Carmel was well-known as a Christian refuge over the centuries. But for Costentenus and Aspasia, it was not to be.

> A jagged rock, hidden just below the surface of the waves, tore the bottom of our boat into a huge chasm, and before I could even snatch at Aspasia a great green wave came sweeping over us, caught us up like straws and dashed us to and fro, as helpless as feathers in a tornado.

Costentenus made it to shore alive, but "there, stretched on the sand, was the body of my lost Aspasia, drowned."

••

*Costentenus finds the body of Aspasia washed up on shore, from* The Life and Adventures of Captain Costentenus, *(Thr 1229.2.10*, Houghton Library, Harvard University)*

# CHAPTER IX.
## SLAVERY.

It seemed to me as if all the light had departed out of my own life as I knelt by her pale, beautiful corpse, tore my hair and longed for death.

••

The pamphlet doesn't give Costentenus long to mourn Aspasia. In the very next sentence, he is surrounded by Kurdish slave merchants. Young Costentenus has been orphaned, hidden in a harem, captured by pirates, shipwrecked, and lost his first love. Now it's time for slavery.

Costentenus, so the story continues, "fought, bit, and tore at them like a wild beast," but he was quickly knocked unconscious. When he awoke, he found himself tied to the back of a mule. The slavers took him east over 1,000 miles, out of the Ottoman Empire into Persia, to what is now Iran.[214] Persia was another "exotic" locale the average American reader of the time would have been familiar with. Throughout the 1800s, Persia was famously caught in the middle of "the Great Game"—the struggle between Britain and Russia over trade routes in the Middle East.

When the slavers reached the Persian capital city, our hero was sold into the household of no less than the shah of Persia himself. Costentenus was "kindly treated" and worked his way up for several years, eventually becoming a member of the shah's bodyguard. Now a bearded young man of about 20 years old, his physical prowess was astounding.

My strength became remarkable, as it has remained ever since. I could ride the most vicious horse, draw the stiffest bow, lift the greatest weights, beat any swordsman in Persia, and throw the most powerful wrestlers. And to all this, I joined a success with the ladies so remarkable that I was known all over Teheran as the "Heart-Stealer."

---

214 Konstantinus, *Life and Adventures*, 11.

He may have been strong and accomplished, but not humble. Naturally, this "Heart-Stealer" stole the heart of none other than the shah's youngest daughter, Princess Gulfirouz.

If we follow the rough timeline of the narrative, we have reached the mid-1850s. Persia's leader at this time was Shah Naser al-Din, who ruled from 1848 until his assassination in 1896. Naser al-Din had dozens of children, but none of them was named Gulfirouz. The timing is also wrong. Naser al-Din's first child was only born in 1847—too young to be Gulfirouz. Even going back a generation to the previous Persian ruler, Mohammad Shah, does not turn up such a daughter. Princess Gulfirouz is, unsurprisingly, pure fiction.

The drama our hero encounters in Persia includes a harem rivalry, a Circassian slave, bribery, faked illness, a fallen veil, a sentence to 500 blows, yet another gender-swapping disguise, horse theft, and a nighttime escape with Princess Gulfirouz in the caravan of an English gentleman called Lord Harley—whose true name, Costentenus says, has been concealed "in compliance with the wishes of his family."

••

*Map showing the approximate route of Costentenus's journey, according to* The Life and Adventures of Captain Costentenus, *(Drawn by the authors)*

## CHAPTERS X - XI:
## OUR CARAVAN, THE COSSACKS.

Little did I think that I was the only one of our party who would ever return alive from Kashgar, marked for life with the impress of a barbarian's cruelty.[215]

••

After their escape from the shah, Lord Harley wanted to head east, "cross the plains of Turkistan and enter China by the way of Kashgar, a road never traveled by Europeans before that time." (Never mind that Marco Polo had been to Kashgar hundreds of years earlier.) Gulfirouz, disguised as a boy, "seemed to be incapable of fear." And Costentenus was "willing to go anywhere and do anything... I longed only for excitement."

As their caravan made its way east, the author of the autobiography gave Costentenus a rare respite from melodrama. He crossed fields covered in flowers, finding "nothing but hospitality from the wandering Kirgis Tartars" (the Kyrgyz people, a Turkic ethnic group). It's as if the author suddenly remembered that most curiosity pamphlets and popular travel stories of the time included some actual information on distant people and places. Thus, the story meanders into a few detailed (and accurate!) descriptions. Our travelers spent many nights in "kibitkas," a type of yurt used by the Kyrgyz people, joined them in hunts with their trained eagles, and drank "koomis," fermented mare's milk that is still popular in Central Asia.

They spent summer and part of autumn with the Kyrgyz people, but news of an Englishman living among them reached the Russian frontier. Continuing the pamphlet's rare run of historical accuracy, "in those days the Russians had not conquered Khiva [a neighboring area], and they were always afraid of British intrigues with the Turcomans and Tartars." The travelers were warned that the Russians were going to send a group of Cossacks to kill them.[216]

Costentenus, Gulfirouz (still in disguise), Lord Harley, and his men, raced eastward, but a group of 30 or 40 Cossacks caught up

---

215 Konstantinus, *Life and Adventures*, 13.

216 Konstantinus, *Life and Adventures*, 13-14.

*Costentenus, Gulfirouz, and Harley pursued by Cossacks, from* The Life and Adventures of Captain Costentenus. *(Thr 1229.2.10\*, Houghton Library, Harvard University)*

with them. Costentenus set up an ambush in the dark. They killed four of the Russians and the rest fled. But in yet another plot twist, Costentenus discovered that the dead men were not actually Russians, but Persians—sent by the shah to catch the two lovers. "He must have tracked us to the frontier and appealed to the Russian government to help him. And I knew that henceforth there was no safety for us in Turkistan anywhere under the Russian influence."[217]

Costentenus decided he had to come clean with Lord Harley and revealed that he and Gulfirouz (apparently now husband and wife) were the reason the caravan had been attacked. He asked Lord Harley to turn them in to save himself, but the gentleman refused, finding it all an amusing adventure.

> He swore that he had taken me and my wife under his protection, and that he would see us through our troubles if he had to invoke the whole power of England for another Crimean War.[218]

And so they raced on toward Kashgar together.

---

217 Konstantinus, *Life and Adventures*, 14.

218 Konstantinus, *Life and Adventures*, 15.

••

## CHAPTER XII.
## KASHGAR.

I have seen Damascus from the Desert, Naples from Vesuvius, Vienna from the spire of St. Stephen's, Paris from Notre Dame, but all of these, in their first impression of beauty to the traveler, are as nothing to the wonderful loveliness of the valley and city of Kashgar...

••

Costentenus's tale has taken him from Albania to Egypt, around the Mediterranean, and 1,000 miles east to Persia. Another 1,300 miles brings him, at long last, to where he claims he was tattooed. The travelers rode past Khiva and Bokhara toward western China, eager to "see the famous chief, Yakoob Beg... the creator of a new nation, a man who had thrown off the yoke of China and set up an independent kingdom."[219]

Yakoob Beg was another real person inserted into the narrative. He was born in 1820 in the Khanate of Kokand (in what is now Uzbekistan). Taking advantage of Muslim uprisings in China in 1864, he went into northwest China and established the kingdom of Kashgaria. The Ottoman sultan declared him the emir of the region. But by the end of 1877, his kingdom had been retaken by the Chinese and Yakoob was dead, perhaps from illness, perhaps from poisoning or suicide.[220]

Unfortunately, just like Ali Pasha, Yakoob Beg can't have actually appeared in Costentenus's story as described. The pamphlet puts their meeting in Kashgar in 1857, seven years before Yakoob Beg even set his sights on taking over the region. Once again, the dates don't work.

So, with an enthusiastic disregard for historical accuracy, the weary travelers rode on. At the Kashgarian frontier, they were

---

219 Konstantinus, *Life and Adventures*, 15.

220 "Yakub Beg," *Encyclopedia Britannica*, https://www.britannica.com/biography/Yakub-Beg, accessed December 16, 2021.

*Night interview with Yakoob Beg, from* Visits to High Tartary, Yârkand, and Kâshghar *by Robert Shaw, 1871, (American Geographical Society Library, University of Wisconsin-Milwaukee)*

taken prisoner and languished in jail for three weeks. Finally, they were summoned to Kashgar to appear before Yakoob Beg.[221] They were welcomed into his large home and told that he liked foreigners, especially if they had skills he could use to his advantage.

The man who welcomed them was not Yakoob himself, but "a tall, thin man with a light beard and a long narrow face."[222] He was, surprisingly, an American. He introduced himself as Jared Bunce from Southport, Connecticut. (An actual Connecticut Yankee in someone's court?[223]) Bunce said he had been in service to Yakoob Beg for ten years, ever since he had escaped into Kashgar from forced labor in Russia.[224]

During the 19th century, stereotypical Connecticut Yankee characters appeared in many stories. The name Jared Bunce, specifically, was plucked from the popular novel *Guy Rivers: A Tale*

221 Konstantinus, *Life and Adventures*, 15.

222 Konstantinus, *Life and Adventures*, 16.

223 Mark Twain's *Connecticut Yankee in King Arthur's Court* was not published until 1889.

224 Konstantinus, *Life and Adventures*, 16.

*of Georgia* written by William Gilmore Simms. Simms was a prolific Southern writer who was a major force in antebellum literature. He was also unabashedly pro-slavery. *Guy Rivers* was the first of his books to explore the culture clash on the frontier in Northern Georgia. Originally published in 1834, the book had been republished at least nine times by 1882.[225]

Simms's Jared Bunce combined two stereotypes of Northerners—the "Jonathan" and "the peddler." The Jonathan was inspired by the song "Yankee Doodle" and various short stories that appeared in almanacs. He was "shy, awkward, bumptious, yet good-natured and helpful," a shrewd man with a good heart.[226] The peddler stereotype appeared in Southern oral tradition, traveler's narratives, and exaggerated newspaper stories. He was a con artist from the north, "a wily, cozening trickster, posed under a mask of ingenuousness and seeming good will for a shrewd deal or an act of mischief."[227] In *Guy Rivers*, Jared Bunce starts out as "slippery and deceitful" like the peddler. But as his story arc continues, Bunce shows his benevolent, "Jonathan" side and becomes a hero of sorts.[228] In Costentenus's story, Bunce has been lifted from the American South and deposited in Kashgar. Like Lord Harley, Bunce is a stereotypical character who ultimately serves as a contrast to our hero's courage, strength, and stamina. All three, Bunce, Harley, and Costentenus, will end up tortured under the tattooist's needle, though only one will survive.

When Bunce finally led the travellers in to meet Yakoob Beg, the Yankee translated, asking each of them what they wanted from the Khan of Kashgar. Harley replied that he just wanted to see the country and tell the world about "the greatness of Yakoob Beg."[229]

---

225 "Publication History," The Simms Initiatives, University of South Carolina Libraries, 2011, www.simms.library.sc.edu/display/view_item.php?item=128577 &tab=publicationhistory, accessed February 11, 2022.

226 Mary Ann Wimsatt, "Native Humor in Simms's Fiction and Drama," *Studies in American Humor* 3, No. 3, (1977): 158-159.

227 Wimsatt, "Native Humor," 159.

228 Wimsatt, "Native Humor," 159.

229 Konstantinus, *Life and Adventures,* 16.

Costentenus, having been a cavalry leader in Persia, wanted to enter into Yakoob's service. What Gulfirouz wanted, the pamphlet does not say.

Yakoob Beg apparently didn't care what they actually wanted. When Harley mentioned that he knew something about mining, Yakoob told them that they were all going to work in his depleted copper mines. If they could get anything out of the mines, they could have half the profits. Once they were dismissed, Bunce had a warning—and a promise—for them: "It's a good sight easier to get *into* Yakoob Beg's service than *out* of it... but I don't intend to stay much longer. Hold your horses, all of you, and we shall see."[230]

••

CHAPTERS XIII - XV:
THE MINES, THE MUTINY,
ENTRAPPED.

You have dared to raise a revolt against the best government the sun ever shone on. In his infinite mercy, however, our illustrious monarch offers you the choice of life and death. You may be starved to death, stung to death by wasps, killed by tigers, cut to pieces - beginning at the toes - impaled on spears, burned to death, or tattooed. If you survive the last the khan will give you liberty. You have leave to choose. Speak!

••

Costentenus and Harley, with Bunce joining them, managed the mines until winter. They gained the support of the local workers by paying them fair wages and making sure everyone was well-fed. They had great success, mining new veins of copper and silver, and Costentenus and Gulfirouz even had a child. But then a man named Gholab Sing, who claimed to be Yakoob Beg's Inspector of Mines, rode into town. His tone was insolent and his smile was sinister, with his teeth turned black from chewing betel nuts. Sing ordered them to pay the workers less and still deliver as much copper. The three refused, and sent him back to Yakoob Beg. Gholab Sing however, was

---

230 Konstantinus, *Life and Adventures,* 16.

not who he claimed to be. Bunce had recognized him! He was none other than Nana Sahib, "the Butcher of Cawnpore," Yakoob Beg's prime minister in disguise. And he coveted Princess Gulfirouz![231]

Nana Sahib is the final name plucked from history to appear in Costentenus's autobiography. Born in India, he was a leader in the First War of Independence (also referred to as the Indian Rebellion of 1857), an unsuccessful attempt to throw off British rule. Early in the uprising, he led the sepoy forces (British-trained, Indian-born soldiers) who attacked the British East India Company soldiers in Cawnpore (now called Kanpur). The British soldiers surrendered and were promised safe passage out of the region. Instead, Nana Sahib had everyone massacred, including the women and children.[232] He eventually fled toward the Nepalese border and disappeared, his fate unknown. There is no evidence that he ever made it to Kashgar and into the service of Yakoob Beg. But many writers of the time, including Jules Verne in his 1880 novel *The End of Nana Sahib*, wrote about the Butcher of Cawnpore and imagined what became of him.

SREENATH alias NANA SAHIB.

Back in our hero's story, Costentenus, Harley, and Bunce were convinced that Nana Sahib would have them killed. They decided to strike first and raised a rebellion against Yakoob Beg. They told their loyal mine workers that Yakoob wanted to make them work for starvation wages again, and asked if the workers

*Portrait of Nana Sahib, from* Harper's Weekly, *October 24, 1857,* (Collection of the author)

231 Konstantinus, *Life and Adventures*, 18.

232 "Nana Sahib," *Encyclopedia Britannica*, https://www.britannica.com/biography/Nana-Sahib, accessed December 22, 2021.

would help fight.[233] The answer was a resounding yes. With the motto "Living wages for workmen!" (a phrase that would have resonated with American readers due to the rise of labor unions in the late 19th century), they marched toward Kashgar, their forces growing as they went.[234] At 100,000 strong, with 1,000 of them armed with muskets, they surprised Yakoob Beg and had him at their mercy. But their mistake was trying to negotiate with him instead of killing him outright. The group was drawn into an ambush by Yakoob and Nana Sahib. Suddenly surrounded by artillery and almost 8,000 armed soldiers, the workers fled in terror. Bunce, Harley, and Costentenus were captured and put into Yakoob's dungeon, "left to meditate over the uncertainty of life in Asia."[235]

Bunce, the American, wept with despair, while Harley, the Brit, was determined to die with a stiff upper lip. But Costentenus had an inner voice that told him he'd survive. It was Nana Sahib, his face now disfigured by a cut from Costentenus's sword during the recent battle, who offered them the choice of how they would die. Would they rather perish by starvation or burning, by wasps' stings or tigers' bites, cut to pieces, or impaled on spears. Their final option, tattooing, sounded innocent enough. How bad could it be? Harley spoke up: "'Why, of course we will choose that. It is better to live than to die.'"

**Nana Sahib smiled again in a still more evil fashion.**

The three men were given hot baths and directed to three narrow tables. An old Mediterranean sailor named Antonio came in. He had rings in his ears, his black hair was in a braid coiled around his head, and his bare arms were covered in blue tattoos. He had pots of indigo and cochineal dye, a set of needles, a small mallet, and several wooden stamps with animal figures on them.[236]

Costentenus, Harley, and Bunce were tied down to the tables. They could not move.

---

233 Konstantinus, *Life and Adventures*, 18.

234 Konstantinus, *Life and Adventures*, 18.

235 Konstantinus, *Life and Adventures*, 18.

236 Konstantinus, *Life and Adventures*, 19.

Antonio started with their faces.

# CHAPTER SIX

# BARRELS OF BLOOD AND INK

Antonio dipped a stamp in blue ink and set it on Harley's forehead. Using a mallet and a block of wood "set with needles like a brush," he started tapping the design into Harley's skin. The old sailor repeated this operation with an alligator stamp on Bunce—and then moved to Costentenus.

In that instant I first realized the terrible fate in store for me. The pricks of those sharp little needles, fifty or a hundred to the inch, just going deep enough to touch the nerves and draw tiny drops of blood, seemed to set all my brain on fire...

The tattooist returned to Harley and soaked his hair with indigo ink.

Then, with the same coolness with which he always worked he pricked in the dye all over his victim's head under the hair, in rows of parallel lines... We began to realize that tattooing was no light punishment.

••

# CHAPTER XVI.
## A LINGERING TORTURE.

*Groan away; yell; curse; pray for mercy; I like to hear it. Go on.*

••

Yakoob Beg and Nana Sahib came in to watch. Yakoob urged Antonio to keep the three men alive, because he wanted to send them to Kashgar's northern frontier as a warning to Russian soldiers. Nana Sahib was betting that the Greek was more likely to survive than the Englishman or the American. He also casually mentioned that Gulfirouz had been captured. That so upset Costentenus that he almost broke his bonds, but his struggles were in vain.

After finishing Bunce and Harley's scalp tattoos, Antonio turned and spoke to Costentenus for the first time: "Do you remember Captain Perikles?" In a stunning coincidence, Costentenus's torturer was... none other than the pirate captain's brother! Somehow, years later and thousands of miles away, fate had put Captain George at Antonio's mercy. And somehow, the old sailor had recognized this grown man with a full beard as the boy who had killed his brother. Antonio would finally avenge Perikles's death!

*Of what followed it makes me, even now, shudder to think.*

While Harley and Bunce shrieked and moaned, Costentenus mercifully lost consciousness. A second tattooist joined the torture and "calmly hammered away, till [Harley's] whole beard was a mass of gore and blue from the flowing blood mixing with the indigo."

By the end of the first day, all three men were tattooed from scalp to neck, and a doctor came in to get them through the night. Somehow, their wounds had healed by morning—and the torture continued. Harley was in bad shape, ravaged by a fever, and didn't think he could survive another day.

The tattooers abandoned their alligator stamps and started drawing freehand, inking elephants, tigers, and sphinxes on their victims' torsos. The pain was worse than ever. Nana Sahib returned to taunt them and was also certain that Harley would die the next day.

••

## CHAPTER XVII.
### THE FIRST DEATH.

By sunset the whole front of our bodies as far as the waist was covered with tattooing, and we felt as if all the skin had been stripped off.

••

Harley was delirious and "all the punctured surface of his body was swelled up and fearfully inflamed." He was wrapped in oiled bandages and carried away, leaving Bunce and Costentenus to further torture. But they, too, became senseless with fever. When Costentenus regained consciousness a week later, an attendant told him that Harley had died.

Bunce was the next to go. The repeated tattooing had made the already thin man "a mere skeleton." After four more days of torture and inflammation, the doctor ordered Bunce be given time to recover. But it was too late.[237] When Costentenus woke up after three more weeks of fever, he was alone.

Antonio and his assistants had tattooed the Greek down to the waist, front and back. Only his legs remained. It was a wonder to Costentenus "how I ever survived... a third of my body was turned into a veritable furnace of fiery pain."

He was marked for life, his two friends were dead, and his wife was captured... Costentenus vowed to survive so he could get revenge.

The last of the tattooing took place more slowly, as Yakoob Beg wanted Costentenus to live. Finally, after three months, he was completely covered—but alive.[238] The Tattooed Greek was "as I am now, and as Yakoob Beg had threatened to make me—a wonder to all

237 Konstantinus, *Life and Adventures*, 22.

238 Konstantinus, *Life and Adventures*, 22.

the world..."[239]

Captain George was still weak, though. He rested for another month, carefully disguising from his captors that his strength was returning. When he was finally summoned to see Yakoob Beg, he was led through the streets dressed in nothing but slippers and a loincloth. He was surprised to find that he was not an object of fear or pity, as Yakoob Beg had intended. Instead, he was admired by all who saw him. In trying to disfigure him, his torturers had made him "a beautifully-colored statue," and "the story of my endurance of the torture had gained me hosts of friends..."

While Costentenus had his life, he did not have his liberty. Yakoob Beg announced that he had sold Costentenus as a slave to the Turks. The Khan of Kashgar asked if the Tattooed Greek had any last requests before he was sent back west. Costentenus had just one: to fight Nana Sahib to the death. Strangely, Costentenus blamed Nana Sahib for all his suffering, not Yakoob Beg.

Nana Sahib was overweight and out of shape, but Costentenus's strength had returned. And his fury was fed by a certainty that Gulfirouz must be dead. He believed she had killed herself—and their child—to avoid becoming Yakoob Beg's wife. "Therefore, I was alone in the world, ruined in my prime of early youth, and it was to Nana Sahib that I owed all this misery."

"No one interfered to part us, and it was nearly ten minutes ere the desperate struggle was over." Nana Sahib, the infamous Butcher of Cawnpore, lay dead, and Yakoob Beg seemed oddly pleased by this. Costentenus's story in Kashgar had come to its end. A slave merchant from Constantinople took him back through Persia and eventually sold him to a stranger—"who proved to be a friend in disguise."[240]

Before we reach the conclusion of Captain George's pamphlet, it is worth remembering that this story was almost entirely made up. Costentenus never would have met Yakoob Beg, Nana Sahib, Ali Pasha, or the shah of Persia. Perikles, Aspasia, and Gulfirouz were

239 Konstantinus, *Life and Adventures*, 22.

240 Konstantinus, *Life and Adventures*, 23.

undoubtedly made up. And Costentenus's tattoos would not have been made by an old Mediterranean sailor in Kashgar.

There are also problems with the basic description of the tattooing itself. While stamps were sometimes used as a way to transfer a design to the skin before tattooing, using a block of wood "set with needles like a brush" is highly unlikely. Tattoos of the time were traditionally done with a single needle mounted on a long rod. A mallet pounding in a block of needles "fifty or a hundred to the inch" is simply there to maximize the horror of the story.

Parts of Costentenus's scalp were indeed tattooed, but there's no way that dye was smeared into his hair and beard and then poked into his skin. Then, as now, all of Costentenus's hair would have been shaved before he was tattooed, to allow the tattooist to see the skin. Also, each tattoo is essentially a wound with a foreign substance in it and would have taken several weeks to heal, never just one night as Costentenus described for his first tattoos.

None of this can be real.

•

## The Truth of His Tattoos

So how did Captain George actually acquire his tattoos? What do the designs themselves tell us? What would the animals and inscriptions have meant to Costentenus and to those who inked them into his skin? And what would the tattooing process have truly been like? It is possible to make several educated guesses that paint a more plausible picture than Captain George's melodramatic tales of torture.

Looking at the designs, they were most likely done in Burma (now Myanmar), over 1,500 miles southeast of Kashgar. Dr. Müller, who guessed this when he saw Costentenus in Vienna back in 1870, was correct. Costentenus's tattoos match descriptions and illustrations of Burmese tattoos in 19th century sources such as *The Burman: His Life and Notions* and Burmese artworks. The specific style that matches best is that of the Shan people, who are today the largest minority in Myanmar.[241]

In the 1800s, most Shan men were tattooed as part of their coming-of-age ceremony. Traditionally, they were covered with red and blue animals from their navels to their knees. This made them look as if they were wearing short pants made of tattoos. One 19th century observer described these as "a skin-tight pair of caleçons [boxer shorts], fitting better than the best glove ever made."[242] Sometimes, Shan men also had tattoos on their chests and arms, but these would have been one or two separate designs, not a carpet of images like Costentenus had.

Like many coming-of-age rituals around the world, such extensive tattooing is no longer very common in Myanmar. These types of tattoos, however, are still applied in more limited ways in Theravada Buddhist communities in Myanmar, Thailand, and Cambodia.

*Painting of a wrestling match, showing traditional tattoo designs, by an unknown Burmese artist, 1897 and an enhanced detail from the same image, (Bodleian Library, University of Oxford)*

---

241 "Shan," *Encyclopedia Britannica*, https://www.britannica.com/topic/Shan, accessed December 11, 2023.

242 Yoe, *The Burman*, 39.

There were a few tattooed performers with this style of tattoos who came after Captain George. In particular, Frank De Burgh (born James Burke in England in 1850) had some strikingly similar tattoos that he had acquired in Burma—with no melodrama involved. The majority of De Burgh's tattoos were typical 19th century Western designs. He had a reclining woman on his chest holding a banner that said "Forget Me Not." There was an eagle with outstretched wings across his stomach, with his wife's name "Emma" above it. (Emma De Burgh was also a well-known tattooed performer.) Frank De Burgh's legs, though, were another story. His thighs were inked with a variety of animals surrounded by lines, the same "menagerie of strange animals" that covered Costentenus's body.[243] De Burgh "was tattooed from his neck down to his toe-nails... His thighs were covered with idhols [sic], etc., placed there when he was in Burmah."[244] He had been there in 1876, likely as a soldier taking part in the slow British encroachment into the country.[245]

Both Captain George and Frank De Burgh seem to have started with a set of traditional Shan "pants." While De Burgh's other tattoos were varied, Captain George was unique in having his entire body inked in the same style. While it's possible Costentenus met a Shan tattooist elsewhere in Asia, it's most likely he was tattooed in or near Burma, where the Shan tradition was common and the artists were numerous.

Shan tattooing was done by a master and apprentice who traveled from village to village. Many tattooists had also trained as Buddhist monks, though they didn't always take vows. Like Western tattooists of the time, they carried a book of designs with them that the person receiving the tattoos could choose from.[246] A master tattooist would have started by drawing the outlines of the image on Costentenus's skin. Then he would have dipped a long brass rod with

---

243 "PT Barnum and the Glorious Fourth of July in Lowell," *Lowell Daily Citizen*, June 24, 1876.

244 "Art Extraordinary: Where Tattooed People in the Museum Come From," *Frederick Weekly News*, July 10, 1884.

245 "Art Extraordinary," *Frederick Weekly News*.

246 Sylvia Fraser-Lu, *Burmese Crafts: Past and Present*, (Oxford University Press, 1994): 138-139.

a needle at the end into black or red ink, made from lampblack or vermillion mixed with oils or animal fats. An apprentice would have stretched Costentenus's skin while the master carefully poked the ink-dipped needle into his skin. Tattooing this way would have been slow, particularly compared with a modern tattoo machine that can move up and down into the skin up to 3,000 times per minute.

The Shan animal figures were typically a mix of tigers and other large cats, along with monkeys, elephants, snakes, dogs, and various mythical creatures. Each animal was surrounded by inscriptions from the Buddha's teachings. Unfortunately, none of the writing tattooed on Costentenus or De Burgh was photographed well enough to be translated. The ink colors were limited to red and black (which, like all black ink tattoos, faded to blue over time, thanks to the body's absorption of ink, accelerated by sun exposure.

Shan tattoos were decorative medicine, meant to safeguard their wearers. They fell into three types: protective (acun), persuasive (yapeya), and barrier (kat and pik) tattoos.[247] Acun images were mostly tattooed in red ink and were believed to have the power to make others act in certain ways toward the tattooed person. For example, a shopkeeper might have gotten acun tattoos on his lower arms to have kindness directed toward him. Acun tattoos were also said to protect the wearer from malice and disease, which were thought to be spread by evil spirits.

Yapeya tattoos were meant to help someone speak well and persuasively, giving them the ability to influence others. There were two subtypes: the Sarasati, to help people remember words, and the Anathi, to increase the wearer's speaking ability. The Sarasati had a very specific design: the head of the Shan goddess of wisdom on the right shoulder, the head of the Mother Earth on the left shoulder, and a katha (a Buddhist story or text) on the chest.

---

247 Nicola Tannenbaum, "Tattoos: Invulnerability and Power in Shan Cosmology," *American Ethnologist* 14, no. 4 (1987): 694, 699; Fraser-Lu, Burmese Crafts, 138; Acun translates as "ability to accomplish," yapeya is ya "medicinal" and pe "to prevail, conquer, overcome," kat is "to be proof against a weapon or a blow, to be charmed," and pik is "to close up,stop up, shut up," J. N. Cushing, *A Shan and English Dictionary*, (Gregg International Publishers, 1971).

The third type of Shan tattoos served as a defensive barrier. These kat and pik tattoos were believed to prevent animals of all sorts from biting, knives from cutting, or even bullets from entering the body.[248] (And if the barrier were broken, the injury was said to hurt less.) Kat tattoos were anti-poison and anti-bite tattoos, while pik tattoos were "said to close off the body... prevent[ing] dangerous objects from entering."[249] More modern pik tattoos included imagery of guns and bullets, while older images were of knives and swords. Kat tattoos were often images of the animals that they protected against: snakes, cats, dogs, tigers, and insects. The tattoos changed to reflect the threats, but the protection they offered was the same.

Costentenus seems to have been covered in kat barrier tattoos, since most of his imagery was of animals and mythical creatures surrounded by incantations. He was also tattooed with a number of boxes with text in them. The text in the boxes were likely numbers for astrological calculations, as well as letters and symbols that were shorthand for spells.[250] With these tattoos covering him completely, far beyond the traditional pants, did he think of them as a suit of armor?

That Costentenus continued with Shan designs on his entire body is another reason to think he was tattooed in Burma. Such extensive tattooing would have taken many months to create—and to heal. Only in Burma would he have had long-term access to the Shan artists needed for such an involved process.

Despite the popular stories of forced tattooing, all the tattooed performers before Costentenus had picked up inked designs because they had lived with a group of people to whom this was an important tradition. Similarly, Captain George most likely got his first tattoos as a rite of passage while living among the Shan people in Burma.

But the truth of it is we will never know for sure where or why Costentenus was tattooed. Likely, he was in Burma with time and

---

248 Tannenbaum, "Tattoos: Invulnerability and Power," 696.

249 Tannenbaum, "Tattoos: Invulnerability and Power," 6978.

250 Susan Conway, *Tai Magic: Arts of the Supernatural in the Shan states and Lan Na*, (River Books, 2014): 196-197.

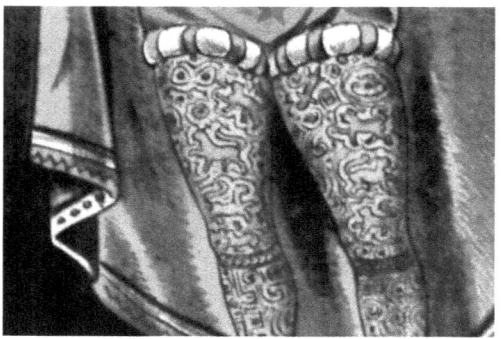

*Poster of Emma and Frank De Burgh, 1888, and an enhanced detail of his legs from the same poster, (Bibliothèque Nationale de France, Department of Prints and Photography)*

130

money to spare. Maybe he was a sailor like earlier tattooed performer Joseph Kabris or a soldier like Frank De Burgh—sent far from home. He probably started with a few traditional Shan tattoos and just kept going. At some point, he looked at himself and realized that he could charge money for others to look at his remarkable body, and his career took off from there.

All this is far more likely than torture in Kashgar at the hands of the brother of a murdered Mediterranean pirate. The truth must, itself, have been a fascinating tale. Unfortunately, it has been lost. It's been replaced by a more sensationalized story, to help sell more tickets.

••

CHAPTER XVIII.
CONCLUSION.

My memories of the past, connected as they are with as many deaths of friends and loved ones, are too painful to be lightly revived. Aspasia and Gulfirouz, sleeping beneath the bare plains of Asia, Harley and Bunce, lying in unnamed graves under the iron rule of the tyrant of Kashgar, are to me sacred forever.

••

The Turkish slave trader brought Costentenus from Kashgar back to Constantinople, his namesake city. In one last incredible coincidence, Captain George's pamphlet reveals that the stranger who bought him was an agent of none other than... the Great Farini, the wildly successful promoter and inventor of the human cannonball act. In an act of surprising selflessness, Farini's agent gave the Tattooed Greek his freedom, with no conditions. Costentenus was turned loose with clothes, money, and Farini's address in Vienna.

However, there is once again a problem with the dates. In the mid-1850s, Signor Farini was still plain old William Hunt of Canada, learning to be a tightrope walker and acrobat. He did briefly live in Vienna, but not until 1872, after Costentenus had already made his debut there. Farini probably didn't meet Captain George until 1881—not-so coincidentally when the pamphlet was published.

*Photograph of a Burmese tattooing process, from* Among the Burmans, A Record of Fifteen Years of Work and Its Fruitage, *by Henry Park Cochrane, 1904, (American Geographical Society Library, University of Wisconsin-Milwaukee)*

This is not the only performer pamphlet to list a promoter or circus owner as a savior. Tattooed performer Nora Hildebrandt's pamphlet credited circus owner Adam Forepaugh's business manager for giving her $50 to help her regain her sight after she lost it due to her (supposedly) forced tattooing.[251]

His supposed savior's identity aside, Captain George's pamphlet does, for once, get something right here: Costentenus went to Vienna to start his performance career. According to the booklet, he was soon exhibited before Emperor Napoleon III of France, King Wilhelm I of Prussia, and Czar Alexander II of Russia, each of whom presented him with a ring.[252] Jewelry was apparently a common gift from rulers to tattooed performers. Nora Hildebrandt was supposedly given a pair of diamond solitaire earrings by President Gonzalez of Mexico when she appeared before him around 1883 or 1884.[253]

251 Nora Hildebrandt, *Miss Nora Hildebrandt, The Tattooed Lady*, (Merchant's Gargling Oil Liniment, date unknown), collection of the author.

252 Konstantinus, *Life and Adventures*, 23.

253 "Mexico's Great Sensation, Miss Nora Hildebrandt," *New York Clipper*, March 22, 1884.

> From that day to the present I have wanted for nothing. The very punishment which was intended to ruin me for life has become the means of my elevation to prosperity.

After several years of success in Europe, Costentenus made his way to the United States, where he started working with G. B. Bunnell (the pamphlet gets something right again!). While he was in Philadelphia, his friend and agent "Dr. G. O. Starr" introduced the Tattooed Greek to the American medical community. At first, they were skeptical, thinking that his tattoos were merely paint.[254] But like so many other performer pamphlets, Captain George's then reassures the readers that these distinguished doctors verified his absolute authenticity. "Applying every test which science is capable" at a private viewing convinced the Philadelphia medical men of the reality of his tattoos.[255] Like his examinations in Boston and elsewhere, perhaps this took place or perhaps it was yet another typical invention in the life of a sideshow curiosity.

"Dr. G. O. Starr" was a real person, however, and someone who was absolutely in Costentenus's life. But he was not a doctor at all. Rather, George O. Starr was the Bunnells' press agent. He had been with the Bunnell brothers at least as far back as the 1878 season with the *Greatest Show on Earth*. He continued to work with them until 1887, before returning to the newly renamed Barnum & Bailey Circus in 1888.[256] Starr would also go on to marry Rossa Richter, a.k.a. Zazel, Farini's human cannonball protégé.

It's likely that Starr, as the Bunnells' press agent when the pamphlet was published, was involved in some way in the creation of Costentenus's narrative. Given the glowing terms with which the ghostwriter described both George Bunnell (Costentenus's longtime employer) and Farini (his future employer), they also may have been involved.

---

254 Konstantinus, *Life and Adventures*, p. 23.

255 Konstantinus, *Life and Adventures*, p. 23.

256 "Starr, George Oscar," William Slout, *Olympians of the Sawdust Circle: A Biographical Dictionary of the Nineteenth Century American Circus*, https://www.classic.circushistory.org/Olympians/OlympiansS2.htm; "GB Bunnell's New Museum," *New York Clipper*, October 15, 1881.

There is one obvious question that is, oddly enough, not answered by this pamphlet: when and how did Costentenus become a captain? While he was supposedly in the cavalry in Persia, a military rank is never mentioned. Throughout the story, he never commands a ship or crew. Not once is he referred to as a captain—a strange oversight.

*The Life and Adventures of Captain Costentenus*, almost entirely a fiction, concludes on a contemplative note:

I alone of all men have survived the torture of tattooing, and I am the only human being of my kind in all the wide world.

But I am alone, and the last of my race.

In me the blood of Constantine the Great, the first Christian Emperor of the Roman world, flows its last drops ere it dries up forever.

Such as I am, I will do no dishonor to my blood to the last. The cruelty of man has driven me to the necessity of living by the exhibition of my scarred body; but no man can say that George Costentenus is not at all times and places a brave, courteous gentleman.

In the hope that my adventures, thus briefly described, may interest and amuse the idle hours of many a man, I close my task.

DJORDGI KONSTANTINUS

[THE END.]

But his real story is far from over. While the Great Farini most certainly did not free Costentenus from slavery and start his career in Vienna, he would be the man who helped Captain George harness the hype for British audiences. After five years in America with Barnum, the Bunnells, the Flatfoots, and the *Greatest Show on Earth*, Costentenus now set sail with Farini—a tightrope walker, trapeze artist, promoter, inventor, painter, botanist, explorer, and one of the most remarkable characters in 19th century circus.

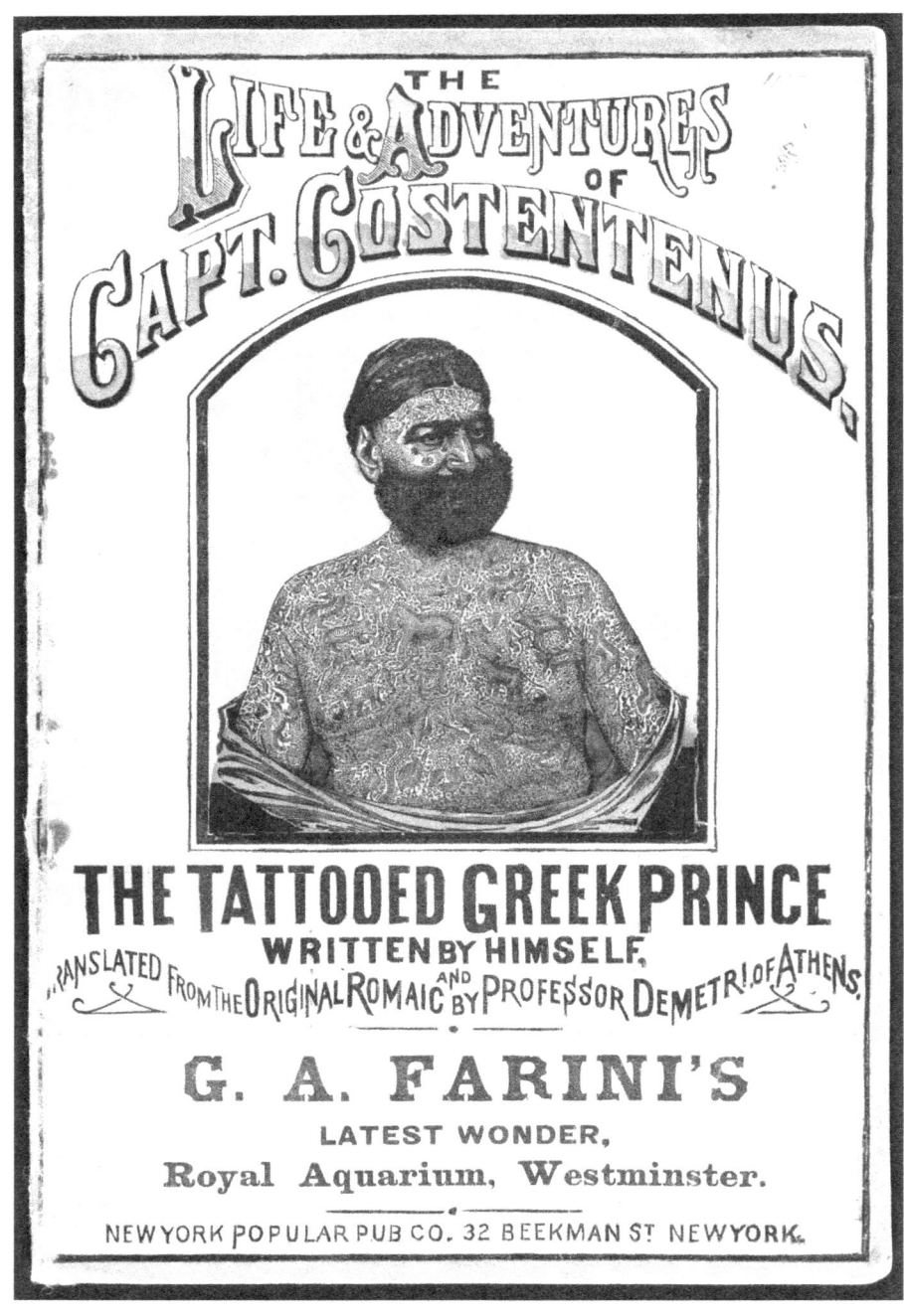

*Costentenus's pamphlet with "G. A. FARINI'S LATEST WONDER, Royal Aquarium, Westminster." pasted on the cover, 1881, (Collection of Syracuse University Library)*

# CHAPTER SEVEN

# LONDON AND THE GREAT FARINI

"The steamer *Queen* numbered among her passengers yesterday Capt. Costentenus, the tattooed Greek, the Leopard Boy, and Zazel of Bunnell's Museum, and G. A. Farini .... The curiosities are booked for the Royal Aquarium."[257]

- *The New York Sun*, November 3, 1881

On his voyage back across the Atlantic, Captain George may have passed the time in his cabin pasting labels for the Royal Aquarium on the covers of his pamphlet. Several surviving copies of the pamphlet have these added strips advertising "G. A. Farini's Latest Wonder."

Costentenus opened at the Royal Aquarium in London on November 21, 1881, and was declared "well worth seeing and talking

---

257 "Curiosities Gone to Sea," *The New York Sun*, November 3, 1881.

to."[258] For six months, he performed four times a day, at 2:30, 5:30, 7:45, and 9:45, with Farini lecturing about his tattoos and his torture.[259] At various times, the "Leopard Boy" showed his mottled skin, magicians made ladies disappear, and swimmers demonstrated their skills in the fish tanks.

Five years earlier, when the Royal Aquarium first opened, an aquarium craze had been sweeping Europe and the United States. (This was also when Barnum's former partner William Coup opened the New York Aquarium.) But the Royal Aquarium's imposing two-story brick building was also intended to be a respectable entertainment venue. It combined an aquarium with a theater, an art gallery, and a reading room. It had not only exotic species of fish, but also performances of classical music and drama, exhibits of fine art, and a collection of literature to supply "mental food." In the winter, it even had a skating rink.[260] But its distinguished board of directors had quickly discovered that its high-brow performances didn't pay the bills.[261]

Barely a year after it opened, the board had hired the Great Farini as a "technical advisor," but in reality, he was in charge of the entertainment.[262] Under his direction, sideshow attractions began taking the place of more high-minded exhibitions. Classical music was replaced by popular bands and music hall artists, and before long, the stage was filled with acrobats, dog trainers, and sword swallowers.

Today, Guillermo Antonio Farini is relatively unknown, but he had a long and eclectic career. He was a daredevil acrobat and inventor. He was a shrewd promoter of innovative circus acts like the first human cannonball—and a few problematic sideshow acts like "Krao, the Missing Link" and the "Friendly Zulus." In his later years, he claimed to have discovered a lost city in the Kalahari Desert,

258 "Sporting Notes," *Sporting Times*, Nov. 26, 1881.

259 "Royal Aquarium, England's Palace of Amusement," *The Pall Mall Gazette*, March 8, 1882.

260 Raymond Mander and Joe Mitchenson, *The Lost Theatres of London*, (Taplinger Publishing Co., 1968): 208-209.

261 Peacock, *The Great Farini,* 225-226.

262 Peacock, *The Great Farini*, 223, 226.

became an expert on growing begonias, invested heavily in Canadian mining, and wrote an unpublished 30-volume history of World War I. But his first claim to fame was crossing Niagara Falls gorge on a tightrope.

Like Barnum, Farini had a flair for exaggeration and a knack for creating hugely successful acts. Unlike Barnum, however, Farini understood how to create an honest thrill. He gave each of his many projects all of his attention, working harder than anyone to perfect an act.

•

## From Niagara Falls to Human Cannonballs

Born William Hunt in New York State in 1838, Farini grew up on a farm in Ontario with strict parents who discouraged his early interest in thrills. Despite this, he taught himself how to walk a tightrope using a rope that stretched from the ground to the top of the family barn. By 1859, he was walking a high wire across the nearby Ganaraska River and calling himself Signor Farini. (What's a great circus act without a theatrical name?) Just a year later, he became the second person to complete a tightrope walk across the gorge below Niagara Falls. This started an escalating competition with Charles Blondin, the first acrobat to accomplish the feat. They both repeated the stunt many times, adding to it by walking blindfolded, stopping to cook an omelet, or carrying someone else on their backs.

During the American Civil War, Hunt/Farini joined the Union Army. He later said he had demonstrated two of his inventions (a rope bridge and pontoon shoes to help soldiers cross rivers quickly) in front of no less than Abraham Lincoln himself. He also claimed he had gone on dangerous spy missions into enemy territory—even enlisting as a rebel soldier before deserting to bring information back to the North. As with Barnum and Costentenus, we must take many of Farini's claims with a grain of salt.

After his first wife's tragic death in Cuba (she fell while they were performing a high wire act), he patented a safety net for acrobats. Over the coming years, he would step away from performing to focus on promoting several young protégés.

The most successful of his early apprentices was a young man named Sam Wasgate (or Wasgatt), who first appeared as "El Niño Farini" in 1866. But at age 15, Wasgate was transformed into—and found fame as—a girl named Lulu.[263] There were very few female acrobats in the 1870s, since the prevailing attitude was that women were too delicate for this kind of stunt work. Farini saw an opportunity to astound and scandalize audiences with a young woman on the trapeze, without having to find a young woman to train.

Simply dressing Wasgate as a young woman would not be enough. At the beginning of 1870, Farini took El Niño away from the public eye and had him grow his hair, pierce his ears, and don a new wardrobe of girl's clothing. After receiving lessons on walking and acting like a woman, from this point on, Lulu was a girl. She only appeared in public dressed as a girl, and she only performed as a girl.

Farini had also created a new act for his protégé: "Lulu's Leap." This stunt was powered by a seven-foot-long piston attached to huge rubber straps, all concealed inside a pedestal. This propelled Lulu up about 25 feet in the air, where she landed on a plank. Lulu's Leap proved to be spectacularly popular.[264] She toured across Europe and the United States until the mid-1870s, when it was finally difficult to disguise her rapidly developing masculine appearance. After a near-fatal accident during a performance in Dublin, Lulu was unmasked by a doctor treating her injuries. Now publicly a man, sporting short hair and a mustache, he recovered and was able to continue performing. But curiously, he continued to use the name Lulu, without any attempt to conceal his masculine appearance. He married Farini's sister Edith and they had a daughter in 1877, though he returned to performing in women's clothing several times as an adult and later published travel photographs under the name Lulu Farini.

---

263 Peacock, *The Great Farini*, 198.

264 Peacock, *The Great Farini*, 200-201.

*Photograph of Lulu, 1870s (© National Portrait Gallery, London)*

As Farini toured with Lulu and the patented Leap in the early 1870s, competitors tried similar acts with less success. The first advertised "human cannonball" act was presented in March 1875 as part of Old Yankee Robinson's Circus at Wood's Museum in New York. It's unclear, however, if this was really a human cannonball act or just something pretending to be. It was described in the press as a "ghost illusion" and didn't generate much publicity—or income. (Robinson's tour that year ended in bankruptcy.)[265] Another act in Paris in late 1875 tried to launch an acrobat out of a "mortar" to a trapeze bar, but the acrobat narrowly escaped death after landing on his head.

Farini's ultimate goal was to launch an acrobat out of a device that looked like a cannon. He just needed to add a barrel. Where Lulu's Leap was vertical, the "cannon" would be angled to send the acrobat across the stage into a net—and a dramatic explosion would release the hidden springs. By March of 1877, just months after Farini took over the Royal Aquarium, this new act was ready. Advertisements trumpeted Farini's latest protégé: Zazel, the Beautiful Human Cannonball.

Zazel (rhymes with gazelle) was born Rossa Matilda Richter. She had performed as a child singer and dancer in London's best theaters before learning gymnastics and making her trapeze debut at age 11.[266] Now almost 15, she was about to take the world by storm.

On April 2, 1877, the day of Zazel's debut, aquarium spectators were in for a surprise. After she performed her trapeze act, Zazel joined Farini and his assistant on the floor of the hall. A huge cannon was suspended from the wall and ceiling. The tiny girl climbed up a ladder and lowered herself into the mouth of the cannon. Farini asked for quiet. "'Are you in?' he asked. There was absolute silence. Then a small, sweet voice said, 'Yes,' and Farini... lit the powder."[267] While the audience held their breaths, there was a terrifying explosion, and Zazel came shooting out of the cannon. She flew across the hall and safely landed in a net.

---

265 Peacock, *The Great Farini*, 227.

266 Peacock, *The Great Farini*, 229.

267 Peacock, *The Great Farini*, 233.

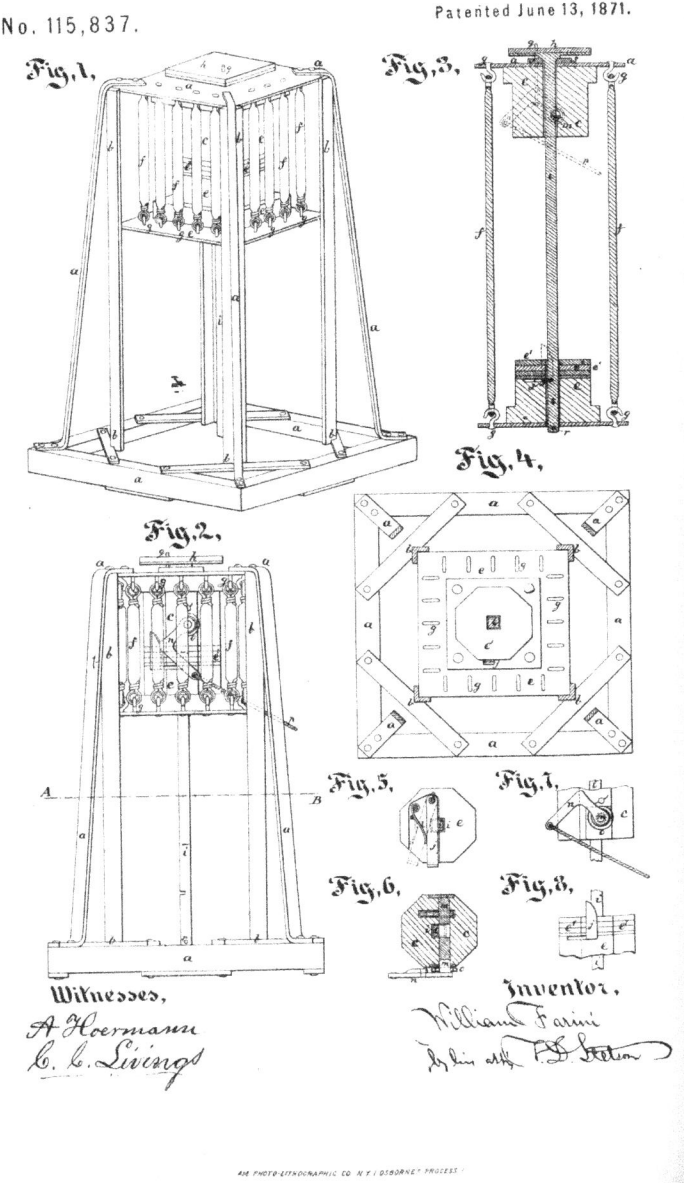

*Diagrams from Farini's U.S. patent for the Lulu's Leap mechanism, a "certain new and useful Apparatus for Projecting Persons and Articles into or through the Air," June 13, 1871, (Milwaukee Public Library, Milwaukee, Wisconsin)*

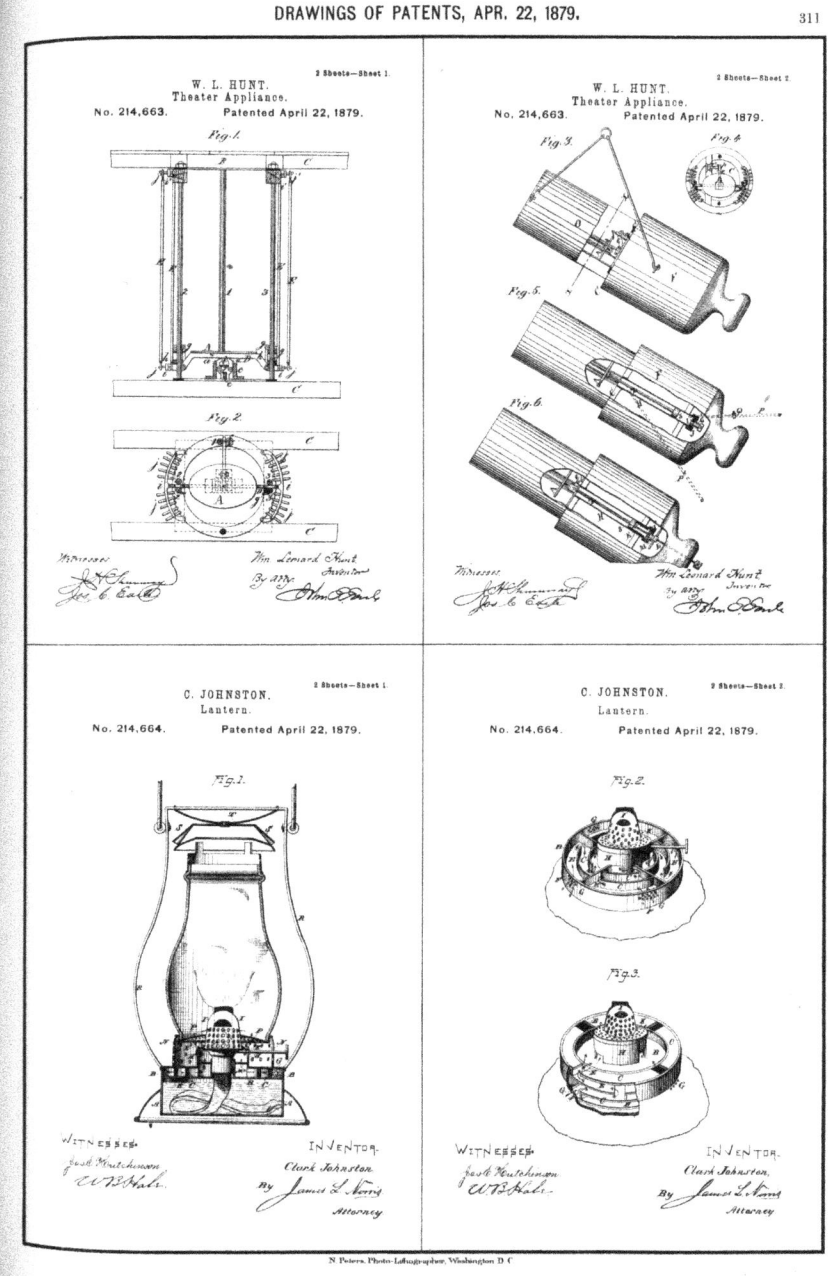

*Diagrams from Farini's U.S. patent for the human cannonball mechanism, under his original name, William Leonard Hunt, April 22, 1879 (he had been issued a British patent in 1875,) (Milwaukee Public Library, Milwaukee, Wisconsin)*

ZAZEL

*Photograph of Zazel and her cannon, with Farini in the lower right, date unknown, (Collection of the John and Mable Ringling Museum of Art, Tibbals Circus Collection)*

The rubber springs were powerful enough to send Zazel about 20 feet through the air. That's a far cry from the 200 feet that today's compressed-air cannons can reach, but the effect was still astonishing. The Aquarium's crowd went crazy, and Zazel launched Farini's career even further than Lulu's Leap had. Pun intended.

Barnum was soon trying to entice Farini into bringing Zazel over to America. Due to Farini's patents (and his aggressive defense of them), Barnum had to either hire Zazel or license the device from Farini. After several years of negotiations, they reached an agreement, and Farini, Zazel, and all their patented equipment made the trip. Zazel opened in New York with Barnum's show in 1880—joining Captain George on his last season with the *Greatest Show on Earth*.

One of Barnum's competitors, Adam Forepaugh, hired "The Australian Marvels," Ella Zuila and George Loyal, who also claimed to be the first human cannonball act. But their act was more like Lulu's leap than Zazel's flight. Regardless of the Australians' claims, Zazel became the one remembered as the original human cannonball, thanks to both Farini and Barnum's relentless and skilled promotion.

Costentenus and Farini would have gotten to know each other during the 1880 season with Barnum. But in early 1881, the Tattooed Greek went off with the Bunnells, while Farini teamed up with Barnum's old partner, William Coup. Farini had first connected with Coup a few years before, when he tried to bring a beluga whale from Coup's New York Aquarium to the Royal Aquarium. The unfortunate animal barely survived the journey across the Atlantic and did not last long after its new tank was unknowingly filled with fresh water rather than salt water.

For the 1881 season, Coup and Farini put together a massive touring circus that they alternately called *The New Monster Shows* and *The Grand United Mastodon Shows*. Trying to challenge Barnum and his new partners, the show reportedly covered eight acres. It was so popular that, even on eight acres with a massive main tent, they routinely had to turn away paying customers.[268]

---

268 "W. C. Coup's New Monster Shows," *New York Clipper*, April 16, 1881; "Circuses," *New York Clipper*, June 4, 1881.

Despite this success, Farini needed to make a quick trip back to the Royal Aquarium for the winter, so Coup bought him out of their joint venture. Eager to hire a few curiosities who hadn't appeared in England before, Farini stopped in New York and consulted with the Bunnells.[269] Thus, Farini and Zazel made the journey back to London with Captain George and "the Leopard Boy," who Farini had also met during his time with Barnum.

•

At a private viewing for the British press, Farini reminded the reporters that "Captain George Costentenus is very amiable, but he will not be pinched."[270] They got as close as they could, inspecting "this remarkable specimen of humanity- he is stalwart and well-proportioned and fat... we took as much advantage as possible... stopping short always of pinching."[271] While the Tattooed Greek drew crowds, some reviewers were less kind, stating that Costentenus was "now falling somewhat into flesh."[272] Costentenus even (supposedly) appeared before Queen Victoria, who hosted many curiosities at Buckingham Palace, and likely was amused with the Tattooed Greek.[273]

Two separate visitors to the Royal Aquarium thought they had already seen Costentenus and his tattoos, despite Farini's claims that Captain George had never been to England before.[274] A letter from someone calling themselves H.W.A. appeared in the Era that December saying that a similar tattooed man had appeared five years earlier at the Shrewsbury Show in western England. This traditional town event had been running annually for several hundred years and

269 Peacock, The Great Farini, 277-279; "Wait for Nothing—The BIG Show is Here!" Cairo Bulletin, October 19, 1881.

270 "Westminster Aquarium," Era, Nov. 26, 1881.

271 "Westminster Aquarium," Era, Nov. 26, 1881.

272 "A Tattooed Man and a Spotted Boy," Morning Post, Nov. 22, 1881.

273 Woolf, The Wonders, 3-4; "G.B. Bunnell's," ht4000221, Tibbals Circus Collection.

274 "The Tattooed Greek Nobleman, to the Editor of the Era," Era, December 3, 1881; "The Tattooed Greek Nobleman, to the Editor of the Era," Era, December 10, 1881.

was attended by thousands of people each June.[275] H.W.A.'s description was corroborated by another letter, a week later from someone named Albert Becher, a comedian, who also claimed to have seen a tattooed man at Shrewsbury. Is it possible Costentenus had been there? It's unlikely. The Shrewsbury Show had been officially abolished "for the sake of public morals and the reputation of the British."[276] In 1876 and 1877, the last two years the show was held, Captain George was in America working for Barnum. The description of the Shrewsbury man also doesn't match Costentenus: the man mentioned in the letter was "tattooed from the neck downwards," with no facial tattoos.[277] The Shrewsbury Show was a loosely organized event, so it's entirely possible that a different man with tattoos had set up a booth and exhibited himself. Who this might have been remains a mystery.

An additional correspondent, Auld Reekie, claimed to have seen Costentenus displayed in a shop "in the company of a fat pig" in Edinburgh in 1872.[278] The man with the pig may have had tattoos of animals, but he was described as "very spare and haggard

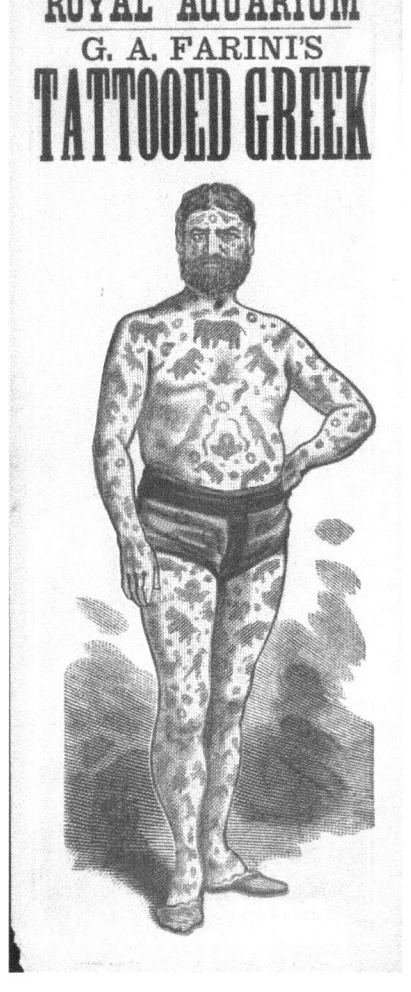

*Royal Aquarium poster of G. A. Farini's Tattooed Greek, undated, (Wellcome Collection)*

275 Pattie Price, "The Decline and Fall of the Old Shrewsbury Show," *Victorian Shrewsbury: Studies in the History of a County Town*, ed. Barrie Trinder (Shropshire Libraries, 1984): 145-155.

276 "Popular Holidays," *Eddowes' Salopian Journal*, June 6, 1877, quoted in Price, "The Decline and Fall of the Old Shrewsbury Show, 152.

277 "The Tattooed Greek Nobleman," *Era*, December 3, 1881.

278 "The Tattooed Greek Nobleman," *Era*, December 17, 1881.

looking," so he, too, was probably not Captain George.

A drawing in the *Illustrated Sporting and Dramatic News* showed Costentenus at the Royal Aquarium, performing alongside Ashbury Benjamin, "the Leopard Boy." Benjamin was a young Black boy who most likely had either piebaldism (where some pigment-

*Royal Aquarium poster of Farini's Latest Novelty, Captain Costentenus, undated, (Wellcome Collection)*

THE TATTOOED GREEK.

*Drawing of Costentenus and Ashbury Benjamin at the Royal Aquarium,*
The Illustrated Sporting and Dramatic News, *December 3, 1881, (Collection of the author)*

producing skin cells are missing from birth) or vitiligo (where some pigment-producing cells are destroyed over time). Both cause patches of pale skin. While these skin conditions appear in people of all races and skin colors, they are more visible in people who have darker skin. Benjamin was not the first Black "Leopard Boy" to be exhibited, nor was he the last. Once again, the troubling question of whether people like Benjamin had any choice in exhibiting themselves surfaces.

Ashbury Benjamin was supposedly born in the West Indies around 1864. Barnum claimed that the boy had been stolen and taken to Australia—and that Barnum had both rescued and hired him.[279] Benjamin worked for Barnum until 1880 and then, with Costentenus, went to the Bunnells' museum in 1881 and on to the Royal Aquarium. His stay in London was short. Benjamin returned to New York after just two months and took up his previous position with the Bunnells.

---

279 "The Wonderful Leopard Boy," *Nebraska State Journal*, Sept. 25, 1877.

150

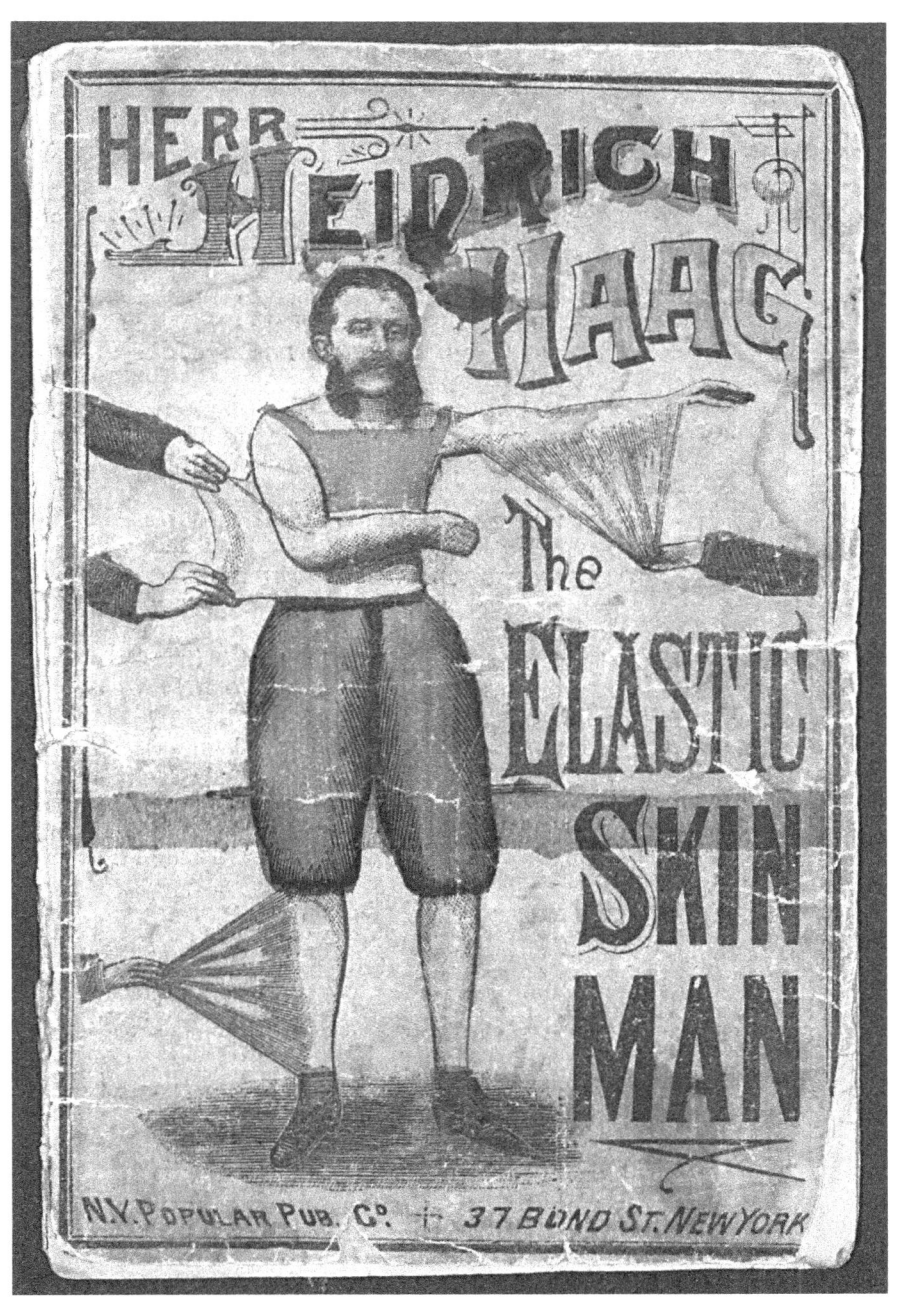

*Cover of Heinrich Haag's promotional pamphlet, New York Popular Publishing Co.,*
*1880s, (Collection of Princeton University Library)*

He went on to have a long career in the sideshow and museum business, including being part of a boxing act in the late 1880s with William Johnson ("Zip the Pinhead") and a stint with Barnum and Bailey in the early 1890s that took him back to Europe for a season.

When Benjamin left the Aquarium, Farini brought in another performer with unusual skin: Heinrich Haag, "The Elastic-Skin Man." Haag likely had Ehlers-Danlos syndrome, which made his skin hyperelastic.[280] Unlike Benjamin, Haag had probably chosen the performing life.

In February of 1882, Farini once again departed London for New York, having obtained another lucrative contract with Barnum. He left Costentenus and Heinrich Haag behind, but brought Zazel, Lulu, and "Farini's Friendly Zulus," all of whom joined Barnum's show for the upcoming season. Like the "Australian Bushmen" who Costentenus worked with in 1877, these were a group of men from South Africa who demonstrated their customs and dances. Farini had recruited these Zulus at the height of the First Boer War, when the Zulus were fighting to remain independent from the British Crown. This group of men were said to be loyal to Britain and came over voluntarily, and the act was promoted as a cultural exhibition, but yes, the act was really as racist as it sounds. The men reportedly also argued with Farini over pay and ability to perform at other locations.

Costentenus stayed on at the Royal Aquarium until April, then also made his way back to the U.S. But when he got there, things had changed. For the first time, the Tattooed Greek had competition.

280 Peacock, *The Great Farini*, 280.

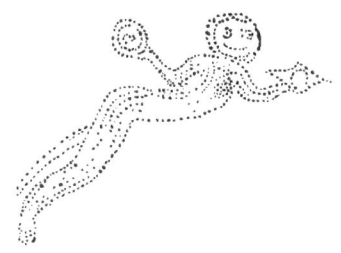

# CHAPTER EIGHT

# A NEW GENERATION

When Costentenus returned to New York on April 24, 1882, he was in for a shock. During his absence, another tattooed "Captain" had rolled into town. And then a tattooed woman appeared, threatening to eclipse them both.

For over a decade, Captain George had dominated the sideshow scene as the only tattooed performer. But his long success finally inspired imitators. A few enterprising Americans accumulated their own tattoos and started to copy Costentenus's formula—complete with their own equally absurd origin stories. Some even pretended to be Greek. One went so far as to call himself "the Tattooed Greek, Jr." Captain George had been such a powerful presence in the sideshow that "working the tattooed Greek racket" became sideshow slang for working as a tattooed performer. What must Costentenus have thought, suddenly being just one tattooed man in a growing crowd of rivals?

•

## Captain Harry DeCoursey

The first signs of competition had appeared just before Captain George left for London. "Captain Harry DeCoursey" came on the scene in Philadelphia, with his body covered in conventional Western-style tattoos. That summer, a number of newspapers carried a story claiming that renowned Philadelphia tattooist Stephen Lee had tattooed DeCoursey earlier in 1881.

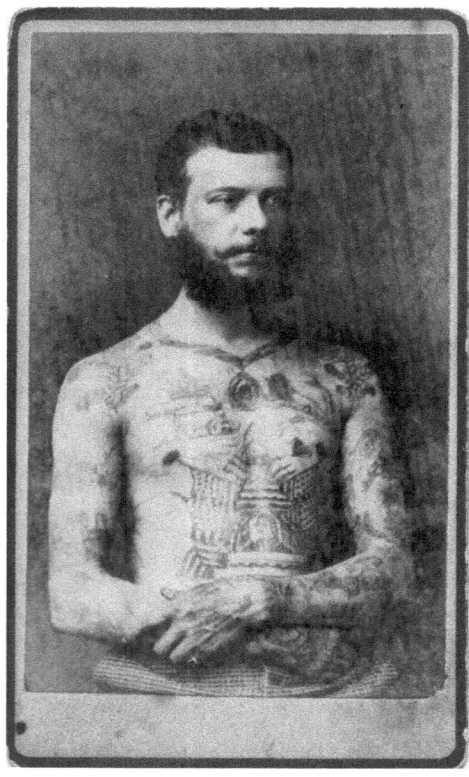

*Photograph of Captain Harry DeCoursey, undated, (Collection of Syracuse University Library)*

Around Christmas, someone, possibly DeCoursey, was pretending to be Costentenus at Philadelphia's Great European Museum.[281] The tiny advertisement read "Captain Costentenus, The Tattooed Man of Burmah." But Captain George had been in England since early November—and he had never referred to himself as "The Tattooed Man of Burmah," despite how accurate that might have been.[282] In 1882, DeCoursey wasn't appearing as Costentenus, but he was still trying to cash in on Costentenus's fame by calling himself "The Greek Tattooed Man."[283]

Of course, Harry DeCoursey wasn't his real name. His real name was William Denny, and he, too, wasn't a captain. He was born

[281] "Tattooing," *Daily Union-Leader*, June 17, 1881; "Captain Costentenus," *Philadelphia Times*, December 23, 1881.

[282] "Captain Costentenus," *Philadelphia Times*, December 23, 1881.

[283] "New Dime Museum," *Sunday Herald and Weekly National Intelligencer*, January 21, 1883.

in 1851 in Connecticut, the only son of a jeweler. Like Costentenus, he also had a pamphlet printed by the New York Popular Publishing Company. Written the year after *The Life and Adventures of Captain Costentenus*, the *Life and Adventures of Captain Harry Decoursey* even mentions Captain George, saying that both of them are "wonders of the Nineteenth Century."[284]

The reliably unreliable authors of the New York Popular Publishing wrote a story for DeCoursey that was almost as fanciful as Captain George's. At least they came up with a new location: the guano fields of Peru. While out seeing the world, young Harry was shipwrecked and imprisoned by Incas in Peru. Cue the melodrama. His two companions in this misadventure just so happened to be legendary tattooists: Martin Hildebrandt from New York and the aforementioned Stephen Lee. The Incas forced the two to torture DeCoursey by covering him in tattoos (hence the American style of his tattoos). Here, DeCoursey claimed that he suffered even more than Costentenus had, because the process took longer. After two years, DeCoursey and his companions escaped and undertook an implausible sea voyage in a small fishing boat back to the United States. Finally, he made his way back to his parents' home in New York. His sister fainted at the sight of him. Only his mother recognized him. She cried out, "It is my boy," and he responded, "Yes, I am the Prodigal returned."[285] He then got a job as a tattooed performer in New York, where "the beautiful marks on me at last... put me in the show business."[286]

Three months before Captain George returned to New York, DeCoursey put an advertisement in *The New York Clipper*, declaring himself available for hire as "the only tattooed man now in this country."[287] He briefly worked at the Bunnells' Brooklyn museum, then moved on to Philadelphia and Pittsburgh.[288] When Costentenus

---

284 *Harry Decoursey, Life and Adventures of Captain Harry Decoursey: A Book Containing a History of My Life, Accounts of Tattooing, How it is Performed and by Whom*, (New York Popular Publishing Co: 1882).

285 Decoursey, *Life and Adventures*, p. 11.

286 Decoursey, *Life and Adventures*, p. 12.

287 "The Only Tattooed Man Now in This Country," *New York Clipper*, January 14, 1882.

288 "At the Dime Museum," *New York Clipper*, January 21, 1882; "New Museum,"

returned in 1882, Captain George regained his spot with the Bunnells, and Captain DeCoursey went back to taking out ads looking for work.[289] He did, however, work steadily as a tattooed man until a few years before his death in 1903.[290]

•

## *Irene Woodward*

A month before Costentenus's return, the Bunnell brothers had also hired a young woman. On March 19, 1882, they held a special reception to introduce her to the world at Sinclair House, a hotel around the corner from their museum. Irene Woodward (formerly Ida Levina Lisk, born in Philadelphia in 1857) stunned audiences with her many tattoos—and a shocking amount of bare skin.[291] A tattooed floral wreath went across her chest like a necklace. Stars, hearts, angels, harps, and a fully-rigged ship decorated her arms. Her back was completely covered with a large cross, heart, and anchor. Newspapers had said Captain George's skin looked like he had a tight fitting shawl wrapped around him.[292]For Irene Woodward, the overall effect was described as looking like a "beautiful dress."[293] She, too, had a long and successful career. She worked all over America and Europe for over twenty years, before she died of cancer in 1915.

Like her male counterparts, Irene Woodward also had a pamphlet created by the New York Popular Publishing Company. *Facts Related to Irene Woodward, The Tattooed Lady* claimed that her

---

*New York Clipper*, February 25, 1882; "At the Fifth Ave. Museum," *New York Clipper*, August 5, 1882.

289 "Captain DeCoursey," *New York Clipper*, June 24, 1882.

290 "Deaths in the Profession," *New York Clipper*, November 7, 1903; "Nickelodeon," *The Boston Globe,* January 3, 1899.

291 "The Tattooed Woman," *New York Times*, March 19, 1882.

292 "Local Matters," *Bangor Daily Whig & Courier*, Tuesday, July 25, 1876.

293 Irene Woodward, *Facts Related to Irene Woodward, The Tattooed Lady*, (New York Popular Publishing Company, 1882).

*Photograph of Irene Woodward, undated, (Collection of the author)*

father, a retired sailor, tattooed her while she was a girl. They lived in Colorado, and her father supposedly thought her tattoos would protect her from capture by Native Americans.[294] After he was killed by Utes, Irene and her brother were supposedly captured, but "the emblems upon her body were to them objects of fear," so the two were released.[295] She then said she saw Costentenus in Denver in 1880 (which would have been during his last tour with the *Greatest Show on Earth*) and was inspired to become a tattooed performer herself.

However, in 1880, Irene Woodward was still Ida, living in Chicago with her husband and young son. It is possible that she saw Captain George out west, but this is probably another example of the New York Popular Publishing Company playing fast and loose with the facts. Most likely, they just wanted any excuse to insert Captain George into her story.[296]

Had Ida indeed seen the stout Greek man in front of her on the stage, covered in strange red and blue animals—and thought that she could do it better? Did she already have a small tattoo? Did she look at it and imagine herself covered with more? A *New York Times* reporter, after seeing Captain George in 1880, remarked that "half the people who visited this specimen of Grecian art looked as if they would be quite willing to go through the process of having their skins embroidered if... they could insure a comfortable living without labor."[297] A later article claimed that someone wanting to go into the business could get a full set of tattoos for between 300 and 400 dollars (about $10,000 in today's money).[298] Was this the path that Irene Woodward had chosen? Did she realize that she could, in fact, rival Costentenus as one of the top tattooed performers in sideshows across America?

•

---

294 Woodward, *Facts Relating to Irene Woodward*, 3.

295 Woodward, *Facts Relating to Irene Woodward*, 3.

296 Woodward, *Facts Relating to Irene Woodward*, 3.

297 "Incidents at the Island," *New York Times*, August 8, 1880.

298 "Living Chromos," *Public Press*, April 11, 1884, p. 1; $10,000 - $13,000 in 2025, per Measuring Worth.

# And Many More...

Harry DeCoursey and Irene Woodward were just the first two to follow in Captain George's footsteps. Throughout the 1800s, there had been at most one well-known tattooed performer at any given time. But now the floodgates opened. Nora Hildebrandt, Dora Dailey, Frank and Emma De Burgh, Lulu Kramer, Wesley Baum, Mary and William Brooks, Frank and Annie Howard, George Karlavagn, George Cardoza, Mademoiselle Aimee, and Tom Sidonia (one of the first to be tattooed with a new electric needle) came racing in. And those are just the performers active in the 1880s and 1890s whose names are still known today. Tattooed performers popped in and out of dime museums and circuses with great frequency—many of them claiming Greek connections and spinning dramatic tales of captivity and torture.

Nora Hildebrandt's pamphlet claimed she and her father were captured by Sitting Bull and his tribe. The famous Lakota leader supposedly ordered her father to tattoo her. He did so for 365 days—while she was tied to a tree—but he finally refused to continue. He was killed and she was rescued by the cavalry.[299]

Ida Mae Busey, who performed as Mademoiselle Aimee, didn't even bother creating a new version of the old stories. Her pamphlet was literally a reprint of Irene Woodward's with a different cover. Woodward's name

*Photograph of Nora Hildebrandt, undated,*
*(Collection of the author)*

299 Hildebrandt, *Miss Nora Hildebrandt: The Tattooed Lady.*

was simply cut out of the text, leaving conspicuous blank spaces throughout.[300] It's impossible to tell if that pamphlet was actually authorized by the New York Popular Publishing Company or was a pirated version produced by someone else.

With this younger generation of tattooed performers challenging his supremacy, Captain George must have seen the writing on the wall. In the spring of 1882, the Bunnells had him work alongside Irene Woodward, exhibiting supposed "royal gifts" that he'd collected in England from the Queen and the Prince of Wales.[301] In May, the Bunnells alternated Costentenus and Woodward between their original museum in Manhattan and their Brooklyn location.

American newspaper coverage of the Captain was also changing. *The Daily Inter Ocean* now said, "The tattooed Greek... has saved his money... and will retire from show business and settle down as a private citizen."[302] *The Waco Daily Examiner* and *The Chaff Farmer's Review* reported that the Tattooed Greek, supposedly now 53 years old, was about to be admitted as a Mason and would be settling down in New York.[303] His competitors and their agents may have encouraged these stories. They had a vested interest in emphasizing his advanced age and how close to retirement he was. Captain George's response? He took a summer vacation and then headed back to Europe in the fall.

It was a short but successful trip. Costentenus appeared in Berlin with Cirkus Renz, performing in a former market hall that could accommodate 4,000 people.[304] [305] He was seen in talks with Botho von Hülsen, who managed the royal theaters in several German cities, but there is no record that anything came of those discussions. The

300 Mlle. Aimee [Ida May Busey], *Facts Related to The Tattooed Lady*, (New York Popular Publishing Company, undated).

301 "G.B. Bunnell's," ht4000221, Tibbals Circus Collection.

302 "Capt. Costentenus," *Daily Inter Ocean*, May 24, 1882.

303 "Some Legal Decisions," *Waco Daily Examiner*, May 26, 1882; "Chaff," *Farmers' Review*, June 8, 1882.

304 "Der Tätowirte Griechenfürst," *Berliner Börsenzeitung*, October 10, 1882.

305 Steve Ward, *Opulence and Ostentation: Building the Circus*, (Modern Vaudeville Press, 2023): 140-141.

Captain was even seen spending evenings strolling along the streets near Café Keck, a popular coffeehouse in Berlin—causing a sensation among the passing crowds.

By the New Year, Costentenus was back in the United States, appearing at the brand new Dime Museum in Washington, DC.[306] They had just opened on Christmas Day with "a host of novelties on the stage and living curiosities in the museum."[307] Crowds were good, drawn in by the Tattooed Greek as well as "art-pictures" and trained dogs.[308] Captain George stayed near the nation's capital for the spring, also appearing at the Baltimore Dime Museum in March of 1883.[309]

Then, almost three years after he last toured with the *Greatest Show on Earth*, Costentenus returned to the traveling circus life for the final time. This was not planned or promoted as a farewell tour. His career was simply drawing to a close. For his last summer season, he signed on with Nathans and Co.—"The Great One Ring Show." It was a promising small show, packed with decent, if aging, performers and a plan to tour New York, Pennsylvania, Ohio, Illinois, Kansas, and Missouri.

It did not go well.

306 "Latest News by Telegraph," *New York Clipper*, Jan. 27, 1883.

307 "The New Dime Museum," *Evening Star*, Dec. 23, 1882.

308 "The Dime Museum," *New York Clipper,* Jan. 20, 1883.

309 "Dime Museum," *Baltimore Sun*, March 26, 1883; "Amusements," *Baltimore Sun*, March 30, 1883.

# CHAPTER NINE

# AD NATHANS, DAN RICE, AND DISASTER

On March 3, 1883, the *New York Clipper* announced that Addison "Ad" Nathans had hired "the Tattooed Greek Capt. Costentenus" and "the greatest old-time living clown, Dan Rice" for his latest show.[310] Nathans & Co. would open in Geneva, New York, on April 25, starting one of the most disastrous seasons in circus history.[311]

•

---

310 "Nathans & Co., Items," *New York Clipper*, March 3, 1883.

311 "Circuses," *New York Clipper*, April 28, 1883.

## Ad Nathans, Manager

Costentenus had first met Ad Nathans when they both worked for Barnum and the Flatfoots from 1877 to 1880. It was Ad Nathans who had waded into the fight between Captain George and the giant Colonel Goshen, demanding that they either stop or take it into the ring.

Ad wasn't the only Nathans in the circus business. Of his 16 siblings and half-siblings, his older half-brother Thomas was the first to enter the circus world. Around 1821, young Thomas was apprenticed to an acrobat and wirewalker. His eclectic circus career would go on to include working with snakes, monkeys, ponies, and caged animals—and comic singing.

John J. Nathans followed his brother Thomas into the business at age 12. The most successful of the family, John also started as a performer but soon rose to the role of manager. He would become

*Poster for Nathan's & Co., 1882, (Collection of The John and Mable Ringling Museum of Art, Tibbals Circus Collection)*

"one of the outstanding personalities in 19th century circus history."[312] As one of the original Flatfoots, he was among the top circus managers in the country for over 50 years.

Addison Nathans, called Ad, born in Florida in 1835, was about 20 years younger than John. As a young man, he worked as a painter and enlisted in the Confederate Army days before the Civil War broke out. After the war, he moved to New York, where John introduced him to circus management.[313] Given Ad's family connections and his experience as a quartermaster managing supplies during the war, he didn't start at the bottom of the circus ranks. He worked on his brother's Great European Circus until 1871 and stepped into a variety of roles for the Flatfoots over the following years.[314] When they started managing the *Greatest Show on Earth* for Barnum in 1877, John was the Director of Amusements and Ad was Assistant Manager. After the Flatfoots split with Barnum, Ad and Costentenus both worked with Coup and Farini in 1881.[315]

All this circus management work had convinced Ad Nathans that it was time to run his own traveling show. He found worthy partners in Erasmus Colvin and Wesley Jukes, who he had worked with at a museum in Brooklyn. Colvin had served as treasurer for John J. Nathans from 1862 to 1864 and as manager for Coup's 1877 and 1879 shows.[316] Jukes had created and maintained Barnum's vast collection of automatons, which were exhibited along with Costentenus from 1876 to 1880.[317] The three partners got a big head start with their own show by purchasing almost every bit of equipment they would need at once. They bought all the tents, rigging, wagons, and more from the late John Hayes Murray's show, which the *New York Clipper* had

---

312 "Circuses," *New York Clipper*, April 28, 1883.

313 *Gadsden County, Florida, U.S., Compiled Marriages, 1851-1875*, Ancestry.com.

314 "The Nathans, A Circus Family," *Stuart Thayer's American Circus Anthology*, ed. William Slout, http://classic.circushistory.org/Thayer/Thayer3b.htm.

315 "The Nathans," *Stuart Thayer's American Circus Anthology*.

316 "Colvin, Erasmus Darwin," William Slout, *Olympians of the Sawdust Circle*, https://www.classic.circushistory.org/Olympians/OlympiansC2.htm.

317 "Jukes, Wesley L.," Slout, *Olympians of the Sawdust Circle*, https://www.classic.circushistory.org/Olympians/OlympiansJ.htm.

called a "first class railroad circus and menagerie."[318] Nathans & Co. were off to a good start.

One of the first performers they hired came from family connections: Philo Nathans, "the only six horse rider in the world." Born Philo Rust, he had adopted the family name after apprenticing with John J. Nathans.[319] Ad also brought in equestrienne Mademoiselle Martha, Cheltra the Contortionist, three giants, and a large menagerie, which supposedly included 20 elephants.[320]

For their first season in 1882, the show traveled through New York and New Jersey. The tour made enough money to start planning for 1883. But Erasmus Colvin departed in March, selling his share to W. E. Sinclair and Richard Dockrill.[321] Sinclair had been Barnum's treasurer for the 1879 and 1880 seasons, and he took on that role with Nathans & Co. He would prove to be a poor choice for the job. Richard Dockrill was the husband of equestrienne Elise Dockrill, who had toured with Barnum and Costentenus in 1879. The Dockrills had managed their own show in the past, but they stepped in as equestrian director (Richard) and performer (Elise) with Nathans & Co.[322]

For 1883, Nathan's Great One Ring Show was going to be bigger and better than before. Along with Captain George (now probably about 50 years old) and Elise Dockrill, they hired trick rider Fred Barclay, acrobats Harry and William Ashton, aerialist Madame Le Fevre, Sam Reinhart and his Cunning Canine Congress, and arguably the most famous circus performer of the 19th century, veteran clown Dan Rice.

•

---

318 "Circuses," *New York Clipper*, February 4, 1882.

319 *Nathans and Co. Herald*, CWi 6498 A-B, Circus World Museum Library, Wisconsin Historical Society; Stuart Thayer, "The Nathans, A Circus Family," *Bandwagon* 29, No. 2 (March-April 1985): 26.

320 *Nathans and Co. Herald*, CWi 6498 A-B.

321 "Circuses," *New York Clipper*, March 17, 1883. ["Mr. St--Clair, formerly treasurer of the Barnum show" which is actually W. E. Sinclair.]

322 "Will Exhibit at Mt. Carmel," *Mount Carmel Register*, August 9, 1883.

# Dan Rice, Talking Clown

Born Daniel McLaren in 1823, Dan Rice started performing in 1841 with a trained pig that could supposedly tell time. Rice sang, danced, and joked, performed parodies of Shakespeare, and did tricks on horseback. He exhibited the first rhinoceros in America, presented an elephant that walked on a tightrope, and trained his horse Excelsior to climb stairs. At his peak in the 1850s, he owned several shows and his fame often outshone rivaled Barnum's. Rice frequently talked politics with his audience, but he tried to play to both sides during the Civil War. That hurt his popularity, but it didn't stop him from running a short—but legitimate—campaign for president in 1867.

Photograph of Dan Rice, 1865, (National Portrait Gallery, Smithsonian Institution)

When he joined Nathans & Co., Dan Rice's career was on its downward slide. Years of bad business decisions had taken their toll, and the clowning tastes of the nation had changed. In 1883, the *Cincinnati Commercial Gazette* declared that "the silent clown [was] now usurping his place."[323]

The 1870s had been particularly tough for Rice. Growing debts followed him as he repeatedly tried to resurrect his career. By 1875, he owed $85,000 (about $2.5 million in today's money) and filed for bankruptcy.[324] Rice's financial problems were compounded by a slide

---

323 "Clowns and Clowns," *Cincinnati Commercial Gazette*, June 3, 1883.

324 David Carlyon, *Dan Rice: The Most Famous Man You've Never Heard Of* (Public

into alcoholism. At the end of 1879, he tried attaching himself to the temperance movement, traveling around giving lectures evils of alcohol.[325] But this may have been just another form of performance to Rice. There were rumors that his water pitcher on stage was actually filled with gin.

Whatever was in the pitcher, temperance did not stick. Rice hit bottom and disappeared for several months. He found small shows to work for in 1880 and 1881, but he was homeless and broke in 1882.[326] One of his circus employers, John Robinson, advised other circus owners to keep him busy if they wanted to keep him away from alcohol. Robinson supposedly said, "I took him out sober; I kept him sober; I brought him back sober!"[327] It seems to have been a big job.

•

## Rain, Wind, Fire, Death, and Drunkenness

So while Nathans & Co. had some star power for 1883, Captain George was getting older and Dan Rice was a risk. But the first problem occurred in the menagerie. When the show reached Albany, New York, on May 4, one of the elephants died.[328] The elephant was likely part of a group of animals purchased at auction in Detroit after Coup's 1882 show failed. One elephant shorter, the show continued on through Troy, Cohoes, and Schenectady, making short hops on local railroad lines.

As they passed through Green Island, New York, Fanny Conley, an African-American woman performing as the "Zulu Giantess," was

Affairs, 2001): 374; $2.5 million in 2025, per Measuring Worth.

325 Carylon, *Dan Rice*, 379.

326 Carylon, *Dan Rice*, 380-382.

327 John Kunzog, *One Horse Show: The Life and Times of Dan Rice, Circus Jester and Philanthropist, a Chronicle of Early Circus Days*, (n.p., 1962): 340.

328 "Circuses," *New York Clipper*, May 12, 1883.

"insulted" by a railroad engineer. So she "knocked him out with a blow from her fist."[329] In Troy, young "hoodlums" broke into a wagon and stole some game prizes, peanuts, and clothing, but they were soon arrested and the property was recovered.[330] On May 8, Elise Dockrill had a bad night and fell from her foremost horse during the show. Fortunately, "the animals leaped over her without touching her."[331] But these incidents were all just hiccups.

The spring so far in New York had been wet, and the lots where the circus set up their tents were muddy. In Rochester, what should have been a two-day run became a two-show run, thanks to a severe rainstorm. Down the road in Brockport, there was so much mud on the Harvester Grounds that they couldn't even set up the tent. Instead, they took a handful of performers and a few animal cages into town and performed on a street corner in the menagerie tent. The local paper reported, "The actors were all very skillful, and the entertainment very good, considering the circumstances."[332] With fewer, smaller performances in Brockport, the show's financial struggles began.

However, the show must go on. Trudging forward through the mud and the rain, Nathans & Co. made their way toward the Canadian border. On June 5, they set up for performances at Niagara Falls. Here, disaster struck. "During the performance... the canvas tents were struck by a terrific rain squall and utterly demolished."[333] Newspapers estimated that there were about 1,500 people in the audience. Although there were injuries in the panic after the tent fell, surprisingly, no one died. The story was big news. It was covered in newspapers across the country for several weeks—which was not great publicity for Nathans & Co.

Coincidentally, this was not the only circus disaster that occurred that day. Barnum's show was in Chicago and caught fire in the middle of the night. A lamp was still lit, and the flame jumped to

---

329 "Circuses," *New York Clipper*, May 19, 1883.

330 "Circuses," *New York Clipper*, May 19, 1883.

331 "Circuses," *New York Clipper*, May 19, 1883; Kunzog, *One Horse Show*, 341.

332 "The Circus," *Brockport Republic*, June 7, 1883.

333 "Panic at a Circus," *Boston Daily Advertiser*, June 6, 1883.

the canvas. Circus tents at this time were waterproofed by coating them in a melted mixture of paraffin and white gasoline, making them dangerously flammable.[334] So this was a big fire. Michigan Avenue was reportedly lit up like daytime.[335] The fire department arrived at 2 a.m. and managed to keep the fire from spreading, but the main tent was completely consumed. Thankfully, it was empty at the time, and the animals were housed in a separate tent, safe from the fire.

Back in New York, Nathans & Co. limped into Buffalo the next day, where they had to skip a performance so they could fix their damaged tent.[336] Here, newspapers revealed a new problem: Captain George was going blind.

Costentenus had lost his sight in one eye and the other was fading.[337] While the crew worked on the tent, he went to see Dr. Lucien Howe at the Buffalo Eye and Ear Infirmary. Dr. Howe had attended Harvard University and trained in Europe before joining the staff of the University of Buffalo and founding his clinic.[338] He diagnosed the Captain with cataracts, cloudy clumps of proteins that can form in the lenses of the eyes as people age. As with other news stories about the Tattooed Greek, this one spread far and wide, and by mid-summer, newspapers across the nation were reporting that America's elder tattooed man was going blind.

Blindness caused by cataracts was common at the end of the 19th century—and could end the Captain's career. Today, surgeons commonly remove a cloudy lens and replace it with an artificial one. What could be done in 1883? There were a couple of options, both of them risky and not very effective.

A procedure called couching (one of the oldest known

---

334 Stewart O'Nan, *The Circus Fire: A True Story of an American Tragedy*, (First Anchor Books, 2001): 30.

335 "Barnum's Circus Scorched By Fires," *Wisconsin State Journal*, June 5, 1883.

336 "Circuses," *New York Clipper*, June 16, 1883; Kunzog, *One Horse Show*, 341.

337 "The Man About Town," *Buffalo Sunday Morning News*, June 10, 1883.

338 "Howe, Lucien," Museum of the Eye Biographies, American Academy of Ophthalmology, accessed September 2, 2022, https://www.aao.org/biographies-detail/lucien-howe-md.

surgeries, first described in an ancient Indian medical text) used "a sharp needle... to push the cataract back into the vitreous portion of the eye."[339] This allowed light to enter the eye, but didn't replace the damaged lens. A modern study found that traditional couching is dreadfully ineffective. Over 70% of patients are left blind, and none regain good vision.[340]

The other 19th century option was full removal of the lens through a small incision. This had first been done in the mid-1700s, but the risk of infection was high. And without a new lens to put in place of the old one, patients would need thick glasses afterwards.[341] Removal had become more common in the 1840s with the invention of general anesthesia. But it wouldn't be until 1884 (the year after Costentenus visited Dr. Howe) that the use of topical cocaine to anesthetize the eye would make the surgery much easier to perform.[342] With either removal or couching, the recovery involved bathing the eye in a mixture of wine and water and covering it with a dressing. Patients then had to lie on their backs in a dark room for at least eight days.

In the end, Captain George left the clinic without undergoing either procedure. Perhaps he was reluctant to take the risk or perhaps he was going to wait until the season ended. Either way, both Costentenus and Nathans & Co. stumbled onward.

They were managing to survive the rains and the publicity of all their problems. But what Ad Nathans could not handle was

339 Elisabeth Brander, "Couching Cataracts: Cloudy with a Chance of Infection," Bernard Becker Medical Library, Washington University School of Medicine in St. Louis, accessed September 18, 2022. https://becker.wustl.edu/news/couching-cataracts-cloudy-with-a-chance-of-infection/.

340 JF Schémann, S. Bakayoko, S. Coulibaly, "Traditional Couching Is Not an Effective Alternative Procedure for Cataract Surgery in Mali," *Ophthalmic Epidemiology* 7, no. 4 (December 2000):271-283.

341 Eugene Straus, Alex Straus, *Medical Marvels: The 100 Greatest Advances in Medicine*, (Prometheus Books, 2006): 284; CT Leffler, A. Klebanov, W.A. Samara, A. Grzybowski, "The History of Cataract Surgery: From Couching to Phacoemulsification." *Annals of Translational Medicine*, 8, No. 22, (November 2020): 1551.

342 Leffler, "The History of Cataract Surgery," 1551.

a drunken Dan Rice. "One of the employees said that he had been with the circus for six weeks and [Rice] had been drunk for four and a half."[343] The newspapers jumped on Rice, who fired back that he was sick, not drunk.[344] Other reports suggested that he wasn't getting paid. Whatever the reasons, three days after the disastrous storm in Niagara, Rice left the show and returned home to Pennsylvania.

Two weeks later, in Salamanca, New York, the show lost another performer. Fanny Conley, the giantess who had previously punched a railroad employee, was found dead on the morning of June 22. Newspapers speculated that, due to her size, she had been unable to turn herself over in bed and suffocated.[345] It's more likely she died from heart trouble in her sleep. There was a coroner's inquest, but the city records from 1883 are no longer available. Conley was buried in Salamanca, with her husband traveling in from Ohio for the funeral.[346]

Fanny Conley's death made nationwide news, adding to the tales of tragedy coming out of Nathans & Co. that season: a dead elephant, a tent collapse in the middle of a rain squall, and Dan Rice apparently fired for drunkenness. Nearly lost in the coverage of Conley's tragic death was that, also in Salamanca, a cage of hyenas fell off the train car, one of the workmen broke his arm, and some showmen and "town boys" got into a fight.[347]

Without Fanny Conley and Dan Rice, the remaining company moved out of New York and into Pennsylvania. While they were loading their wagons after the June 29 performance in Sharon, a "near riot" broke out. "The employees were engaged in loading" when "about 250 roughs attacked the circus men."[348] The sheriff and his posse chased

---

343 "Local Notes," *Middletown Daily Argus*, June 13, 1883; "Circuses," *New York Clipper*, June 16, 1883.

344 "Dan Rice's Prayer," *Philadelphia Times*, June 20, 1883.

345 "Death of a Giantess," *New York Clipper*, June 30, 1883; "Human Obesity," *Milwaukee Journal*, August 28, 1883; "Telegraphic Notes," *Evening Telegraph*, June 23, 1883.

346 "The Pretended Zulu Princess," *Watertown News*, July 25, 1883.

347 "State and Vicinity," *Buffalo Evening Telegraph*, June 26, 1883.

348 "Brevities," *Record Argus*, July 5, 1883; "The Circus Rows" *Daily City News*, July 2, 1883.

away the "roughs", but one circus employee was cut on the head and another hit by a brick.[349]

Ad Nathans, Costentenus, the Dockrills, and the rest continued on without incident for about a month, traveling through Ohio, West Virginia, and then into Virginia. Professor Rienhart's performing dogs did get sick, but it seems they recovered and continued performing.[350]

It was in Portsmouth, Virginia, on July 24 that the next disaster struck. Another storm came up. This one, however, didn't just knock down the tent. It also set it on fire. The show had just begun, with 4,000 to 5,000 people in the audience. Elise Dockrill rode into the ring on horseback. The wind started to howl. Dockrill's horse was spooked and bolted out from underneath her, throwing her and causing a season-ending injury.[351] The force of the wind then tore the tent from the center pole to the side wall and toppled several other poles. Part of the tent must have fallen on a lantern, starting the fire. This is where the rain, for once, helped them out. It extinguished the fire overhead. But the audience had already panicked. As they tried to flee, many of them cut gashes in the tent walls to escape. Outside, however, a ditch full of briars ran along one side of the tent. A number of people ended up falling in the dark—bleeding, bruised, and covered in mud. The city's residents were alerted via fire bells and storm whistles, "throwing the city into great excitement and turning out great numbers of citizens."[352]

Miraculously, while many audience members and performers were injured, no one died. This storm, like the one earlier in the season at Niagara Falls, became big news throughout the country.

Like the professionals they were, Nathans and Co. did their best to continue on. "After the disaster the showmen took up their tents... and left the city for the next place of exhibition."[353] There

349 "Brevities," *Record Argus*, July 5, 1883.

350 Kunzog, *One Horse Show*, 342.

351 Kunzog, *One Horse Show*, 342.

352 "A Circus on Fire," *New York Clipper*, August 4, 1883.

353 "The Panic at the Circus Tuesday Night – Nobody Seriously Injured," *Norfolk Virginian*, July 26, 1883.

were notices in the local newspaper that several ladies' hats had been recovered after the catastrophe. Those missing a hat should inquire at the mayor's office. And one Miss Nellie Tabb published a notice looking for a silver bracelet that she had lost in the panic.[354]

The show made it to their next stop in Weldon, North Carolina, but they had to use an improvised canvas that wasn't large enough to cover all the seating.[355] Ad Nathans advertised in the *New York Clipper* that the show was looking for replacement acts, "curiosities, specialty people, free-show attractions, etc." as well as musicians, specifically "first-violin and alto, who is well up in variety business... also other musicians. Must be good and reliable."[356]

In the meantime, Dan Rice had returned, apparently sober. But it's unclear if this was a good thing. A review from Norfolk, Virginia, said that Rice "addressed the audience (perhaps too long) for the people want to see the exhibition, not hear speeches."[357] Nathans & Co. limped across North Carolina, Kentucky, Indiana, Illinois, and Missouri, reaching Kansas in early September. In many towns, the turnout was low, and the show was getting closer and closer to the financial breaking point.

•

## The Final Straw

At the September 11 show in Garnett, Kansas, people "turned out to the 'grand parade' in good force... and then they went over to [a local] auction booth, leaving a beggarly array of empty benches

---

354 "The Panic at the Circus," *Norfolk Virginian*.

355 "The Circus," *Roanoke News*, August 2, 1883.

356 "Wanted for Nathans & Co.'s Show," *New York Clipper*, June 30, 1883; "Musicians Wanted Immediately," *New York Clipper*, July 21, 1883.

357 "Nathans and Co., Circus Yesterday Afternoon and Night," *Norfolk Landmark*, July 24, 1883.

etc., under the canvas."[358] The amount of money taken in was so low that W. E. Sinclair, the show's treasurer, was unable to pay the $100 that the Missouri Pacific Railroad required to take them on the next leg of the tour.[359]

The show was stranded.

Employees "made a raid for wages due," but most went unpaid. Those without savings and unable to sell belongings for cash were stuck there in Garnett.[360] Most of the performers and employees—about 100 people—were fed by sympathetic townspeople. They started planning a benefit performance at a local hall to help everyone move on to other jobs.[361] In the meantime, someone got word to the advance advertising team, which was up ahead in Palmyra, Missouri,

*Photograph of Garnett, Kansas, Memorial Day 1882, (Kansas State Historical Society)*

---

358 "A Busted Circus," *Ottawa Daily Republic*, September 13, 1883.

359 $3,300 in 2025, per Measuring Worth.

360 "A Busted Circus," *Ottawa Daily Republic*.

361 "The Circus," *Garnett Republican-Plaindealer*, September 14, 1883; "Show Stranded," *Evening News*, September 17, 1883.

to stop promoting upcoming shows. All the animals and wagons were kept on Garnett's town square for a few days, until everything was moved to the county poor farm.

Dan Rice, trick rider Fred Barclay, and clown Thomas Miaco sued for back wages. This tied up the show's assets in the court system for months. Rice claimed that he was owed $1,600 and attached his name to 20 horses as part of his payment.[362] The show's New York lithographers, Samuel Booth and James Snedden, also sued for $11,000 they were owed for printing posters for the season.[363] The large amounts owed suggests that the show had been short of money for quite some time.

Captain George was among the lucky ones to have enough money to leave. He made his way to Kansas City, where he found work at a dime museum. Dan Rice also left, launching a lecture tour. This was poorly received but made him enough money to get out of Kansas.[364] Several newspapers reported that other circus employees were angry at Rice for starting the lawsuits that kept everything tied up for so long. But the show's failure could not have been much of a surprise. Rice was just an easy target for their anger.

A special term of the district court was convened to figure out how to handle the mess that was left. The judge decided that the show's remains would be auctioned off to pay the suits and the bills.[365] The sheriff notified Ad Nathans, John Nathans, W. E. Sinclair, and Richard Dockrill of this in early October. All four denied that they'd ever been partners in the business (how they did that with straight faces is a mystery). Then all four of them quickly left the state.[366]

Two auctions were scheduled, and the appraisal for everything—the animals, train cars, wagons, and tents—was a mere $20,000.[367]

---

362 $53,000 in 2025, per Measuring Worth.

363 "Short Stops," *Marion County Herald*, September 21, 1883; $360,000 in 2025, per Measuring Worth.

364 Carlyon, *Dan Rice*, 384.

365 "The Case of Dan Rice," *Garnett Journal*, Sept. 20, 1883.

366 "Only Big Show Coming: A Mighty Mammoth Monarch and Gigantic Colossus," *Bandwagon*, Jan/Feb 1989: 44-45.

367 $660,000 in 2025, per Measuring Worth.

One of the Sells Brothers (of Sells Brothers' Quadruple Alliance, Museum, Menagerie, Caravan and Circus—quite a mouthful) from over in Topeka was spotted browsing in town. So was H. S. Fargo, "the hippodrome man of Paola." The first auction, on October 31, sold off the 20 horses that Rice had claimed for his back pay.[368] The second, on December 18, was for everything else: monkeys, goats, tigers, buffalo, deer, ponies, rabbits, a kangaroo, a gorilla, an eagle, a bear, and a camel, as well as the seats, canvas, train cars, and wagons.[369]

Of course, the story of Nathans and Co.'s disastrous 1883 season closes with one final misfortune: a bad snowstorm blew in and kept many buyers away from the second auction. The two auctions together brought in only $6,186.90—less than a third of the appraised value.[370] Town residents bought the majority of the horses, and a local named Jake Blum decided he needed the young black bear (only ten dollars!).[371] The New York printers Booth and Snedden clearly saw the writing on the wall, so they bought a number of the horses to try to unload later for a profit. They also picked up an elephant and the bandwagon, which they then sold to to the Sells Brothers. However, they certainly didn't make back the money they'd lost to Nathans & Co.[372] Most of the show's bills didn't get paid, and the stranded performers got almost nothing.

•

## Picking Up the Pieces

After this disastrous season, Ad Nathans got out of the circus business entirely. He returned to his wife and children in New York

---

368 "Sheriff's Sale," *Garnett Republican-Plaindealer*, October 12, 1883.

369 "Sheriff's Sale," *Garnett Republican-Plaindealer*, December 7, 1883; "Sheriff's Sale," *Garnett Republican-Plaindealer*, December 8, 1883.

370 "The Circus Sale," *Garnett Republican-Plaindealer*, December 21, 1883; $200,000 in 2025, per Measuring Worth.

371 $330 in 2025, per Measuring Worth.

372 "The Circus Sale," *Garnett Republican-Plaindealer*, December 21, 1883.

and got into the jewelry trade. His older brother John shook off what was, for him, a relatively small loss and retired. When John died in 1891, he left a substantial estate.

Richard and Elise Dockrill put together their own show and took it to South America in 1885. But in Venezuela, Elise dislocated her knee, ending her riding career. After yellow fever ran through their company, they returned to the U.S. having lost over $100,000 in just seven months.[373] Richard continued to work as an equestrian director for a number of shows, and their daughter Rose went on to perform, dancing on horseback for Barnum & Bailey and the Ringling Brothers.[374]

The biggest surprise here is Nathan & Co.'s treasurer, W. E. Sinclair. First, he dropped out of sight for a few years. Then in 1886, he was re-hired by Barnum as an assistant treasurer, but he didn't last long.[375] In early April, when the show started its monthlong stand in New York, Sinclair took $6,500 of the show's money and disappeared. And this was not the first time he had stolen from an employer.[376] It emerged that, before his circus career, he had embezzled somewhere between $40,000 and $60,000 from the Wall Street firm of H. L. Horton & Co.[377] Sinclair was clearly a fast talker and had told H. L. Horton that "he had not intended to do wrong, but he had got into the stealing habit before he knew what he was about."[378] Horton forgave him, gave him $500, and "urged him to begin life over and be an honest man."[379] Sinclair clearly hadn't followed Horton's advice.

373 "Dockrill, Elise," and "Dockrill, Richard H.," William Slout, *Olympians of the Sawdust Circle*, www.classic.circushistory.org/Olympians/OlympiansD2.htm; $3.4 million in 2025, per Measuring Worth.

374 "Variety, Minstrel, and Circus," *New York Clipper*, February 6, 1892; "Circus Personalities," *New York Clipper*, October 5, 1912.

375 "From Saturday's Daily" *Garnett Republican-Plaindealer*, January 8, 1886; *Route Book of P. T. Barnum's Greatest Show on Earth and The Great London Circus Consolidation 1885.* http://classic.circushistory.org/History/PTB1885.htm.

376 $230,000 in 2025, per Measuring Worth.

377 "Crimes and Casualties," *Superior Times*, December 8, 1876; $1.2 million to $1.8 million in 2025, per Measuring Worth.

378 "An Old Trick of His," *New York Times*, April 4, 1886.

379 "An Old Trick," *New York Times*; $15,000 in 2025, per Measuring Worth.

Were some of Nathans and Co.'s financial troubles in 1883 due to their treasurer being a seasoned embezzler? Did Sinclair keep out of sight from 1883 to 1886 because he was worried he might get caught? In 1886, Sinclair was rumored to have fled to Canada with the money he had stolen from Barnum, but where he went and what he did is unknown. He did eventually make his way back to New York City, where he died in 1892 at age 40. He was buried in his family's plot in Green-Wood Cemetery in Brooklyn, though without a headstone.[380]

Captain George fared better than the partners in Nathans & Co. He made his way slowly back to New York, after appearing at the Kansas City Dime Museum in September of 1883 and at another museum in Columbus, Ohio, that November.[381] He probably never got paid what he was owed by Nathans and Co., but he landed on his feet. However, his eyesight was still failing, there were rumors in the newspaper that he had died, and his competition continued to dog him.[382] Captain Harry DeCoursey, for instance, had also been working in the Midwest that fall.[383]

In December, Costentenus made a different type of appearance in New York's Superior Court. There, he completed the naturalization process that he'd started in 1880. The man now legally known as George Costentenus was officially a citizen of the United States, with his occupation listed as "showman" and his address given as Earl's Hotel in New York City.[384] The front page of *The Sun-Journal* in Lewiston, Maine, even announced the event: "The Greek Tattooed Man Sings Hail Columbia and Renounces...his allegiance to the King

380 "William E. Sinclair, 1851-1892," *Green-Wood Cemetery Burial and Vital Records: 1840-1937*, accessed April 13, 2024, https://www.green-wood.com/burial-and-vital-records/.

381 "Kansas City Dime Museum," *Kansas City Journal*, September 30, 1883, "Professionals' Bureau," *New York Clipper*, November 3, 1883.

382 "Professionals' Bureau," *New York Clipper*, November 3, 1883; "Capt Geo Costentenus" *New York Clipper*, November 3, 1883.

383 "St. Louis Dime Museum," *St. Louis Post-Dispatch*, September 3, 1884.

384 New York, Naturalization Petitions, 1794-1906, New York, U.S., *Index to Petitions for Naturalization filed in New York City, 1792-1989*, Ancestry.com, Provo, UT, USA. Index to Petitions for Naturalization filed in New York City, 1792-1989, New York, Naturalization Petitions, 1794-1906, New York, U.S., Ancestry.com.

of Greece."[385]

Despite gaining his citizenship, Captain George wasn't planning on staying long. He made arrangements to appear in Boston at Austin and Stone's Museum ("The Best Known and Most Successful Amusement Resort in America") before returning to Europe. Austin and Stone were pleased to have Costentenus before he left the country, supposedly paying him $500 per week.[386] [387] He performed for them until mid-February and then sailed for Liverpool on the White Star Lines' ship *Republic*.[388]

Over the past eight years, Costentenus had changed the look of American sideshows and museums. He made decorated skin a main attraction—and a fixture—on their stages. When he departed in early 1884, there were at least a dozen tattooed performers working in the U.S. Perhaps Captain George thought that Europe would be a less crowded place to work as a tattooed man. Had this disastrous season with Nathans and Co. soured him on the world of the traveling circus? Or was he seeking an eye surgeon who could repair his failing vision? It's hard to say why, but off to Europe he went, where he would stay until the end of the decade.

385 "The Greek Tattooed Man," *Sun-Journal*, December 22, 1883.

386 Dennett, *Weird and Wonderful*, 104.

387 Dennett, *Weird and Wonderful*, 104; $17,000 in 2025, per Measuring Worth.

388 "City and Suburban News" *New York Times*, February 17, 1884.

# CHAPTER TEN

# A FADING CAREER

On his return to England in February of 1884, Costentenus contacted his former employer, Farini. The promoter was back at the Royal Aquarium and he had adopted (literally) a new protégé: "Krao, The Missing Link." She was a young girl, about seven to nine years old, dark-skinned, and very hairy. She may have been from Laos, but like Captain George, her actual origins are obscured by all the cifferent stories told to promote her.

Wherever she was from, Krao had hypertrichosis, a medical condition where an unusual amount of hair grows all over the body. In an era filled with problematic sideshow acts, hers was a particularly egregious, pseudo-scientific mess. According to her promotional pamphlet, Krao was the "long-sought-after 'missing link' between monkeys and human beings whom many Victorians believed existed somewhere on earth."[389]

Like Costentenus, Krao drew huge crowds at respectable venues throughout the United States and Europe. Unlike Costentenus, she

---

389 Peacock, *The Great Farini*, 292.

*Photograph of Krao Farini, taken by Julius Gertinger, Vienna, undated,*
*(Library of Congress)*

was charismatic, cheerful, and much-loved by her fellow performers.[390] As so many other sideshow workers did, she found community and financial success there. But she also had no choice in her early exhibition or in the pseudo-Darwinian nonsense that sold her to an eager public. Krao's long career—and her "missing link" label—would last into the 1920s.

---

390 "Circus Folk Mourn 'Best Liked Freak,' Krao, the 'Missing Link,' Buried With Tribute of Tears From Side-Show Associates," *New York Times*, April 19, 1926.

Back at the Royal Aquarium, Captain George returned to its exhibition halls in early April of 1884. This time around, he appeared with acrobats, ventriloquists, a comic ballet troupe—and "Professor Fred Beckwith's Natatorial Entertainment," a.k.a. swimming demonstrations.[391] Since the death of the beluga whale in 1877, the Aquarium had continued to struggle with the health of its aquatic residents.[392] But swimming exhibitions had become so popular that the tanks at "the Tank," as the Royal Aquarium was commonly called, often held human swimmers instead.

"Professor" Fred Beckwith and his seven children were the most famous of the 19th century British swimmers. Daughter Agnes ("the premier lady swimmer of the world") had recently come back from a tour of the United States, giving "ornamental swimming" exhibitions with various circuses. Her publicity stunts included a 25-

MR. FRED BECKWITH.                    MISS AGNES BECKWITH.

*Photographs of Professor Fred Beckwith and daughter Agnes Beckwith, in* Swimmers and Swimming, or The Swimmer's Album, *1899, (Collection of the author)*

---

391 "Dramatic and Musical Gossip," *Referee*, April 13, 1884.

392 John Sands, "Sullivan and the Royal Aquarium," *The Gilbert and Sullivan Archive*, accessed September 27, 2002, https://www.gsarchive.net/articles/sull_aquarium/index.html.

mile swim from Sandy Hook, New York, to Rockaway Pier.[393] Agnes's performances in the Royal Aquarium's whale tank would have included demonstrating a variety of swimming strokes, an aquatic waltz, and an imitation of a seal, along with eating, drinking, and "smoking" under water (this was actually blowing a mouthful of milk into the pool).[394]

Between Krao, the Beckwiths' swimming demonstrations, and the Tattooed Greek's celebrated return, the Royal Aquarium continued to draw good crowds. Farini had also found himself a live walrus, which he billed, somehow, as a "talking walrus.". It's not clear if the walrus was longer-lived than the whale. The swimmers were likely the better long term bet.

Costentenus was still in demand in England, but after about a month at the aquarium, he dropped out of sight. That only encouraged newspapers to speculate about his location, his health, and his wealth. *The London Era*, for example, wrote, "Captain Costentenus, the original tattooed Greek, retired upon a fortune, and is now living on a fine estate in Greece, but has become blind."[395] A later article in *the Boston Globe* said that Costentenus's "eyesight failed him four years ago and [he went] to Europe for the best medical treatment but he was robbed by a supposed friend and did not even partially recover his eyesight until lately."[396] All these articles are vague and shouldn't be taken at face value. They are probably the 19th century equivalent of tabloid coverage—more in the long series of mostly-made-up stories about the Tattooed Greek.

One quite different—and similarly dubious—article was published in various American newspapers in March and April of 1885. It claimed that Costentenus had had a terrible accident. Supposedly, he had been hit by a hackney cab in London "some 18 months ago... [He was] picked up insensible and taken to St. Thomas' Hospital, where he

393 Dave Day and Margaret Roberts, "A Swimming Family: The Beckwiths," *Swimming Communities in Victorian England*, (Springer: 2019): 65-102.

394 "Royal Aquarium," The Sportsman, April 1, 1884; Day, *Swimming Communities*, 92.

395"Living Curiosities," *Era*, December 26, 1885.

396 "Dramatic Offerings," *Boston Daily Globe*, November 17, 1889.

lay at the point of death for thirteen weeks."[397] Unfortunately, there's no way to confirm this story. For that, we can blame the Nazis.

In September of 1940, the German Luftwaffe began the Blitz—a series of massive air attacks on Great Britain. For 56 of 57 consecutive days and nights, the Nazis dropped bombs all over London. On September 9, they hit St. Thomas' Hospital, killing four staff members. Over the coming months and years, the hospital was hit repeatedly. While it never closed, the northern section of St. Thomas' was damaged and three ward blocks were completely destroyed. Also destroyed? All the admission registers and patient records from the 19th century. An archivist confirmed in 2018 that these were lost in the bombing, so there is no way to verify if Captain George was ever a patient there.

There is also a reason to doubt the accident story: there's a problem with the dates. If we use the newspaper article's first publication date (March 1885) as a guide and work backwards, "some 18 months ago" would have been around October 1883. This was when Costentenus was working in Kansas City, not London. However, if the article simply got the dates wrong, St. Thomas' Hospital was quite close to the Royal Aquarium, just a few minutes away on the opposite side of the Thames.

If Costentenus really was run down in the street, he would have gotten state-of-the-art medical treatment at St. Thomas'. It also had a well-respected ophthalmic department, so maybe the article got the right hospital but the wrong reason for his stay. Perhaps, while he was out of the public eye (no pun intended) in 1884 and 1885, Costentenus was receiving treatment for his increasing blindness. Cataract surgeries (and medicine in general) were more advanced in Europe than the U.S.

While Dr. Howe, whom Costentenus had consulted in Buffalo the previous year, had trained at Harvard and in Europe, most American doctors of the day were rather casually trained. There were few schools in the U.S., and those relied on lectures only. In 1851, a medical reformer estimated that nearly half of all American medical

---

397 "Freaks' Bequests," *Daily Saratogan*, April 9, 1885.

school graduates had not had any hands-on training with patients. Most had just two years of studies—with only three to four months of lectures each year. There were no exams and no formal certifications. In 1869, not even Harvard Medical School had a written exam.[398] In Captain George's travels all over the United States, he had probably encountered many poorly-trained doctors and was not in a hurry to have them anywhere near his eyes.

In Europe, however, doctors had many well-respected schools to choose from and received hands-on training at teaching hospitals. Dr. Howe had experienced this first hand. He had trained in Edinburgh under Lord Joseph Lister, the "father of modern surgery", whose antiseptic techniques decreased the risks of infection.[399] He had also studied at several ophthalmic clinics in Germany with Hermann von Helmholtz, who had invented the ophthalmoscope for viewing the interior of the eye.[400] Outside of a very few specialists in the U.S. like himself, Dr. Howe probably would have recommended Captain George seek treatment in Europe for the most up-to-date techniques.

While there's no way to know when, where, or even *if* Costentenus had eye surgery, perhaps, while in London or later in Vienna, he was able to get the treatment he needed.

•

## Vienna, 1885

Over a year had passed since Captain George had last appeared

398 John C. Walker, *Health and Wellness in 19th Century America*, (Greenwood: 2014): 34-35.

399 F. F. Cartwright, "Joseph Lister." *Encyclopedia Britannica*, accessed October 7, 2022, https://www.britannica.com/biography/Joseph-Lister-Baron-Lister-of-Lyme-Regis.

400 L. Pearce Williams, "Hermann von Helmholtz." *Encyclopedia Britannica*, accessed October 7, 2022, https://www.britannica.com/biography/Hermann-von-Helmholtz.

at the Royal Aquarium. Bostock and Wombwell's Royal National Menagerie, an English company that had toured both Europe and the United States, posted a wanted ad in the *Era*. They were looking for various workers and "the address of the Tattooed Greek Nobleman."[401] He never replied. Unfortunately for Bostock and Wombwell, Costentenus had moved on.

Just when you thought maybe he had vanished for good, the Tattooed Greek resurfaced again, this time in Vienna. On June 30, 1885, "der berühmte Tätowierte"—the famous tattooed one—appeared at H. Präuscher's Museum.[402]

Costentenus was back in the city where he had made his first appearance 15 years before, and H. Präuscher's Museum was the perfect place for him to exhibit. Hermann Präuscher was a former lion tamer from a circus family, who ran his incredibly popular museum from 1871 until his death in 1896. It continued on under his descendents until it was destroyed by a fire during World War II.[403] The museum had the typical wax figures and taxidermied animals, but what set it apart was the separate, adults-only Menschenmuseum (Museum of Humans). This displayed skeletons, three-dimensional models of fetuses, wax casts of internal organs and muscle groups, and unusual anatomical specimens.[404] Präuscher was teaching the public anatomy, catering to voyeurs, and making money off of all of it. Costentenus would have fit right in. He worked there until the end of the summer of 1885—and then disappeared again.

For the rest of the decade, Costentenus seems to have stayed in Europe and continued to work sporadically. There were good lengths of time between jobs when he was off the public radar. Likely, he appeared at various museums and in rented rooms, as curiosities

401 "Bostock and Wombwell's *Royal National Menagerie*, Wanted," *Era*, July 19, 1885.

402 "H. Präuscher's Museum im K. K. Prater," *Morgen-Post* (Vienna, Austria), June 30, 1885; "H. Präuscher's Museum im K. K. Prater," *Morgen-Post* (Vienna, Austria), August 15, 1885.

403 Alys X. George, "Anatomy for All: Medical Knowledge on the Fairground in Fin-de-Siècle Vienna," Central European History 51 (2018) p. 537; "Präuschers Panoptikum," Wein Geschichte Wiki, https://www.geschichtewiki.wien.gv.at/Pr%C3%A4uschers_Panoptikum, accessed Oct. 13, 2022.

404 "Anatomy for All," *Central European History*, 552-553.

*Photograph of H. Präuscher's Panoptikum, Vienna, undated, (Austrian National Library)*

had throughout the 19th century. But the records here are scarce. Like St. Thomas' patient records, many European archives were lost in the wars. Many others can only be searched in person—particularly the smaller town newspapers that would have carried notices of Captain George's appearances. Without going from town to town and scouring their individual archives, there's currently no way to follow exactly where he was during these years. At times, he was probably taking a well-deserved break, and at others, he may have been working somewhere off the beaten path.

To make matters more confusing, while Costentenus was doing whatever he was doing in Europe, someone was using his name in the United States. Mixed in with the dubious articles that Costentenus was blind, rich, or in the hospital were advertisements for a "Captain Costentenus," a "Tattooed Man of Burmah," and the obvious imitator "Captain George Cardoza."

Cardoza (not to be confused with that other tattooed copycat,

Captain Harry DeCoursey) is a bit of a mystery man. From the few surviving pictures, it looks like George Cardoza (likely not his real name) was also covered in animal tattoos. Had he, too, traveled to Burma? The style—and the animals—say no. For starters, there are no inscriptions among Cardoza's tattoos. And the giraffe on his leg is not exactly a native Burmese animal. Cardoza's style seems to have been his own. He was one of the few tattooed performers of this generation, aside from the original Captain George, who didn't have traditional sailor-style tattoos—no ships, women, or banners. He even appears to have had his face tattooed—again, just like Costentenus. Some photographs of Cardoza are even labeled "George Cardozaus Constantini" or "George Constantine." Many other imitators simply referred to themselves as "tattooed Greeks." Cardoza was trying to be as close to the original as he could.

And like Costentenus, Captain George Cardoza also had multiple origin stories. Handwritten notes on various photographs stated, " Tattooed on the island of St. Vincent in 1857 by the Native Indian women" or, alternatively, "Tattooed in 1860 by the Arabs in Eastern Asia."[405]

•

What little is available about Cardoza's work history starts in 1884 in St. Louis, where he was working at Gregory's Dime Museum in early January.[406] He was in St. Joseph, Missouri, in early 1885, and then in St. Louis again a year later.[407] Cardoza was hired by Miller, Okey, and Greeman's show for the 1886 season, along with Professor Smith's trained goats and an all-female brass band.[408] He also worked for S. H. Barrett & Co.'s Circus for the 1887 season. With newspapers across the country talking about Costentenus retiring in Europe with a fortune, it's no wonder Cardoza went into the imitation business.

---

405 Nick Vaccaro's collection of American Circus Photography.

406 "Missouri," *New York Clipper*, January 3, 1883.

407 "Cole's Dime Museum," *St. Joseph Gazette*, January 21, 1885; "The Palace Museum," *St. Louis Globe-Democrat*, April 5, 1886.

408 "Minstrel, Variety and Circus," *New York Clipper*, 31 July 1886.

*Photograph of George Cardoza, front and back, undated, labeled Packard Photographer, Kalamazoo, Michigan, with handwritten text on the back:*

George Cardozaus Constantini

Born on the rock of Gibraltar. Tattooed on the island of St. Vincent in 1857 by the Native Indian women; it occupied between 3 & 4 mos. and was done with "SHARKS" <u>Teeth</u>.

The scar on my left leg is where I was stung or bit by a most poisonous snake called "HABUE." So deadly is the bite of this snake that anyone bitten dies within 24 hours if the flesh is not cut out.

The little boy in the picture I once saved from drowning. He fell into the sea and I plunged after him.

*(Courtesy of Nick Vaccaro's collection of American Circus Photography.)*

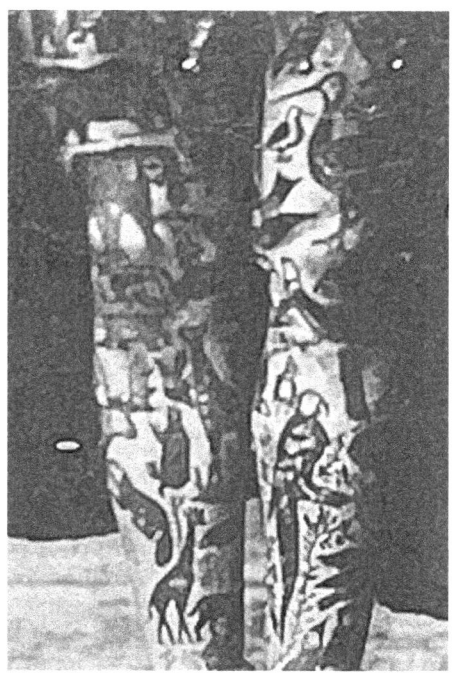

Detail of George Cardoza's chest and legs, showing a butterfly, a ram, an elephant, a giraffe, various birds, and other animals

Photograph of George Cardoza, front and back, undated, labeled Jones, Fort Wayne, Ind., 44 Calhoun Street, with handwritten text on the back: George Constantine, The Tattooed Greek, (Courtesy of Nick Vaccaro's collection of American Circus Photography)

An actual "Captain Costentenus" appeared again at the Great European Museum in Philadelphia in 1886, in a show "for gentlemen only" (a red flag that the venue was less-than-respectable).[409] This museum had hosted an imposter back in 1881, and later advertised appearances of this "Tattooed Man of Burmah" from December 26, 1888 to New Year's Day of 1889.

Was this really Costentenus? Was it Cardoza? Was it another tattooed man altogether? Or was it just a wax figure or an automaton? The museum had a number of these. It's impossible to say who (or what) this tattooed man was, though it likely wasn't the real Costentenus. To start with, the original Tattooed Greek usually appeared at quality museums. The Great European Museum, with its "gentlemen only" designation, was distinctly not up to his usual standards. And while there are no records of Costentenus appearing in Europe during these dates, more importantly, there are no records of him traveling back to the United States. His trips across the Atlantic usually left a paper trail.

Also, this museum was the only venue to ever bill "Costentenus" as "the Tattooed Man of Burmah."[410] Throughout all the thousands of performances in his career, Costentenus was always billed as the Tattooed Greek—and occasionally as "A Noble Greek Albanian"—but he never admitted in public that his tattooing was Burmese.[411] So while it's not impossible that these appearances were the real Costentenus, it seems unlikely.

In January of 1887, the real (or perhaps it would be more accurate to say "the original") Captain George Costentenus was back in Vienna. This time, instead of appearing at a popular anatomical museum or in front of a group of learned men at the university, he was appearing at the offices of Dr. Viktor Urbantschitsch, at Kolowratring 4. Urbantschitsch was an otologist (an ear specialist) and had trained at the University of Vienna. He may well have met Captain George when Costentenus first appeared at the university in 1870—during

409 "See Captain Costentenus," *Philadelphia Times*, December 24, 1886.

410 "See Captain Costentenus," *Philadelphia Times*, December 24, 1886.

411 "P. T. Barnum at Gilmore's Garden," ht4000127, Tibbals Circus Collection, The John and Mable Ringling Museum of Art, Sarasota, Florida.

Urbantschitsch's final year of studies.[412]

"Costentenus, der interessante Tätowierte"—the interesting tattooed man—took up residence at Urbantschitsch's offices, performing there until April.[413] The exhibition started with Costentenus wrapped in a blanket, so that just his head was visible. He slowly removed the blanket, revealing a mostly nude tattooed body.[414] He was still using the story that he had been tattooed in Chinese Tartary as punishment, though several newspapers included a titillating new detail: he'd been tattooed by "wilden Frauen mit glühenden Nadeln," or "wild women with glowing needles."[415] It seems that the Captain was, even now, embellishing his history.

His presence in Vienna was noted repeatedly by the newspapers that spring, and he had a number of famous visitors. In March, Princess Pauline von Metternich, a socialite and patron of the arts and fashion, came and reportedly spoke to him in several foreign languages. And in April, Archduke Ludwig Viktor visited repeatedly.[416] Ludwig Viktor was the brother of both Emperor Franz Joseph I of Austria-Hungary and Emperor Maximilian of Mexico. He was more-or-less openly gay and rejected his family's attempts to marry him off to women of various royal houses. The visits of such socially important visitors demonstrated that curiosities had drawing power for all classes—and that Costentenus was still in demand.

•

---

412 "Fonograf," *Allgemeine Sport-Zeitung* (Austria), January 2, 1887.

413 *Allgemeine Sport-Zeitung.*

414 *Allgemeine Sport-Zeitung.*

415 "Ein Tätowirter," *Innsbrucker Nachrichten* (Austria), March 26, 1887.

416 "Ein Tätowirter," *Neues Wiener Tagblatt* (Austria), March 24, 1887; "Der Tätowirte," *Neue Freie Presse* (Vienna, Austria), April 23, 1887.

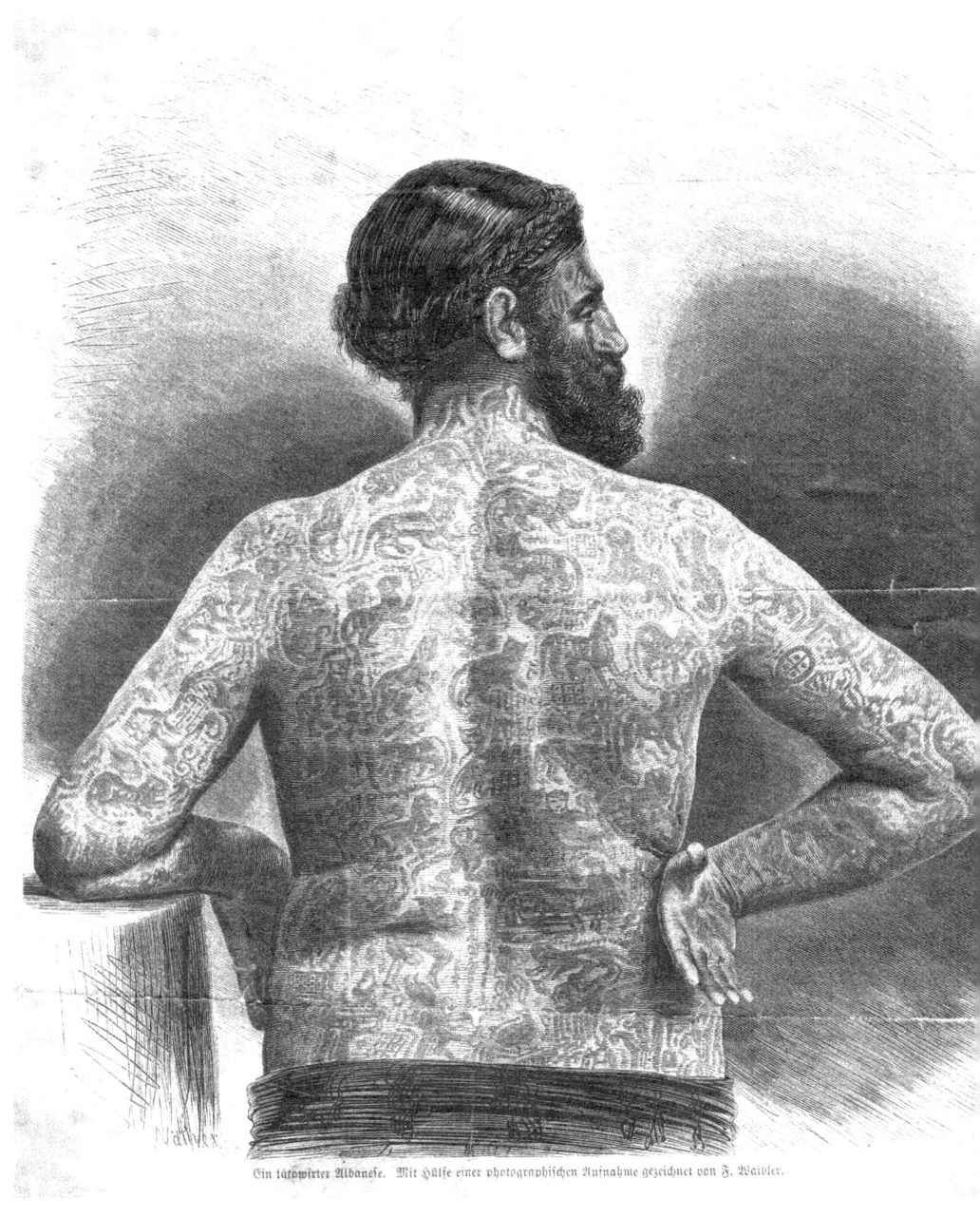

Ein tätowirter Albanese. Mit Hülfe einer photographischen Aufnahme gezeichnet von F. Waibler.

*Image of Captain George Costentenus, undated (George Burchett's Scrapbook, McMaster University, Ontario, Canada)*

## Bucharest and Baden, 1887-1888

After spending the spring in Vienna, Costentenus vanished again, reappearing that fall in Bucharest, Romania. It's not clear if he was there for business or pleasure, but he appeared at the United States Legation in Bucharest on October 24, 1887, to update his travel plans and was issued a new passport.[417] Passports in the 19th century were nothing like the modern versions. They were oversized letters that identified the bearer as an American. The large size frustrated many travelers, with one commenting that "no pocket of any sex would tolerate them."[418] Captain George's original, which had been issued in the United States when he became a citizen, had very little information on it. But passports issued overseas contained all sorts of details. The information on Costentenus's new passport, however, was often dubious or downright contradictory—as should be expected at this point. He now claimed, for example, that he was born on July 4, 1833 in Suli, Albania, rather than March 15, 1833 in Athens, Greece.

He also struggled to recall details of his travels over the past decades. Costentenus guessed at his first arrival in the U.S., saying he'd sailed over on a "German steamer from Hamburg" sometime in May 1870. The May arrival was correct, but 1870 is clearly six years too early. He did verify that he next sailed to Liverpool on the White Star Lines steamer in January 1884 and that he had been in Europe ever since. (That's another sign that the supposed "Captain Costentenus" appearances in the U.S. during these years were not him.)

Passports at this time also asked the bearer when they were planning on returning to the United States. Here, Captain George predicted that he would be returning in the summer of 1888. But curiously, he said he wanted the passport so he could go to Turkey. What awaited him there? He was 54 years old (perhaps), 5 feet 8 ½ inches tall, with his "face and body tattooed," still traveling, and still

---

417 *U.S., Passport Applications, 1795-1925,* National Archives and Records Administration (NARA); Washington D.C.; Roll #: 1; Volume #: Volume 002: Africa to Honduras, Ancestry.com.

418 Craig Robertson, *The Passport in America: The History of a Document,* (Oxford University Press, 2012): 36.

performing. He signed his X on the line of passport number 29, and off he went.[419]

But the next sign of Captain George was back in Austria, in Baden bei Wien, one of Europe's most famous spa towns. On March 11, 1888, Costentenus checked into the Herzoghof Hotel and spent several weeks enjoying the town's sulfur baths.[420] Baden bei Wien (which translates literally as "bath near Vienna") was a short train ride from Vienna and had been renowned for its hot springs since Roman times. The idea of going to a spa for a month may now conjure images of getting a massage with cucumbers on your eyes, but in the 19th century, "taking the waters" had long been considered a medicinal treatment, not just pampering.

Spa towns like Baden had also become social centers with lavish hotels, casinos, and theaters—places to see and be seen. Viennese newspapers even reported on who visited there and how long they stayed. Baden bei Wien had its own publications that listed when individuals arrived, where they stayed, and what treatments they received. "Herr Georges Costentenus, Capitän [sic] aus Griechenland" (Captain from Greece) was on the Fremdenliste (list of foreigners) in 1888. Was he exhausted? Was he hoping the mineral baths would help his eyesight? Whatever his ills—and whatever the results—Costentenus checked out of the Herzoghof Hotel on April 14, 1888, and left for Constantinople.[421]

•

## Back to Paris and the U.S., 1889

There is only a third-hand report that Costentenus actually

419 *U.S., Passport Applications, 1795-1925*, National Archives and Records Administration (NARA); Washington D.C.; Roll #: 1; Volume #: Volume 002: Africa to Honduras, Ancestry.com.

420 "Ein Tätowirter, *Baden Bezirks-Blatt* (Austria), March 13, 1888.

421 "Der Tätowirte," *Baden Bezirks-Blatt* (Austria), April 14, 1888.

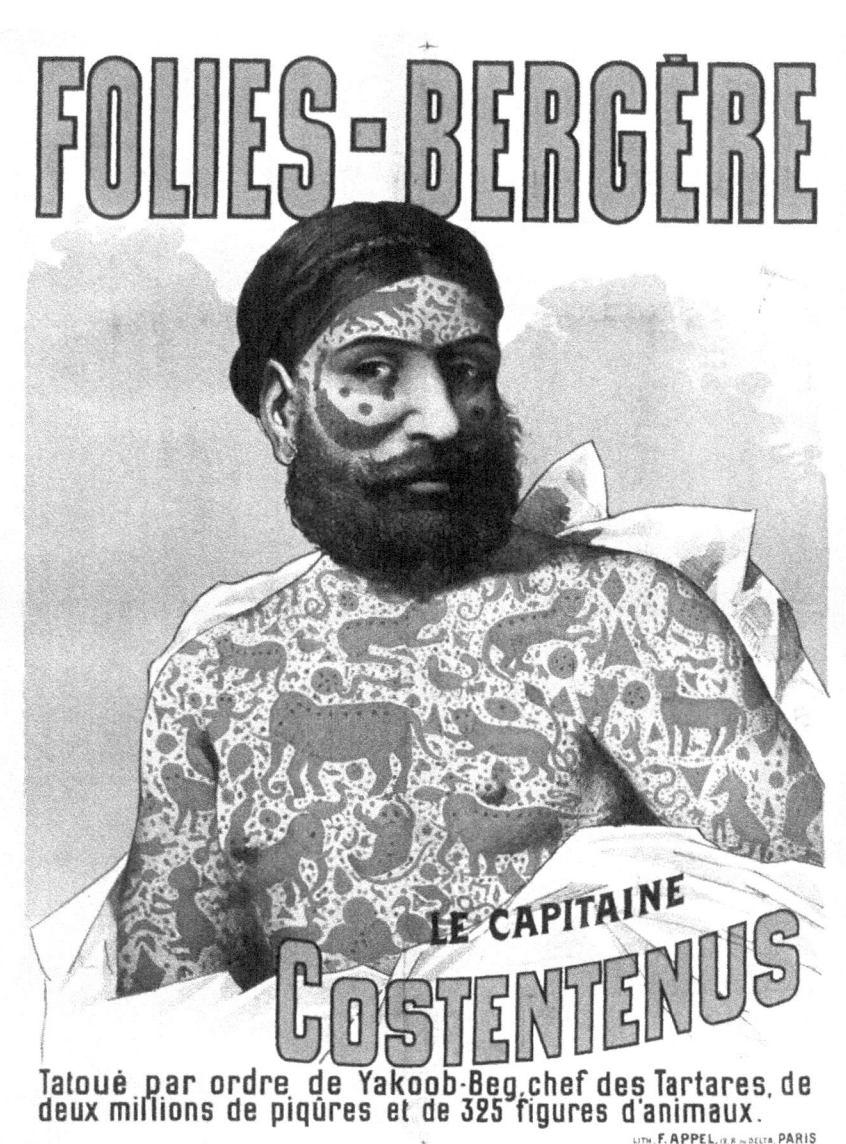

*Folies-Bergère poster of Le Capitaine Costentenus, undated (Bibliothèque Nationale de France, Department of Prints and Photography)*

arrived in Constantinople in the spring of 1888. Ethnographer

Wilhelm Joest, who was there that May, wrote that Captain George had apparently just left the city.

Costentenus resurfaced in Paris in June 1889, returning to the Folies Bergère where he had made waves back in 1874. He headlined at the famous club with the renowned Hanlon-Lees troupe (a group of brothers who combined tumbling, juggling, and comedy). French newspapers reported on his performances throughout the summer.[422]

Captain George also made a triumphant return to his adopted homeland. On October 9, 1889, he sailed back to New York aboard the steamship *Egypt*.[423] Just as he had on his first trip to the U.S. back in 1876, he traveled in a second class cabin. Still surly and private, he likely kept to himself once again. His celebrity status was also still strong. Newspapers were trumpeting his arrival within days.

He found work quickly, appearing at the Grand Dime Museum in New York City from October 28 to November 3, 1889, before moving up to Boston in mid-November.[424] Austin and Stone's Museum in Boston was thrilled to have him back. "Manager Austin struck what he thinks will be the big feature of the museum season in Costentenus... who for the past three or four years has been credited with having been dead."[425]

The Tattooed Greek allegedly explained his absence by saying that his eyesight had failed and he had gone to Europe for treatment—but then a "supposed friend" had robbed him and that had delayed his medical care until recently.[426] Should we believe this statement? It's dubious, since he'd been working on and off in Europe since 1884. Regardless, Boston crowds ate up the Captain's return, flocking to

422 "Spectables du 8 Juiilet," *Gil Blas* (Paris), July 9, 1889.

423 New York, U.S., Arriving Passenger and Crew Lists (including Castle Garden and Ellis Island), 1820-1957; Microfilm Serial: M237, Steamship Egypt; Line: 42; List Number: 1392, ancestry.com.

424 George C. D. Odell, *Annals of the New York Stage Volume 14* (AMS Press, 1970): 396; "Dramatic Offerings," *Boston Daily Globe*, November 17, 1889.

425 "Dramatic Offerings," *Boston Daily Globe*, Nov. 17, 1889.

426 Derin Bray and Margaret Hodges, *Loud, Naked, and in Three Colors: The Liberty Boys and the History of Tattooing in Boston*, (Rake House: Portsmouth, NH) 2020.

Austin and Stone's to see him.

Coincidentally, Scollay Square, where Austin and Stone's was located, would become the heart of tattooing in Boston after the turn of the century. Famous tattooed man Frank Howard, along with tattooist Edward "Dad" Liberty and his sons, decorated the skin of Boston residents out of shops in Scollay Square for decades. But in the early 1960s, the Boston Redevelopment Authority demolished the entire neighborhood to build the Boston Government Center.[427]

From Boston, Costentenus moved on to Philadelphia, though *not* to the Great European Museum where his copycat had appeared. He showed off his tattoos on stage at one the city's premier museums, the Ninth and Arch Museum. He performed there from Christmas Eve though the beginning of 1890.[428]

The Ninth and Arch Museum had opened originally in 1869 as Colonel Joseph H. Wood's Museum, with a large collection of objects and a menagerie. In 1885, Charles A. Brandenburgh transformed it into a popular destination.[429] The first floor was filled with trick mirrors and penny arcade machines; the second floor was home to the menagerie; and the third floor was where Costentenus would have exhibited himself, among the human oddities. The museum also had a "Theatorium," where sketch comedy teams and singers performed.[430] While Costentenus was there, he shared billing with the "Human Joint Dislocator" and the "Woman with the Iron Jaw."[431] The "dislocator" would have used his hyperflexibility to twist his body in alarming ways. The woman with the "iron jaw" would have suspended herself from a leather strap gripped only in her teeth, performing mid-air spins and other tricks.[432]

Despite tales of his having been robbed, it seems Costentenus

427 Bray and Hodges, *Loud, Naked*, 72.

428 "Ninth and Arch Museum," *Philadelphia Inquirer*, December 25, 1889.

429 Dennett, *Weird and Wonderful*, 42.

430 Dennett, *Weird and Wonderful*, 42.

431 "Ninth and Arch Museum," *Philadelphia Inquirer*, December 24, 1889.

432 Aíne Norris, "The Tenacious Women of Iron Jaw," *Bandwagon* 61, No. 3 (2021): 29.

had invested in a new wardrobe while in Europe. The Captain impressed admirers with a Greek skull cap, "a cutaway coat decorated with braid and patent leather boots adorned with nickel-plated spurs on French heels."[433]

From Philadelphia, Costentenus moved further west, to St. Joseph, Missouri, for a month or so at the Eden Musée. The original Eden Musée had opened in New York in the early 1880s and was renowned for its shocking "chamber of horrors" waxworks. It proved so popular that the owners took the concept to various cities across the nation, including St. Joseph. That particular Eden Musée had a "Curio Parlor" where Costentenus entertained visitors in February. He then moved on to another Eden Musée in Omaha, Nebraska, and yet one more in Lincoln during March.[434]

*Image of the Ninth and Arch Museum, "Philadelphia's Pleasure Palace Containing Countless Curiosities," 1883, (The Library Company of Philadelphia)*

433 "Gossip of the Corridors" *The Times* (Philadelphia), December 23, 1889.

434 "Eden Musée," *St. Joseph Herald*, February 24, 1890; "The Jones Tragedy," *Omaha*

Continuing his westward tour of popular museums, the Tattooed Greek showed up in Denver in mid-March at the Wonderland Dime Museum—for supposedly his "last visit to the WEST."[435] Wonderland, like the Eden Musée, was a popular and lucrative dime museum that had become a chain business.[436] Denver was indeed the most westward city Costentenus visited that spring, on what was to become a farewell tour of sorts. But Wonderland was the only location billed as any sort of last appearance for the Captain.

From there, he swung south and east to Hutchinson, Kansas, and then went on to Topeka in late April and early May of 1890.[437] The Capital City Museum in Topeka bragged that he was "direct from Paris... laden with jewels... and $55,000 worth of largest diamonds."[438] Back in 1878, his rumored jewels had supposedly been worth $3,000.[439] So either the Captain had moved up in the world or, more likely, his exaggeration had exceeded the rate of inflation. This advertising also mirrored language used to promote tattooed ladies Nora Hildebrandt and Irene Woodward. Both women supposedly had expensive jewelry and gifts from famous people. However, this was likely a ploy to legitimize their appearances before the public, in a time when no "respectable" woman would ever take off any of her clothes in front of an audience.

Captain George's dime museum tour ended in Chicago at Epstean's Dime Museum on Randolph Street from May 26 to May 30, 1890.[440] His last performance at Epstean's was promoted by a tiny newspaper ad on page seven of Chicago's *Daily Inter Ocean* newspaper.

*Daily Bee*, March 2, 1890; "Eden Musée," *Lincoln Daily Nebraska State Journal*, March 14, 1890.

435 "10 Cents Admits All," *Rocky Mountain News*, March 16, 1890.

436 Dennett, *Weird and Wonderful*, 154.

437 "Museum," *The Independent*, April 21, 1890; "Another Extraordinary Exposition," *Topeka Daily Press*, May 3, 1890.

438 "Another Extraordinary Exposition," *Topeka Daily Press*, May 3, 1890; $2 million in 2025, per Measuring Worth.

439 "Capt. Costentenus Beaten" *New York Times*, March 31, 1878; $100,000 in 2025, per Williamson, Measuring Worth.

440 "Epstean's Dime Museum," *Daily Inter Ocean*, May 26, 1890.

Without any fanfare, Captain George Costentenus's American career had come to an end.

The famous Tattooed Greek quietly returned to New York and applied for a new passport on June 9, 1890. The passport clerk, a man named George W. Russell, noted that Costentenus was leaving the United States and intended to return "in about 2 years." This time around, when asked when he had first arrived in the United States, Captain George answered "do not remember 1875." As to what ship he had traveled on, he answered, "name of ship I do not remember"[441] These were much more honest answers.

With that, he returned to Europe.

Maybe Costentenus really did have a fine estate somewhere that he could retire to. Or perhaps he had museum appearances lined up in Europe. People had turned out in droves to see him on his last tour across the United States. He had been hired by the best of the dime museums in the cities he visited. And the newspapers still couldn't stop talking about him.

But he was also nearing 60 (give or take, given the uncertainty of his origins). Ever since he had first appeared in Vienna 20 years earlier, he had lived a life of almost constant travel and exhibition. Likely, he'd been traveling for much longer, at least to Burma and back as a younger man. Was he tired? Was he done with audience members pinching and poking at him? Like so many older circus and sideshow performers, he may not have had a choice. Unless he was one of the few who had saved enough money to retire on, he may have needed to keep exhibiting himself. He may have traveled until the work dried up and been forced to settle down wherever he was when his money ran out.

Whether he kept traveling or put down roots somewhere, Captain George had marked himself in such a distinctive way that he would be unable to disappear easily.

---

441 George Costentenus, U.S., Passport Applications, 1795-1925, National Archives and Records Administration (NARA); Washington D.C.; Roll #: 353; Volume #: Roll 353 - 10 Jun 1890-16 Jun 1890, ancestry.com.

*Poster of L'Homme Tatoué, undated, (Bibliothèque Nationale de France, Department of Prints and Photography)*

But disappear, he did.

If Costentenus did have any further appearances lined up in Europe, I'm unable to find any record of them. It appears that his shows in Chicago were his last. In 1891, Bostock and Wombwell's in London put out another wanted ad, trying once again to hire the Tattooed Greek.[442] It looks as if they didn't get him this time around, either.

Back in the United States, the Great European Museum in Philadelphia began 1893 with their reliable Costentenus imposter. Someone was pretending to be him at Doris's Eighth Avenue Museum in New York that August.[443] And in September 1894, there was a puzzling "Captain Costentenus and his tattooed dogs" performing at the South Street Globe Museum in Chicago. Yet another Tattooed Greek (most likely a man named Tom Sidonia from Nova Scotia) was advertised with the Sells Brothers Circus in Galveston in November 1894.[444]

Tattooed Greeks were mentioned in circus and museum advertising into the 20th century. But none of them were the original.

•

## Cairo, 1894

I have found only one sure sighting of Captain George after 1890. On March 6, 1894, passport number 18 from the United States Embassy in Cairo was filled out for George Costentenus. There are no

442 "Edmond's, Late Wombwell's, and Sir James W. Bostock's Monster United Shows, Menagerie, Circus, and Museum... Wanted," *Era*, July 11, 1891.

443 "Captain Costentenus," *Philadelphia Inquirer*, January 27, 1893; "At the Theatres," *World*, August 20, 1893.

444 "Amusement Addenda," *Chicago Inter Ocean*, September 9, 1894; "Fun for the Boys," *The Galveston Daily News*, November 13, 1894.

clues to how or why he had ended up in Egypt. He still had his 1887 passport from Bucharest. It's not clear what had happened to his 1890 passport from New York.

He said that he'd been traveling and his occupation was "tattooed man." He wanted the passport "for the purpose of travelling home to America" in a few months.[445] He said he was 61 years old. His hair was still black and long, he still had a beard, and the tattoos on his face and body were still visible. But now, he had only one brown eye.

And after this, he was never seen again.

Did he die in Cairo before returning home? Did he return to the United States unobserved? Did he travel to Athens, Vienna, or London on his way to the U.S., and die somewhere in Europe?

For a man so widely known throughout much of his life, his end was quiet. Newspapers did not celebrate him and mourn his passing the way they had other sideshow stars. They did not retell his spectacular and absurd stories. There were no engravings of his amazing tattoos plastered on front pages. Like those old tattoos, he had simply faded away.

George Costentenus, the original Tattooed Greek, was gone.

—————
445 George Costentenus, Emergency Passport Applications (Issued Abroad), 1877-1907; National Archives and Records Administration (NARA); Washington D.C.; Roll #:8; Volume #: 11, Belguim to Egypt, ancestry.com.

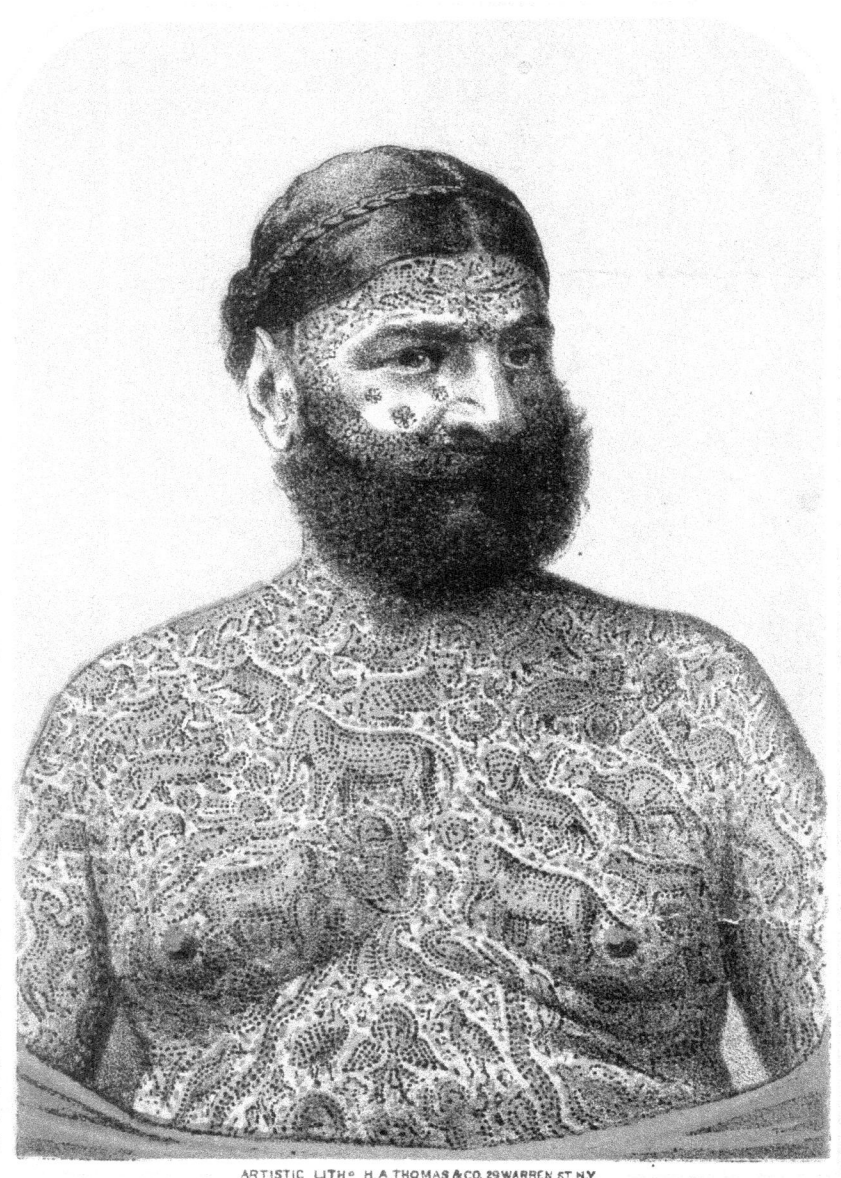

ARTISTIC LITHº H.A.THOMAS &CO. 29 WARREN ST. N.Y.

# CAPTAIN COSTENTENUS
## THE GREEK ALBANIAN

*Tattooed from Head to Foot in Chinese Tartary as punishment for engaging in Rebellion against the King.*

*Color postcard of Captain Costentenus, the Greek Albanian, undated
(Collection of Syracuse University Library)*

## CHAPTER ELEVEN

# FINAL STORIES

I've been searching for Captain George for a long time, and every time I've gotten closer, it has felt like he's tried to move further away. Some big questions still linger. Where did he come from? Why did he get such an extreme tattoo suit somewhere in Myanmar? His life story is disguised by so many outlandish sideshow tales that, all too often, the truth has simply been lost.

There are glimpses of the real man behind the celebrity, like the stories of his anger at being touched and pinched, storming off to the railroad station in protest... Little moments of his humanity surface, like the reports of him wrapped up in fur in the summer heat of Europe, watching a parade and smiling... Pieces of the puzzle connect, like his visit to a respected eye doctor in Buffalo and then him turning up in Cairo a decade later with only one eye. But if you put all the clues together, parts of him still remain shrouded in mystery. Throughout his decades in the spotlight, he kept so much of himself hidden.

Newspapers continued to talk about him for years. They interviewed nostalgic "old-timers" who remembered seeing him during the golden age of the American circus.[446] They speculated about his wealth. They wondered how and why he got his 388 tattoos. And he was used as a frightening example of someone who went "too far"—to try to scare young men from getting anchors inked into their skin.[447] Well into the 20th century, whenever tattooing was mentioned, his name popped up.

Generations of tattooed performers continued to "work the tattooed Greek racket." In addition to the tattooed men and women of the 1880s and 1890s, there were several more waves of performers in the 20th century. Artoria Gibbons worked for sideshows and circuses like Ringling Brothers and Barnum & Bailey Circus starting in the 1910s. Her tattoos ranged from a portrait of George Washington to images inspired by Renaissance paintings. Betty Broadbent, who looked like the girl next door—covered in more than 500 tattoos—worked from the early 1920s into the late 1970s.[448] Mae Vandermark, Lady Viola, Trixie Richardson, Fred Clark, Cindy Ray, Ted Hamilton, and Jean Carroll... All these tattooed performers had careers thanks to George Costentenus.

Even the current popularity of tattoos among the general public in the United States owes a debt to the Tattooed Greek. A number of performers like Amund Dietzel, the "Master in Milwaukee," started tattooing customers on the side to make extra money.[449] Then, instead of going out on the dime museum circuit during the winter months the way Costentenus had, they settled down in the off-season and set up tattoo shops. This brought a permanent presence of professional tattooists to cities across the United States. In 1943, Dietzel said that he had himself inked tattoos on over 20,000 customers.[450] Today, an

446 "50 Years Ago Today," *Lafayette Journal and Courier*, July 28, 1927; "In New York," *Rock Island Argus*, December 30, 1927.

447 "Firing the Freaks," *The Pomona Daily Review*, March 1913.

448 Amelia Osterud, *The Tattooed Lady: A History*, (Taylor Trade, 2014).

449 Jon Reiter, *These Old Blue Arms: The Life and Work of Amund Dietzel*, (Solid State Publishing, 2010): 25.

450 Don Doorbrook, "War is Booming Skin Art, Says Man Who Has Needled 20,000," *Milwaukee Journal*, December 24, 1943.

estimated 32% of people in the United States have one—or more.[451] George Costentenus helped set all this in motion.

·

I'll leave you with two final tales—from people who claimed to know the *real* story of George Costentenus. One is from an ethnographer who reported that he had met Costentenus's sister in Constantinople. The other is from a Boston tattooist who said that he had met a man in Burma who had actually tattooed Captain George.

·

## Wilhelm Joest, Constantinople, 1888

At the July 1888 meeting of the Berliner Gesellschaft für Anthropologie, Ethnologie, und Urgeschichte (The Berlin Society of Anthropology, Ethnology, and Prehistory), the members discussed a letter from German explorer and ethnographer Wilhelm Joest, reporting several new details of George Costentenus's life.[452]

Joest had an ongoing interest in tattooing, having published a book the year before titled *Tätowiren: Narbenzeichen und Körperbemalen (Tattooing: Scars and Body Painting)*. This book is a delightfully open-minded study of tattooing practices around the world, both ancient and modern.[453]

---

451 Katherine Schaeffer and Shradha Dinesh, "32% of Americans Have a Tattoo," *Pew Research Center*, August 15, 2023, accessed April 27, 2024, https://pewrsr. ch/3QFg5w1.

452 Wilhelm Joest, "Tättowirten von Birma," *Verhandlungen der Berliner Gesellschaft für Anthropologie, Ethnologie und Urgeschichte* (1888) V 20 (Berlin: 1888): 319-321.

453 Wilhelm Joest, *Tätowiren: Narbenzeichen und Körperbemalen, Ein Beitrag zur*

Not surprisingly, Joest mentioned the world's most famous tattooed performer in *Tätowiren*. But he saw through the absurd sideshow stories and called out Costentenus on his deceptions. "It may be permitted... to mention at this point the Greek swindler who was fond of tattoos and who caused a lot of talk a few years ago..."[454] He didn't call Costentenus a swindler because his tattoos were fake, but because he was lying about how he had gotten them. Joest was offended by all the tall tales told in the name of entertainment.

Joest also says in his book (without revealing where this information came from) that the Tattooed Greek had been a vagabond in Mandalay (Burma's capital at that time). Too lazy to work, Costentenus had gotten himself covered in tattoos. So now he led a "carefree existence" where he deceived scientists and the general public with his stories of tattoo torture.[455]

In his 1888 letter to the anthropological society in Berlin, Joest reported that he had traveled to Constantinople that May. Frustratingly, he found that he had arrived just *after* George Costentenus had been there.[456] However, Joest had been fortunate enough to meet Costentenus's sister. Finally, here is someone who knew Costentenus before he became the Tattooed Greek! Joest was surprised to learn that Costentenus did not lie as much as he had previously suspected.

According to the sister, George Costentenus was indeed Greek, though a native of Constantinople. He grew up in the historically Greek neighborhood of Tatavla, now called Kurtuluş, near St. Demetrios Church. He had enlisted as an Ottoman soldier in 1842 and fought in the Crimean War. (She said he was ten years older than he claimed, so he would have been 19 years old in 1842, not nine.) He had then traveled around, eventually arriving in Mandalay, but his family lost track of him.

---

*Vergleichenden Ethnologie* (Berlin: Asher, 1887): 107-109.

454 Joest, *Tätowiren*, 109. Translation by the author.

455 Joest, *Tätowiren*, 99. Translation by the author.

456 According to scholar Carl Deußen, Joest was in Istanbul on May 10-12, 1888. Correspondence with the author, October 30, 2022.

(10) Hr. W. Joest schreibt aus Ragatz, 19. Juli: „Während meines jüngsten Aufenthalts in Constantinopel stiess ich zufällig auf die frische Spur eines Mannes, der seiner Zeit in der wissenschaftlichen und Laienwelt grosses Aufsehen erregt hat, den ich aber längst todt oder verschollen glaubte, des sogenannten

### Tättowirten von Birma.

Dieser Mann tauchte, soviel mir bekannt ist, in Europa im Jahre 1872 zuerst in Wien auf (vergl. den Aufsatz von Dr. Kaposi (Moritz Kohn) in der Wiener Medicin. Wochenschrift 1872 Nr. 2 S. 39 und Hebra-Elfinger, Atlas der Hautkrankheiten, Wien 1856—76. Heft VIII Tafel 10, „Homo notis compunctus") und wurde von dort nach Berlin empfohlen. Von Berlin, wo seine Tättowirung von Prof. Bastian sofort als eine birmanische erkannt und dadurch seinen romantischen Aufschneidereien von den Qualen der „Strafe der Tättowirung" in der chinesischen Tartarei u. s. w. ein plötzliches Ende gemacht wurde, verschwand er aber nach zwei- oder dreitägigem Aufenthalt für immer. In der anthropologischen Gesellschaft war mehrmals von diesem, in so aussergewöhnlicher Weise tättowirten Manne die Rede (vgl. Bd. IV S. 201; Bd. XII S. 37); Dr. Jagor bezeichnete ihn damals als „ein in Mandalay wohl bekanntes faules Subject, welches sich lange dort herumtrieb und sich endlich tättowiren liess, um sich in Europa u. s. w. für Geld sehen zu lassen".

Wie ich jetzt in Constantinopel erfuhr, hat der Mann doch nicht ganz so viel gelogen, wie auch ich früher vermuthete. Er heisst wirklich Georg Constantin und zählt heute etwa 70 (nicht 60, wie er sagt) Jahre; er ist aber weder Suliote, noch Albanese, sondern seine Wiege stand in Tatawla, einer an Pera anstossenden Vorstadt von Constantinopel, von welcher Meyer's neuester Führer durch die Türkei sagt: „sie besteht aus einem Gemisch schmutziger und enger Gässchen mit elenden Häusern und ist als Wohnort allerhand schlechten Gesindels verrufen".

*Correspondence from Wilhelm Joest, in the proceedings of the Berlin Society of Anthropology, Ethnology, and Prehistory, written July 19, 1888. (University of Minnesota Libraries)*

Costentenus's sister still lived in their old neighborhood. When her long lost brother had come home again earlier that spring, he was covered in tattoos and talking about his vast fortune.[457] His whole family had been shocked, and not just by the tattoos. They had thought he had died 20 years before.

She also reported that Costentenus was not received well in Constantinople. He was mocked at the port and he refused to recognize his family. A hoped-for exhibition before the Sultan did not materialize. He limped badly, he was blind in one eye, and he was actually broke. His "entire fortune consisted of a fake diamond ring."[458] Life had been hard on George Costentenus. Although he was

---

457 Joest, "Tättowirten," 319-321.

458 Joest, "Tättowirten," 319-321.

still able to travel and work, that spa treatment in Baden bei Wien did not seem to have cured him of his ills. And perhaps he had never gotten that cataract surgery—or if he had, it hadn't worked.

Here, at long last, is a story of his past that rings true. While it doesn't explain how or why he got his tattoos, it reveals his origins. Here, without any sensational nonsense about being kidnapped by Ali Pasha of Tepelena or escaping from a harem in Egypt, is a glimpse of his childhood.

•

## Elmer Getchell, Boston, 1894

A few years later, shortly after George Costentenus's last passport was issued in Cairo, a *Boston Post* reporter interviewed a tattooist on Hanover Street who also claimed to know the "true story of the tattooed man."[459]

The unnamed artist in question is undoubtedly "Electric" Elmer Getchell, Boston's oldest and best known tattooist at the time.[460] It was Getchell who had completed Frank De Burgh's tattoo suit, started years before in Burma.

The reporter began by asking Getchell a number of general questions about tattooing. He even had Getchell use his electric tattooing machine (based on an electric doorbell mechanism) on his arm without ink, just so he could experience the sensation. After talking about skin and ink in general, the reporter came to his big question, "How did the original tattooed man come to be so profusely illustrated?"[461]

Getchell said that he himself had been in British Burma, in Rangoon, some years ago. He had met a local artist there—who had

459 "Needle Pricks," *Boston Post*, March 18, 1894.

460 Email correspondence with Derin Bray, November 17, 2022.

461 "Needle Pricks," *Boston Post*, March 18, 1894.

been one of the men to tattoo Costentenus. "Then he proceeded to tell the following story, which is as wild a tale... as ever was put in print. ... It differs very materially from the published book, but it hangs together with considerable probability."[462] Now, we finally have a true expert on tattoos speaking about this part of Captain George's history.

According to Getchell and his Burmese friend, while

# NEEDLE PRICKS.

## Tattooing Rendered Pain-less by Electricity.

## A POST REPORTER TRIES IT.

Wonderfully Romantic Story of the Tattooed Greek, as Related to a Boston Man in Burmah--- Tricks of the Trade.

*Newspaper headline for"Needle Pricks," Boston Post, March 18, 1894, (Newspaper Collection, Boston Public Library)*

*Tattooing Rendered Painless by Electricity.*
*A Post Reporter Tries It.*
*Wonderfully romantic story of the Tattooed Greek, as Related to a Boston Man in Burmah---Tricks of the Trade.*

462 "Needle Pricks," *Boston Post*, March 18, 1894.

Costentenus's father was Greek, his mother was Malaysian. Young George had worked as a pearl dealer, traveling throughout Southeast Asia. However, he fell in with a group of pirates, eventually becoming their captain. (What's a seafaring story without pirates?)

Then the story takes a dramatic turn. "It seems in Rangoon... there was a woman."[463] Of course there was. And another pirate named Dom Pedro was in love with the same woman. Like a princess in a fairy tale, the woman set her two suitors a task. Captain George and Dom Pedro were to go out into the world to make their fortunes. In a year's time, she would marry the one who brought back the most money.

A year later, Dom Pedro was the winner. But he wasn't content with just marrying the woman. He decided that he must also kill Captain George. But at the last moment, he had a change of heart and decided merely to have him tortured. So Dom Pedro ordered his eunuch to take Costentenus away and have his face tattooed. Of course, Costentenus bravely fought back. But his struggles were in vain, and the eunuch took revenge for the fight by having not just Costentenus's face tattooed, but his entire body.

Seven men tattooed him for seven hours. Costentenus developed a fever from the tattooing but was strong enough to pull through.

After all this, Dom Pedro died and the woman disappeared. So the now-tattooed Greek went back to piracy and pearl dealing. He ended up in London looking to sell some pearls and was irritated that everyone kept staring at him. But he ran into the Great Farini, who promptly hired him, launching his long and illustrious career.

In the end, Getchell says Costentenus went blind, and "is said to have died, not long ago, in France... Such is said to be the true story of the tattooed man."[464]

So that turns out to be just another of the hundreds of

---

463 "Needle Pricks," *Boston Post*, March 18, 1894.

464 "Needle Pricks," *Boston Post*, March 18, 1894.

•

sensational stories about Captain George that cannot be true. Clearly, Getchell's story of pirates and torture is just more humbug. Glorious and ridiculous humbug.

Joest's story of meeting Costentenus's sister, on the other hand, has none of the these melodramatic absurdities. But does that make it any more true? Did Joest really manage to track down Costentenus's long lost sister in Constantinople? I want to believe he did. The story she told him feels right. But can we take either of these reports at face value?

Joest and Getchell's stories are just two of many "true stories" of the Tattooed Greek that were told in the years after he disappeared from view. One of the more creative tales claimed that he was actually a French Canadian who had been tattooed in a Bridgeport barn at Barnum's request.[465] One particularly boastful tattooist claimed that "they sliced up his skin when he got through with it and I have seen some of the best pieces."[466]

There is so much misinformation to untangle in all the stories of Captain George. With all the lies and the contradictions, the only thing I can say with certainty is that we will never know exactly where this man came from. It's tempting to think that Joest's story of Costentenus growing up in Tatavla and joining the Ottoman army is true. It's certainly simpler and more believable than his "autobiography." But there's no way to prove Joest's version—or any of the other versions of Costentenus's story. This research has taught me that, particularly when it comes to the sideshow, sometimes admitting that you don't actually know the truth is the most honest thing. In the sideshow, the truth wasn't important. The story was. They cared about the image they projected to a paying public. So after a decade of research, George Costentenus's life outside the public eye remains largely a mystery.

---

465 "If Barnum Were Alive!" *Boston Globe*, February 17, 1895; "The Stolen Fat Woman," *Nebraska State Journal*, October 5, 1895.

466 "Weeping Willow Tattooed In Side," *Buffalo News*, September 27, 1908; "Freaks Always Popular," *Sun*, January 3, 1897; "The Trade in Tattooing," *Colfax Chronicle*, June 7, 1902.

He appeared out of the blue in Vienna, covered from head to toe in Burmese tattoos. For twenty years, he performed across Europe and America, becoming perhaps the most famous tattooed performer of all time. At the dawn of the golden age of American circus, he traveled with the *Greatest Show on Earth*—and then he got stranded in Kansas with one of the worst. He drew huge crowds, from the Royal Aquarium in London to the Folies Bergère in Paris. He spoke many languages, but he had a reputation for being a confrontational loner. It seems he never married or started a family, at least not while he was performing. His success spawned a host of imitators, but it would be decades before anyone duplicated the extent and artistic unity of his tattoos.

But there is no evidence that he was ever a pirate or a pearl dealer. He wasn't sold into slavery and freed by the Great Farini. Barnum didn't have him tattooed in a barn in Bridgeport. He couldn't have met Ali Pasha or Yakoob Beg. He surely didn't kill Captain Perikles and escape with his Aspasia. There's no evidence that he was tortured by seven Burmese men for seven hours. He wasn't tattooed by a beautiful Chinese princess. He couldn't have had masses of needles hammered into his skin by a Mediterranean sailor who just happened to be Captain Perikles's vengeful brother. That simply can't be true.

But when has that ever stopped someone from telling a good story?

Captain George created himself. He, Barnum, the Bunnells, Farini, and others created his story. And then they rewrote it many times. When his time in the public eye came to an end, Georg Konstaninos, Djorji Costentenus, Yolos Constantinos, Captain George Costentenus, the Tattooed Greek, "The Most Memorable of Mortal Marvels"... all of them disappeared.

His 388 tattoos—and all of the incredible stories he told—are all that remain.

*Artist's rendering of a tattoo from the 5th century BCE that was preserved on the skin of a mummified Pazyryk chieftain from the Altai Mountains of Central Asia*

# A BRIEF HISTORY OF TATTOOS

The earliest direct evidence of tattooing is more than 5,000 years old, on the preserved skin of "Ötzi the Iceman."[467] Around 3250 BCE, high in the mountains on what is now the Austrian-Italian border, Ötzi was struck in the shoulder by an arrow—and most likely bled to death. His body remained there, frozen in the snow and ice for over five millennia, until it was found by two hikers in 1991. Careful examination revealed that his skin was marked with 61 tattoos. While many of these are now difficult to see with the naked eye, multispectral imaging showed 19 groups of black lines, made by rubbing soot and fine ash into punctures or incisions in his skin. These tattoos were initially thought to be medicinal, perhaps to ease Ötzi's arthritis. But developing understanding of tattoo traditions from a variety of Indigenous cultures shows that tattoos like these can have many more

---

467 Aaron Deter-Wolf, Benoît Robitaille, Lars Krutak, Sébastien Galliot, "The World's Oldest Tattoos," *Journal of Archaeological Science: Reports* 5 (2016): 19-24.

complex meanings.[468] For example, lines tattooed on Inuit women's fingers may appear to be lines like Ötzi's, but they symbolize women's places within the origin story of the ocean spirit and remind the tattooed to follow cultural practices.[469] So it is difficult to speculate on what Ötzi's tattoos would have meant to him.

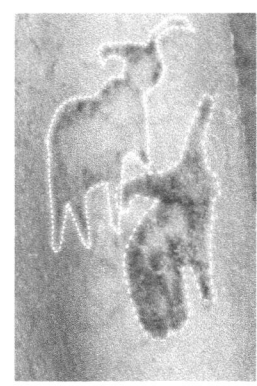

*Photograph of the upper body of "Gebelein Man A" from Egypt, from 3351-3017 BCE, showing tattoos of a wild bull and a sheep on his upper arm, with an enhanced closeup with outlines drawn to show the tattooed areas (© The Trustees of the British Museum)*

In 2017, two Egyptian mummies—a woman and a man from about the same time as Ötzi—were also found to have tattoos just barely visible on their ancient skin. Where the cold had preserved Ötzi, the dry heat of the desert naturally mummified the bodies of these Egyptians. The skin of the woman shows four small S-shapes tattooed on her shoulder, and the young man has images of a wild bull and horned sheep on his arm. While the purpose of these tattoos—decorative or medicinal—is unknown, they are the earliest figurative tattoos yet to be found.[470]

---

468 Marco Samadelli, Marcello Melis, Matteo Miccoli, Eduard Egarter Vigl, Albert R. Zink, "Complete Mapping of the Tattoos of the 5300-year-old Tyrolean Iceman *Journal of Cultural Heritage* 16 (2015): 753-758; Aaron Deter-Wolf, Benoît Robitaille, Danny Riday, Aurélien Burlot, Maya Sialuk Jacobsen, "Chalcolithic Tattooing: Historical and Experimental Evaluation of the Tyrolean Iceman's Body Markings," *European Journal of Archaeology* 27 no. 3 (2024): 267–288.

469 "Chalcolithic Tattooing," *European Journal of Archaeology*, 271.

470 Renée Friedman, Daniel Antoine, Sahra Talamo, Paula J. Reimer, John H. Taylor, Barbara Wills, Marcello A. Mannino, "Natural Mummies from Predynastic Egypt Reveal the World's Earliest Figural Tattoos" *Journal of Archaeological Science* 92

*Photograph of a blue bowl from Egypt, circa 1300 BCE, showing a woman with an image of the god Bes on her thigh, (National Museum of Antiquities, Leiden)*

Later mummies show a tradition of tattooing among ancient Egyptian women—and only women—going back to around 2000 BCE. Tattooed dots on their abdomens and the image of the god Bes (protector of women and children) on their thighs may have been seen as protection against evil spirits during pregnancy and childbirth.[471]

Other mummified remains show that tattoos were common all over the ancient world. From Chile to China, from Russia to Greenland, various peoples were marked with everything from simple facial tattoos to elaborate images of mythical animals.

(2018): 116-125.

471 Cate Lineberry, Sonja Anderson, "The Worldwide History of Tattoos: Ancient Ink Exhibited Religious Faith, Relieved Pain, Protected Wearers and Indicated Class," *Smithsonian Magazine,* October 18, 2023, https://www.smithsonianmag.com/history/tattoos-worldwide-history-144038580/.

*Photograph of a Chimú mummy arm with bird/fish tattoos on the fingers and geometric designs on the forearm and wrist, from the El Brujo Archaeological Complex, Chicama Valley, Peru, circa 1000-1470 CE, Milwaukee Public Museum, (Collection of the author)*

In Peru, for instance, examples of tattoos on mummified remains span a large range of times (from as early as 2500 BCE to as late as 1470 CE) and cultures (Chinchorro, Inca, Moche and Chimú). The imagery includes complex geometric designs, such as wrist bands, as well as images of animals, birds, and fish, found on multiple sections of the body.[472]

But that's just the direct evidence from preserved skin. Japanese figurines from around 5000 BCE[473] and Egyptian artworks from around 4000 BCE[474] depict people with decorations on their bodies, suggesting that tattooing goes back even further than Ötzi.

•

Turning to written historical records, finding references to tattoos can be tricky—because they weren't called tattoos until the 1700s. The word *tattoo* is from the Polynesian *tatau* and first appeared in the West in Captain James Cook's writings after his 1769-1771 voyage to the South Pacific.

The ancient Greeks used the word *dermatostiksia*, from

472 Madison Auten, "Ancient Andean Tattooing Practices," (Master's thesis, University of Wisconsin Milwaukee, 2018), 24, 28-36, UW Milwaukee Electronic Theses and Dissertations Database.

473 Amy Olson, "A Brief History of Tattoos," Wellcome Collection, April 13, 2010, https://wellcomecollection.org/stories/a-brief-history-of-tattoos.

474 Lineberry, "The Worldwide History of Tattoos."

*derma* (skin) and *stigma* (a mark, prick, or dot). The Greek historian Herodotus, circa 450 BCE, noted that the neighboring Scythians and Thracians used tattoos as a sign of nobility. But for the Greeks and Romans, tattoos were punitive, marking the lesser and the outcasts for all to see. Greek slaves would be marked with a delta for *doýlos* (slave). Criminals might have their transgressions tattooed on their foreheads.[475]

The Roman emperor Constantine the Great banned this penal tattooing in 316 CE, and that was reiterated in the collected laws of the Theodosian Code a century later. Some early Christians had decided that, because humans were created in God's image, tattoos were not appropriate—even for the lowest members of society. But despite the ban, penal tattooing continued for centuries into the Byzantine period.

Even with the idea that a tattoo marred the human body, many early Christians adopted tattooing as an expression of their religion. Some Christian slaves marked by the Romans turned their tattoos into subversive symbols—badges of honor that showed how they had suffered for their faith. This tradition is still alive in parts of Egypt, where Coptic Christians mark their arms and wrists with crosses, as do Kurdish women living in the Balkans. Their hands, arms, chests, and occasionally faces bear black linework in complex circular designs as well as decorative crosses. The Balkan practice, called *sicanje*, is likely older than Christianity, with the religious symbols incorporated into their existing tradition.

During the Middle Ages, tattooing continued to flourish around the world, but in Europe, it largely disappeared from public view. A few markings showed up on the arms of pilgrims and soldiers returning from Jerusalem during the Crusades. But it wasn't until the late 1500s that tattooing started to reemerge in Europe—when decorated foreigners were captured and put on display.

●

---

475 G. Kyriakou, A. Kyriakou, Th. Fotas, Dermatostiksia (Tattooing): An Act of Stigmatization in Ancient Greek Culture" *Actas Dermosifiliogr.* 112 (2021):907–909.

In the Age of Exploration, as Europeans sailed around the world, they encountered people with tattoos everywhere they went. Explorer and artist John White was part of the first attempts to establish a permanent English colony in North America at Roanoke Island in the 1580s. His watercolors of the Algonquin people provide a window into the tattooing traditions of native North Americans. White's paintings show geometric bands tattooed on their arms and legs, as well as symmetrically placed dots on their faces.

Many of White's images were copied by other Western artists into engravings, spreading the idea of tattooing across Europe. White also copied paintings (the originals are now lost) by Frenchman Jacques Le Moyne from the 1560s. These depict the Timucua people from what is now Florida. However, the renderings of their tattoos appear to have been influenced by Elizabethan patterns, and they look more like armor or embroidered fabric than tattoos. But since

there are no other remaining representations of Timucuan tattoos, it's impossible to say for certain if the images are accurate.[476]

Several people from North America and the South Pacific were captured and exhibited in Europe, while others voluntarily visited as dignitaries. The earliest were captive Inuit women brought to

*Watercolor by John White, "One of the wyves of Wyngyno" (Wingina was the Native American leader the English met at Roanoke), 1585-1590, (© The Trustees of the British Museum)*

476 Kim Sloan, *A New World: England's First View of America*, (The University of North Carolina Press, 2007.)

Antwerp and England in the 1500s. In the late 1600s, Jeoly, an enslaved Pacific Islander, was exhibited in England as "Prince Giolo." And about 100 years later, Mai, a man from the Pacific island of Ra'iatea, accompanied Captain James Cook to England, where he became a popular sensation. Jeoly had traditional geometric patterns tattooed across his torso, arms, and legs, while portraits of Mai show only lines and dots inked on the backs of his hands.[477]

In the early 1700s, a group of four Haudenosaunee (Iroquois) and Mohican leaders visited England to meet with Queen Anne and request aid in fighting the French in Quebec. Like Mai, the men caused a sensation while they toured London as visiting diplomats. Their portraits by Dutch artist Jan Verelst, now in the National Archives of Canada, were originally displayed at Kensington Palace and Hampton Court for many years. One of the paintings shows "Sa Ga Yeath Qua Pieth Tow, King of the Maquas" with symmetrical geometric tattoos across his face, torso, and arms.[478]

These visitors—and the earlier exhibited captives—brought new awareness of a wide range of tattoos to Europe. And as more

477 Hampton Sides, "The Polynesian 'Prince' Who Took 18th-Century England by Storm," *Smithsonian Magazine,* September 13, 2021, https://www.smithsonianmag. com/history/polynesian-prince-who-took-18th-century-england-storm-180978618/.

478 *Drawing With Great Needles: Ancient Tattoo Traditions of North America*, ed. Aaron Deter-Wolf and Carol Diaz-Granados, (University of Texas Press, 2013.)

and more sailors returned home with their own tattoos, inked skin became a more common sight in the West.

•

There is a surprising record of American tattoos starting in the late 1700s: sailors' "protection certificates." These certificates, created between 1779 and 1818, were a type of identification, with each one naming and describing the person holding it. Long before people commonly carried any ID cards, sailors carried protection certificates in case of death, kidnapping, or impression into slavery. And their detailed descriptions of the bearers included any tattoos.

Surviving records, from the Philadelphia Seamen's Protection Certificate Applications held in the National Archives, show that about 10% of the men carrying protection certificates were tattooed. However, the word "tattoo," still new in the West, doesn't actually appear anywhere in these records. Instead the sailors were described as "marked with ink."[479]

Just under half of the men marked with ink had just one tattoo, and a quarter had two. Only one person in these records had enough tattoos to be considered totally "covered": William Gaines from New York was listed as having 30 individual tattoos by the age of 24.[480] Was he a tattooist? Or did he simply have the same impulses as Costentenus?

The most common tattoo designs among these sailors were personal to them: just under half were tattooed with initials (theirs or someone else's), and about one third had a full name tattooed on them. Many sailors tattooed their own names as the ultimate form of identification in case the ship sank and their bodies washed

479 Ira Dye, "The Tattoos of Early American Seafarers, 1796-1818," *Proceedings of the American Philosophical Society,* 133, No. 4 (Dec., 1989): 528.

480 Dye, "The Tattoos of Early American Seafarers," 536.

*Photograph of preserved skin tattooed with a flower and the initials "A. T.," circa 1850-1920, (Wellcome Collection)*

ashore.[481] Another popular theme revolved around things from the sea: mermaids, fish, and ships. Other tattoos described on the certificates included patriotic imagery, professional and fraternal symbols, sentimental images (such as hearts or clasped hands), drawings of ladies, and depictions of nature (such as trees and flowers).

•

While many Eastern tattooists apprenticed to a master to learn traditional techniques, Western tattooists at this time were casually trained. They typically learned from someone on board a ship or in a neighborhood tavern. There is very little record of the designs they used, but it was generally simple folk art.

By the 1880s, we can see what imagery was popular from the wealth of photographs that Captain George and other tattooed performers left behind. There are even a few sketchbooks drawn by tattooists that survive from this time. Known as "flash," these sketchbooks allowed prospective customers to choose which design they wanted on their skin.

These tattoos fall into fairly neat categories that mirror the

---

481 Dye, "The Tattoos of Early American Seafarers," 542.

*"Hope" design from a tattoo pattern book, circa 1850, (Courtesy Winterthur Museum, Garden & Library)*

designs worn a century earlier: religious, patriotic, professional, and sentimental. While the techniques and artistry of tattoos have grown so much since the 1800s, these categories remain among the most popular to this day.

Religious tattoos in the 19th century would look familiar to us now: simple crosses and images of Christ with a crown of thorns, or more elaborate designs like the Rock of Ages. Patriotic designs included American eagles, shields, Lady Liberty, and Columbia (a female personification of the United States). Professional tattoos vary from traditional anchors and stars for sailors to Masonic and Odd Fellows symbols. Sentimental images include images of clasped hands, initials or names of a loved one, and hearts.

Looking at my own arms, I've got a smattering of most of these: a mermaid, a heart with a name, flowers and bees, and a lodge symbol. I guess tattoos haven't really changed all that much in 200 years, have they?

•

While many of the designs haven't changed much, the materials and technology used to make the tattoos has. Today, inks are manufactured in a rainbow of colors, but in the 19th century, tattooists were limited by their ability to make their own ink. The earliest known tattoo design book, in the collection of the Winterthur Library in Delaware, includes a handwritten recipe for making a basic blue/black ink from around 1850:

> 2 ½ oz. of blue vitrol
> 200 c.c. measures water
> 1 c.c. measures sweet spirits niter
> 2 oz Pulvire Rosen
> 2 oz beeswax
> 1 pint boiled oil
> Boiled together until "desolve"[482]

Many of these ingredients are now unfamiliar. "Blue vitrol" (vitriol) is copper sulfate, which was used for dying fabric and is still used for intaglio printmaking. It was commonly available then as an emetic (medicine that induces vomiting). Copper sulfate is also toxic when inhaled and can cause skin irritation and eczema. "Sweet spirits niter" is a centuries-old, ethanol-based cold remedy that was banned by the FDA in 1980. It can be fatal to infants—and doesn't seem to help with a cold.[483] "Pulvire Rosen" most likely refers to pulverized rosin, a powdered form of the substance used by violinists, gymnasts, and acrobats to increase friction.

Is this a safe concoction to put into a wound in the skin? Who knows! There are many stories about tattooists making ink out of questionable or odd ingredients, such as graphite, witch hazel, vodka, and Listerine. Tattooists, like the one who wrote down the recipe above, have always mixed their own combinations of inks, dyes, thickeners, stabilizers, and other chemicals in the pursuit of strong, consistent colors that don't fade over time or change their hue in the skin.

American tattooists in the 1800s would have taken a bundle of needles, dipped the ends into one of their homemade concoctions, and tapped them into the skin. (The first mechanized tattoo machine wasn't patented until 1891.) Nineteenth century New York tattoo legend Martin Hildebrandt used "some half dozen No. 12 needles bound together in a slanting form, which are dipped as the pricking

---

482 Nicholas Schoenberger, Inking Identity: Tattoo Design and the Emergence of an American Industry, 1875-1930, Thesis University of Delaware, Summer 2005, 44.

483 "Old-Time Remedy Ruled Off Market," *St. Joseph News-Press*, Oct. 8, 1980.

is made into the best India ink or vermillion."[484] These needles were sewing needles, with the number referring to the thickness. Number 12 needles are very fine and sharp. India ink is a traditional black ink from China, originally made from soot as early as the 3rd millennium BCE. It is prized for its deep black color. In the skin, however, India ink has a tendency to turn green over time and the quality is not consistent.

Martin Hildebrandt had his own recipes and techniques—and his own book of designs. He offered tattoos of the crucifixion, portraits of women, Masonic and Odd Fellows emblems, anchors, cannons, and weeping willows. He even did custom work: "sometimes there comes to me a man who don't like any of my pictures in my book, but is willing for me to invent something for him."[485]

After performers like Captain George and tattooists like Martin Hildebrandt made images of inked skin more and more familiar to everyday people, tattooing started its slow climb in popularity in the West. Today, nearly one third of Americans have at least one tattoo.[486] The FDA now inspects the ink to make sure it's safe. Machines can

*Photograph of preserved skin with a tattooed portrait of a woman surrounded by garland, circa 1850-1920, (Wellcome Collection)*

484 "Tattooing in New York," *New York Times* January 16, 1876.

485 "Tattooing in New York," *New York Times*.

486 Katherine Schaeffer and Shradha Dinesh, "32% of Americans Have a Tattoo," Pew Research Center, August 15, 2023, accessed April 27, 2024, https://pewrsr. ch/3QFg5w1.

now puncture the skin up to 3,000 times per minute. Many of the same themes, from crosses to eagles to hearts, remain popular. But now there are also trained tattoo artists, expanding the possibilities of the craft far beyond what even the Captain could have imagined.

•

In 1871, Charles Darwin wrote that tattooing and other permanent body marking was one of the "tastes, dispositions, and habits" that people all over the world share.[487] Modern study of these global traditions affirms that tattooing developed independently in different places, at different times, from ritualistic or religious practices, cultural celebrations, and medical treatment.

Because there are so many distinct traditions, tattoos can represent achievement or misfortune, distinction or shame. They can symbolize age, class, marital status, family background, or religious expression. They can serve as a group's visual link, showing who belongs—or they can be used to mark those who don't belong. They can be used to beautify. They can be used to scar.

Indigenous tattoos

*Photograph of unidentified woman with a small butterfly tattoo on her leg, 1920s, (Collection of the author)*

487 Charles Darwin, *The Descent of Man*, (D. Appleton and Co., 1871): 232.

have played a huge part in cultures all across the globe for millenia. There has been as much variety in those tattoos as there has been in the humans themselves. Tattoos have been central to many cultures' traditions of expression, and yet the art form adapts and changes with time. From Ötzi's tattooed lines to Costentenus's animals to today's trends, tattoos illustrate human experiences.

As many cultures are reviving their tattoo traditions and adapting them to modern life, new ideas and expressions continue to develop. The artistry is ever expanding and the meanings are ever more rich and varied. For me, as for so many others, tattoos can help tell your story—who you are and where you came from.

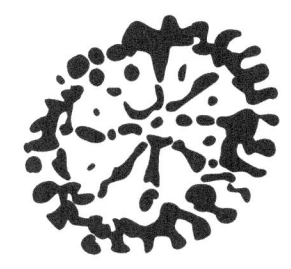

# A BRIEF HISTORY OF CAPTAIN GEORGE'S PREDECESSORS

Before George Costentenus, there were only four tattooed people who chose to exhibit themselves in the West. And just like the Captain, they had traveled to distant lands and told far-fetched tales of torture and escape. Joseph Kabris, John Rutherford, Barnet Burns, and James O'Connell set the standard. They helped develop the tropes that would be used by tattooed performers for decades to come.

•

## Joseph Kabris

In 1817, a heavily tattooed Frenchman arrived in Paris. Half his

JOSEPH KABRIS (1780-1822)

VICE-ROI ET GRAND JUGE DES ILES MENDOÇA

D'après une lithographie de Martinet

*Drawing of Joseph Kabris, from* Revue philomathique de Bordeaux et du Sud-Ouest *[Scholarly Review of Bordeaux and the Southwest], 1933, (National Library of France)*

*"Joseph Kabris (1780-1822), vice-roi et grand juge des iles mendoça, D'après une lithographie de Martinet" [Viceroy and Grand Judge of the Marquesas Islands, after a lithograph by Martinet]*

forehead and the skin around one eye were completely tattooed black. His body was covered in lines, spirals and other patterns. Joseph Kabris (or Cabri) had been born in Bordeaux around 1780 and went to sea when he was about 14.[488] In May of 1795, he joined a whaling ship leaving Portsmouth, England, for the South Pacific. But he deserted in the Marquesas Islands in French Polynesia. He went on to live there, on the island of Nuku Hiva for six years, from 1798 to 1804.

He told a version of his story in his pamphlet, *Précis Historique et Véritable du Séjour de Joseph Kabris, Natif de Bordeaux* [*Historical and True Summary of the Soujourn of Joseph Kabris, Native of Bordeaux*]. In it, he claimed that a gale sprang up out of nowhere and dashed the ship on the rocks of an island.[489] The survivors were fed freshly cooked pork while women pinched their pale skin, planning for their tattoos.[490] The islanders reportedly wouldn't consider Kabris a man until he was tattooed. Once he was covered with designs, he was

---

488 Jennifer Terrell, "Notes and Documents: Joseph Kabris and His Notes on the Marquesas," *Journal of Pacific History* 17 No. 2 (1982): 105.

489 Terrell, "Notes and Documents, 106.

490 Terrell, "Notes and Documents, 108.

## PRÉCIS

HISTORIQUE ET VÉRITABLE

DU SÉJOUR

## DE JOSEPH KABRIS,

NATIF DE BORDEAUX,

*Dans les îles de Mendoça, situées dans l'Océan Pacifique, sous le 10ᵉ degré de latitude sud, vers le 240ᵉ degré de longitude.*

Six mois après la malheureuse affaire de Quiberon, je m'embarquai sur un vaisseau anglais pour la pêche de la baleine dans la mer Pacifique. Notre navigation fut heureuse jusque dans les parages des îles de Mendoça. Après avoir pêché six baleines, notre capitaine

Précis Historique et Véritable du Séjour de Joseph Kabris, Natif de Bordeaux, *supposedly written by Joseph Kabris, circa 1817, (National Library of France)*

welcomed into Nuku Hivan society, where he married a local woman and had several children.

However, in 1804, ships from the first Russian circumnavigation of the Earth arrived on Nuku Hiva. The Russians used the French Kabris as a local translator, along with a British man who was also living there. (Knowing that the British and French were enemies, the Russians tried to use the two men as opposing translators, so that neither could deceive them.) There are conflicting reports on how Kabris ended up on board the Russian ship *Nadezhda (Hope)* when it set sail from Nuku Hiva. He might have been kidnapped, or he might have gotten drunk and fallen asleep.

Regardless, the heavily-tattooed man returned with the expedition to the Kamchatka Peninsula on the far eastern edge of Russia. Unable to get back to Nuku Hiva, he had to make his way in Russian society. He tried exhibiting himself. He gained the patronage of royal officials and passed from one governor to another on a slow overland trip westwards to St. Petersburg.[491] There, Kabris performed before Czar Alexander I, who gave him a yearly salary as a curiosity. His fame didn't last long, but he landed on his feet.

Though Kabris was now tantalizingly close to his homeland, he couldn't make his way back to France because of the Napoleonic Wars. He had learned to swim while in the Marquesas, so he was given a position teaching swimming at a Russian military training school.[492]

---

491 Terrell, "Notes and Documents, 105.

492 Christophe Granger, *Joseph Kabris ou Les Possibilités d'Une Vie: 1780-1822* (Ana-

He was finally able to sail to Calais in 1817 and then continued on to Paris. His arrival there created a sensation.

In Paris, Kabris met Duke Amedee de Durfort and his wife Claire, and with their assistance, he started performing at salons and telling his strange story.[493] He gained the attention of King Louis XVIII, who, like the Czar, gave him a salary. While his tattoos were the main attraction, his stories of traveling with the Russians also proved quite popular, given the recent end of the Napoleonic Wars.

Kabris published his pamphlet and became a regular attraction at Paris's "Cabinet of Illusions." He performed holding a bamboo spear, nearly nude except for a feathered headdress. His backdrop was a series of panorama paintings of island scenes. Over time, he added acrobats and a performing dog to his show, though what, if anything, they had to do with his story is unclear.[494]

He left Paris in 1818 and joined the ranks of traveling entertainers in France for a few years. In 1822, at age 42, he died in Valenciennes, where he was buried in a common grave.[495] Kabris had brought together most of the elements that would guide tattooed performers for the rest of the century: a Westerner with tattoos from a culture not his own, an act on stage, and a travel narrative steeped in adventure and danger.

•

## John Rutherford

The next tattooed performer in Europe was Englishman John Rutherford, who returned from the South Pacific in 1826 or 1827 decorated with Māori tattoos. Rutherford was born in Manchester or Lancashire between 1792 and 1796.[496] As a young man, he was arrested

mosa, 2020): 318-321.

493 Granger, *Joseph Kabris,* 344-345.

494 Granger, *Joseph Kabris,* 352-354; Terrell, "Notes and Documents," 107.

495 Granger, *Joseph Kabris,* 407.

496 C. A. O. Fox, *Bibliographical Notes on John Rutherford and Barnet Burns,*

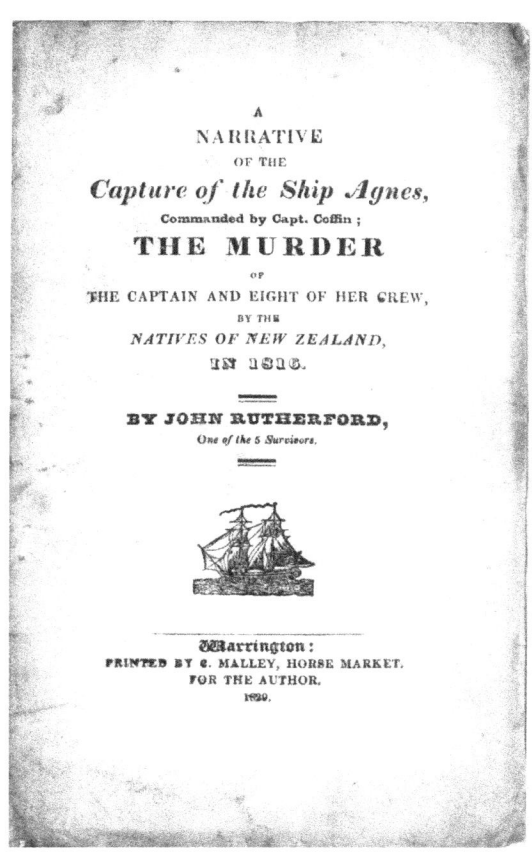

A
NARRATIVE
OF THE
Capture of the Ship Agnes,
Commanded by Capt. Coffin ;
THE MURDER
OF
THE CAPTAIN AND EIGHT OF HER CREW,
BY THE
NATIVES OF NEW ZEALAND,
IN 1816.

BY JOHN RUTHERFORD,
One of the 5 Survivors.

Warrington:
PRINTED BY C. MALLEY, HORSE MARKET.
FOR THE AUTHOR.
1829.

John Rutherford's promotional pamphlet, 1829, (National Library of Australia)
"A Narrative of the Capture of the Ship Agnes, Commanded by Capt. Coffin; The Murder of the Captain and Eight of Her Crew, by the Natives of New Zealand, in 1816. By John Rutherford, One of the 5 Survivors. Warrington: Printed by C. Malley, Horse Market. For the Author. 1829."

for theft and sent to prison multiple times.[497]

British prisons were so desperately overcrowded in the 18th and 19th centuries that convicts were sometimes sent to decommissioned ships to serve their sentences. These floating prisons had their rigging, masts, and rudders removed and were outfitted with jail cells. Rutherford served two of his sentences on one of these "prison hulks," the *Captivity*.

Rutherford's trips to prison didn't change his ways, so he was finally sentenced to penal transportation to Australia in 1822. But in his autobiographical pamphlet, *A Narrative of the Capture of the Ship Agnes*, he conveniently omitted his criminal past. He claimed he had been in the British Navy before voluntarily sailing to the South Pacific on the *Agnes*. According to Rutherford, they attempted to trade with the Māori in New Zealand, but the natives overran the ship. The crew was hauled ashore and stripped of their clothes. The Māori "immediately proceeded to cut the buttons from our clothes as precious ornaments to hang in the ears of the chief women of the

Christchurch, History and Bibliography, 1950.

497 England & Wales, Crime, Prisons & Punishment, 1770-1935/Captivity For Year 1809-1811 & 1812, findmypast.co.uk.

horde" and ominously started digging large holes in the ground.[498]

Here Rutherford introduces the final element of what would become the standard narrative for so many tattooed performers, being tattooed against your will by "savages":

> [Our] arms and legs were held by numbers whilst four operators went to work upon us. The instruments used in tattooing were made of bone or shark's teeth some were sharp like a Chisel; and others indented like a Saw. They are dipped into a black liquid composed of charcoal and water, and then applied to the skin; they are then struck smartly with a piece of wood, till the blood flows copiously.[499]

498 John Rutherford, *An Account of the Capture of the Ship Agnes, Commanded by Capt. Coffin; The Murder of The Captain and Eight of Her Crew by the Natives of New Zealand in 1816*, (C. Malley, 1829): 7-8.

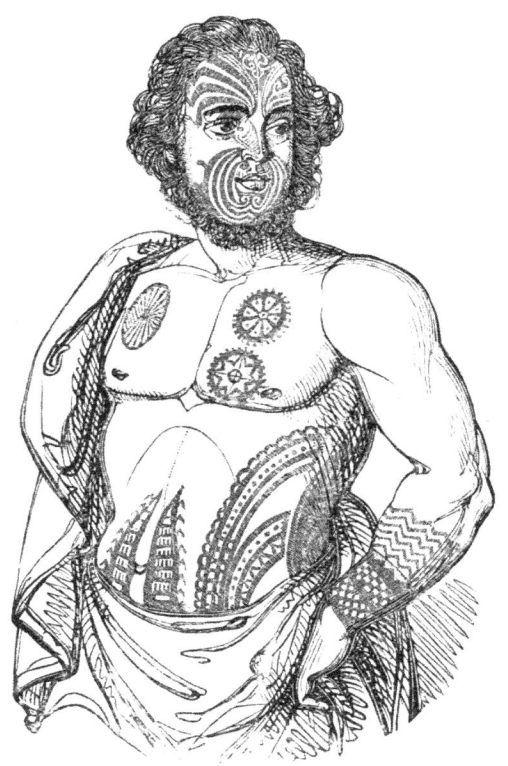

*Illustration of John Rutherford in G. L. Craik's* The New Zealanders, *1830, (Alexander Turnbull Library, Wellington, New Zealand)*

499 Rutherford, *An Account of the Capture*, 8.

236

Not only did he claim he was forcibly inked, he said the Māori then offered him a meal of cooked potatoes—and the roasted body parts of a dead crew member. While Kabris had at least kept his story plausible, Rutherford fully embraced sensational nonsense.

Rutherford eventually went to the interior with one of the chiefs, "whose property I had become," and married two of the chief's daughters.[500] He lived in New Zealand for 10 years before he finally spotted a British ship at sea and escaped back to England. Rutherford was a changed man when he returned, at least in appearance. His face was covered in Māori tattoos, with other parts of his body decorated with Tahitian tattoos.

Rutherford started his career as a tattooed performer around 1828 in Lancashire, but he couldn't quite shake his earlier impulses to steal. Unfortunately for him, his prominent facial tattoos made him exceptionally easy to catch–especially after he tried robbing a man on the street when he was performing at a fair in the same town.[501] He was arrested several times in 1828, "a dark complexioned little man with a shaggy beard, tattooed after the manner of the South Sea Islanders..."[502] He was arrested again in 1830 before fading into obscurity.

•

## Barnet Burns

The next inked performer was a bold character named Barnet Burns. Like Rutherford, Burns had Māori tattoos, but he went so far as to bill himself as "Pahe-A-Range, the New Zealand Chief." Once, he even tried to pass himself off as a king.

Burns claimed that he was born in 1805 in England's Lake District. He went to sea as a cabin boy and made his way to Jamaica. There, he worked for the anti-slavery activist Louis Celeste Lecesne,

---

500 Rutherford, *An Account of the Capture,* 9.

501 "Street Robbery by a New-Zealand Chieftain," *Lancaster Gazette,* May 24, 1828.

502 "Trial," *Manchester Courier and Lancashire General Advertiser*, July 28, 1828.

who supposedly made it possible for Burns to attend school in England. But Burns also later claimed that he was born in "Sidney Grove, New Holland [Australia], son of a European and a native of the country who were married in 1807."[503] As with Rutherford before him and Costentenus after him, it's unclear what was true.

In his 1835 pamphlet, *A Brief Narrative of the Remarkable History of Barnet Burns,* Burns said that he landed in Australia in 1831 and signed up to work as a flax trader in New Zealand.[504] What came next? Sensational stories of tribal warfare, cannibalism, and forced tattooing, of course. He ended up settling in New Zealand under the protection of a Māori chief and marrying the chief's daughter. He said that his tattoos then gave him the freedom to travel and trade throughout New Zealand.

In 1834, Burns left his wife and children to conduct business in Sydney and then sailed on to England. Whether he ever intended to return is unknown. But he clearly didn't miss his Māori wife too much, since he married a woman named Bridget Cain a few months after his return to England. They were wed in London on June 1, 1835, with one of his brothers serving as a witness.

Shortly after this bigamous marriage, Burns started exhibiting himself at the Royal Surrey Zoological Gardens.[505] Set on 15 acres, the gardens included a lake, many exotic plants, and a giant glass dome that housed lions, tigers, giraffes, and more.[506] Burns and his tattoos joined the animals, plants, fireworks displays, and paintings of the world's wonders. The performances he gave were simple: he talked about his time in New Zealand, showed off his tattoos, and brought out what he called a "war cloak" and, supposedly, a Māori Chief's

503 "Shearman, Police to Provincial Secretary—inquiry being made for whereabouts of Barnet Burns, interpreter. Filed with 1847 (Colonial Secretary), 1847.1 to 1847.3–17 November 1873," Reference: CAAR 19936 CH287/CP 139 ICPS 1902/1873, Te Rua Mahara o te Kāwanatanga, Archives New Zealand.

504 Barnet Burns, *A Brief Narrative of the Remarkable History of Barnet Burns, an English Sailor, Who Has Lately Been Exhibiting at the 'Surrey Zoological Gardens,' and Other Place of Amusement,* (E. Justins and Son, Printers, 1835): 5-6.

505 "Union-Hall," *Morning Chronicle,* July 23, 1835.

506 Mogg's New Picture of London and Visitor's Guide to it Sights, 1844, https://www.victorianlondon.org/entertainment/surreyzoologicalgardens.htm

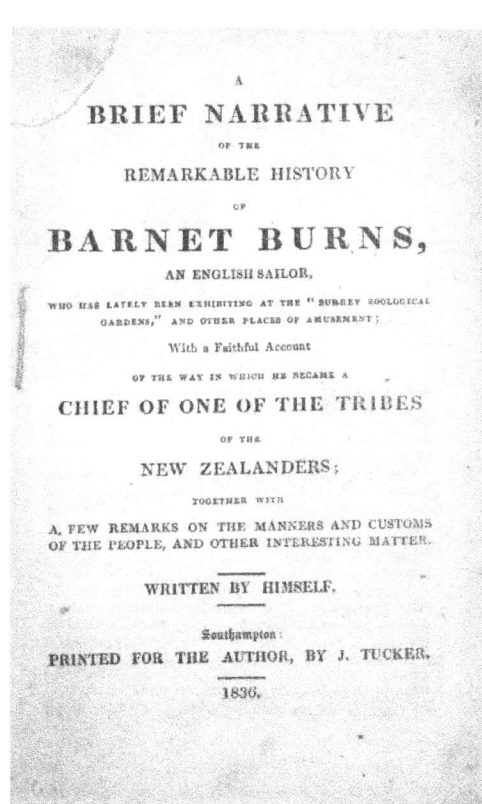

Barnet Burns's promotional pamphlet, 1836, (National Library of Australia) "A Brief Narrative of the Remarkable History of Barnet Burns, an English sailor, who has lately been exhibiting at the 'Surrey Zoological Gardens,' and other places of amusement; With a Faithful Account of the way in which he became a chief of one of the tribes of the New Zealanders; Together with a few remarks on the manners and customs of the people, and other interesting matter. Written by himself. Southampton, printed for the author, by J. Tucker. 1836."

shrunken head.[507] Weirdly, Burns may not have had to bring back this head from abroad. There seem to have been a number of them in circulation in the West, including one at Barnum's American Museum in 1860.[508]

Burns took his act across England, but his early reviews were not great. One newspaper reported that his lecture was a "jumble of impudence, ignorance, low wit, and bare-faced presumption."[509] In the face of this less than enthusiastic press coverage, Burns decided to move to France, where he tried (unsuccessfully) to convince "the Academy" that he was the King of New Zealand.[510]

---

507 "Union-Hall," *The Morning Chronicle.*

508 "Amusements: Barnum's American Museum," *Brooklyn Evening Star,* September 8, 1860.

509 "Mechanic's Institution," *Hampshire Advertiser,* May 14, 1836.

510 "Barnet Burns," *Bath Chronicle and Weekly Gazette,* November 17, 1836.

*Drawing of Barnet Burns, used to advertise his appearances in England, 1842-1844, (Alexander Turnbull Library, Wellington, New Zealand)*

BARNET BURNS.

Having left his new wife Bridget behind in England, Burns settled down in Paris—and married wife number three, Anne Amelie Boval, in 1838. But by October of 1840, he had returned to England and married wife number four, Rosina Crowther.[511] England had very strict divorce laws at the time, and Burns was not wealthy enough to navigate the legal system. Undeterred, he went for serial bigamy instead. This was a crime—one that could have gotten him transported back to Australia—but convictions were rare. There was no centralized record keeping, so if Burns kept quiet about his concurrent marriages, he was unlikely to be caught.

From 1840 to about 1857, Burns performed throughout England in lecture halls, town halls, clubs, and hotel auditoriums—essentially anywhere he could book a show. He often went by the name "Pahe-A-Range" and spoke about the manners and customs of New Zealand, showing off his tattoos, various war clubs, and other artifacts. His wife

511 "Bradford Exhibition," *Leeds Mercury,* October 17, 1840.

Rosina (sometimes called "Madame Pahe-A-Range") also performed, playing the "musical glasses."[512]

Barnet Burns's last recorded performance was in 1857 in Leicester. He was visibly ill, "suffering from severe bodily affliction" but like any performer dedicated to both the performance and making a living, the show went on.[513]

Years later, his third wife Anne wrote to the British Ambassador in Paris looking for her husband. Her letter was forwarded to the Constabulary Department Commissioners Office in Christchurch, New Zealand in 1873:

> I solicit your kindness for the following requested information... My husband... was summoned by her Majesty the Queen of England, to be part of an English expedition to New Zealand in the capacity of interpreter... My husband then left for this expedition, telling me that he had assured me a fixed maintenance allowance. Since that time I have written often and have received no answer and no remedy, although my husband must have left me and the two children of our marriage enough money to ensure our existence. But slowly I found myself in a very precarious position that has since worsened because of a lack of information my uncertainty whether he is dead or alive. I cannot even access a small amount of money from my family without producing a death certificate with year of death, if it happened. In a word, my position is unfortunate and complicated in that I cannot in any way change my position... I ask of you... to do all that you can to relieve this unmerited position, I beg you to take into consideration that my husband departed for service to England leaving me almost without resources.[514]

Authorities in New Zealand were asked to find aged French settlers and see if they knew anything about Burns. A notice was placed in the *South Australian Police Gazette*, but they were unable

---

512 "Corn Exchange," *The Preston Chronicle and Lancashire Advertiser,* December 4, 1847.

513 "New Zealand" *Leicester Chronicle or Commercial and Leicestershire Mercury*, April 18, 1857.

514 "Shearman, Police to Provincial Secretary," Archives New Zealand.

to find any trace of the missing man. [515] The officials couldn't locate Burns, alive or dead, because they were looking in the wrong place. "Pahe-A-Range" had died in England in 1860 of cirrhosis of the liver. He was buried in a common grave in Devonshire.[516]

•

## James O'Connell

While Barnett Burns was performing around England, an Irishman was working in the United States as America's first tattooed man. James O'Connell, in his own melodramatic autobiographical pamphlet, said that he was born into a circus family in Dublin in 1808. After leaving school to join the family business for a few years, he went to London and sailed with the ship *Phoenix* as a cabin boy— bound for Botany Bay in Australia with 200 female convicts.[517]

At this point, you won't be surprised to hear that even this was not true. In reality, O'Connell was convicted of robbery in Ireland in July of 1828. He was given a life sentence of transportation and shipped off to Sydney.[518]

But in his pamphlet, *The Life and Adventures of James F. O'Connell, the Tattooed Man,* he claimed that he joined a whaling vessel in 1822, only to be shipwrecked off a remote stretch of the Australian coast.[519] He lived with the natives for eight or nine months before finally making his way back to Sydney. He joined another ship, but this time, the captain was a drunk who ran the ship aground. Most of the crew were killed, but six survivors made it to the island of

---

515 "Missing Friend," *The South Australian Police Gazette*, December 17, 1873.

516 "George Barnet Burns - Death," *Plymouth and Devonport Journal*, Thursday, 3 January 1861.

517 James O'Connell, Life and Adventures of James F. O'Connell, the Tattooed Man, During a residence of eleven years in New Holland and the Caroline Islands, (W. Applegate, Painter, 1845): 5-6.

518 New South Wales, Australia, Convict Indents, 1788-1842, ancestry.com.

519 O'Connell, Life and Adventures, 13.

*James O'Connell's promotional pamphlet, 1845, (Library of Congress) "The Life and Adventures of James F. O'Connell, the Tattooed Man. During a residence of eleven years in New Holland and the Caroline Islands. New York: W. Applegate, Printer, 17 Ann Street. 1845."*

Pohnpei, now part of Micronesia.

They were greeted by a group of islanders, who offered them food. The other survivors took the natives for cannibals and were afraid they would soon be roasted and eaten, but O'Connell was sure the islanders meant them no harm. To prove his theory and calm his shipmates, he jumped up and started to dance a traditional Irish jig to the song "Garry Owen." According to the pamphlet, "my new acquaintances were amazingly delighted thereat."[520] Such dancing would be a part of O'Connell's performances throughout his career in America. An 1849 newspaper enthused that, "Every person that has witnessed the agility, muscular power, and uncommon brilliancy of execution exhibited in Mr. O'Connell's dancing will never forget him."[521]

After several days, the islanders took O'Connell and George Keenan, another Irish survivor of the shipwreck, to a different island. There, they feasted and celebrated—and several women began tattooing the two men.

One woman "produced a small flat piece of wood with thorns pierced through one end; this she dipped in the black liquid then rested the points of the thorns on the mark on my hand, and with a sudden blow from a stick, drove the thorns into my flesh... I summoned all my

---

520 O'Connell, Life and Adventures, 11.

521 "Franklin Theatre," *New York Daily Herald*, October 21, 1849.

fortitude, set my teeth, and bore it like a martyr. Between every blow my beauty dipped her thorns in the ink."[522]

As in Costentenus's story of his tortured companions, O'Connell's compatriot was weaker: "He swore and raved... He wished all sorts of bloody murder to light on his tormentors... The operators suspended their work to mimic him, and mocked his spasmodic twitches of the arms and horrid gestures."

After eight days, O'Connell had been inked on his "left hand, on both arms, legs, thighs, back and abdomen."[523] George Keenan had also survived, but he had only been able to withstand a few unfinished stripes on his left arm.

O'Connell claimed that he lived on Pohnpei for four or five years, married, and had several children. Despite this, he jumped

*Drawing of James O'Connell performing an Irish jig for the islanders, from* Life and Adventures of James F. O'Connell, the Tattooed Man, *1845, (Library of Congress)*

522 O'Connell, Life and Adventures, 12-13.

523 O'Connell, *Life and Adventures,* 17

on a passing ship at the first opportunity and made his way to North America. Keenan came with him–but was left behind when he took ill in Canada.

O'Connell arrived in the United States sometime in 1835. He gave his first performance in Boston in February of 1836. He tried out his story and his dancing at the New England Museum, a dime museum on Court Street that featured wax figures, presidential portraits, and curiosities like him.[524]

Through the museum, he connected with the Boston Lion Circus, a small show that toured across New England.[525] He also performed publicity stunts: "[he ran] from the State House... to the lower end of Long wharf- climbed to the main top gallant yard of a ship, and there danced five complete steps, all in the space of four minutes and forty two seconds!"[526]

O'Connell went on to have a long, successful career. He worked for a wide variety of circuses and museums throughout the country– even going across to Cuba–and appeared at Barnum's American Museum as their first tattooed man in 1840 and 1842.[527] He traveled with a riverboat circus on the Mississippi River, worked for legendary showman Dan Rice, and made New Orleans his home base for many years.[528]

O'Connell's last few years were mostly with Rice's various shows, except for a brief return to Barnum's American Museum, where he was promoted alongside the famous Feejee Mermaid.[529] Rice

---

524 "The Tattooed Man," *Boston Post*, February 16, 1836.

525 Stuart Thayer, *Annals of the American Circus, 1793-1860* (Dauven and Thayer, 2000): 256, 263; "St. Patrick's Evening," *Boston Post*, March 16, 1837.

526 "Agility" and "At the Lion" *Boston Post*, March 31, 1837.

527 "Barnum's American Museum," *New York Herald,* November 15, 1842; "American Museum," *Evening Post*, September 25, 1840.

528 Thayer, *Annals,* 161, 255.

529 Annals of the American Circus, p. 529; "American Museum," *New-York Tribune*, November 14, 1842; Carlyon, *Dan Rice*, 148-149.

took O'Connell into the new state of Texas in 1852 with his Star State Circus.[530] In between tours, O'Connell continued to return to New Orleans, often performing for local museums and benefit shows.

That was where the first performing tattooed man in America died in late 1853 or early 1854. Rice's show finished the season without him. At the end of January 1854, mourners were invited to see him off for a final time: "It is thought by those who knew him while living, that a few of his many friends may like to attend and see his remains finally placed at rest. He will be buried at four o'clock this evening from No. 22 Philippa Street."[531]

•

These four tattooed performers laid the foundation that Captain George Costentenus would build on so spectacularly. The Captain would bring together elements of Joseph Kabris's accounts of distant lands and danger, John Rutherford's tales of torture, a bit of Barnet Burns theatrical flair, and a big dose of James O'Connell's melodramatic storytelling. While all four of the Tattooed Greek's predecessors had found fame–and Burns and O'Connell had long, successful careers–the stage was set for Costentenus to surpass them all.

530 "Star State Circus" *Times-Picayune*, October 10, 1852.

531 "Death of the Tattooed Man," *New Orleans Crescent*, January 30, 1854. The address, 22 Phillipa Street, would be on the present-day 100 block of Roosevelt Way, between Canal and Common Streets. The Orpheum Theater relocated there in 1921.

# THE ANNOTATED AUTOBIOGRAPHY OF CAPTAIN GEORGE

Being "THE LIFE & ADVENTURES OF CAPT. COSTENTENUS"
—His Autobiography—

Reprinted Here for the First Time Ever,
UNABRIDGED and in its ENTIRETY,
Complete with Odd Spellings, Creative Grammar,
and Antiquated Turns of Phrase.

—With Explanatory Notes by the Authors of this Book—

As we mentioned in chapter 5, The Life and Adventures of Captain Costentenus has only a passing resemblance to the truth. The ghostwriter who crafted this lengthy pamphlet recast Captain George Costentenus, surly tattooed performer, as a man of action and adventure—and let his imagination run wild. This "autobiography" is both a work of delight and loaded with problematic narratives.

Like his tattooed predecessors Kabris, Rutherford, Burns, and O'Connell, the Captain used a popular trope of the time: the captivity narrative. Each man had been traveling somewhere exotic and was captured by "savages." These stories were grounded in the racist idea that Westerners were "civilized" and somehow superior. Many sideshow acts and the pamphlets they sold reinforced these attitudes.

The Life and Adventures of Captain Costentenus offers many insights, despite (and because of) its issues. The tales that sideshow talkers used to pull in audiences were never just about the performers themselves. Often, the narratives reveal more about the audiences— their beliefs, their knowledge, and what entertained them—than they do about the performers. They are a way to get inside the minds of 19th century audiences and understand why the acts were structured and presented the way they were. The narratives were built around themes in popular books and prominent news stories of the day. They often threw in cameos by real, well-known people, to add exciting brushes with fame—or infamy—with little regard for the truth. In the sideshow business, giving the audience a fantastic story was always part of the game of making more money.[532]

•

---

532     Robert Bogdan, *Freak Show: Presenting Human Oddities for Amusement and Profit*, (Chicago, 1988): 95-96 and Amelia Klem Osterud, "The True Life and Adventures of Tattooed Performers," in *Tattoo Histories: Transcultural Perspectives on the Narratives, Practices, and Representations of Tattooing*, ed. Sinah Theres Kloß, (Routledge, 2020): 136-154

*George Costentenus's "autobiographical" pamphlet, 1881,*
*(Collection of A. Bruce Tracy)*

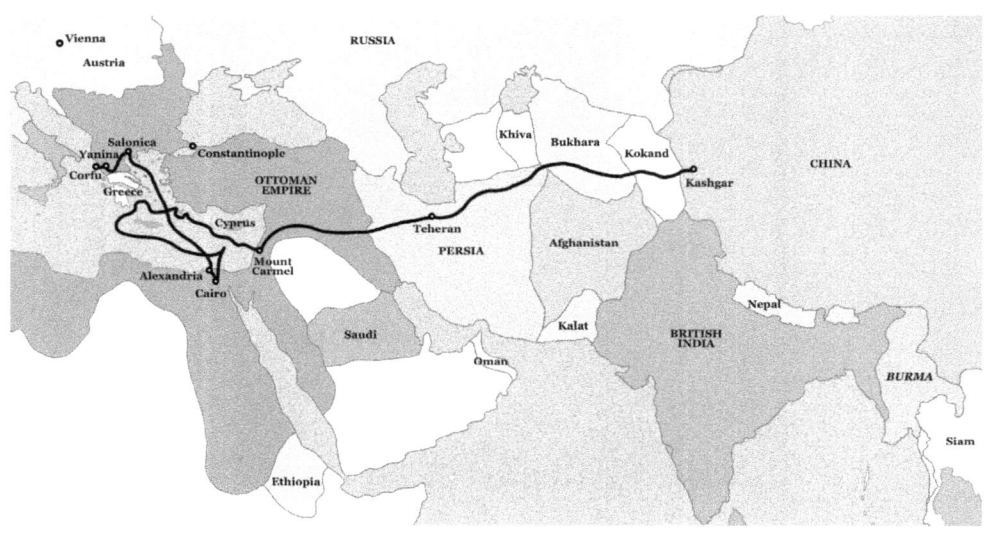

*Map showing the approximate route of Costentenus's journey, according to* The Life and Adventures of Captain Costentenus *(Drawn by the authors)*

The Life & Adventures of Capt. Costentenus,
The Tattooed Greek Prince
Written by Himself,[533]
And Translated from the Original Romaic[534]
By Professor Demetri of Athens.

———— • ————

For The Past Year One of The Leading Features of
Geo. B. Bunnell's Museum
Broadway Corner of Ninth St.
New York City.

———— • ————

New York Popular Pub Co. 32 Beekman St. New York.

•••

Handsomely Illustrated with Fine Engravings. Price Ten Cents.[535]

•••

Entered, according to Act of Congress in the year 1881, in the office
of the Librarian of Congress at Washington, D.C., by the New York
Popular Publishing Co.

•••

---

533 Costentenus was illiterate, so it's unknown who actually wrote this pamphlet. The New York Popular Publishing Company employed writers to produce such works on demand. Other publishing companies employed journalists and authors to turn out pamphlets and dime novels. Louisa May Alcott, for example, wrote around 30 dime novels under a pseudonym before the publication of *Little Women*. Costentenus's longtime employers, the Bunnell brothers, may have had a hand in the creation of his pamphlet. Even more likely, however, George O. Starr, the Bunnells' press agent at the time, may have been involved.

534 Romaic was a word commonly used in the 19th century to describe the language of the common people of Greece and Albania, which Lord Byron referred to as a dialect "as notoriously corrupt as the Scotch of Aberdeenshire," quoted in "Childe Harold's Pilgrimage," Canto the Second, 202 in *The Works of Lord Byron*, ed. Ernest H. Coleridge (Scribner's, 1899).

535 Equivalent to about three dollars in 2025, per Williamson, Measuring Worth.

# INTRODUCTORY.

Urged by the importunities of many thousands of people in all parts of the civilized globe, and in a spirit of gratitude to the great American people to whom I owe, under Providence, the preservation of my life and liberty from the oppressions of barbarian tyranny, I have consented, with much reluctance, to give to the world the particulars of my strange and most eventful life. I have hitherto refrained from the task, because I am aware that many of my adventures are so much out of the common course that they will be deemed incredible.

On this head I can only say that truth is frequently much stranger than fiction. The very fact of my now being alive and in good health is so extraordinary, that many eminent surgeons and doctors have refused to believe in the indelible nature of the patterns which cover my body from the very crown of my head—beneath the hair—to the tips of my fingers and toes, till convinced by ocular examination and the strictest tests of which science is capable.

Before my appearance settled the question it was asserted to be IMPOSSIBLE for any living man to survive the operation of tattooing when extended over the whole surface of the skin. The inflammation well known to accompany it is so severe, that its continuance for a period of three months[536] was deemed necessarily fatal to the most powerful constitution.

Yet the *facts remain*, and, as they exist in me, they are a living contradiction to all the doctors of Europe and America. I was tattooed in one operation, as is proven by the unity of the pattern which covers my body; and yet I live, as thousands—nay, millions—can witness, a hale man, without one square inch of my skin from which blood has not flowed under the torturing points of the tattooing-needles.

I am myself alone a living contradiction of all humanity. No

---

536 In reality, Costentenus's tattoos were likely done over a period of years. The healing process alone would have taken many months, and most people with similar coverage obtained their tattoos over several years. The style of the Captain's tattoos is remarkably consistent, indicating a long period of time with the same tattooist (or tattooists).

man ever suffered as I have suffered, and it need excite no wonder that no man ever had such a strange life as mine. With this brief explanation let me proceed to my task.

DJORDGI KONSTANTINUS.[537]

•••

# CHAPTER I.

### MY CHILDHOOD.

I WAS born in the Turkish province of Albania, in Turkey,[538] in the year 1836.[539] The village in which I first saw the light no longer exists even in name, save for the mouldering ruins of a few cottages, from which forty years' rains have removed the black smoke-stains which once told of the torch of the incendiary.

Marked almost from my birth for misfortune and vicissitude, my after life fulfilled the promise only too well.

Our little hamlet was the sole remnant of a once flourishing colony of Greek nobles and their dependents who had fled from Constantinople when it was taken by the Turks, under Mahomet II,

---

537 Even within his own pamphlet, Captain George used multiple versions of his own name. *Djordgi* and *Djorji* (used later on) are variants of the name George. His last name is twice spelled as *Konstantinus* (here and at the end) rather than Costentenus. His father's name is given as *Constantinus*. Spelling in the 19th century could be an adventure.

538 The Ottoman Empire was often referred to as Turkey. During the 19th century, there was considerable resentment by Westerners against the Ottoman Empire, which was seen as despotic and heathen—and the oppressor of nations like Albania and Greece.

539 The birth year that Costentenus gave on each of his passport documents was 1833, not 1836.

in 1455.[540] These resolute patriots had cut their way sword in hand out of the city at the time of its storming, and after a thousand perils, such as only Greeks could overcome, had settled in the wild fastnesses of the Pindus Mountains, overlooking the ancient plains of Pharsalia, where Caesar once defeated Pompey and won the empire of the world.[541]

In these remote recesses, then almost uninhabited, the Greeks had made themselves a home, where they reared their flocks in peace, introduced the culture of silk-worms, and trained up their children to love Greece and to hate their infidel invaders.

For three hundred years they lived and prospered, till the great Turkish and Russian wars[542] began to desolate the land. After that there was no more peace.

The Turks tried to press the young Greeks into their armies; the colonists resisted; and from that arose a series of border feuds, in which the wild Moslem Albanians tried to exterminate the peaceful Greek colonists, till every Greek became a warrior in self-defense.

It was under Ali Tebelen, the bloody Pasha of Yanina,[543] that

---

540 Constantinople actually fell in 1453, to the Ottoman Sultan Mehmed II after a 55-day siege.

541 In *The Pharsalia*, the Roman poet Lucan wrote of the civil war between Julius Caesar and Pompey the Great. Caesar won the decisive Battle of Pharsalus in 48 BCE.

542 The ongoing Russo-Ottoman wars flared up 12 times between 1568 and 1918. Many Greeks were conscripted into the Ottoman forces.

543 *Ali Pasha of Tepelena* was a real person, born around 1750 in Albania. His appearance as a villain in Costentenus's tale makes sense given Ali's bloodthirsty reputation in the West. But unfortunately for the story's credibility, Ali died in 1822, before Costentenus was even born. The British poet Lord Byron met Ali in 1809 in Tepelena, the southern Albanian town that Ali's family controlled. Byron's description of Ali was one of many which introduced this minor Ottoman despot to the Western world. Ali rose to prominence as the leader of a band of brigands. Through murder, threats, and military force, he expanded his wealth and power to become an important Ottoman governor (pasha), ruling over the Pashalik of Yanina (parts of Albania, Greece, and Macedonia). For many years, he fought to control the Souliotes, a group of Christian Albanians from whom Costentenus (sometimes) claimed to be descended. For a time, Ali was largely independent from the Ottomans. Eventually, the sultan sent troops to reign in Ali's unchecked power, and Ali was killed in the ensuing conflict.

the woes of my native village came to their culmination a few years after my birth. My family, as direct descendants of Constantine the Great,[544] had been considered the heads of our little band from time immemorial. From them had been chosen the successive chiefs of our tribe, and on my father devolved the defense of our village. His name was Constantine Constantinus, corrupted by the Turks into its present form, Costentenus.

My mother—alas! my poor mother had the misfortune to be too beautiful to escape the eye of the tyrannical Pasha of Yarina. One day, in an interval of peace, during which our people traded with the Turks, it happened that she took me—only four years old at the time—before her on a mule, in company with a train of our people, to sell the year's silk crop in the markets of Yanina. Our trade had been very successful, prices good, and our people were about to return home, well satisfied, when Ali Pasha, accompanied by a troop of his Dellies or Turkish cavalry,[545] rode through the marketplace, coming back from hunting.

He noticed the costume of our people, so different from that of his Turks, and halted in front of us, as it happened, close to my mother.

Child as I was, I can still see his long gray beard, fierce eyes, glittering dress, and the ferocious faces of the Dellies behind him. Of course, I cannot clearly remember his words, nor what followed, but I have heard the story too often from the remnants of our people not to know it now. Fixing his eyes on my mother, who already began to tremble, he asked:

"Who art thou, woman, with thy face unveiled? Art a Christian?"

---

544 *Constantine the Great* ruled the Roman Empire from 306 to 337 CE and founded the city of Constantinople. He was the first Roman emperor to convert to Christianity. Here, the story tries to inflate Costentenus further in the eyes of his readers, adding this claim of noble Roman and Christian ancestry to his claim of being a Greek prince.

545 A *Deli* was a type of Ottoman cavalry soldier. They were frontline fighters and acted as personal guards for high ranking Ottoman officials in the Balkans. The unit was established in the mid-15th century and abolished in 1829.

"Yes, my lord," answered she, mildly.

"Who are these people?" he went on.

"They are my friends and neighbors, my lord. We came hither to sell our silk."

Ali Pasha frowned as he answered:

"A curse on all Christian dogs! I know your rebellious horde. Ye are the followers of the robber chief, Costentenus. Whose child is that?"

He pointed to me as he spoke.

My mother, now pale as a corpse, could hardly muster strength to answer, as she clasped me closely in her arms:

"Mine, my lord."

The pasha smiled; and men used to say that the smile of Ali Tebelen was more dangerous than his frown.

"I knew that ere I asked. But who is its father?"

My mother was silent. She knew the absolute power of the cruel Ali and how he hated her husband, who so long defied the Turks.

One of our men who stood by, thinking to screen his chief's wife, said to the smiling pasha:

"This is only a poor widow of one of our men, killed by your highness' soldiers. She is not worth your notice. I have a daughter, my lord, if you will but deign to turn your eyes this way, much more fair to look at."

Ali Pasha deigned no reply, but continued to look at my mother.

"Whose child is that?" he asked again.

Still my mother was silent, looking at him like a tigress at bay.

One of the Dellies suddenly spoke to his chief:

"It is the robber's child, highness. The woman is Maryam Costentenus. I have seen her before."

Ali Pasha smiled in his most cruel way as he turned his face on poor Nicolon, who had tried to shield my mother, and demanded:

"Hast any more lies to tell thy lord, son of a Greek swine? Where is this daughter of whom thou told'st?"

Nicolon could make no answer, and the pasha, his face suddenly turning black as night, hissed out to his Dellies:

"Cut the dog to shreds!"

A moment later the terrible order was literally obeyed by the fierce Dellies with their razor-like sabers, as coolly and remorselessly as if they were slaughtering a sheep.

Our men—what few were present—were unarmed; my father

was away with his band, and there were none to resist the fierce pasha's will.

Nicolon having been hacked to pieces in the midst of a silent, staring crowd, the pasha observed:

"Take the thief's wife and the thief's son to my house. We will make a good Moslem of this young infidel. Drive the rest forth. I have spoken."

He coolly turned his horse's head and rode on while my poor mother and myself were seized and carried off.

Not without resistance, however. I can still remember my mother's frantic entreaties to the merciless Turks, her appeals to Heaven to save her, and my own outcries, frightened by her tears.

It was all in vain. That night found my mother and myself lodged in the luxurious harem[546] of Ali Pasha, surrounded by luxury, but *prisoners*.

Of course I was too young to fully understand what had taken place. I can dimly remember my mother, her pale, beautiful face bending over me, always in tears, all that day while I was awake. The next thing I remember was being suddenly aroused from my sleep to find myself snatched up by a burly negro slave in a room full of shrieking women of the harem; while Ali Pasha, his face pale, blood falling from his breast, stood supported by two more negroes, facing my mother, who curried in her hand a dagger, dripping with gore.

"Kill the accursed witch!" I heard the pasha say hoarsely. "She has stabbed me to death. Kill her!"

And then—I shall never forget it—my poor mother, who had never been to me aught but an angel of love, laughed aloud in the pasha's face.

"Kill me!" she cried. "Kill me! I am the wife of Constantine Costentenus, and you are a coward."

How it happened I know not, but there was a flash, then a report. My mother fell dead before my eyes, shot through the heart. For myself I knew no more. A tender child, not five years old, I must have fainted away in my terror.

When I next remember things clearly, I lay on a sick bed, tenderly nursed by the women of the harem, and it was not till years

---

546 The mystique of the harem loomed large in 19th century Western literature, as did the "evil" of Islam. The harem was viewed with considerable prurient interest by Western men, who not only saw it as a space for polygamy but for lesbianism.

afterward that I learned the real events that had taken place that night.

It seems our people had met my father outside Yanina, told him of his wife's abduction, and that he had tried, with only thirty desperate followers, to break into Ali Pasha's harem. He arrived just as my mother, in defense of her honor, stabbed Ali. The wicked pasha shouted for help, and was at once surrounded by the inmates of the harem and all his black guards. And then it was that my father, knowing that death in a more cruel form was certain for his faithful wife, shot her dead, engaged in a desperate contest with the overwhelming forces of Ali, and finally, after seeing all his men fall dead amid heaps of foes, defied the Turks with his last breath, and killed himself in the midst of Ali Pasha's harem.

So ended the hero Constantine; and I, poor little waif that I was, knew not that the murderers of my family had become my protectors. Even the stern heart of Ali Tebelen was accessible to remorse. He destroyed our village, drove our people out of Albania, but he brought me up as his adopted son, and I never knew the difference for many years after. How the knowledge came to me will be told in the next chapter.

•••

# CHAPTER II.

### MY BOYHOOD.

AS a child, after the memory of these terrible events had died away, I was as happy as a spoiled child could be. The women of the harem petted and indulged me to my heart's content, and I grew up in the enjoyment of every sort of luxury.

Even after the death of Ali Pasha,[547] which happened within a year of the time of our sad tragedy, I was no worse off; for his whole harem was transferred, by his will, to the care of his friend and fellow Albanian, Mehemet Ali, Viceroy of Egypt.[548]

---

547 Here, the narrative doesn't line up with historical events. Ali Pasha died in 1822, but the Captain's story puts his death around 1840.

548 *Mehemet (Muhammad) Ali*, also a real person, was born in 1769 in what is now Greece, though he was likely an ethnic Albanian. He rose through

I was too young then to realize what took place; but I remember the fun and excitement of the first sea voyage I ever made, when the pasha's household was transported from Salonica to Alexandria.

Ah, how often since that have I sailed the salt sea, and how I have learned to love the bounding billows! On the sea there is but one grade of nobility, and it is founded on courage and knowledge.

When we arrived in Egypt we were taken to Grand Cairo, where I passed my boyhood till the year 1848, under the protection of the great Viceroy Mehemet Ali. I was treated like a young prince, taught to read the Koran, to ride and handle arms like a true Mameluke,[549] and at the same time, like all Oriental[550] children, had the free run of the harem.

I was considered—and I say it without any vanity—a beautiful child. Indeed, the only fault found with me at this period by my male preceptors was the effeminacy of my appearance.

The women of the harem were fond of dressing me up like a girl and passing me off as such,[551] and many a funny escapade was I concerned in when the ladies of our harem paid visits to the families of the great officers of the state.

I was very tall of my age, and was always taken along by the

---

the ranks of the Ottoman military, arriving in Egypt in 1801 as second in command of a regiment of Albanian soldiers sent to fight the French. There, his rise continued. In 1805, he was named the Ottoman pasha and viceroy of Egypt and proceeded to brutally suppress any opposition to his rule. By 1831, Ali's position was strong enough for him to rebel against the Ottoman Sultan Mahmud II. Ali took control of Syria but was ultimately pushed back. While Egypt remained subject to Ottoman rule, Ali and his family were given hereditary rights to govern Egypt and the Sudan. His descendants would rule Egypt until 1952, and today, Muhammad Ali is thought of by many as the founder of modern Egypt.

549 The *Mamluks* (the name comes from the Arabic word for slave) began as armies of slaves who rose to rule Egypt and Syria from 1250 to 1517. Mehemet Ali killed the remaining Mamluk leaders in Egypt in 1811, but the Mamluks continued to be renowned fighters.

550 Now considered offensive, the term *Oriental* originally referred to the Near East, then came to include Central Asia, and eventually became a derogatory reference primarily to the Far East.

551 Perhaps this was inspired by Byron's *Don Juan*, where Juan is disguised as a woman by the sultana to sneak him into the harem.

Hanoum[552] Zuleika,[553] the old viceroy's favorite, as her waiting maid, for no one ever suspected but what I was a girl of sixteen.

Now the Hanoum (Princess) Zuleika was, like myself, a Greek, and a very beautiful woman besides. She ruled the old viceroy (Mehemet Ali was eighty) with absolute power, and he adored her.

When she called me in, dressed as a girl, and introduced me to the old pasha as her new slave, Fatima,[554] I was frightened to death, for I feared the old man would see through the trick. But Zuleika knew his dim vision better than I, and the viceroy made no remark. From thenceforth it became the fashion in the harem to pretend I was a girl and call me Fatima at all times.

Being a boy and fond of manly exercise I rebelled stoutly against this, but was pacified by my mistress with many caresses and the promise that I should know in time what it all meant.

At last it came out in an unexpected fashion. Mehemet Ali, in August, 1848, sustained a paralytic stroke from which he died in the following year, but was immediately succeeded by his eldest son, Ibrahim Pasha, who became viceroy.[555]

The first act of the new viceroy was to choose but the Princess Zuleika, who was still a slave like myself, and make of her a present to the sultan at Constantinople, in honor of his coming to the throne.

The custom of giving presents to the sultan is universal in the

---

552 A female honorific, sometimes meaning princess.

553 The name *Zuleika* was likely drawn from Byron's poem *The Bride of Abydos*, the second of his Turkish tales, which tells the story of Selim and his love for his cousin Zuleika. Though published in 1813, this was still a popular work of romantic literature near the end of the century. Many readers of Costentenus's story would have known the name from the poem and understood her to be a beautiful woman from the East. Byron likely chose the name from the medieval Islamic story of the prophet Yusuf and the woman—Zuleika—who tried to seduce him. Byron's travels through Greece and Turkey had inspired the writing of *Childe Harold's Pilgrimage* and *The Bride of Abydos*. For more information, please see Fiona MacCarthy's *Byron: Life and Legend*, Farrar, Straus and Giroux, 2002.

554 Fatima is a common name in the Muslim world. The Islamic prophet Muhammad's daughter Fatima is often seen as a model of compassion and generosity.

555 The real Mehemet Ali did actually retire from his post in 1848 due to senility, and his son Ibrahim Ali, or Ibrahim Pasha, was appointed viceroy of Egypt. But Ibrahim died only 40 days later. Mehemet Ali himself died the following year.

East, and Ibrahim Pasha wished to make his seat sure in the disturbed state of Europe; for it was then in the heat of the German, French, Italian and Hungarian revolutions,[556] and the sultan wanted to get back Egypt into his own hands.

Zuleika was allowed the privilege of taking with her two slaves of her own choice. She chose me (under the name of Fatima) and a black mute.[557] The new pasha did not care to enter the harem to see for himself, and thus it came to pass that in September, 1848, I found myself, under the name of Fatima Costentenus, apparently unsexed, in company with my mistress and the black slave, Saad, on board a brig[558] bound for Constantinople.

It was not till we were out of sight of land that I learned the reason of all these strange mysteries. It was then that my mistress, we being alone in the cabin, suddenly spoke.

"Ali, do you know who you are and who I am?"

I must remark here that I had been called Ali in the harem, and did not know anything of my parents, save that I was always told I was the son of Ali Pasha. The events of my mother's death had been concealed from me, and if I spoke of them the women told me I was dreaming.

Now, however, the sudden address of Princess Zuleika excited me strangely. I began to tremble and said:

"Indeed, madam, I wish I did."

"Do not call me madam," she replied looking at me in a strange, yearning way. "Ah, my sweet boy, what a history is ours!"

I was still more disturbed.

---

556 Europe saw a wave of revolutions in 1848 and 1849. Though short-lived, they did introduce democratic and liberal reforms.

557 *Mute* was commonly used to mean deaf in the 19th century. Deaf people were often used as servants/slaves in the Ottoman court because they were unable to overhear what was discussed around them and could not pass on information or gossip. They developed a system of signing so the sultans could communicate with these servants. This system was so sophisticated and popular, it came to be used by hearing people as well. Travelers to the Ottoman Empire wrote about these deaf servants and their sign language in various accounts. For more information, please see M. Miles's "Signing in the Seraglio: Mutes, Dwarfs and Jestures at the Ottoman Court 1500 - 1700" currently on the website of the Independent Living Institute: https://www.independentliving.org/docs5/mmiles2.html (accessed 2-6-2025), originally published in *Disability & Society*, Volume 15, Issue 1 (2000).

558 A two-masted, square-rigged ship.

"For Allah's sake," I stammered, "tell me what you mean, in Mahomet's name."

She beckoned me to her side, put her arms round my neck and kissed me. Then she whispered, in a low tone:

"Ali, we are both Christians. You are Djorji (George) Costentenus, son of the King of the Mountains, and I am your cousin Aspasia.[559] Don't start or cry out. We may be watched. Listen. Do you remember your mother?"

I trembled more than before, and began to cry. Remember, I was but a boy, brought up among women.

"Yes," I whispered.

Then I told her all I remembered; for I had brooded over those faint traces of the past many a night when they thought me asleep. She listened to me attentively and then replied:

"Your mother was my father's sister. I was ten years old when Ali Pasha killed all of our people he could catch, and carried off the young girls to his harem. We are both orphans and I am your cousin. My real name is Aspasia, but these wicked Turks called me Zuleika. I have planned our escape for years, Djorji, and the time has come at last. To induce Ibrahim Pasha to send me to the sultan I told him some of his father's state secrets, and I have intrigued with the English minister, Lord Stratford de Redcliffe,[560] to interfere on the way and claim us as British subjects.

"How?" I interrupted. "We are Greeks, not English. What do you mean?"

Aspasia (as I must now call her) smiled as she answered:

_____

559 *Aspasia* is a name plucked from ancient Greek history. The actual Aspasia was a philosopher and contemporary of Socrates and Plato, romantically attached to the renowned Athenian politician Pericles. Several 19th century authors used Aspasia and Pericles as characters in romantic novels and poems such as *Philothea* (1835) by American abolitionist and novelist Lydia Child, *Pericles and Aspasia* (1836) by British poet Walter Savage Landor, and *Aspasia* (1876) by novelist Robert Hamerling. The latter was published just five years before Costentenus's narrative. The name conjured beauty and sensitivity as well as intelligence, and would have been recognized by many readers.

560 Stratford Canning, 1st Viscount *Stratford de Redcliffe*, was a British diplomat to the Ottomans in several capacities between 1810 and 1858. Canning, like many of the individuals inserted into this narrative, was also involved in the Greek Revolution and advocated for the Greek cause with the Ottoman sultan.

"We were both born in the Island of Corfu, under the British flag.[561] I have done many favors for Lord Redcliffe with the viceroy, and he has promised to send a British frigate[562] to intercept and search this vessel before we reach Constantinople. Then we must both claim the protection of the captain."

"But why did you dress me up as a girl!" I asked; "and what are we to do when the captain takes us away?"

"If I had not prepared for this by making people believe you a girl, I could never have carried you off with me. As for what we are to do, I have provided for that also."

She looked around apprehensively, went to the door to be sure there were none to listen, and then showed me something which fairly astounded me, used as I was to the sight of jewels.

Wound round her waist, inside all her garments, were strings of diamonds, rubies, emeralds and other precious stones that fairly dazzled my eyes.

Some I had seen before. They were the state jewels of the viceroy. Young as I was, I understood our danger.

"Did you steal these?" I whispered.

She nodded triumphantly.

"Trust a Greek woman to outwit a Turk. Ibrahim Pasha will not find out till to-morrow."

"And then?" I faltered.

"Then we shall be out of his reach. The English frigate *Leopard*[563] will meet us at Cyprus."

Almost as she spoke these words, the deep sullen doom of a distant gun came rolling over the sea. The sound reached us through the open stern windows of the brig, and made Aspasia start. It was very faint and far off, but it came so suddenly in the midst of her words that it sounded like an omen of evil.

My cousin turned pale, and both of us hurried to the cabin

---

561 Corfu and the other Ionian Islands had been controlled by Venice for centuries, keeping them from Ottoman rule. After the Napoleonic Wars, they were controlled by the British until they were ceded back to Greece in 1862. Here, the narrative is further elevating young Djorji to Western readers of the time: he was not only a Greek prince and descendant of Constantine the Great, he was also a Christian and a British subject.

562 A warship.

563 There actually was a British first class frigate called *HMS Leopard* which was launched in 1850 and sailed the Mediterranean until 1854.

windows to look out.

Nothing was to be seen but the wide tossing waves of the sparkling Mediterranean.

The low, sandy shores of Egypt had been out of sight for several hours, and the only sails visible were those of a few humble Levant[564] traders, standing toward Alexandria.

We listened intently, and presently the distant boom was repeated. In our inexperience we could not locate it, but our fears told us that it must come from Egypt. Had I been a sailor then, as I was afterward, I should have interpreted it as we then interpreted it.

The gun was an alarm signal.

Aspasia knew it, for she whispered:

"They have found it out. They will chase us. What shall we do?"

I know not how it was, but the moment my cousin showed fear my own spirits rose.

"Do?" I answered. "I will fight for you. I will be a girl no longer."

•••

# CHAPTER III.

## THE CHASE.

ASPASIA looked at me with a new expression. She, who had been the leader and protector up to that time, had become the helpless one. She looked up to me in admiration, and whispered:

"Oh, Ali, how brave you are! But what can a boy like you do?"

"I will show you when the time comes," I answered, proudly. "I have my sword hid away, and a pistol, too. We are on the seas, and we can fight. Tell me of my father, Aspasia. What would he have done in such a strait?"

She seemed to be much pleased at my spirit—I was only a boy, but I verily believe that the soul of my brave father entered into me at that moment—and she readily consented.

Then it was that I learned for the first time, from the lips of my

___
564 *The Levant*, most broadly, referred to the lands of the Eastern Mediterranean.

beautiful cousin Aspasia, all the particulars of my family and my early life which I have set down above. We talked and talked away in the cabin of the brig till the sun began to near the horizon. And still I kept asking for more, more.

At last came a knock at the door; Aspasia, with the instinct of the harem, hastily veiled herself, and signed me to do the same.

Our black mute, Saad, entered the room, with our afternoon meal on a salver, and set it down on the cabin table. I noticed that the slave looked excited and uneasy, and that he frequently glanced through the stern windows while he was laying the table.

Involuntarily my eyes followed his, when I noticed, out on the horizon, a black line of smoke that streamed away like a pennant.

In my ignorance of the sea I did not understand the meaning of this smoke, and asked my cousin what it was.

She had been sitting in a thoughtful attitude, and my question made her start and look out. No sooner did she see the smoke than she turned deadly pale, and murmured, in a low tone:

"It is a steamer.[565] We are lost."

Saad looked quickly up, and nodded his head, with a grave face. I hastily asked Aspasia:

"Does he know?"

"Yes," she whispered; "he hid the jewels."

"And you think they are coming after us, Aspasia?"

"I am sure of it."

"Very well, then," said I," we must confide in the captain and try to escape. See, it is almost sunset now. We can get away in the dark."

Aspasia nodded.

"It is our only hope. Let us send for the captain. I will receive him. Let me do the talking."

Saad was dispatched to summon the captain, which he did by signs; and the sailor soon made his bow to us in the cabin.

We were both closely veiled, of course; and the captain, a big, swarthy Italian from Naples, imagined that we were great ladies of the court going to Constantinople; for Aspasia told me she had taken my passage as a sultana, though to the Egyptians I was only a slave.

Therefore, the captain was full of obsequious politeness, and Aspasia found him a willing tool. The present of a jeweled ring made

---

565 A *steamer* or *steamship* used a steam engine to power a propeller or paddlewheel. Being able to move independent of the wind, steamers helped drive a huge increase in global trade in the late 1800s.

him ready to promise anything, and when she told him that she wanted to escape from the steamer that could be seen on the horizon, he told her that was easy enough.

Night was at hand and he would answer for the steamer in the dark.

To quiet any suspicions he might have had as to the jewels, my cousin told him a part of the truth in other respects. He was a bigoted Christian. She told him we were escaping from the infidels. He was avaricious. She promised him a jewel worth a thousand English pounds as soon as she met the English frigate Leopard.

Finally he swore by all the saints he would be true to us, and went on deck, where he crowded on every inch of canvas possible, till the swift vessel seemed fairly to leap out of the water.

As for me, I soon became too full of excitement to stay in the cabin. The advancing shades of evening and the altered course of the vessel had taken the column of smoke out of our sight, and I easily persuaded Aspasia to go on deck, where our vision would be unimpaired.

When we reached the open air I looked around with surprise and pleasure. It was my first sight since early childhood of a ship in full sail, and nothing in nature is more lovely.

The white canvas bellying out, the wind whistling through the cordage, the heavy motion of the brig as she rode over the little waves, the silent stars overhead, and the musical wash of the sea on the cut-water, all formed a picture pleasant to eye and ear.

I looked around for the smoke of the steamer. There in the west still lingered the crimson and purple flush of sunset, though the short twilight was almost over, and across the purple we could see the black smoke, now in a thick cloud, while the outlines of the steamer herself were plainly discernible.

But even I, ignorant as I was, could see that she was not heading toward us, and involuntarily I asked the captain, who stood near us:

"Where is she going?"

The Italian laughed as he told us that he had altered his course soon after the sun set, and that the steamer was pursuing a phantom now.

"She is after another vessel bound for Cyprus," he pursued, "and before it is midnight we shall be safe."

And it turned out to be as he had told us, for when morning dawned we seemed to be alone on the sea, save for the ordinary run of small craft that ply the Mediterranean in different directions.

But alas! little did we know the trap into which we had fallen. Better had the Egyptian steamer caught us than to suffer what we afterward did.

For three days and nights we sailed along over the tranquil sea. The captain was obsequiously polite as ever; but we noticed, after the first day, that he became inquisitive about our habits and paid us frequent visits in the cabin, under pretext of inquiring after our comforts.

It was on the third day that he at last threw off the mask and revealed himself as he was.

We were in sight of some low islands, which I now know must have been in the Greek archipelago. Saad, who had been growing very sullen of late, had taken away our breakfast, when there came a rap at the door, and in walked Captain Gianetti.

Without asking pardon he took a seat, looked at us fixedly, and said:

"I have found you out at last. Which is the boy? Take off your veils."

Aspasia rose indignantly.

"What do you mean?" she said. "Leave the cabin."

He laughed hoarsely.

"You wish to keep your little lover to yourself, I see. Bah, I am worth a hundred boys. I am a man."

As he said this, he leered horribly at my beautiful cousin, who retreated to my side.

The brute laughed again.

"Ah, I see which is the boy now. I have found it all out, and I am going to have my share of those jewels. Come, don't be shy. I won't give you up to the Turks, but you shall come to Italy with me, and I'll make a lady of you. I won't hurt the boy, either."

He rose as he spoke, and we could see that he was somewhat drunk. He made a snatch at Aspasia and tore off her veil.

My blood rose to fever heat of a sudden.

As I had told Aspasia, I had weapons hidden away, and one of these was a dagger.

In a moment I had flown at the gigantic Italian, and was stabbing fiercely at him with my puny strength.

He uttered a snarl of rage, turned on me with his vast power, and, in a trice, had me by the throat.

"Little viper!" he roared, savagely," I will cut your heart out for this."

And, as he spoke, he wrenched away my little dagger with one grip of his brawny hand, as he shook me violently.

I thought my last hour had come, when loud voices came down the cabin hatch.

•••

# CHAPTER IV.

## THE PIRATES.

THE shouting on deck became louder, and Captain Gianetti wavered a little.

I was nearly strangled by his fierce grip, though I struggled hard. Strange to say, once engaged in the fight, I felt no sort of fear, though I had trembled much before it. This peculiarity has clung to me through life.

He hated to release me, for I had sent the knife deep into his arm, but we could hear the men shouting:

"Capitano! Capitano! Gli Pirati! Gli Pirati!" (Pirates!)

That terrible cry brought even the wild Gianetti to his senses, for he knew where we were.

He shook and threw me off, growling:

"I'll pay you for this yet."

Then he rushed up on deck, where we heard him giving orders while the men ran hurriedly about.

As for me, no sooner had he gone than I deliberately stripped off my woman's garments, and said to my frightened cousin Aspasia.

"I will be a man henceforth and fight. Don't try to stop me."

She did not, poor girl. She wept over and kissed me heartily, but none the less she helped me to assume the proper garments of my sex, and to put on my little cimeter[566] and pistol.

In the meantime the noise on deck increased, and presently black Saad came running down the stairs, his face blue with terror,

---

566 Alternative spelling of *scimitar*, which is a curved sword with origins in Persia.

and hid himself under one of the berths in the cabin.

I was disgusted with the treason of this scoundrel, who had evidently told our secret to Gianetti, but that was no time for recrimination. I knew the danger must be imminent, so I hastily told Aspasia to hide herself while I ran up on deck.

Then I saw the cause of Saad's terror.

The ship, under all sail, was yet hardly moving through the water on account of the faint breeze, while four large row-boats, full of black haired Greeks, in their picturesque velvet jackets, white kilts and scarlet sashes, bristling with weapons, came pulling up to us astern and on either side.

The Italian captain and all his men had fallen on their knees and were praying fervently, but doing nothing till I came on deck, while the Greeks were coming closer.

I must have looked quite a striking figure as I came on deck in my rich Turkish dress, for I seemed to give courage to the trembling cowards.

"Up and fight," I cried, in my shrill boy's voice. "I will lead you, for I am the son of Costentenus, the Palikar.[567] Get your pistols and shoot these pirates."

The name of Costentenus rallied them, for my father had been renowned in the Levant. They began to get up, and one called out:

"We have only two muskets and our knives, signor. We can do nothing."

"Shame," I answered boldly. "You are twenty men here. Stab them as they climb up. Knock them on the head. I will show you how to do it."

I ran to the quarter-deck, took careful aim with my long Turkish pistol, and fired into the foremost boat.

To my great delight one of the pirates fell back, and I shouted aloud in triumph, while the Italians took courage and brought out their two muskets. The only real coward on board seemed to be the big captain, who kept on saying his prayers.

But my little triumph was of but short duration. The pirates took no notice of our feeble fire, but rowed grimly on, and presently were alongside.

Then our men lost their courage, though I stormed, entreated,

---

567 A *Palikar* was either a soldier in the Greek War of Independence (1821-1828) against the Ottomans or, subsequently, a Greek or Albanian soldier serving the sultan.

wept for rage. They made a sort of half effort to repel one assault, but in another moment three boats had hooked on, and the Italians had huddled into a frightened mass on the forecastle,[568] while I, surrounded by ferocious pirates, was cutting and slashing away, as they told me afterward, like a fiend incarnate, all alone.

Of course there was but one issue to such a contest. Boy that I was, I killed two pirates and wounded another, when the blow of a pistolbutt from behind stretched me on the deck and I knew no more.

How long I lay insensible I cannot now tell but I awoke at last as from a deep sleep, with a dull pain in my head, which made me try to put up my hands to it.

To my surprise I could not move them; they were fastened down in front of me, and I felt that thin cords were cutting my wrists and ankles. I was bound hand and foot, and lying on my back on hard planks.

I looked around, but could see nothing. All was pitch dark.

I listened and could hear, close to my head the washing of waves, while the creaking and groaning of timbers all around told me that I was still at sea and in the bottom of some vessel.

I was learning quickly, you see, for a boy brought up in a harem.

With nothing to do but to lie and listen, I soon found out where I was.

Every now and then the heavy steps of men sounded overhead, and I could occasionally hear the muffled sound of voices.

I began to remember, dimly, the events of the day, and, as I tried to think, my head got confused again, and I seemed to doze off. I suppose I really must have fainted again.

I awoke a second time with a blaze of sunlight right in my eyes, while two men were laying me down on the deck of some strange vessel, and a crowd of wild-looking Greek sailors, knives in their sashes, were staring at me not unkindly.

Overhead swelled two huge sails of triangular shape, striped red and yellow, and the rocking sway of the vessel showed that there was a good breeze on.

I was only half sensible of all this when I heard some one say:

"He will live. It were a pity he should not, for he's worth a good ten thousand piasters."[569]

---

568 The forward part of a ship, containing the living quarters.

569 Used here as a generic term for currencies of the time.

The language spoken was Greek or Romaic, with which, of course, I was familiar, as well as with Turkish and Arabic, while Italian is too commonly spoken in Egypt not to be understood by all. Since my childhood I have added Spanish, French, Tartar, Russian and Chinese to my stock of tongues, with all of which I am fully conversant.[570]

My bearers laid me down in the shadow of a huge sail, and then a tall, handsome man, who seemed to be a chief among the pirates, came and looked at me. He did not seem unkindly disposed, for he smiled at me as I looked up and said:

"Well, little tiger-cat, how do you like having your claws cut?"

I made no answer at first, but stared at him in amazement.

He continued looking down, with a smile curling his black mustache.

"If I did right I should flay you alive for the men you killed, but your fair sister has pleaded for your life."

Vaguely I remembered what had passed, and my first whisper was:

"Aspasia!"

The pirate laughed, as he said:

"Aspasia is happy with her Perikles.[571] I am Captain Perikles, you know, and your sister is to be the queen of the *Egean*. What say you, little man—will you be killed or will you join us? You have mettle in you and would make a good rover."

Still I could only whisper:

"Aspasia!"

The pirate chief nodded to one of his men, who disappeared.

A moment later my own sweet Aspasia was bending over me in tears, kissing my pale face, and calling me her darling brother, while in the interval between her sobs she whispered softly to me:

---

570 What languages was Costentenus really able to speak? In Vienna in 1870, the academics noted that he spoke "his mother language (Greek), albeit incorrectly, also French, Italian and English, some words of German, however he is very familiar with Arabic and Persian." Chinese was perhaps added because they were in Eastern China? "Der Tätowirte von Birma," *Wiener Medizinische Wochenschrift*. Nr. 2, 1872., p. 40.

571 *Perikles* is a clear reference to the historical Aspasia's romantic partner, also spelled Pericles. The real Pericles was an orator and statesman from Athens, whom Thucydides, one of Pericles's contemporaries, called "the first citizen of Athens." In keeping with history, sort of, the pirate Captain Perikles of Costentenus's narrative will fall in love with Aspasia.

"Consent. I will show you how to escape. The captain will do anything for me."

Indeed, Captain Perikles seemed to be entirely infatuated with my lovely cousin, for he maintained the most rigid politeness among his men, and behaved to Aspasia as if she had been his queen and he her willing subject.

The moment I saw her again I seemed to revive at once, and it was with a clear voice that I now said to the pirate captain:

"I will join your band if you will let me and my sister see each other often."

"You shall be with her always, and teach her to love me," he answered.

So the contract was closed.

•••

# CHAPTER V.

### THE PIRATES' DEN.

SO there I was, a boy of twelve, in full fellowship, whether I would or no, with a band of the most ruthless pirates that ever roamed the seas.

Not that they were a bad-looking lot of men. Oh, no! Their manners were of the most polite description to each other, and no one ever dreamed of calling his neighbor a liar.

Had he done so, the answer would have been a stab in an instant. But there were no loud words heard aboard the pirate felucca,[572] which, by the way, was called the Athene.

If a quarrel took place between the men, it was over in a moment, and the unlucky person that got the worst of it was quietly dumped into the sea, while the survivor was expected by his comrades to wash down the deck in the vicinity, and remove all the stains of blood found.

But none of the men ever troubled me. In fact, as the youngest on board, I soon became a pet of the crew and did about as I pleased.

---

572 A traditional wooden sailing boat with a single sail used in the Mediterranean.

Captain Perikles was especially kind to me, in order, as I soon found, to ingratiate himself with Aspasia, who had saved my life by proclaiming me as her brother.

I soon had reason to admire more than ever the singular power which my beautiful cousin exercised over these wild sea-rovers.

Using as a talisman the name of my illustrious father, whom I found to have been famous all over the Levant, she kept Captain Perikles at a distance by promising to marry him in a year's time, if he would do as she wished meanwhile.

Before we joined the pirates, they had been in the habit of robbing peaceful traders of all nations, but Aspasia raised and ennobled their calling by inducing them to confine their warfare to the Turks alone, the old enemies of our race.

The mode of life of these Greek rovers in those days was sufficiently wild and romantic. They were not always at sea, but lived on the little islands of the Archipelago, from whence they sallied forth on their expeditions in a number of small vessels rather than in any one bark[573] of a size to be recognized elsewhere.

In those times there were few steamers in use, and gunboats of light draught were needed to follow up these bold rovers. The Turks had none such, and the consequence was that the Greek pirates of those times made the Levant a dangerous place, till the English and French navies took up the task of suppression in 1849.[574]

It was in the course of that year that I succeeded in making my escape from this robber's den in the following manner:

We had had a very successful year, during which the band of Captain Perikles had destroyed so many vessels that our spoils were immense. It was under this state of things that the pirate chief

---

573 A ship with three or more masts, mostly square-rigged.

574 This may be a reference to the Epirus Revolt of 1854. In the midst of the Crimean War between the Russians and the Ottomans (1853-1856), peasants in Epirus rebelled against their local Ottoman government. The British and French, who were on the Ottoman side of the war, captured a ship of rebels and determined that they were actually pirates. After turning the captives over to the Greek government, the Greeks decided that they were patriots instead of pirates and set them free. This led to the British and the French becoming involved in suppression of Greek pirates/patriots in an effort to protect their commercial trade with the Ottomans in the Mediterranean. For more information on this, please see Leonidas Mylonakis, "Transnational Piracy in the Eastern Mediterranean, 1821-1897," PhD dissertation (University of California San Diego, 2018): 103-109.

proposed to his men to break up the band, divide the spoils, and go to some other country to enjoy our wealth.

Aspasia, to induce him to do this, had promised to marry him as soon as he quit the sea; and he, madly in love with her, consented willingly.

The men were not loth to get a chance of dissipation on shore, but knew that it was necessary to lose themselves in some way before they could hope to escape detection in any large city.

It was finally determined to do the boldest thing imaginable— to sail for Constantinople itself, and by going in small parties in different vessels to elude the efforts of the clumsy Turkish police.

When this plan was arranged, Aspasia came to me one day when we were ashore. I had got into the habit of wandering away from the rest of the pirates in our retreat to sit fishing on a rock in a cove of sight of our main body, and Aspasia had so often followed me there that our absence was not noticed.

This day her beautiful face wore an expression of great anxiety, and we were no sooner alone than she said to me, hurriedly:

"Djorji, we must do it to-night."

"Do what?" I asked

"Escape. Perikles will wait no longer. The year is up to-morrow."

I felt a singular thrill of anger at her words. That year had turned me from a boy into a young man in the fierce climate of the south.

"Perikles shall never have you," I answered, grinding my teeth. "I will kill him first. I can shoot better than he."

This was true. I had taken great pains to perfect myself in shooting, knowing that I was not strong enough to fight men single-handed with knives.

I had managed to hide away a fine pair of double-barrelled pistols, stolen from a French yacht we had surprised one night, and I knew where to find them.

Aspasia looked at me with pride, for we had long since owned that we dearly loved each other.[575]

---

575 This love affair would not have scandalized readers of the day. Cousin marriage, including first-cousin marriage, was common when this narrative was written. Communities were small and isolated, and your choices for a partner were often relatives. Conventional wisdom over the past century has said that, as Americans began to spread out over the frontier during the middle part of the 19th century, cousin marriage became less common. Newer studies in genealogy reveal that this increase in genetic diversity

"My Djorji is braver and handsomer than a hundred Perikles." she said; "but we can do better by escaping than by killing him. If you shoot him they will shoot you."

"What do you propose then?" I asked.

"I propose," she said, "to wait till it is dark. The men are to have a grand carouse to-night, and have collected all their boats to scatter in the morning. Captain Perikles has told me that I must go in his boat, and that Father Basil, the degraded priest[576] who joined us last month, is to marry us before we start. I will never marry Perikles, Djorji; I will never marry any but you, my darling little lover."

You may judge what was my answer. I kissed Aspasia a hundred times, and we swore to be true to each other till death—a vow she kept, poor girl.

We laid our plans for the night, and separated so as to divert any kind of suspicion. That evening, as Aspasia had said, the pirates held a grand parting carouse in our place of assembly. We had learned that the English and French men-of-war had been ordered to our coasts to put down piracy, and we well knew that our organization could not long stand a serious attack.

Therefore we had gathered all the gold, jewels and silks that we had accumulated into a common stock, which was to be divided equally among the pirates, after which we were to take our boats and feluccas, all in the guise of simple fishermen and scatter every man where he wished, all to come together within three months in the Greek quarter of the City of Constantinople.

There Perikles proposed to set up another band of footpads and robbers, to knock down rich Turks at night and take their money.

I had heard of all these plans, and it was to overturn this villainy that I made up my mind.

Our meeting-place was to be in a deep, winding cave, the mouth

_____

didn't start to happen until the mid-1870s, indicating that social norms took longer to change than geographic mobility. In the United States, many states have outlawed cousin marriage, as communities grew to understand the genetic risks of close family members having children together. For more information, please see Martin Ottenheimer's *Forbidden Relatives: The American Myth of Cousin Marriage*, University of Illinois Press, 1996.

576 Father Basil is likely a generic anti-Catholic character. Anti-Catholicism waxed and waned throughout the nation's history, and by the middle of the 19th century, large numbers of Catholic immigrants from Ireland and Eastern Europe brought back a rise in anti-Catholicism.

of which came down to the sea at low tide. At high tide it was quite invisible, the water covering it.

Inside this cave the ground rose up so that there was a room nearly three hundred feet square at the end, secure from the sea in the wildest storms.

On this night all our people had gathered there, and the boats were moored in a line at the mouth, for the tide was still falling.

There the pirates met—a wild cut-throat crew—all dressed up in the spoils of their victims, while heaps of costly silks and velvets lay on the white sands, as being too cumbersome to carry away. Nothing but the clothes on their backs, gold, and jewels were to be removed.

But in the end of this cave stood a row of black casks, from which every one kept at a very respectful distance.

It was the powder magazine, and it was in that magazine Aspasia and I founded our hopes of escape.

The night came, bright and moonlit, and the revels began. All the pirates had assembled in honor of their chief's bridal, for Aspasia's year of waiting was over, and she had promised to marry him at last.

Father Basil, a priest who had been expelled from Italy for immoral practices, had lately joined the band, and had offered to perform the ceremony, and all the pirates were drinking healths to the bridal pair.

I, boy that I seemed, was held in honor that day, as the brother of the bride, the more so that I had killed a pirate in the afternoon for speaking disrespectfully of my sister, as they thought Aspasia.

To kill a man was a sure title to the love of these pirates.

They voted me a man at once. I showed it that night.

The time had come for Father Basil to perform the ceremony, and all the men were very drunk, when, on a sudden, I stood up in the midst of the crowd, and announced that I was going to make a speech.

They all began to cheer and laugh, and I made a long complimentary address to Captain Perikles, under cover of which Aspasia silently slipped off down the cave to the water's edge and got ready for our boat.

Unknown to anyone, I had secretly laid a train of powder from the magazine along the side of the cave to the water's edge, and thence up a cord, soaked in pitch and covered with powder, to the open air outside the cave.

I listened during my speech for the signal which Aspasia had promised to give me when she was ready, and just as I was turning an extravagant compliment to Captain Perikles I heard her give the rap on the gunwale[577] of the boat on which we had agreed.

Then I suddenly changed my tone, and said to the pirates:

"Such is your chief, but I am more than he, for I am Costentenus, the Palikar. Perikles has striven to dishonor my race by a mock marriage with Aspasia, and thus I avenge the insult."

As I spoke, I drew my pistol and shot the pirate chief stone dead, then turned, and ran down to the water.

For a moment the drunken robbers were too much amazed to follow; then with a howl of fury they began to fire their pistols after me.

But ere a bullet whistled close enough to endanger our safety, I was at the water's edge, and had leaped into the boat.

*Illustration from* The Life and Adventures of Captain Costentenus: *Costentenus kills Perikles, with Aspasia ready in their boat, (Thr 1229.2.10\*, Houghton Library, Harvard University)*

•••

---

577 The top edge of the side of the boat.

# CHAPTER VI.

## THE EXPLOSION.

ASPASIA was already in the boat, with the oars in the rowlocks, and two or three strokes swept us out of the sight of the pirates behind the felucca, which lay at anchor outside the boats.

We heard them cursing and swearing as they examined boat after boat, but found every one full of water, with a plank started in the bottom.

I knew that if they once got the felucca out they would show us no mercy, and it was only as the last resort that I had contemplated the necessity of blowing up the cave. It soon came.

Shouting out imprecations on my head, they dashed into the sea, swam to the felucca, climbed up her sides, and opened a vicious fire at us in the boat.

My answer was to fire my own pistol close to a cord that hung over the felucca's side, after which I plied my oars as fast as I could to get away.

The effect of my shot was all that I could have desired. The cord, soaked in pitch and covered with powder, blazed up in a moment, and the flame went leaping over the felucca's deck.[578]

The pirates knew what it was in a moment, and forbore to fire at me. With yells of terror they dived overboard, while the lighted train burned on, the flame darting over the water to the side of the cave, while I rowed desperately on out to sea.

I had calculated on a minute, and I had a minute and a half.

Aspasia labored with me, and we were more than a hundred yards from shore when up shot a vast column of red flame, followed by

---

578 This is reminiscent of a fireship, which was a popular weapon revived during the Greek War of Independence (1821-1832). To combat the superior Turkish navy, the Greeks would load a ship with powder and explosives. A trough on the deck would be filled with combustible material, like pitch and oil. The fireship would then be rammed into or affixed to the enemy vessel. At the last possible moment, the captain and crew would light the trough and jump overboard as the ship exploded in flames. Fireships proved crucial in Greek naval victories, notably in the destruction of the Ottoman flagship in 1822, which killed about 2,000 sailors and the admiral of the Ottoman navy.

a terrible concussion, which felled us both senseless into the bottom of our boat in the midst of a thick pall of black smoke.

For my own part, I think I must have lain there for about ten minutes. When I came to myself the moon was shining down on a tranquil sea amid an awful silence.

My head hurt me, and I felt something warm trickling down my neck.

It was blood from a cut on the temple, received I know not how.

Then I looked into the stern sheets of the boat and there lay Aspasia, her face pale and calm as if she were dead. For a moment I thought her so till she stirred and moaned.

Then I caught her up in my arms and kissed her back to life, for she was only stunned, after all. At last we looked around us again.

We were alone on the sea, floating on the ebb tide further away every moment from the pirates' island, amid a chaos of floating spars and fragments of wreck.

Where the rocky point had been, under which was our cave, now was nothing but a yawning pit, like the crater of a volcano, surrounded by a fringe of rocks and splintered stumps of trees, blackened and twisted.

But we were alone at last. Not a pirate had survived, and we were free to go where we would.

"At last," said Aspasia, with a sigh of relief—"at last we are together, my Djorji, with none to part us."

And we were indeed.

Ah! I shall never forget the joys of that night when we hoisted our little sail and sped away over the Mediterranean, neither knowing nor caring whither we went, so long as we were together in our love.

The boat was large enough to hold us both with provisions and water for three weeks, and the wind was fair. What more could we ask?

We sailed on all that night, and when we felt sleepy just hauled down the sails and let the boat drift, for the weather was so mild that we had no fear of accident.

When morning broke on us I found that Aspasia had wakened before me, had set sail, and that we were steering straight toward the east, as I could notice from the rising sun.

I cast a quick glance around me, with a sailor's instinct—for my year among the pirates had made a rover of me—and I noticed, on the southern horizon, two columns of smoke, that I knew in a moment could only be steamers.

Aspasia nodded toward them and remarked:

"They must be the English vessels that we heard were to be sent after the pirates, Djorji. What shall we do?"

"Keep on," I answered; "they will not hurt us."

But as the day wore on and we continued to advance, we spied two more columns of smoke from the north, and before noon twelve or fourteen steamers were in sight, about two miles apart, evidently coming on in a line to sweep the seas for every strange craft.

Still we kept on our tranquil way. Our boat was of a very swift model, with one huge lateen sail.[579] The wind was just strong enough to put her to her best speed, and the steamers seemed to gain on us but little, for they were cruising at only half speed.

At last, in the afternoon, when we had passed at a respectful distance several Levanters bound in all sorts of directions, we were startled by hearing a gun and seeing one of the steamers leave the line and run directly down on us.

In half an hour she was within hailing distance, when she hoisted, to our dismay, the Egyptian flag, and we were hailed in stentorian tones in Arabic, crying:

"Stop, you accursed children of Satan! You are pirates and cannot escape."

Aspasia looked up and said to me, in a low voice:

"We are lost. They will recognize us both, and Ibrahim Pasha will have us executed!"

As she spoke a grapnel flew aboard our boat. We were taken prisoners.

•••

# CHAPTER VII.

### OUR SECOND ESCAPE.

IT was, of course, as yet uncertain if we had been recognized by

---

579 A *lateen* or *latin rig* is a large triangular sail, mounted at an angle to the mast. It originated in the eastern Mediterranean in the 2nd century and proved more versatile than the ancient square sails.

any of the crew of the Egyptian steamer; but it was clear that they took us, and very justly, too, for members of the pirate crews.

The rudeness of our dresses and the arms that were scattered about in the boat told their own story.

We had both resumed the costume of our ancestors, and they could see we were no common sailors or fishing folk.

I whispered to Aspasia to be of good cheer, and when the officer of the deck hailed us to come on board I readily obeyed, Aspasia following with the ease of one who had lived an active life for a year past.

When we arrived on board we were taken to the quarter-deck, where we found the captain and his officers waiting to inspect us.

I recognized him in an instant. His name was Abdul Melek, and he had once been connected with the viceroy's staff in Cairo.

Would he recognize me?

That question was soon decided. He looked at me from head to foot and slowly observed:

"I have seen you before. What is your name, young man?"

I saw that he was doubtful, and I knew that Aspasia was safe.

"Your excellency is mistaken," I said, boldly; "I am a Greek, born and bred. My name is Perikles Stavros."

He frowned thoughtfully and looked sharply at Aspasia.

"Who is this?" he asked.

"This is Aspasia Stavros, my wife," I answered, with equal boldness.

A grim smile curved his lip.

"You are too young to have a wife. This woman is older than you. I say I have seen you. Have you ever been in Egypt?" "

"No," I said coolly.

"Then how is it you talk Arabic so well?" he asked, in a sharp tone.

For a moment I was caught, and I must have colored up, for the officers began to nudge each other. I was quick to recover myself, however.

"I learned it in trading to Aleppo, your excellency," I said.

"Whom do you know in Aleppo!" he instantly demanded.

Again I was caught. I had never been there, but I made the best of it.

"I was too young to remember. An old Arab, Hadji Abdallah, taught me."

The captain made no answer to me but he whispered to one of his officers, who went below and presently came back with a wrinkled old black slave, whose face I knew only too well. It was Seyd Hamet, the chief of the eunuchs[580] of the late viceroy's harem.

No sooner had this creature set eyes on Aspasia than he screamed out in his shrill tones:

"Excellency, it is the Hanoum that ran away with the boy Ali. We have found them at last."

Then up started the captain, with a laugh of fierce joy.

"By the head of Mohammed, I thought I knew the young dog. He shall suffer for this. Seize them at once."

In a moment we were surrounded, while my weapons were seized, and I, myself, was pinioned fast. As for Aspasia, no man dared lay his hand on her, for the old eunuch had drawn his keen cimeter, and hurried her down below at once, where she was kept a close prisoner.

I, myself, was tied up to the rigging, while the steamer set off for Alexandria. The captain kindly informed me that it was probable that I should be flayed alive and then impaled, for my sacrilegious crime in carrying off one of the pasha's wives.

The vessel steamed away on her new course, and I was left to my not over-agreeable thoughts all day. I had a great fund of hope and courage, or I should have got very despondent.

I knew that my death was certain if I reached Egypt; but I felt sure that something would happen to avert it at the last moment.

So we steamed on all day, during which I saw nothing of Aspasia; and at night I was left, still tied up to the rigging, to console myself as best I might on an empty stomach.

The sailors went below, and only the night watch paced the deck, or lay, shrouded in their cloaks, under the bulwarks,[581] when I noticed old Seyd Hamet come sauntering by me on his way to the cabin.

I hated the old wretch cordially, and as he passed I muttered a curse.

He showed his white teeth in a grin, and remarked, in a whisper: "You were fool enough to come on board."

"How could I help it?" I whispered back, for I began to see he

---

580 *Eunuchs* were male servants or slaves who had been castrated and, in this case, guarded the women's living quarters.

581 The sides of the ship above decks.

meant something.

"Because I *had* to have you." he said, in the same tone. "If you had a knife now, what would you do with it?"

"Try me and see," I answered, eagerly.

He grinned again; and I felt the cords that held my right wrist cut; then a knife was put in my hand, and Seyd Hamet glided away to the cabin.

Now I began to feel a thrill of hope. I had a knife. Most of the watch were asleep, and the moon did not rise for two hours more. Youth and courage must do the rest.

I waited till everything was quiet and then softly cut the cords that bound me. I remained standing in the same position for some time, and then crept softly aft to the quarter where my little boat was still towing.

I saw that nothing would be more easy than to slip overboard, but I was determined not to stir without Aspasia.

Better death with her than liberty without her.

I turned, stole to the cabin hatch, and looked below. All was silent there, and I crept down the stairs. At the very foot, I stumbled over some one asleep, who started up with a low curse. Before he could repeat it my knife was buried in his throat, and he fell back with a gurgling moan, dead.

Then I listened intently, but there was no other sound. By the dim light of the binnacle lamp[582] that shone through the skylight I saw that I had killed Seyd Hamet, the eunuch.

For a moment I was shocked, but there was too much at stake to turn back. I knew he must be near to Aspasia's prison, and I felt the first state-room door to the right.

It was locked, and I heard her voice saying, in a tone of alarm: "Who's there?"

"'Tis I," whispered I, and then I took from Seyd Hamet's belt a key, with which I easily unlocked the door.

A moment later Aspasia was in my arms, and we were silently feeling our way back on deck.

Silently slept the watch, all but the helmsman, and he nodded over his wheel as he steered.

Two minutes later we were in our boat, cut loose, and drifting away.

---

582 An oil lamp mounted on the ship's *binnacle*, which is a case or stand on the ship's deck containing a compass and other navigational instruments.

...

# CHAPTER VIII.

## WRECKED.

YES we were free again, in the same boat in which we had escaped from the pirates' cave.

The steamer went rushing on her way into the darkness, leaving us tossing about in her wake, for I did not dare to make a motion for fear of being seen or heard.

The night was clear and starlit, but there was no moon. We could see the black hull and huge paddle-boxes of the steamer looming up against the stars for some distance, and then at last she was swallowed up in the darkness, and we could only hear the low rumble of her paddles.

When she was quite out of sight I took the oars and began to pull away toward the east, guided by the stars. My intention was to reach Syria by some means, hoping to hide ourselves in one of the seaport towns and a favorable breeze arising from the west, I hoisted our little sail and we sped on through the night.

But this quiet was not to last long. I noticed that as the western breeze came in a dark cloud was beginning to obscure the stars in that quarter of the heavens.

Before long this cloud rose up as black as ink, overspread the sky above us, shut out the last star, and brought with it a furious tempest.

Giving the helm to Aspasia I was just able to reef the sail closely,[583] when the storm struck us and sent us tearing over the black, foam-streaked waves at racing speed.

We wrapped ourselves in the one solitary cloak which was left to us, clung closely to each other and the helm, and drove on through the darkness of the storm.

I felt quite happy to be left alone with my Aspasia, even if we were fated to die together. She, too, seemed to be quite contented; for ever and anon she whispered:

---

583 *Reefing the sail* is a way to handle strong winds by tying up part of the sail, thus reducing its exposed area.

"Ah, Djorji, this is love indeed!"

My only reply would be a kiss, and so we drove on.

The night seemed very short, great as was our danger. The wind grew fiercer than ever, and the waves came rolling after us as if to devour our little boat; but still she fled on and not a drop of water came aboard.

Hour after hour passed, till at last day broke and showed us a gray, ragged sky, covered with flying scud,[584] a gray sea speckled with white foam-caps, a few feluccas and speronares[585] scudding[586] before the wind, and the black smoke of the very steamer, from which we had so lately escaped, not a mile off on the southern side.

Of course this startled us, but I cheered up Aspasia with the idea that they could not see us from the steamer as we could see them, and so we drove on just as we had all night.

The steamer was riding with her bows to the gale, and seemed to be trying to make headway against it, but only able to hold its own; for we soon passed her by, apparently unnoticed, and within an hour she was hull down on the horizon, while in front of us, to the east, rose the distant summits of a lofty chain of mountains.

The moment I saw those peaks my heart bounded within me, for I knew where we were.

I knew Mount Carmel and the Lebanon chain at a glance, for I had seen them before on voyages with Captain Perikles.

Could we reach those shores alive, we were safe from all the power of Turkey and Egypt, for the brave Druses[587] of the mountains were Christians, who had sworn eternal enmity to the Turks.

Still as we drove on I began to feel some alarm at the possibility of our losing our lives in landing.

The nearer we came the steeper and more forbidding looked the land, the water's edge, all studded with black rocks, standing up as if they only wished a chance to shatter us to atoms.

---

584 *Scud* are fast-moving, low cloud fragments that form beneath storm clouds.

585 A small merchant craft originally from Malta.

586 Here, *scudding* means sailing along swiftly.

587 The *Druze* are a religious group of Arabs from West Asia. The Druze faith is not Christian, however. It developed from Shia Islam, with influences from Christianity and other religions. The Druze remain one of the major religious minorities in Syria, Lebanon, and Israel.

On we drove until we were within a mile of the coast, when we saw a large felucca and two smaller vessels go to pieces almost in an instant at the foot of the cliffs.

Aspasia clung fast to me and whispered:

"Oh, Djorji, we are lost!"

"Not so," I said. "We shall go in much further than they could, and we shall swim to shore. Let us get ready."

We bound the two oars into a sheaf with some ropes, and I bid Aspasia cling fast to them as soon as the boat broke up.

Then I took my post at the helm, and steered straight for an opening I saw among the rocks.

To get more command on the boat I even shook out the reefs of the little sail. For the last half mile we seemed to fly.

At last we were close to the tall black pinnacles of rock that stood like sentinels in advance of the white sands beyond them.

In between two of the tallest we skimmed, and the white beach lay before us. I thought our perils were safely past, when--

Crash!

A jagged rock, hidden just below the surface of the waves, tore the bottom of our boat into a huge chasm, and before I could even snatch at Aspasia a great green wave came sweeping over us, caught us up like straws and dashed us to and fro, as helpless as feathers in a tornado.

I was a good swimmer; but all my skill was useless in the embrace of that watery giant. It tossed me high up on the beach, caught me in its suction, and drew me out to sea again, whirled me out about the rocks till I nearly lost my senses, and finally left me in a cleft of one of those very jagged black pinnacles of rock I had seen nearly a quarter of a mile from shore.

I say left me there, but only because I clung to it with the energy of despair, for every now and then the hungry waves came dashing up, as if anxious to tear me from my place of safety.

For awhile I was so much occupied with barely sustaining my position that I almost forgot to look for Aspasia, but even in the midst of my struggle I felt sure that she was safe. She had oars which would be sure to float.

When, at last I had climbed to a secure position I looked around, but could see her nowhere; and then I realized that death must have come between us.

It came over me in an instant, and in that instant I felt as if I could have leaped into the sea again to die.

But, even as I looked around, a ray of sunlight came across the scene, and I saw that the storm, like all those on the Mediterranean, was breaking as rapidly as it had begun.

In half an hour after I swam to shore without any trouble, and there, stretched on the sand, was the body of my lost Aspasia, drowned.

*Illustration from* The Life and Adventures of Captain Costentenus: *Costentenus finds the body of Aspasia washed up on shore, (Thr 1229.2.10\*, Houghton Library, Harvard University)*

•••

# CHAPTER IX.

### SLAVERY.

I CAN hardly tell what happened to me after I found that Aspasia was dead.

It seemed to me as if all the light had departed out of my own life as I knelt by her pale, beautiful corpse, tore my hair and longed for death.

I was rudely awakened from my sorrow by harsh voices, and I found myself surrounded by a crowd of fierce, brutal-looking people, who spoke a language strange to me, and at once proceeded to strip me of the gold and jewels with which my dress was so liberally covered.

I made no resistance. I felt cowed and stupid. I knew they were wreckers,[588] and I hardly cared whether they killed me or not.

It was only when they began to tear away the jewels from Aspasia that I seemed to recover my senses. Then I rushed at the robbers, fought, bit and tore at them like a wild beast, with inarticulate cries of rage, and received for my pains a shower of blows on the head, under which I speedily fell, stunned, to the earth.

When I recovered my senses I was fastened on a mule, my feet tied under the animal's belly, while we were trotting along a mountain pass.

Aspasia's body had disappeared, and I never saw it again.

I was carried along all day through the mountains by the same company of robbers that had seized me, and at night we encamped in a lonely valley, where I was thrown on the grass to sleep or die as I pleased, for they gave me nothing to eat or drink.

I must pass rapidly over the events of the next few days and weeks, during which I was carried along by the robbers. I at first thought them Druses, but I found out my mistake later. They were Kurdish[589] slave merchants, returning from a trip to Beyrout,[590] and had seized on me as a prize to be carried away as soon as possible.

After a long and toilsome journey, during which I suffered a hundred insults and indignities, we arrived at last on the Persian[591] frontier, and I was sold in the markets of Teheran as a slave to the shah's household.

---

588 Here, people searching for valuables from shipwrecks.

589 The *Kurds* were a traditionally nomadic people, who now primarily live in areas of Iran, Iraq, and Turkey. The division of the Ottoman Empire after World War I failed to create a Kurdish nation.

590 *Beyrout* refers to Beirut, the capital and largest city of Lebanon.

591 *Persia* at this time was an alternative name for the nation of Iran. Persia and the Ottoman Empire fought a series of wars from 1505 to 1823. Persian civilization traces back to the Achaemenid Empire of Cyrus the Great (circa 600-530 BCE).

Once there I was kindly treated and made one of the shah's pipe-bearers, on account of my face and figure pleasing the Master of the Slaves.

There I lived as a petted slave for several years, till I had grown to my present size and my beard had become heavy. The shah was pleased with my polite manner, and promoted me to a position in his body-guard, where I first had an opportunity to renew the exercises I loved so well in my childhood.

At these I speedily became so expert that I could beat all my teachers.

My strength became remarkable, as it has remained ever since. I could ride the most vicious horse, draw the stiffest bow, lift the greatest weights, beat any swordsman in Persia, and throw the most powerful wrestlers.

And, to all this I joined a success with the ladies so remarkable that I was known all over Teheran as the "Heart-Stealer." I became a good poet and musician after the Persian style; and might have risen to high honors at court but for that cause of trouble which has been in my way all my life. It was my fate to love and be loved, "Not wisely but too well."[592]

In brief, when I was a youth of twenty, I had more adventures with ladies than I knew how to manage. I received *billets*[593] by the hands of the black slaves every day, from various ladies, and, as I very often answered the letters,[594] I soon gained a number of enemies among the men.

But all this time my heart was free from any disposition to love. I had lost Aspasia, and though seven years had passed since her death, it seemed as if I could never love another.

At last, however, I became engaged in an adventure which changed my feelings of indifference, if not aversion, to the female sex.

The shah's youngest daughter, the Princess Gulfirouz,[595] was

_____

592 A quotation from Shakespeare's *Othello*, Act V, scene 2, from Othello's final speech before he stabs himself: "Then must you speak of one that loved not wisely, but too well," saying that his love blinded him to reason.

593 Here, from the French, meaning short letters. These were short letters from "various ladies," so they were likely *billet-doux*, or short love letters.

594 The ghostwriter seems to have forgotten that the Captain was illiterate.

595 This *Gulfirouz* is not a historical figure. If this narrative's timeline made sense, the year at this point would be about 1856. The Shah of Qajar Persia, or Qajar Iran, at that point in history would have been Naser al-Din, who

out riding one day, attended by her suite, of which I commanded the escort. I had, of course, never seen this princess to know her face. Persian women are always muffled up in cloaks, veils and other swathings, so that it is absolutely impossible to know one from the other.

The Princess Gulfirouz had a reputation for beauty, but I did not believe in it, having been so often deceived by women who pretended to be houris[596] and turned out hags.

She had been ill, and had been attended by the doctor of the English embassy, who had directed frequent exercise on horseback. Accordingly, the shah had ordered that she should ride out every morning, with only a few of the zenanah[597] eunuchs, and be attended by a strong force of cavalry, which I had to command.

This soon became a regular part of my duty, and, by no means, a disagreeable one. The princess seemed to be very fond of fast riding, and I was soon the only one of the suite that could keep up with her in our morning rides.

The fat, puffy eunuchs of her escort were always left behind, and my escort could not keep up with either of us.

At first I had no idea that anything would come of all this, for I am by nature very modest; but, after the first day, the princess fell into a habit of speaking to me, and I noticed that her voice, through the veil, was very soft and sweet.

On the third day, after we had outridden every one and lost ourselves in a forest, Gulfirouz managed to catch her veil in a branch by accident and it was torn off, revealing to me the most beautiful face I had ever seen in Persia, blushing like a rose.

Of course, according to etiquette, I picked up the veil and handed it to her without lifting my eyes, but, to my surprise, the lady began to laugh at me, and gave me a box on the ear with her open palm, saying:

---

ruled from 1848–1896, and while he had somewhere around 28 children, none of them appear to have been named Gulfirouz, whom the narrative's author names as his youngest daughter. It doesn't even appear that Naser al-Din even started having children with his many wives until 1847, so this detail doesn't fit in the timeline at all. The previous Shah, Mohammed, who ruled from 1834–1848, didn't have any similarly named daughters either.

596 *Houris* are allegorical beautiful virgins in Paradise promised to Muslim men who are true believers.

597 From the Persian for "of the women," a *zenana* is a living area reserved for the women of a Muslim household.

"Meer[598] Djorji, you are not worthy of your fortune."

Full of surprise at the action, I answered:

"Madam, my only fortune is that of a slave."

"You might be a prince, had you any sense," she retorted. "What does this mean?"

She handed me a full-blown rose as she spoke, and I understood her at once.

In Persia, the rose is an emblem of love.

Ah, Gulfirouz! little did you know, when you proffered me that rose, how my love was fatal to all on whom it lighted! Aspasia was dead, and you—but we did not know what was to come of it all.

I shall never forget the bliss of that day, when I found that I was able to love again. I knew my danger in daring to love so high, but we forgot all about it till we returned to Teheran in the evening.

We found the city in commotion about our being lost in the forest. The shah was furious, and had punished all the escort for losing his daughter.

Not daring to visit his wrath on Gulfirouz herself—for the English doctor had warned him that any excitement might kill her— he turned it on me, and I was privately informed that I had been sentenced, for having permitted the princess to run away, to receive five hundred blows of the sticks on the bare feet.

The sentence was to be fully executed the next morning, but I had already made up my mind that I would escape from this country. The British ambassador and doctor were my friends, and one of them had a young English milord[599] staying with him, who desired to see some more of Persia than could be seen by him as a stranger.

That very night, in the character of a charoodar[600] or muleteer,[601] and accompanied by Gulfirouz, who was dressed as a boy, I followed our English friend from the gates of Teheran, our whole party mounted on the best horses we could steal from the stables of the shah himself.

•••

---

598 *Meer*, or *Mir*, is a Persian title derived from Emir, and it indicates that the man is a leader.

599 English nobleman or gentleman.

600 This word remains a mystery, but from context, it refers to some sort of person traveling with pack animals. Perhaps it is a creative spelling of a synonym for muleteer, language unknown?

601 A mule driver.

# CHAPTER X.

## OUR CARAVAN.

IT may seem to some people a very strange and incredible thing that I, having been sentenced by the shah himself to be punished next day, could yet find means to escape on one of the shah's own horses with the shah's own daughter from the capital of Persia.

Yet the explanation is very simple, for truth is stranger than fiction.

The shah, like all Oriental despots, is surrounded with courtiers well skilled in deceit, who flatter and lie to him, and who rule him without him knowing it.

In the zenanah, which takes the place of the Turkish harem, the ruling party is always in the hands of the shah's favorite wife, and at this time it so happened that the favorite was a new Circassian[602] slave, of whom Gulfirouz, the shah's daughter, was very fond.

This Circassian, whose name was Leila, was a designing creature. She saw that the shah was inordinately fond of his daughter, and worked on this fondness to further her own ends. When Gulfirouz confided to her her love for the chief of her father's body-guard, Leila promised to help her, and did so very effectually.

She it was who suggested the shamming sickness; she also bribed the English doctor to prescribe morning rides; she suggested me for commander of the escort; finally, it was she who sent me warning of the shah's intentions, and provided a disguise for Gulfirouz to escape with me.

Leila was keen enough to see that by getting rid of Gulfirouz, if her treason were not found out, she would become Queen of the Zenanah; and I afterward found out that she was right.

But in the meantime, I was full of anxiety till we had put a good day's march between us and Teheran. The young English milord knew nothing of the means by which he was furnished with such splendid

---

602 *Circassia* lay between the Black Sea and the Caspian Sea in what is now the North Caucasus region of Russia. Circassian women were a staple of the sideshow in the 19th century. The act drew on myths about white women being kept as sexual slaves in the Ottoman Empire, as well as racist and now-discounted ideas about humanity's origins in the Caucasus Mountains.

horses and traveled so fast. Our only confidant was the doctor, who received from Leila a heavy bribe to secrecy.

He knew that he was safe enough in the English embassy, even if he were to be found out, which was not likely.

The name of the English milord was Harley,[603] and he was a very fine, handsome fellow, who had lived in Tehran long enough to acquire a little Persian, and who had a passion to be thought a great traveler.

He only knew me as his charoodar, or Muleteer Meer Djorji, and had no suspicion of the way in which Gulfirouz and I had compromised the safety of the whole party. He was anxious to leave Persia, cross the plains of Turkistan,[604] and enter China by the way of Kashgar,[605] a road never traveled by Europeans before that time.[606]

As for me, I was willing to go anywhere and do anything. I was young, strong, skillful in arms; I had the best horse in the shah's stable, and I longed only for excitement.

Gulfirouz ought to have been born a boy, she was so fond of adventure. Indeed, as she rode with us in the guise of a boy, no one would have suspected her sex, so slender was her figure, so bold her air. She seemed to be incapable of fear.

We rode on at the rapid amble of our fine Persian horses all night, and by daybreak were, as I knew, out of all danger of pursuit from the capital.

In various expeditions while in the shah's service I had learned the country throughout the north of Persia very well, and had made up my mind that our only safety lay in reaching the mountains of

---

603 *Lord Harley*, like Gulfirouz, seems to be a generic character—with a name that sounds appropriately British. Later in the pamphlet, the author admits: "The name of Lord Harley is an assumed one. In compliance with the wishes of his family I have done this."

604 Here, *Turkistan* refers to the geographic area of Asia east of the Caspian Sea, stretching west to the Gobi Desert in China and Mongolia.

605 *Kashgar* is one of the westernmost cities of China, long an important link on the "Silk Road," a network of trade routes connecting China with the Middle East and Europe.

606 Never mind that Marco Polo had been to Kashgar hundreds of years earlier.

Khorassan[607] and the Turcoman[608] deserts as soon as possible.

We pushed on, therefore, all next day at a rapid pace, and at night halted at a ruined caravansary[609] close to the borders.

Lord Harley, who was with us, had been much delighted with the rapid way in which we traveled, used as he was to the slowness of Persians. He called me to him that evening, and, in token of his gratitude, presented me with a very handsome revolver, a weapon I had never seen before.

"Go on as you have gone, Meer Djorji," he said, "and the day we reach Kashgar I will make you a rich man, and take you to England, if you like."

I thanked him heartily. Little did I think that I was the only one of our party who would ever return alive from Kashgar, marked for life with the impress of a barbarian's cruelty.

The next day we entered the mountains of Khorassan, where we were forced to take great precautions against the robbers that infest that country. More than once we were followed by small parties, but the rapid pace at which we went enabled us to defy pursuit, and we always took up such a position at night that we could not be surprised.

Finally we escaped from that country and entered the great green plains of Turkistan, where we found nothing but hospitality from the wandering Kirgis[610] Tartars.[611]

607 The eastern province of Persia.

608 *Turcoman* was used interchangeably with other terms for the Turkic peoples and the areas they controlled between Persia and China.

609 An inn serving traveling caravans.

610 The *Kyrgyz* people were originally from the forests of Siberia. In the 9th century, they overthrew the Mongolian Uyghur Empire, though they later became nomadic and many eventually adopted Islam. By the 19th century, they were divided into several groups fighting both the Russians and the Persians, but were little known outside Asia. Today, Kyrgyz people make up the majority of Kyrgyzstan's population of about seven million.

611 *Tartars*, or more correctly *Tatars*, was used broadly in the 19th century to refer to nomadic peoples of the Asian steppes. The first Tatars lived in and around what would become Mongolia in the 5th century. After various Tatar tribes became part of the Mongol Empire of Genghis Khan, Europeans came to refer to the Mongols, confusingly, as Tatars. And Western cartographers often labeled Central Asia as *Tartary*. Today, there are about five million Tatars, mostly living in Russia. The term also made its way into European and American food, with the popularity of *steak tartare* (a French meal of raw meat). The name seems to have come from a rumor that the Mongols/

This was the pleasantest portion of our journey. All day long we used to ride along over the green steppe covered with bright flowers, till at evening we would spy in the distance a faint cloud of smoke.

Whenever we saw this we rode toward it and always found some Tartar encampment; surrounded by flocks of sheep and camels, with innumerable horses straying loose near by the felt tents. Here we were always welcomed by the simple Tartars to the best they had, which was generally milk, cheese, and *koomis*, a sort of foaming wine made out of mare's milk.[612]

These Tartars live in a very simple and comfortable way. Their tents are shaped like beehives and covered with very thick sheets of felt, stretched over a frame of willow basket-work. They are called *kibitkas*.

In summer they are cool, and in the bitterest winter storms they are warmer than any house, while no tempest can upset them.

In these *kibitkas* we passed many a pleasant night, and the way in which the Tartars received us was so kind that Lord Harley was persuaded to join in several hunting expeditions with them.

These Tartars have trained eagles which they employ in the chase,[613] and the birds are so powerful that they do not hesitate to attack and kill wolves.

But it was owing to the very hospitality of our reception in these steppes that we finally came to grief.

Harley was so much pleased with our wild life that he loitered from camp to camp, hunting and hawking, till a part of the summer had passed and autumn was approaching.

On the steppes, where newspapers do not exist, gossip takes its place, and it soon came out that an Englishman was among the Tartars, coming from Persia. The news spread from tribe to tribe, and finally reached the Russian frontier.

In those days the Russians had not conquered Khiva,[614] and they were always afraid of British intrigues with the Turcomans and

---

Tartars ate raw meat that had been stuffed under their saddles to tenderize it. Such meat would have been anything but edible. There is no evidence that people who lived in Central Asia ate this dish, but they may have used raw meat to help with saddle sores.

612 This fermented mare's milk is still popular in Central Asia.

613 Traditional Kyrgyz hunting with golden eagles continues to this day.

614 The Khanate of *Khiva*, with its capital city of Khiva, lay between Russia and Persia. It came under Russian control in 1873.

Tartars.[615]

The first intimation we had of trouble was when we heard in a Tartar camp that the Russians were going to send some Cossacks[616] after us.

The man who told us was very much alarmed, and begged us for our own sakes to go out of the country as soon as we could, for fear of being killed.

Lord Harley laughed at the idea of danger, and said:

"No Russian can catch us in these deserts. What do you care for them? They cannot hurt you; here to-day, there to-morrow. Why should we fear?"

But the old Tartar assured us that we were much mistaken. It was true, he said, that in summer they were independent of Russia, but in winter it was not so. All the tribes had certain places at which they had been wont to winter for a great many years past, and if they offended the Russians the soldiers would cut them off from these places.

Besides, all the flour and gunpowder they possessed was obtained from the Russians, who held them in control on that account.

Finally he begged us, as the only way to prevent an infinity of trouble, to move on next day and pursue our way to Kashgar, as we had at first intended.

To pacify him, we consented, and he promised to supply us with a guide to the next tribe on our way.

Accordingly next day we were just setting forth on our journey, when we spied, advancing from the west, the glittering spears of a party of horsemen, whom our host pronounced with much apprehension to be Cossacks.

"The Russians have found you," he said, in trembling tones.

●●●

---

615 Throughout the 19th century, Central Asian nations were famously caught in the middle of "the Great Game"—the struggle between Britain and Russia over trade routes in the Middle East.

616 *Cossacks* are a semi-nomadic group of Slavic people. Historically, they were Orthodox Christians and militarized. They often traded military service for self-governance and defended the southern borders of Ukraine and Russia from other nomadic peoples.

# CHAPTER XI.

## THE COSSACKS.

FOR myself I was not as much afraid of the Russians as were our Tartar friends. Lord Harley was a rich young man, and had quite a strong, well-armed retinue with him, composed of servants of several nationalities, but all picked for courage.

We had ten carbines,[617] fourteen of the new American revolvers, then just beginning to be fashionable; and our horses were fat and in good wind.

Lord Harley himself was a regular dare-devil and hated a Russian as badly as any man could, for it was just after the Crimean War.[618]

As soon as he spied the Cossacks, he turned to me saying:

"Meer Djorji, let's give those fellows a fight if they want it."

I hesitated, for I knew the danger into which Gulfirouz would be led, and as yet no one suspected her sex. She was only known as "little Houssein, the most impudent boy unhung."

I hardly knew how to evade the desire of this English lord for a fight, but Gulfirouz herself put an end to my doubts by crying out:

"Death to the Russians, mi'lord! Let us fight them and kill them all."

She spoke in Persian, but Harley understood her and looked regretfully at her. She had the appearance of a boy of twelve.

"It won't do to take that child into a fight, Meer Djorji," he said. "We must even ride away. By the way, where did you pick up that boy?"

"He is my cousin, the son of my mother's brother," I said, "and I would not have him hurt to-day."

"All right," answered Harley; "then let us ride away."

Our Tartar host seemed to feel very much relieved as we

---

617 Short rifles developed for cavalry.

618 *The Crimean War* (1853-1856) was fought between the Russians and an alliance of the Ottomans, British, and French. As the Ottoman Empire weakened in the 19th century, Britain and France stepped in to keep the expanding Russian Empire from upsetting the balance of power in the Mediterranean.

cantered off, for by this time the Cossacks were not more than a mile off, and our departure relieved him from responsibility.

As we rode away we looked back over our shoulders and observed that the Cossacks had quickened their pace, and were evidently in pursuit.

We felt no fears on that score, for we knew our horses could easily distance the Cossack ponies in a fair race, but we kept on at an easy amble or canter, not trying hard to escape them, but rather allowing them to close up gradually.

As I had anticipated, this had the effect of urging them to ride hard, and about midday they were only a quarter of a mile behind us.

Then all of a sudden we saw them halt, and the next moment there was a sputter of fire and smoke all along the line, and a shower of bullets came whistling around us, knocking up the dust.

Of course there was no mistake about this. There were thirty or forty Cossacks in the line, and our only course was to put spurs to our horses and endeavor to escape.

Away we went at full speed followed by a yell of triumph from the Cossacks, and in a few minutes we were out of gunshot. They tried a second volley as they galloped after us, but it was so ineffective that

*Illustration from* The Life and Adventures of Captain Costentenus: *Costentenus, Gulfirouz, and Harley pursued by Cossacks, (Thr 1229.2.10\*, Houghton Library, Harvard University)*

they ceased their efforts and rode silently on, as if determined to tire us out.

For the rest of the afternoon we kept on at such a rate that we increased our distance to three miles from our pursuers; but when night came on we turned our course to the south, marched about a mile, and then halted to wait for them.

I had determined to give them the benefit of an old trick of the Kurdish robbers by which I had seen Persian soldiers suffer heavily.

We picketed[619] our horses in the grass, and then stole forward ourselves to lie in ambush for the Cossacks.

Pretty soon we heard them trotting along in a close column, and heard a voice call out in Russian:

"Close up, pigs that you are. They must be near now."

A moment later they were riding by in a dark mass, right into the midst of our little ambush. Our men were crouching in the grass, and, as luck would have it, all around the Cossack column.

Up I jumped and fired my carbine into the mass of dark bodies outlined against the stars.

In a moment our comrades all around, began firing. first with their carbines, then with revolvers, and the volley was so rapid that the Cossacks, thinking themselves attacked by superior numbers, lost heart and galloped away at full speed, yelling to each other and not firing a shot.

We found four dead bodies on the field, and examined them as closely as we could in the darkness, when Lord Harley suddenly called out to me, in tones of surprise:

"Come here, Meer Djorji; this fellow isn't a Cossack; he's a Persian!"

I came to him with some little uneasiness, for the news was quite startling to me, who understood it better than he.

Sure enough, the high fur-cap, the yellow robe and the boots, the gay attire of the dead man, showed that he was a Persian.

More than that; for I soon struck one of Lord Harley's matches to look at the face of the corpse. And there I recognized only too plainly the dark, stern lineaments[620] of Mirza[621] Kassim Zil Busheer,

---

619 A *picket line* is a horizontal rope that horses are tied to at intervals.

620 The lines of the face.

621 Originally meaning a prince or commander, *Mirza* came to be a more general title of importance.

the Master of the Slaves.

In a moment I had realized our position and the danger to which I had exposed my generous English friend. Mirza Kassim could only be out there in the steppes for one object—to catch Gulfirouz and myself. He must have tracked us to the frontier and appealed to the Russian government to help him.

And I knew that henceforth there was no safety for us in Turkistan anywhere under the Russian influence.

Lord Harley was English; England and Russia were bitter rivals in Asia.

The opportunity afforded to the Russians to strike England through this great English lord at the same time that they curried favor with the Shah of Persia by punishing the runaways, was too tempting to be resisted.

Had we been alone we might have gone on forever over the steppes, Gulfirouz and I, and no Russian would have troubled his head about us. But once under British protection, it became a matter of vengeance to get hold of the rash English lord who had helped us to escape, and so punish him.

I saw all this in a moment, and determined to make a clean confession of my whole course to my generous friend, giving him the option of surrendering me to save his own life.

I therefore told him the whole story, to his great surprise, concluding:

"And now, my lord, you can save your life by giving me up. The princess is safe, for no one will dare to harm her if she consents to go back; but my life is forfeited. Let me be tied hand and foot, and then take me back to these Cossacks as a prisoner. They will not harm you then, but otherwise we must go on."

Lord Harley had listened to me with great interest, and when I had finished, he said, drily:

"So that impudent little wretch is a princess after all. I thought no boy could have quite so much tongue. And here I've been assisting in a regular romance without knowing it. I must say you're a bold fellow, Djorji—to turn an English gentleman into a horse-thief without telling him."

I felt very much ashamed of my action at that moment, and began to stammer some apology, when he all at once burst out laughing.

"Egad, what a joke! I'll put it in my book when I get home. Won't my father be proud of it!"

I began to understand him then, for I had heard of these mad Englishmen who were always hunting adventures to put into their books. He went on laughing awhile, and then slapped me on the shoulder, crying:

"Meer Djorji, you're a brick, and I'll stick to you. Let's get to horse at once, and we'll show those Russian idiots that they can't separate a pair of true lovers like you."

Ah, my poor, generous friend Harley! why did you not give me up then? It would have been better for you in the end. But fate is too strong for any man to resist it.

We rode on all the rest of that night at a fast pace, and the next day stopped at the last Tartar camp before we came to the land of the independent Turcomans.

But we observed here that our reputation had preceded us, for our hosts were unmistakably nervous about our reception. The old customs of their race prevented them from absolutely refusing us shelter; but they sent out scouts in all directions to give warning if the Russians came, and we heard from them that more than one party were in pursuit of us

All this news, however, only increased Lord Harley's delight. He swore that he had taken me and my wife[622] under his protection, and that he would see us through our troubles if he had to invoke the whole power of England for another Crimean War.

We were not, however, molested at that camp, where we bought a large stock of supplies necessary to cross the Kyzil Kum Desert,[623] and the next day, guided by a Turcoman who claimed to be a chief among his tribe, we plunged into the wilderness.

•••

# CHAPTER XII.

## KASHGAR.

---

622 Somewhere along the way, Costentenus and Gulfirouz seem to have gotten married?

623 The *Kyzilkum Desert* is an area covering 115,000 square miles southeast of the Aral Sea.

WE had less trouble than I had first anticipated in crossing the great Turcoman desert. To be an enemy of Russia was in the eyes of these wild men to be their friend.

We found them a taller and much handsomer race than the Kirgis Tartars, among whom we had so lately been; and their women were often very beautiful, while their horses are better than any in Asia, except the Arabians.

They were well aware of the value of money and jewels, and we were able to buy several splendid horses on which to pursue our journey; for our own, not used to the desert, began to flag in Turkistan.

We came into the neighborhood of Khiva, but were warned by the wild tribes not to venture into the power of the Khan, who was famous for his cruelty and avarice.

Accordingly, we left Khiva at a respectable distance, and did the same with Bokhara,[624] bent as we were on reaching Kashgar, the object of all our hopes.

It may be asked why we went to Kashgar, of all places? We went there because we were anxious to see the famous chief, Yakoob Beg,[625] who then lived there, and who was said to have done much to civilize his subjects by introducing people from Europe into high places.

It was to Yakoob Beg, the creator of a new nation, a man who had thrown off the yoke of China and set up an independent kingdom in Mantchooria[626] as large as all France, Spain and Germany together,[627] that I looked for help and employment.

Lord Harley, of course, had no such wish; but he had the insatiable curiosity of a traveler bound to see every one and everything.

Therefore we pressed on, week after week, over the brown steppes, till at last we were greeted by the sight of a little mud fort with regular embrasures as in Europe, from which grinned the muzzles of four brass guns, and our guide announced to us that we had reached

624 *Bukhara*, in what is now Uzbekistan, was an important center for trade on the Silk Road.

625 *Yakub Beg* was a real person as well. He was born in what is now Uzbekistan circa 1820 and went to northwest China in 1864 to take advantage of uprisings by the area's Muslims. He managed to establish the kingdom of Kashgaria (Yettishar), and the Ottoman sultan named him the emir of the region. China retook the area in 1877, and Beg died around that time, of uncertain cause.

626 *Manchuria* is a region of Asia that includes parts of China and Russia.

627 A bold—but possibly true—claim.

the frontiers of Kashgar.

The sight of the little fort, and still more of the neat guard of soldiers that garrisoned it, showed us that we had reached civilization of some sort at last.

It was not European, perhaps, but it was far above anything in Persia. The Shah's best troops never looked half as trim as these few soldiers of Yakoob Beg.

They wore a sort of zouave[628] dress, and carried clean, bright muskets that showed good officers. They turned out of the gate of the fort as we approached over the steppe, and we could see behind them something I had never witnessed since I was in Europe—a real road, paved and guttered.

Harley was so much excited at the sight that he actually gave a loud cheer for the first road in Asia; but we soon found that if we had the pleasures of civilization before us, we had also its little troubles to undergo.

A smart-looking officer, who turned out to be a Greek, asked us for our passports, and when he heard that we had none, told us that he was sorry to say we were his prisoners till the Khan or Beg—as he was indifferently called—sent word what to do with us all.

This was not so pleasant, but we saw that we had no recourse but to obey. Before us the land rapidly became more mountainous than it had been, and we were told by the Greek, whose name was Alkibiade Fokion,[629] that the little fort before us was called Sofur-Kara-ool. Strange that I should remember this singular name now after the lapse of more than twenty years; but Sofur-Kara-ool marked my entrance on the land of Kashgar, whence I was never to return, save as an object of wonder to all mankind.

Alkibiade listened to our story of ourselves, and took notes of

---

628 *Zouaves* were French light infantry units that originally served in North Africa. They were formed in 1830 and disbanded in the 1960s. They were known for their fast, unconventional drills and their bold North African-inspired uniforms: short jackets, wide trousers tucked into their boots, and fezes. Van Gogh's well-known painting "Le Zouave" depicts one of these soldiers in uniform. Zouave units were also formed in the British and American militaries, inspired by the originals' methods and uniforms.

629 This character's first name, *Alkibiade*, is likely a version of Alchibiades, an Athenian statesman and military general who lived around 450-405 BCE. *Fokion* may reference Phocion, another Athenian statesman and general, who lived around 402-318 BCE.

it. I noticed that when I spoke of taking service with the Beg he gave me a peculiar glance; but he said nothing to make me believe that all was not right.

He gave us quarters inside the range of the fort; but that was all. We had to buy our food from the neighboring village, and feed was so scarce that our horses suffered considerably from hunger.

All the while Alkibiade answered our questions as to when we would hear from the Beg with a shrug, saying:

"Soon enough—soon enough."

Nevertheless, it was not for three weeks that anything came to our relief, and then appeared a troop of cavalry, armed after a sort of French model, and their officer announced that he came to conduct us to the city of Kashgar, where his Illustrious and Unequaled Majesty, son of the Sun, Yakoob Beg, Khan of the Mantchoo Tartars, would graciously give us an audience.

Of course we thought that our troubles were all over then, and it was with great joy that we followed our conductor for two days over wild mountains, which on the third descended into the fertile smiling plain of Kashgar.

It seems to me, even at this great distance of time, as if the first sight of Kashgar could never be excelled.

I have seen Damascus from the Desert, Naples from Vesuvius, Vienna from the spire of St. Stephen's, Paris from Notre Dame; but all of these, in their first impression of beauty to the traveler, are as nothing to the wonderful loveliness of the valley and city of Kashgar when one comes on them from the fertile mountains that separate them from Kokand.[630]

The plain is about a hundred miles square, and fairly teams with the richest of vegetation, studded as it is, with little streams that run into and out of the lovely lake of Kashgar.

And in the midst, resting on the shores of the lake, like a bird in its nest, lay the city of Kashgar, all aglow in the morning sun, which was reflected back from hundreds of gilded domes and minarets, while the dark green foliage of the trees between the white houses set off the latter to perfection.

We were so much delighted with the distant prospect that we were disappointed as we came closer.

---

630 The Khanate of *Kokand*, with its capital city of Kokand, lay just to the west of Kashgar. The Khanate of Kokand stretched across parts of modern Uzbekistan, Kyrgystan, Tajikistan, and Kazakhstan.

We found the glittering domes and minarets, when looked at close by, were cheap concerns of plaster with brass ornaments; that the houses were small and mean in appearance; and that the only difference between this city and others in Turkistan was that it was kept clean.

We rode through the streets of Kashgar till we came to a large handsome house, which we were told was the royal palace, and in front of this we halted and dismounted.

Then Lord Harley took the lead, followed by Gulfirouz and myself, and we entered the palace, following the captain of the guard, who was a Polish renegade, called Rostosky. He had already informed us that the khan was very fond of foreign officers and mechanics, and that we were sure of employment if we had any special knowledge.

We were conducted through several halls, all more or less full of soldiers and officers, till we came to a green curtain, where our conductor stopped and coughed slightly as a signal.

The curtain moved, and out came a tall, thin man with a light beard and a long narrow face. I had never seen such features before. I saw that he was no Asiatic, but I could not place him among any nation of Europe with which I was acquainted.

He certainly could not be English, yet it was in English he spoke to Lord Harley, who led our party.

It seems only yesterday that I heard his voice, high and nasal, as he said:

"Well, stranger, so you've got here at last. The old man will see you in a moment. How de do?"

He shook hands warmly with Harley, who naturally asked:

"Who have I the pleasure of seeing? You are an Englishman?"

"Not by a blame sight!" replied our tall friend. "I hail all the way from Southport, Connecticut, I do, and my name's Jared Bunce.[631]

---

631 This was published 8 years before Mark Twain's *A Connecticut Yankee in King Arthur's Court,* but stereotypical Connecticut Yankee characters also appeared in many other stories in the 19th century. The name *Jared Bunce* came from the popular novel *Guy Rivers: A Tale of Georgia* written by William Gilmore Simms. Originally published in 1834, the book had been republished at least nine times by 1882. Simms's Jared Bunce combined two stereotypes of Northerners—the "Jonathan" and "the peddler." The Jonathan was inspired by the song "Yankee Doodle" and various short stories that appeared in almanacs. He was "shy, awkward, bumptious, yet good-natured and helpful," a shrewd man with a good heart. In Costentenus's story, Bunce has been lifted from the American South and deposited in Kashgar. Like Lord Harley, Bunce is a stereotypical character who ultimately serves as a

Very much at your service, stranger."

Lord Harley smiled and introduced himself and our party, telling the truth as to Gulfirouz and myself.

Mr. Bunce seemed to be much interested in the story, and explained that he had been in Yakoob Beg's service for ten years, having wandered to Kashgar from Russia. He didn't say how, but I afterwards found out, as I shall tell in its proper place.

We were still talking when a bell sounded within the curtain and our American friend put his finger on his lips and whispered:

"Don't speak till he speaks, but bow and wait for him. Come on."

We followed him into a large and beautifully decorated room, at the upper end of which, on a sort of throne covered with tiger-skins, sat a tall, stern-looking man, with a long beard tinged with gray. This was the Yakoob Beg, Khan of Kashgar.

At the time of our visit he was about forty-two,[632] a man of great stature and strength, dressed in the scarlet uniform of a British general, with a bright steel helmet on his head.

He had a stern, hard look, a cold, gray eye, and the air of a man whose will was law. Yet, strange to say, our leader, Bunce, did not seem to be in any fear of him, for he stood quietly at the foot of the throne and announced us to the khan as coolly as if he were his equal.

Of course we did not understand what he said, for he spoke Mantcho Tartar, but I saw the khans eyes rove to each person in our party as Bunce pointed them out.

Naturally I watched him curiously.

He looked at Harley, I thought, coldly; but smiled on me and Gulfirouz, passing over the rest indifferently.

When Bunce had finished, the khan said something which the American thus interpreted to us:

"The khan wants to know if you have any request to make, and if you wish to live in this country or take service with him. Speak out."

Harley said he was only a traveler, who wanted to see the country, write about it in his book and let all the world know of the greatness of Yakoob Beg.

I said that I wished to enter the service of the Khan of Kashgar,

---

contrast to our hero's courage, strength, and stamina.

632 Yakoob Beg was born circa 1820, so his age being 42 puts this part of our story around 1862. This will shortly be contradicted.

and that I was a leader of cavalry in Persia.

After we had spoken the khan asked Harley if he knew any trade. Harley thought a little and said that he owned a tin mine at home and understood mining. That was all.

This seemed to please Yakoob Beg, who immediately said:

"It is enough. Tell the Englishman he shall work my mines at Oosteem-Keechak. I never got anything out of them, but the Chinese say there is plenty of copper there to make guns. He shall have half the product for his labor. The rest shall go with him. I have said."

It was in vain for any of us to plead that we did not want to go there; that our intentions were averse to mining. We were in the power of an absolute despot, and even the American, Bunce, told us, as we retired from the presence of the khan:

"It's a good sight easier to get into Yakoob Beg's service than out of it. I've been here ten years, but I don't intend to stay much longer. Hold your horses, all of you, and we shall see."

•••

# CHAPTER XIII.

## THE MINES.

YES, we were in Yakoob Beg's service; there was no disputing that. As Jared Bunce had remarked, it was easy enough to enter it, but very hard to escape.

The tyrant of Kashgar was a man of wonderful powers of mind, but a thorough barbarian withal.

Born the chief of a petty tribe of Tartars, he had, by dint of courage and cunning, succeeded in overthrowing the lax Chinese government of Mongolia, and had extended his dominions from Kashgar to the borders of China.

Quick to perceive the advantages of European discipline, he had decoyed English, French, Americans, Poles, Greeks and Russians into his service as officers, and had procured arms from India, so that when we saw him in 1857,[633] he had a well-disciplined army with which

---

633 Here, the dates don't line up. We seemed to be sometime around 1862, but now we're explicitly in 1857. Most importantly, however, Yakoob Beg

he could defy all his enemies.

His power being thus secure, Yakoob Beg found that he could not keep up his army without money; and, as his people were poor, he determined to accumulate riches.

His method was simple and it showed his sense. He determined to keep all the money he could in the country by manufacturing everything needed at home.

Therefore he turned all his officers into manufacturers, whether they wanted it or not. He had cotton, woolen and silk factories, iron-works, powder-houses, all under his own eyes, and made his people buy his goods, instead of buying from caravans of traders.

He was able to do this on account of his army, which suppressed all show of discontent. He had set up a regular monopoly, and he was jealous of any one who tried to interfere with it.

We found this out very soon as we traveled on to Oosteem-Keechak, where the khan had his copper mines.

Under the Chinese these mines had yielded well, but the ignorant Mongols did not understand the business, and so had worked out the old veins, and did not know how to find new ones.

It was thus that the khan had jumped so eagerly at the idea of Lord Harley working his mines for him, as soon as he found the English man understood mining.

We were sent off with a large party of soldiers as escort, and Jared Bunce—who we found out was a sort of assistant-treasurer in Kashgar—was sent with us to report on our methods of work.

It took us two weeks to reach Oosteem-Keechak, which we found to be a half-ruined town, once flourishing, but now much decayed.

The khan's orders were sent into all the surrounding country to compel the Tartars to come in and work in the mines; and Lord Harley, who was a skillful miner, after a few days' exploring, struck two paying veins of copper, one of which had streaks of silver, and began work.

As for myself, I was so happy to be safe with Gulfirouz that I did not think much of the tyranny to which we were subjecting the miserable people around us.

We ourselves were well and generously treated to all seeming. The laborers were told to build houses for us, and provisions were

did not establish Kashgaria/Yettishar until 1864, so none of this is plausible.

plenty as long as fine weather lasted.

But when the winter came on with all the fearful severity of Central Asia, we realized the hardships of our position.

The khan had sent orders that we were to pay the miners only one-half of the wages with which we had commenced, and at the same time he put up the price of food.

The consequence was that before the winter was half over most of the laborers were in debt to the khan, and starving besides.

Lord Harley, myself, and even Bunce, who was naturally rather a hard man, could not avoid pitying their condition, and we held a consultation together as to what we could do to help them and ourselves.

The product of the mines had fallen off, and the khan was grumbling. Bunce knew that a month's grumbling was often followed by a day's executions.

He told us this, and with native Yankee shrewdness suggested a way of escape by bribing the khan.

He knew, as did we all, that the mines could yield five times their present stock of ore, were they properly worked.

He proposed, therefore, that we should offer to give the khan a certain number of pounds of pure copper—double what he was then getting—for the privilege of working the mines ourselves, paying what wages we liked.

We sent him to the khan with the offer, which was greedily accepted, and from that day the mines wore a new look.

The men worked cheerfully, grew fat, paid off their debts, and by the spring we had saved a good hundred thousand pounds of copper, with half as much silver, as profits of our new system.

Besides this, all the Tartars adored us, and a flourishing town of ten thousand people had sprung up around us.

It was in the midst of this tide of prosperity, when everything was smiling, that one day a stout, sensual-looking man, dressed in the khan's uniform and followed by a party of cavalry, rode into Oosteem-Keechak, and announced himself as Gholab Sing,[634] the Khan's Inspector of Mines, come to report to his master.

---

634 While this is soon to be revealed as a false name in the story, it also happens to be the name of a real person. *Gulab Singh* (1792-1857) was the founder of India's Dogra dynasty and the first Maharaja of Jammu and Kashmir, a state created by the British after the First Anglo-Sikh War. Jammu and Kashmir was divided in 1952 and is now split between Pakistan and India.

I happened to be at the mines doing my duty as foreman when this man arrived, and in an insolent tone asked for the English steward, Alee Khan—as they called Harley. He spoke to me in English, which I already understood very well.

I looked at him astonished, for his face was too dark for a European and his accent peculiar. As I made no answer, he repeated his question in French, which he spoke equally well.

"Who are you, and why do you ask?" I said at last in French.

He smiled in a sinister way, showing his teeth, which were blackened with betel-chewing, and replied:

"I am the inspector Gholab Sing, and I want to see this English thief who is robbing the khan."

I was always quick-tempered, and I instantly answered:

"You are a dog and a son of a dog. Alee Khan is my friend and no thief. He has made these mines pay the khan more than any one ever did before."

He turned pale at my defiant answer and laid his hand on his sword.

"Take away your hand," I cried, "or I will take your sword from you, for I am Costentenus the Palikar."

There were several hundred men at work close by, and they had stopped at the sound of our angry voices, so that the stranger judged it prudent to be quiet.

He took his hand from his sword and spoke with the most oily politeness.

"I crave pardon, Signor Costentenus," he said, "but I am a Hindoo and do not love the English, as you know. I am sent here on duty by Yakoob Beg. Where can I see His Excellency Alee Khan?"

I was pacified at once, for I am naturally very polite, and told him I would accompany him to see Harley.

He professed himself charmed at the prospect; so I called for my horse and rode off with him. Gholab Sing's manner having become perfectly unctuous in its civility.

As we passed my house, Gulfirouz came out with our child in her arms[635]—for we were all simple and unaffected there—and asked me when I would come to dinner.

According to our European habits, which we followed unrestrained, she was unveiled, and Gholab Sing saw her face. I noticed

---

635 Somewhere along the way, Costentenus and Gulfirouz seem to have had a child.

his fat countenance change as he looked, and his dark eyes glared.

A moment later he had resumed his polite demeanor and looked away; but I knew the meaning of his glance, and, hastily telling Gulfirouz to go in, I rode on to Harley's house, feeling a vague sense of impending danger.

We found Harley at his house looking over accounts with Bunce, and I formally introduced the Hindoo.

Harley received him with courtesy, but I noticed that the Yankee's face wore a singular expression of gravity and reserve as soon as he set eyes on the Inspector of Mines.

However, he said nothing, but kept in the background while Gholab began to ask all sorts of questions as to our affairs, which Harley parried as well as he could.

At last he said:

"I am ordered by the khan to tell you that you must reduce your wages to the same rate which he pays to all his subjects. Your pay is too high, and there is much dissatisfaction among the people that the men of Oosteem-Keechak are growing so fat."

I was about to answer myself, when I felt Bunce press my foot under the table and caught a look from him which I understood as a signal for silence.

Harley good-temperedly replied:

"I will do what the khan orders; but in that case we must give up the contract to supply him with a certain amount of copper. The men will not work hard for so little."

Gholab Sing smiled in an ugly sort of way as he answered:

"The khan says that you must give him the same amount of copper as before, or he will know the reason why."

Then Harley grew angry and retorted:

"The khan is not able to draw blood from a stone. Let him leave us alone and we will pay what we agreed. We can do no more."

For my part I was so angry at the insolence of the man, especially as I remembered the way he looked at Gulfirouz my wife, that I started up and cried out:

"Tell the khan that we are not Tartars to be beaten like dogs. I am a Greek and know how to fight for my rights, which is what you cowards in India never dared. Go back, or I may lose my temper and kill you."

I shall never forget the look of diabolical malignity that came over the Hindoo's face as he slowly rose, saying to me:

"I will take your answer to the khan, and before the snow falls you will indeed be sorry for it."

Then he bowed to Harley, and soon afterwards rode away, leaving us all more or less uneasy.

But it was Jared Bunce who first revealed to us the full extent of our danger when he said to us:

"That man is Yakoob Beg's prime minister in disguise. I knew him at once. More than that, I firmly believe he is no other than Nana Sahib."[636]

•••

# CHAPTER XIV.

## THE MUTINY.

YOU may imagine our wonder and consternation at this news. The name of Nana Sahib, the Butcher of Cawnpore, was then in everybody's mouth, for the Indian Mutiny had but lately been suppressed.

It was known that this wretch had escaped from India, after Delhi was taken, to Jung Bahadoor, King of Nepaul,[637] from whose court he had disappeared.

Bunce, who had been a great traveler in his day, had seen the

---

636 *Nana Sahib* is the final important character plucked from history to appear in Costentenus's autobiography. Born in India, he was a leader in the First War of Independence (also referred to as the Indian Rebellion of 1857), an unsuccessful attempt to throw off British rule. Early in the uprising, he led the sepoy forces (British-trained, Indian-born soldiers) who attacked the British East India Company soldiers in Cawnpore (now called Kanpur). The British soldiers surrendered and were promised safe passage out of the region. Instead, Nana Sahib had everyone massacred, including the women and children. He eventually fled toward the Nepalese border and disappeared, his fate unknown. There is no evidence that he ever made it to Kashgar and into the service of Yakoob Beg. But many writers of the time, including Jules Verne in his 1880 novel *The End of Nana Sahib*, wrote about the Butcher of Cawnpore and imagined what became of him.

637 *Jung Bahadur* was actually the Prime Minister of Nepal at this time, while Surendra Bikram Shah was king. But Surendra was essentially a figurehead, with Jung Bahadur as de facto ruler.

Hindoo prince in the heyday of his power, and remembered his face when he met him at Yakoob Beg's court a few weeks before our arrival.

Nana Sahib, it seems, had fled from India with an enormous treasure in jewels, with which he had purchased the good will of the avaricious Yakoob, who had made him his trusted friend at once.

The American, after sojourning in India in the year 1848, had gone to Russia, where he foolishly engaged in a political plot, for which he was sent to Siberia to work in the mines of Barnaul.[638]

From thence he had escaped to Kashgar, where he entered Yakoob Beg's service and had forgotten all about Nana Sahib till the fugitive prince had taken refuge at Yakoob's court.

"I am sure it is he," Bunce concluded, "and that he has determined on our being killed, because one of us is English. He will never forgive the English to his dying day."

"Then in that case," observed Harley, in his cool way, "we shall have to fight for our liberty."

"Why not follow and kill this man before he poisons the khan's mind against us?" I asked, impetuously. "If we must fight, let us fight our own way, not the way he wants us."

But both my friends dissuaded me from this. They thought it better to get our people together, arm them and defend our rights. Then, if we triumphed, we could make terms with Yakoob Beg.

"But if we kill his minister at once we put ourselves in the wrong," said Harley, "and our Tartars may not fight for us."

I did not believe them, and I was right in the end; but I could not oppose my noble friend, who had done so much for me. Would I had taken my own way.

We knew there was not much time to lose; for Yakoob Beg's army could be on us in a week. If we acted, we must act quickly. Here, at least, my friends deferred to me, that we must attack Yakoob before he could get ready.

We called the men together and told them how the khan, seeing their prosperity, wished to put them back in the miserable position in which we found them. We asked them if they were willing to take up arms and force that justice from his fears we could not obtain from his love.

Their answer was full of enthusiasm. They would go anywhere and do anything for the friends who had "made men of them."

---

638 *Barnaul* is a Siberian city that was known for its production of silver.

The news flew through the country like lightning, and thousands of people, armed with spears, swords, bows, axes, and a few firearms, flocked to our standards as we set out for Kashgar.

Our motto was:

"Living wages for workmen![639] Down with bad men who tell lies to the khan!"

It was three weeks' march to Kashgar, and our forces grew larger every day we advanced. We overcame every little post that we found by force of numbers, and took away the soldiers' guns, so that we had a thousand men armed with muskets when we reached the city, with more than a hundred thousand wild Tartars from all the country who swarmed round Kashgar.

We completely surprised Yakoob Beg, for his capital was not walled in, and before he could gather up more than his body-guard, we had him invested in his palace and virtually at our mercy.

Then we began to treat with him for terms; for we had no desire to kill him, inasmuch as we could not govern the country ourselves and did not want to.

The khan remained in his palace, surrounded by his body-guards, sullen and defiant. He was at our mercy, but he showed no symptom of fear.

We sent in Bunce, as the one who knew him best, with a white flag to offer him our terms. They were that we were to retain the mines, and agree to give him half as much copper again as we had been in the habit of giving, if we could have our own way as to wages.

The Tartars with us sent in another envoy to state their demands. They were "living wages for all workmen in Mongolia."

We gave him two hours to decide, after which the Tartars threatened to burn the palace and city.

Then we waited for the return of our envoys. In half an hour we saw Bunce coming back, looking happy.

"The khan has consented," he said. "He only wants to see the leaders in person, that he may hear their compliments face to face."

Lord Harley readily consented to go in, but I warned them that it would not be safe.

"Do you not see," I said, "that he only wants to get us into his power, that he may capture us? Don't go in."

This opened their eyes, and my English friend said, uneasily:

---

639 A phrase that would have resonated with American readers due to the rise of labor unions in the late 19th century

"What can we do, then?"

"Make him come out to us," I said. "We are not safe anywhere but in the midst of our men."

Alas! we were yet to learn that safety against a tyrant is found nowhere but in his death.

Bunce was not so much deceived by the apparent submission of Yakoob Beg that he did not see the danger of going back to him with such a message as I proposed to send.

Harley pointed out to him that I was right. If he feared to go into Yakoob now, at our mercy as he was, how could we trust Yakoob after he had made an agreement and our forces had dispersed?

Finally we concluded to send for the Pole, Rostosky, whom we thought our friend, and to make him our emissary.

Rostosky looked frightened, but said he would take our message. He went into the palace and remained there for some time. When he reappeared, he said to us, gravely:

"His Highness is coming."

I directed the Tartars to form a huge circle, in the midst of which Harley, Bunce and myself, with our little retinue of European servants, awaited the coming of the tyrant of Kashgar.

Presently there was a commotion at the doors and a company of guards filed out, preceding Nana Sahib—for, as we soon learned, it was that wretch—who was dressed in gorgeous robes and covered with jewels. All the officers of Yakoob's court followed, and in their midst, borne aloft on a splendid palanquin,[640] sat Yakoob Beg himself.

I had never seen him look so magnificent before.

The palanquin halted in the midst of the square and the khan made a gesture, at which his guards closed in all around him. Then Nana Sahib came to us and said, haughtily:

"The khan has come. What do you wish to ask of his mercy?"

"Nothing," said Harley, firmly. "He is at our mercy, not we at his. Send your guards back, that we may speak to him. We need no interpreters—least of all, a fugitive from justice like you."

The Indian's dark eyes glittered like those of a cobra in the jungle, but his voice took a more polite tone:

"You can advance and speak to the khan face to face. I do not wish to hinder you. But at least dismount, out of respect to what he was yesterday."

---

640 A covered litter carried on poles on the shoulders of multiple bearers, formerly used in eastern Asia.

Harley, always good-natured, was appeased at once, and got off his horse, saying to us:

"It's no good spitting on a man and then rubbing it in. We can get out of Kashgar in a few days and go back to India if we can't trust him, but I think we can trust him."

Jared Bunce looked uneasy, and I made a signal to our Tartars to close in on the guards. I could not help a suspicion of some sort of treachery though what it could be I knew not. The khan seemed to be entirely in our power.

Therefore, we three, accompanied by our servants with cocked muskets, went into the midst of the khans guards, who fell back at our approach.

There sat Yakoob Beg on his palanquin as cold and austere as when in his palace; and as we stood before him he fixed a severe glance on us and said:

"What would ye now? The wages must come down, as I said. I yield nothing. Return whence ye came, and I forgive you. Remain, and ye are all dead men."

•••

# CHAPTER XV.

### ENTRAPPED.

I KNOW not how it was, but no sooner had the khan opened his lips than I saw we were lost. How or why I could not tell, but his defiant air and language told me that he had been deceiving us all along.

The rest of us were so much amazed at this unexpected reception that we could say nothing for a moment and it was Harley who first regained his equanimity. Poor brave Harley!

Instantly realizing some treachery he drew his sword and shouted:

"Kill the guards at once! Take the khan alive!"

Hardly were the words out of his mouth when the reports of cannon echoed all around us, followed by the terrible swish and whirring of grapeshot.[641]

---

641 *Grapeshot* is a cluster of small projectiles (resembling a bunch of grapes,

There was a chorus of yells—of fear and pain—from our Tartars throughout the square, and at the same moment the khan's guards sprang at us three, and our followers fled in all directions like sheep. The tables were turned in the twinkling of an eye, as it were.

Like a flash it came on me that our mob had been trapped. The khan's soldiers and artillery had been hidden in the houses round the square, and we were helpless if we did not get out of the town. In that instant I rushed at Nana Sahib, cut him down with a backhanded stroke, and ran for my horse.

Harley and Bunce, equally quick, had shot down two of the guards, and we had all mounted, when the terrible continuous rattling of volleys all round the square told us that we were in a new danger. Inside that square were packed nearly thirty thousand undisciplined Tartars, armed chiefly with bows and swords. All round them was a double line of soldiers, not eight thousand all told, but all armed with muskets and all firing.

The surprise, the difference of weapons and order, told fatally on us. In ten minutes afterwards, we three, lately triumphant, were prisoners; our men were fleeing in dismay to their homes; and it was Nana Sahib, with his face bound up where I had slashed his nose in half, who now called out to the guards:

"Take them to the palace. We will make such an example of these bold rebels that all the world shall fear the vengeance of Yakoob Beg, and his minister, Nana Sahib."

Then we were taken, all three of us, and thrust into a dungeon under the palace, where we were left to meditate over the uncertainty of life in Asia.

We were cast down very much at our fate. Bunce, generally the most hopeful of our party, was particularly gloomy and despondent.

"I shall never see Southport again," he said mournfully. "Jared Bunce will be forgotten, except as the boy who ran away to sea. We'll be killed sure."

Lord Harley was resigned.

"If we must die let's show these infernal Tartars how men of our race can die game," he said, and he fulfilled his promise.

As for myself, I felt nothing but rage at myself for not seeing through Yakoob Beg's trick. He had come out on purpose to get us huddled in a mass, and he had outwitted me, a Greek. That was my

---

hence the name) packed into a canvas bag that breaks apart when launched from a cannon. The overall effect is like firing a giant shotgun.

chief mortification. I did not fear to die; and the same confidence which had sustained me in other trials kept on whispering to me:

"You will be saved."

We lay two days in the dungeon, and on the third we were taken before the khan, who looked at us coldly and made a signal to Nana Sahib.

The wretched Hindoo, whose face was disfigured for life, smiled in a ghastly, derisive way at us, and said to Harley:

"Englishhman, it is the will of the khan that you three traitors be made an example to the world. You have dared to raise a revolt against the best government the sun ever shone upon. In his infinite mercy, however, our illustrious monarch offers you the choice of life and death. You may be starved to death, stung to death by wasps, killed by tigers, cut to pieces—beginning at the toes—impaled on spears, burned to death, or tattooed. If you survive the last the khan will give you your liberty. You have leave to choose. Speak!"

We stared in surprise at the Indian, and Harley said:

"Tattooed? Why, of course we will choose that. It is better to live than to die. I have seen many men who have been tattooed. Is the khan serious?"

Yakoob Beg, who had been listening, here inclined his head. He did not deign to speak to us.

Nana Sahib smiled again in a still more evil fashion.

"Do you willingly consent to be tattooed?" he asked again.

With one accord, and rather glad to get off, as we supposed, so cheaply, we said that we consented.

Then the minister called up one of the khan's scribes, who read out to us a long decree, by virtue of which the khan graciously consented to spare our lives if we survived the operation of tattooing. To all this we listened, half incredulous at our good fortune, and Harley observed:

"Well, this is a queer freak of the old sinner. To be sure he'll make regular guys of us, but as long as we get out of this country what do we care?"

Ah! little did we know what was in store for us all. "Tattooed" was an innocent-sounding word, but we found out too late what it meant.

No sooner was the edict read than we were taken away to a light and pleasant part of the palace, where we were well lodged and well fed. The attendants made us take a hot bath, combed out our hair and beard, and then led us to a large warm room, where we found a short, stout-built man, whose face had the unmistakable look of an old sailor of the Mediterranean. He wore rings in his ears, his black hair was plaited in a coil, and his bare arms were covered with pictures in blue. He had before him three narrow tables. and a fourth on which rested a pot of indigo dye with another of cochineal[642] scarlet. Beside these pots was a little block of wood, set with needles like a brush, a small mallet and a few wooden stamps made in the figures of animals.

Without a word the attendants seized us and laid us out on the tables, where he fastened us down in such a manner that we could not move a muscle. Then they left us there, and the dark man took up one of the stamps and advanced to Harley.

He dipped the stamp in the blue dye, laid it on the Englishman's forehead, then took the block and mallet and lightly tapped all over the figure.[643]

Harley said nothing till he had finished, when he called out:

"I say, Bunce, that hurts. I hope he's not going to do any more just now. By Jove! it's like a bunch of stinging-nettles, only worse."

The tattooer said nothing, but he grinned in the same evil fashion as had done Nana Sahib, and moved his tools over beside Bunce, where he exactly repeated the operation.

The American looked steadily up at him, and remarked to me:

"The blamed skunk's putting an alligator on my forehead. What'll the folks say in Southport? Whew! Don't the needles hurt!"

With the same evil smile, the tattooer came over to me and put the alligator stamp on my forehead.[644]

He laid it on with the utmost care, as if he wished to make a handsome picture. So careful was he that he even washed it off once and reapplied the stamp till it suited him. Then he took up the block and mallet and lightly tapped all over the figure.

In that instant I first realized the terrible fate in store for me. The pricks of those sharp little needles, fifty or a hundred to the inch,

---

642 *Cochineals* are various insects used to produce red dyes for fabrics and, for a time, tattoos.

643 While stamps were sometimes used as a way to transfer a design to the skin before tattooing, using a block of wood with needles set into it is highly unlikely. Tattoos of the time were traditionally done with a single needle mounted on a long rod.

644 Nevermind that Costentenus didn't have any alligators tattooed on his face, just cats and symbols.

just going deep enough to touch the nerves and draw tiny drops of blood, seemed to set all my brain on fire as the tattooer went on with his remorseless tap, till every hair's breadth of the figure was covered.

Then he calmly turned away to the next table, leaving me with my forehead feeling as if all the skin had been torn off, a sheet of bare, quivering nerves.

I set my teeth hard, and presently Bunce asked me ruefully:

"How does it feel now?"

I answered, quietly:

"It is nothing. I can laugh at this."

The tattooer now went to Harley and began to soak his light hair with indigo, rubbing it down into the scalp.

Then, with the same coolness with which he always worked, he pricked in the dye all over his victim's head under the hair, in rows of parallel lines.

At first Harley kept silent, but as the operation extended over his whole scalp, he gradually began to groan and mutter till I perceived that he must be delirious with the pain.

And all this time Bunce and I lay and listened to his groans and waited our turns. We began to realize that tattooing was no light punishment.

As the operator turned away from his victim, Yakoob Khan and Nana Sahib entered the room and looked curiously at us, the Hindoo smiling sneeringly.

•••

# CHAPTER XVI.

### A LINGERING TORTURE.

TO describe my feelings at the sight of the detestable Hindoo would be in vain at this distance of time.

I knew we were utterly in his power, bound naked and helpless before him I knew from what I had already seen that the torture just beginning for all us three was to be something appalling: yet I felt nothing but the most bitter fury, without a particle of fear.

The khan and Nana Sahib came and looked down at me first,

and the Hindoo observed, mockingly:

"This fellow is the stoutest of the three, and he will last till they have got down to his toes, excellency. He has a fine body for pictures."

The khan looked stonily at me and then spoke to the tattooer, who was just then dyeing Bunce's head, before pricking in the pattern.

"Will any of them live through it till you have finished, Antonio?"

I listened for Antonio's answer, for I could not turn my head to see him. He said nothing but the khan rejoined as if he had made a sign.

"Keep them all alive as long as you can; for I want to send them to Russia to frighten the soldiers away."

Nana Sahib laughed lightly.

"If that Englishman is alive by the time they get down to his waist, I am much mistaken. The Yankee is much stronger, but this Greek fellow will stand most of any."

He came over and stood looking down at me with such a contemptuous, cold-blooded sneer that I fairly boiled with rage, and struggled violently to break my cords.

He only laughed still more tauntingly, and observed to the khan:

"If he recovers he will be a good sight to amuse the court, while your Highness and the pretty Gulfirouz look on at his antics."

These words excited me so much that, with a mighty effort, I had almost broken my fastenings, when the Hindoo observed to the khan:

"To-morrow he will be tamer. They all get quiet under Antonio's hands. I think he will last through it."

Then they turned away, while I heard beside me the hollow groans of poor Jared Bunce, into whose scalp the merciless Antonio was now quietly pricking in the indigo. My last effort had enabled me to move my head so far as to watch the operation with a sort of morbid interest.

The Italian worked with as much coolness and care as if he were using his tool on a block of stone.

He first applied the tattooing block in a circle round the head to the edge of the hair, with the same gentle tap he had used all along, and then ran cross patterns to and fro over the head till every part was covered.

In the meantime poor Bunce, who stood it well as long as the khan was in the room, began to utter hollow groans of pain as the whole surface of his scalp under the hair became one tingling surface of agony.

Slowly and carefully as Antonio went on, it was nearly an hour before he left Bunce and Harley, both raving and shrieking in wild delirium, and came over to me.

Then for the first time he spoke, and it was in my native tongue that he said:

"Do you remember Captain Perikles?"

I stared up at him, and he grinned back at me as he went on:

"I knew your face, beard and all. I am the brother of Perikles, and now I can punish you for his death. Howl as much as you like. I love to hear it."

This he said while he was putting the dye on my head, and, as he closed, he took the tattooing block, and began his devilish torture.

Of what followed it makes me, even now, shudder to think. The tearing off of the whole scalp by a savage Indian could not be half as painful as this protracted merciless prick, pricking that went on, minute after minute, till every particle of the scalp was tingling with agony.

If the reader can fancy that some person took the pains to pull out all his hair patiently and conscientiously, hair by hair, with tweezers, he might have an idea of the awful torment that then went on over my poor head, till, stout as I was, in the effort to keep down my groans, I burst into a roar of rage and swooned dead away.

Ah! could I have kept that merciful insensibility, all would have been over; but I was awakened again by the still increasing pain. Antonio was still tapping stoutly away, and he grinned as he remarked:

"Groan away; yell; curse; pray for mercy; I like to hear it. Go on."

I set my teeth, and he proceeded. in the same cool way:

"You will make a handsome picture. I have not had such an opportunity for a long time. The Englishman is too delicate; the Yankee too thin. You are a figure of a man. I will decorate you so that you shall be a world's wonder if you live through it."

So he kept on till he had quite finished my head; and, strange to say, though I was fairly dizzy with the terrible pain, I made shift to suppress any groans and keep my senses, while both my companions had succumbed to the torture and were delirious.

Our torturer now called in another man, who proved to be

a Spanish sailor, once a pirate like Antonio. This fellow's name was Pepito, and Antonio observed:

"Come, Pepe! I'm tired with doing three heads. You finish them under the beards according to the pattern, and they'll do for the day. The doctor comes at sunset."

Pepito nodded, and came over to examine us before going on. He chuckled at Harley, saying:

"That fellow's near dead now. He won't live through it. He's not worth tattooing. It will be wasted."

"Obey orders, or you may meet the same fate," observed Antonio, drily.

Then the Spanish sailor laughed, and went to his work in the same deliberate and painstaking fashion which had distinguished Antonio, joking and laughing over the mad head of poor tortured Harley, as he proceeded to dye the fair beard of the Englishman with indigo, after which he pricked in the spots as before under the hair.[645]

The renewed torture, in a different place and that so sensitive, roused the poor fellow from his stupor, and he began to shout savagely in his frenzy, trying to escape the block, while Pepito calmly hammered away, till the whole beard was a mass of gore and blue from the flowing blood mixing with the indigo.

Harley, only half conscious, had lost all sense of control and was alternately shouting, cursing and begging them "take those wasps away for God's sake."

Antonio, after a little rest, began work again on my other companion, and there was I, with my own head feeling as if it had been scalped, lying waiting and listening to the cries of my tortured comrades all day.

But why lengthen the terrible and painful recital? By the time that the sun set, we were all tattooed on the same pattern, from the crown of the head to the neck, while inflammation had set in on Harley, swelling his head to a fearful size, and I was at last mercifully almost unconscious from the same cause.

What followed that night I know not. I have a faint memory of some one saying:

"They must rest, or they'll die."

I remember soft oily bandages being placed over my fevered and smarting head, after which I fell asleep from sheer nervous debility.

---

645 Why did these torturers not shave the men?! Hair simply gets in the way of the needle and the artist, making a mess of everything.

When I woke I found my two companions near me, their heads tied up; all in bed, but all tied down. I called out to Harley, and heard him say:

"I'm alive, Meer Djorji, but that's all. I sha'n't get through it alive. One more such day and I must kick the bucket, though it's a beastly shame."

Bunce groaned out from his cot:

"'Tain't the pain so much; but to have a blamed alligator on my face. Such a disgrace! I could stand all the rest."

I tried to raise my hand to my face, but found we were still bound down where we had been kept for a night and a day.

On the next morning, with all our multitude of little wounds healed up, we looked at each other and realized that we were marked for life.

Then came the French surgeon, who inspected us carefully with Nana Sahib, and remarked:

"They can stand another day; but keep away from the vital organs till they get stronger if you wish to complete the tattooing alive."

Nana Sahib smiled and said:

"It is of little consequence. The Englishman will die first."

Indeed, any one could see that poor Harley, nervous and delicate, looked haggard through the disfiguring tattoo: his white body, set off by the dark ring round his neck, was already wasting with a fever, and it seemed impossible he would survive any further operations.

Nevertheless, having been washed and combed again, we were once more laid on the well-remembered torture-tables, while Antonio and Pepe began to decorate our breasts with those strange figures which have since, on my body, attracted so much wonder wherever seen.

They no longer used the alligator stamps, but drew the designs by hand—elephants, tigers, sphinxes, opposed to each other in symmetrical patterns.

The pain was, if possible, worse than at the beginning, but it did not affect the brain. The whole surface of our breasts was raw and inflamed at the same time, and no merciful insensibility came to relieve us.

As the lines of blood-drops extended further and further over the white sensitive skin, and all the nerves together began to twitch, the sweat stood out on Harley's brow, and at last he groaned aloud with pain. He was followed by Bunce, and even I was at last forced to groan in spite of all my determination to be silent.

Just as we were all groaning together, Nana Sahib came in and laughed heartily.

"These dogs do not like tattooing after all," he said. "Hear them yell under the whip."

I heard him, gnashed my teeth, and kept silent till he came by, when I spit at him hard. I hoped to provoke him into killing me.

He only laughed again, and told Antonio to take special pains with me and my pictures.

"As for the English dog, he will die to-morrow," he went on, pointing to Harley, whose breast had swelled up frightfully.

•••

# CHAPTER XVII.

### THE FIRST DEATH.

IT was indeed true. My noble comrade was again insensible, and all the punctured surface of his body was swelled up and fearfully inflamed. They took him off the table, wrapped him up in oiled bandages and carried him away but continued their devilish work on Bunce and myself.

By sunset the whole front of our bodies as far as the waist was covered with tattooing, and we felt as if all the skin had been stripped off.

The difference between this and the ordinary tattooing as practiced by sailor's was slight, but it was enough to cause terrible torture.

Ordinary tattooing designs are traced in outline only; ours were solid and made up of blue dots close together over the whole surface of the skin.

That day more than three square feet of each body was a mass of needle-pricks, every puncture poisoned with indigo.

The consequence was that by sunset inflammation had set in both with me and Bunce, and that night we were both in a raging fever, which lasted, as I was afterwards told, for a week.

When I recovered my senses I felt as helpless as a child. They had not even bound me as I lay in bed. I looked at my body and found it a mass of blue figures, beside which the whiteness of my arms and legs seemed preternatural.

Bunce lay sleeping beside me, but Harley had disappeared. A Tartar attendant was watching us, of whom I asked for my English comrade. He gravely replied:

"The Englishman is dead. You are to go on the tables to-morrow. Allah preserve you, poor men!"

We found unexpectedly that our sufferings had raised us up a friend, for the Tartar spoke in a compassionate tone.

The next day, weak but recovered, we were placed on the tables again, and the tattooing was extended from our shoulders down each arm to the elbows. This time Antonio and Pepito traced the designs while assistants used the mallets. Moreover, the work was done rapidly.

But in our weakened state the pain was as bad to bear as before. The long strain on the nerves had told on us both, and poor Bunce was already a mere skeleton.

We were returned to our beds for that night and next day the torture was continued, till the patterns were complete on our arms, down to the ends of the fingers. Then once more inflammation set in, and poor Bunce found his arms swelled up to a frightful size.

That inflammation lasted four days, at the end of which time he was so nearly dead from exhaustion that the doctor ordered him a week's rest, during which he was to be fed up carefully.

But I, being stronger, paid the penalty of my strength. The tattooing was to be continued on me.

Therefore, I was turned over on my face, and in a single day the patterns were pricked in all over my back by Pepe and Antonio working together.

It is a wonder to me to-day how I ever survived that operation, by which in a few hours more than a third of my body was turned into a veritable furnace of fiery pain.

It very nearly killed me as it was, for it threw me into a fever of which I was not free for some three weeks, at the end of which time I woke up—alone with the Tartar attendant.

He looked at me mournfully as I pointed to Bunce's bed.

"Dead," he said. "They tattooed his back like yours and he died the next day."

Then I looked at my hands, arms and body. I found that I

was colored all over down to the hips. Only my legs remained to be tattooed.

"I shall live through it," I said to myself; "and then—vengeance!"

Strange that I only thought of the Hindoo in that connection. I had no grievance against Yakoob Beg.

Two days afterward I was taken back to the table, and while there was visited by Yakoob Beg himself. He seemed milder than his wont and spoke to the doctor, who was with him.

"They were fools to let the other man die. This man must be kept alive, at any cost. I want him to live as a monument of my power. I give you orders to see he is not hurt so as to endanger his life."

The doctor bowed and promised. From that day forth I never saw Nana Sahib in the room, and they proceeded in the tattooing with care, only one figure at a time, with frequent rests.

The consequence was that, whereas the decorations on the upper part of my body had only occupied four days' actual work with three weeks nearly fatal inflammation between them, the rest of the patterns were not finished in six weeks, and it was three months from the day when we were first laid on the tattooing-table before I came forth indelibly marked as I am now, but alive.

Only the palms of my hands, the soles of my feet, and a few square inches of my face were left as Nature made them. Otherwise I was as I am now, and as Yakoob Beg had threatened to make me—a wonder to all the world, civilized and savage.

But I was nearly spent, spite of all the doctor's care. From the bed on which I was laid, sore and smarting from the last touches of the needles, I rose not for nearly a month; and it was not far from a year after the famous riot at Kashgar that I had regained my full strength.

Then, however, I was as well as ever; in fact, better. I had carefully husbanded and concealed my strength under an affectation of sickness, that I might at last be able to seize the opportunity of vengeance when it came to my hand.

I felt a secret presentiment that it would come, and it did.

At last, when I could no longer conceal the fact that I was well and strong again, I was summoned before the khan and his court.

They gave me no clothing but a pair of slippers and a small waist-cloth, and I was led through the public streets for all the people to stare at.

But then it was that I began to realize for the first time that instead of having become an object of pity and scorn, as the khan had undoubtedly intended me to be, I was actually the center of universal admiration. The devilish ingenuity of Nana Sahib, hoping to disfigure me for life, had made of me a beautifully-colored statue, and the story of my endurance of the torture had gained me hosts of friends, even among the soldiers of the khan.

I found Yakoob Beg and all his courtiers in the throne-room, and the evil face of Nana Sahib was the first that caught my view beside his master.

The khan motioned to me to turn around that he might see all the patterns on my body, and then said:

"Enough; you are worse punished alive than dead. I promised you your life. You shall have it, but not your liberty. I have sold you for a slave to the Turks. Have you any boon to ask before you depart? Ask on."

I looked at Nana Sahib and said:

"Sire, I have an enemy whom I wish to fight in your presence. Give me leave to do it and I am content."

The khan laughed—the first time I had ever seen him even smile—while he said:

"You may fight him. Who is he?"

I pointed to Nana Sahib. Yakoob Beg turned to him with a smile, for the selfish tyrant was pleased with my audacity. He said to Nana Sahib:

"Go and fight my picture man at once, but don't kill him. I can get many such as you, but he is the only one in the world. Strip and beat him, if you can."

My time of vengeance had come. The fat and sensual rajah was no match for me and he knew it.

He hesitated; but in a trice, at a signal from the cynical khan, he was stripped of his robes and set out opposite to me, while the courtiers clapped their hands for glee in imitation of their savage ruler.

Nana Sahib was trembling with fear. I quivered with eagerness.

Yakoob Beg gave the signal, and in a moment more I had the false Hindoo by the throat and was beating out his brains on the stone floor.

He was like a child in my hands, and in that moment of vengeance I wiped out the memory of all the wrongs done to me by that wretch.

I knew that Gulfirouz was or must be dead, or I should have heard from her. The Tartar who befriended me had told me how the khan had bought a new wife lately and that the woman had killed her child and herself to avoid entering the zenanah. I know that could only be my Gulfirouz. Therefore, I was alone in the world, ruined in my prime of early youth, and it was to Nana Sahib that I owed all this misery.

No one interfered to part us, and it was nearly ten minutes ere the desperate struggle was over.

The Hindoo fought with all the energy of despair, but I was a perfect maniac in my fury and at last had throttled him to death, and beaten a jagged hole into his skull on the stone steps at the foot of the khan's throne.

Then I rose and salaamed to the khan as I said:

"Now I am willing to go anywhere your highness sends me. I have slain my enemy and I am happy."

Yakoob Beg smiled in his grim way and observed.

"You are a stout fellow. I wish I had an army of men like you. Rostosky will take care of you and conduct you to the frontier. All the world shall know the power of Yakoob Beg."

He dismissed me with a wave of his hand, and Rostosky, Commander of the Guard, took me away according to his orders.

I was clothed and mounted, and turned over to a guard who conducted me to the frontier of Kashgar, where I met my new master, a Turk named Redif Effendi.[646]

Redif Effendi was a slave merchant of Constantinople, and by him I was taken through Persia, and finally sold in the slave bazar to a stranger, who proved to be a friend in disguise.

An American of great wealth, gained in the show business, had heard of my existence, and knowing the singular nature of my experience, redeemed me from slavery and restored me to freedom without any condition.

Heaven bless that generous American! I, for one, shall never, in all my life, forget my obligations to him.

His agent set me at liberty in Constantinople, provided me with clothes and a purse of money, and gave me his employer's address.

It was in Vienna, and there it was that I met my rescuer and friend, to whom I have adhered ever since.

From that day to the present I have wanted for nothing. The very punishment which was intended to ruin me for life has become

---

646 A *redif* is a Turkish soldier, and *Effendi* is a Turkish title of respect.

the means of my elevation to prosperity.

Instead of an object of fear and aversion, as it was hoped I should become, I have found myself a theme of admiration wherever I went, and every sovereign in Europe has honored me with interviews. The story of my checkered life is nearly over.

•••

# CHAPTER XVIII.

## CONCLUSION.

I WAS only too glad to make a contract with my generous friend, by which he was to undertake the expense of exhibiting me in Europe, paying me a munificent salary and expenses.

The Emperor Louis Napoleon of France was pleased to express great admiration of what he called my heroic endurance, and he it was who presented me with the fine diamond ring I now wear.

The King of Prussia—he was not then Emperor of Germany[647]—and Czar Alexander of Russia also expressed great interest in me, and each gave me a ring.[648]

After a successful tour over Europe, occupying several years, I came to America, where I have traversed all the Northern States, year after year, showing in all the principal cities.

---

647 If we critically examine the timeline again, which is probably a bad idea, this point in the story seems to be happening in the early 1860s. Louis Napoleon (Napoleon III) was the Emperor of France from 1852 up to 1870. The King of Prussia, specified here as "not then Emperor of Germany," would have been Wilhelm I, who was king between 1861 and1871. The overlap of these two spans places this part of the Captain's story between 1861 and 1870. Earlier, the pamphlet states that Costentenus met Yakoob Beg in 1857. This would put the rebellion, torture, and journey back to Constantinople in 1858 or 1859–perhaps 1860, at the latest. That puts the beginning of Costentenus's career in the early 1860s in Vienna, although he didn't start there until 1870. Once again, the pamphlet seems to have only a passing resemblance to the truth.

648 Jewelry was apparently a common gift from rulers to tattooed performers. Nora Hildebrandt was supposedly given a pair of diamond solitaire earrings by President Gonzalez of Mexico when she appeared before him around 1883 or 1884.

In Philadelphia, thanks to the efforts of my friend and agent, Dr. G. O. Starr,[649] himself a physician, I became the center of attraction to the medical fraternity, who refused at first to believe in the genuineness of my markings.

One and all were of the opinion that there must be some sort of deception; that the figures were only painted on.

They pronounced it "an impossibility" for any human being to survive the process of tattooing when extended over the entire body.

Well, these gentlemen were invited to a private view in the parlors of the Continental Hotel in the city of Philadelphia, and in a very short time the most stubborn disbelievers were convinced that their "impossibility" was a fixed fact.[650]

After applying every test which science is capable, they pronounced my tattooing to be genuine, and from thenceforth became my warmest friends and supporters.

Need I say to the inhabitants of Great Britain that the American was none other than their greatest showman, G. A. Farini.[651] Through

---

649 *Dr. G. O. Starr* was a real person, but he was not a doctor at all. Rather, George O. Starr was a press agent. He had been with the Bunnell brothers (Costentenus's employers when the pamphlet was published) at least as far back as the 1878 season with the *Greatest Show on Earth*. He continued to work with them until 1887, before returning to the newly renamed Barnum & Bailey Circus in 1888. It's likely that Starr, as press agent, was involved in some way in the creation of Costentenus's pamphlet. Given the glowing terms with which the ghostwriter described both George Bunnell (Costentenus's longtime employer) and Farini (his future employer), they also may have been involved.

650 Perhaps this was a version of the viewing that supposedly took place in Boston in 1876, where the learned men of Harvard Medical, including Dr. Oliver Wendell Holmes, Sr., viewed the tattooed man and attested to his authenticity for Barnum's publicity machine. Or perhaps it was just another invention for the pamphlet.

651 *G. A. Farini* managed Costentenus at the Royal Aquarium in Westminster, but he could not have been the Captain's savior as this story says. There is once again a problem with the dates (and the credibility). In the mid-1850s, Signor Farini was still plain old William Hunt of Canada, learning to be a tightrope walker and acrobat. He then fought in the American Civil War in the early 1860s. Farini did briefly live in Vienna, but not until 1872, after Costentenus had already made his debut there. Farini probably didn't meet Captain George until 1881—not-so coincidentally when the pamphlet was published. This is not the only performer pamphlet to list a promoter or circus owner as a savior. Tattooed performer Nora Hildebrandt's pamphlet

his efforts I have traveled all through Europe and America. While in the latter country, by his advice I placed myself under the protection of youngest and greatest museum manager of that land, G. B. Bunnell.[652]

My memories of the past, connected as they are with as many deaths of friends and loved ones, are too painful to be lightly revived. Aspasia and Gulfirouz, sleeping beneath the bare plains of Asia, Harley and Bunce, lying in unnamed graves under the iron rule of the tyrant of Kashgar, are to me sacred forever. The name of Lord Harley is an assumed one. In compliance with the wishes of his family I have done this.

So long as Yakoob Beg lived and was accessible to an increase of power, I forbode to publish the facts of my life. The publicity given to his name would have pleased that savage potentate, and I did not care to let him have such an advantage.

Therefore neither in Europe nor America did the name of Yakoob Beg ever cross my lips. I let all sort of absurd stories pass current about me, but I never told any one how I was tattooed or by who.

Since the death of Yakoob Beg, in 1877, the reason for my silence has been removed. The bloody tyrant has gone to his long rest, and the kingdom of Kashgar is broken up.

The Chinese, who once controlled it, have reconquered the kingdom and the copper mines, which once belonged to Harley, Bunce and myself, have returned to their original owners. Yakoob Beg can feel no more pride now.

It is in gratitude to Americans, to whom I owe my liberty, that I have at last consented to give the world my life, which will, I trust, be found interesting.

I am the only living man of a civilized stock that saw Nana Sahib die, and it was my bare hands, nerved by the desperate fury of a bereaved husband and father, that rid the earth of that villain.

Almost alone of civilized men, I traversed the plains of Turkistan long before the Russians took Khiva.

I alone stole the shah's daughter from Teheran, and married a princess in spite of all the power of an empire.

---

credited circus owner Adam Forepaugh's business manager for giving her $50 to help her regain her sight after she lost it due to her (supposedly) forced tattooing.

652 *George B. Bunnell* had managed Barnum's sideshow during Costentenus's time with *the Greatest Show on Earth*. The Captain continued to work for the Bunnell brothers at their New American Museum in New York.

I alone of all men have survived the torture of tattooing, and I am the only human being of my kind in all the wide world.

But I am alone, and the last of my race.

In me the blood of Constantine the Great, the first Christian Emperor of the Roman world, flows its last drops ere it dries up forever.

Such as I am, I will do no dishonor to my blood to the last. The cruelty of man has driven me to the necessity of living by the exhibition of my scarred body; but no man can say that George Costentenus is not at all times and places a brave, courteous gentleman.

In the hope that my adventures, thus briefly described, may interest and amuse the idle hours of many a man, I close my task.

DJORDGI KONSTANTINUS

# [THE END]

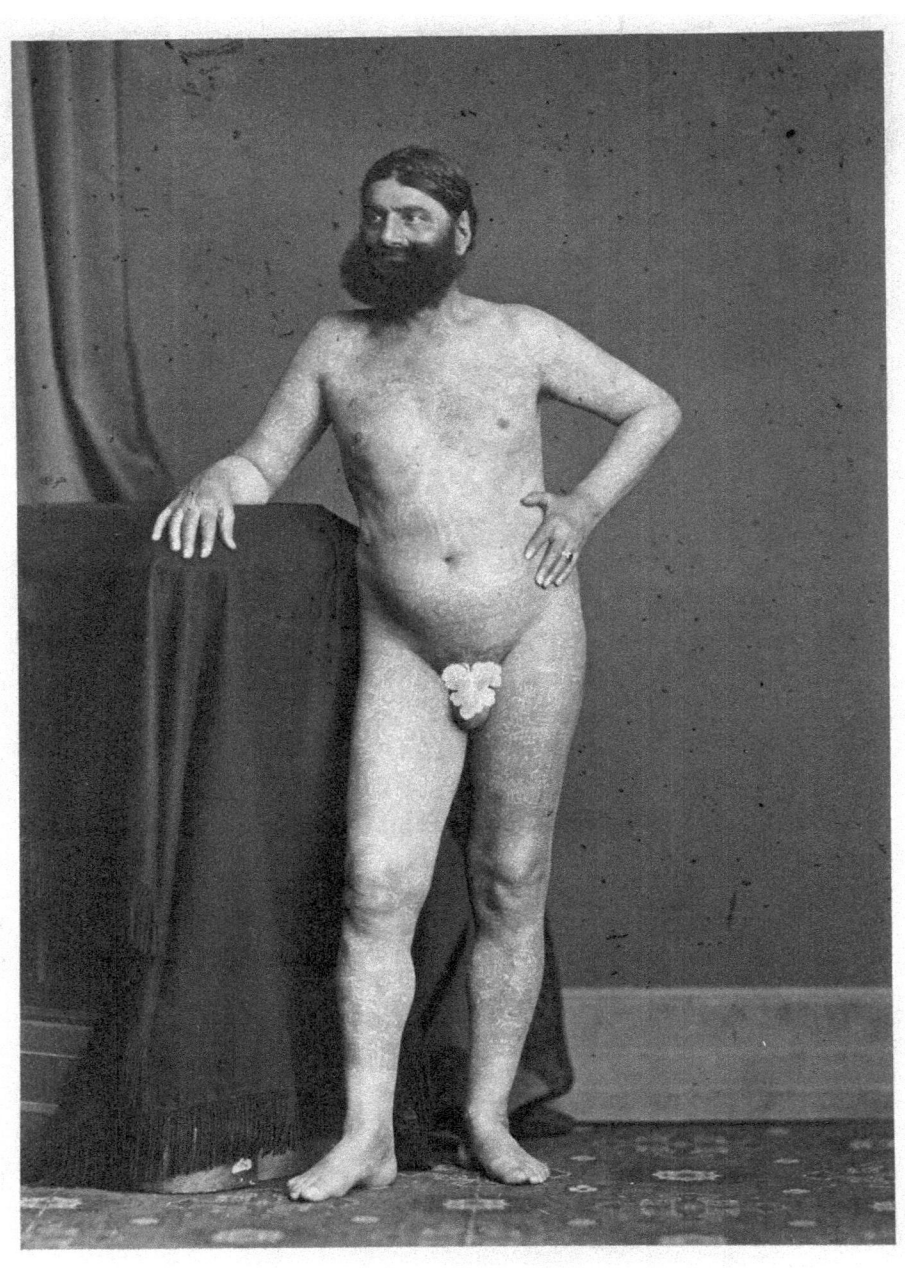

*Photograph of George Costentenus taken by Ludwig Angerer, Vienna, 1870,*
*(Collection of Adam Woodward)*

# ACKNOWLEDGEMENTS

The journey this project took was a long one. I started researching the Captain in 2013, after that fateful trip to the University of Chicago's Library of the Health Sciences' Special Collections and Archives Department with my friend and fellow tattoo history researcher Anna Felicity Friedman. Many events interrupted my progress, including the five long years of remodeling a home with my husband. The early days of COVID gave me the time to write the first three chapters, which gave me the momentum I needed to keep writing.

I'm very grateful to all those who encouraged and helped me along the way.

Librarians and archivists Pete Shrake and Jen Cronk at Circus World's Parkinson Library and Research Center in Baraboo always seemed pleased to see me and were so helpful in finding images, plus are fun to drink with. Jennifer Lemmer Posey and Susan O'Shea at the Circus Museum at the John and Mable Ringling Museum of Art in Sarasota are super knowledgeable of everything circus in their collections, and kept finding me amazing images and documents. I loved coming back to the library after taking a short break to see "my guy" waiting for me at a table. Adrienne Saint-Pierre and Kathy Maher of the Barnum Museum in Bridgeport, Connecticut were so very generous with their newly identified tiny French Costentenus image.

So many knowledgeable people answered my really random questions and gave their time and energy to helping me track down information. I am a Pfenning Pfan because Fred Pfennig III took the time to read one of my chapters and give me helpful feedback, as well as answer random questions about Barnum, the Bunnells, route books, and W. E. Sinclair, the swindler. Thank you to Maureen Brunsdale and Mark Schmitt, both librarians at University of Illinois Bloomington/ Normal's Special Collections Department, especially Maureen for finding a third copy of Costentenus's pamphlet for me to use from the collection of A. Bruce Tracy. Bob Cline and Fred Dahlinger answered obscure wagon and tent stake questions. Carl Deußen, from University College, Freiburg, answered my emails about Wilhelm Joest, and Nicola Tannenbaum, Professor Emerita of Anthropology at Lehigh University, answered my questions about Shan tattooing and recommended several books. Matt Reeves, librarian at the Kansas City Public Library, scrolled through newspaper microfilm looking for appearances Costentenus made in 1883 in Kansas City. Julie Mayle, of the Rutherford B. Hayes Presidential Library & Museums, looked for evidence of a meeting between the Tattooed Greek and the President. Nancy Folz, of the Anderson County Historical Society in Garnett Kansas, combed through print records and photographs for me. Daniel Goldin, of Boswell Books in Milwaukee, encouraged me to write about my experiences in tracking down information about the Captain. My dad, Bruce Klem, used his Civil War expertise and connections to help me find the still elusive daguerreotype of Ad Nathans. And Brian Hannemann, from Milwaukee Public Library's Interlibrary Loan department, helped me get access to all kinds of obscure resources.

Nick Vaccaro, Derin Bray, and Dana Brunson generously made photos from their personal collections available for the book. Dale Stinchcomb, the Assistant Curator of the Harvard Theatre Collection Houghton Library, tracked down images I'd looked at over a decade earlier and made them available to me.

I am indebted to Fritz Grobe for working with me for over two years to turn a fairly academic book into something much better, and to Thom Wall for putting Fritz and I together.

Thank you to Sam Tracy, Erin Christman, Ara Kueny, Casey

Turner, and Betsey Grobe who read and gave feedback to the manuscript, and thanks to all my friends who have patiently listened to my weird research rabbit hole obsessions over the years. Lord Byron is, in fact, connected to everything.

My biggest supporter over the years I worked on this project has been my husband, DannO Osterud, who has never tired of hearing about some dead guy.

Finally, the most thanks to the leading ladies of the SubPar Circus: Betsy Golden Kellem, Aíne Norris, Kat Vecchio, and Kristin Lee. You all kept me going with your encouragement, support, and shared love of circus history.

Amelia Klem Osterud
Milwaukee, Wisconsin, October 2025

# ABOUT THE AUTHORS

**Amelia Klem Osterud**

Amelia Klem Osterud is a heavily tattooed freelance historian and public librarian from Milwaukee, Wisconsin, who has become the world's leading expert on tattooed performers. She researches and writes on circus, sideshow, and tattoo history and is on the board of the Circus Historical Society.

She is the author of *The Tattooed Lady: A History* and a contributor to *The World Atlas of Tattoo and Tattoo Histories: Transcultural Perspectives on the Narratives, Practices, and Representations of Tattooing.*

Amelia is a fan of swimming in very cold lakes and has either 421 or 38 tattoos, depending on how you count them. She is always planning her next one.

## Fritz Grobe

Fritz Grobe has been a world-record-setting juggler, a circus director, and a nationally-ranked math geek. He became "internet famous" as one of the Coke & Mentos guys, creating early viral videos featuring the explosive combination of Diet Coke and Mentos that have been viewed over 150 million times. His online video work won four Webby Awards and received two Emmy nominations.

He is the co-author of *The Viral Video Manifesto* (McGraw-Hill) and *How to Build a Hovercraft and 25 Other Amazing D.I.Y. Science Projects* (Chronicle Books) with Stephen Voltz.

Fritz has performed live in 19 countries and appeared on dozens of television shows including *The Late Show with David Letterman, The Today Show, Jimmy Kimmel Live*, and *Mythbusters*. He has more than 250 Lego sets, but—as yet—zero tattoos.

# BIBLIOGRAPHY

"Agility" and "At the Lion." *Boston Post*, March 31, 1837.

"American Museum." *Evening Post*. September 25, 1840.

"American Museum." New-York Tribune. November 14, 1842,

"Amusement Addenda." *Chicago Inter Ocean*. September 9, 1894.

"Amusements." *Baltimore Sun*. March 30, 1883.

"Amusements." *Brooklyn Union-Argus* November 13, 1880.

"Amusements." *St. Louis Globe-Democrat*. September 1, 1880.

"Amusements: Barnum's American Museum." *Brooklyn Evening Star.* September 8, 1860.

"Another Extraordinary Exposition." *Topeka Daily Press*. May 3, 1890.

"At the Dime Museum." *New York Clipper*. January 21, 1882.

"At the Fifth Ave. Museum." *New York Clipper*. August 5, 1882.

"At the Hotels." *St. Louis Globe-Democrat*. August 25, 1879.

"Art Extraordinary: Where Tattooed People in the Museum Come From." *Frederick Weekly News*. July 10, 1884.

"At the Theatres." *World*. August 20, 1893.

"Aus den Wünschen Andern und Wäldern." *Neuen Fremden Blatt*. September 18, 1872.

Auten, Madison. "Ancient Andean Tattooing Practices." Master's thesis, University of Wisconsin Milwaukee, 2018. UW Milwaukee Electronic Theses and Dissertations Database.

"Barnet Burns." *Bath Chronicle and Weekly Gazette.* November 17, 1836.

Barnum. P.T. *Struggles and Triumphs*. Alfred A. Knopf: 1927.

"Barnum's American Museum." *New York Herald*. November 15, 1842.

"Barnum's Behemoth." *City Times*. June 19, 1877. P.T. Barnum Clippings 1876-1880. Circus World Museum Library, Wisconsin Historical Society.

"Barnum's Circus Scorched By Fires." *Wisconsin State Journal*. June 5, 1883.

"Barnum's Day: The People's Holiday." *Omaha Daily Bee*. July 30, 1880.

"Barnum's Great Show." *Rutland Daily Herald*. June 16, 1873.

"Barnum's Great Show." *Vermont Watchman and State Journal*. August 9, 1871.

"Barnum's Great Show: First Day's Performance," *Richmond Dispatch*, September 19, 1876.

"Barnum's Latest: The New and Greatest Show on Earth." *Boston Daily Advertiser*. June 20, 1876.

"Barnum's Show." *Rochester Democrat and Chronicle*. September 19, 1871.

Bogdan, Robert. *Freak Show: Presenting Human Oddities for Amusement and Profit*. Chicago, 1988.

"Bostock and Wombwell's Royal National Menagerie. Wanted" *Era*. July 19, 1885.

Braathen, Sverre O. and Faye O. Braathen. "Circus Monarchs: Wm. Cameron Coup." *Bandwagon*. March-April 1970.

"Bradford Exhibition." *Leeds Mercury*. October 17, 1840.

"Brief Mention," *Hartford Courant*, July 6, 1876.

"Brevities." *Record Argus*. July 5, 1883.

Brander, Elisabeth. "Couching Cataracts: Cloudy with a Chance of Infection." Washington University School of Medicine in St. Louis. https://becker.wustl.edu/news/couching-cataracts-cloudy-with-a-chance-of-infection/.

Bray, Derin and Margaret Hodges. *Loud, Naked, and in Three Colors*: *The Liberty Boys and the History of Tattooing in Boston*. Rake House, 2020.

Brewer, David . *The Greek War of Independence: The Struggle for Freedom from Ottoman Oppression*. Abrams Press, 2022.

Burns, Barnet. *A Brief Narrative of the Remarkable History of Barnet Burns, an English Sailor, Who Has Lately Been Exhibiting at the 'Surrey Zoological Gardens,' and Other Place of Amusement*. E. Justins and Son, Printers, 1835.

"Burning of Barnum's." *New York Herald*. December 25, 1872.

[Busey, Ida May] Mlle. Aimee. *Facts Relating To the Only Tattooed Lady*. New York Popular Publishing Co., undated.

Byron, George Gordon. *The Works of Lord Byron*. Ed. 202 in *The Works of Lord Byron*, ed. Ernest H. Coleridge. Scribner's, 1899.

"A Busted Circus." *Ottawa Daily Republic*. September 13, 1883.

"Capt. Costentenus." *Chicago Daily Tribune*. March 1, 1877.

"Capt. Costentenus." *Daily Inter Ocean*. May 24, 1882.

"Captain Costentenus." *Philadelphia Inquirer*. January 27, 1893.

"Captain Costentenus." *Philadelphia Times*. December 23, 1881.

"Capt. Costentenus Beaten" *New York Times*. March 31, 1878.

"Capt. Geo Costentenus." *New York Clipper*. November 3, 1883.

"Captain DeCoursey." *New York Clipper*. June 24, 1882.

"Card." *New York Clipper*. April 1, 1876.

"The Case of Dan Rice." *Garnett Journal*. Sept. 20, 1883.

Carlyon, David. *Dan Rice: The Most Famous Man You've Never Heard Of*. Public Affairs, 2001.

Cartwright, F. F. "Joseph Lister." *Encyclopedia Britannica*. https://www.britannica.com/biography/Joseph-Lister-Baron-Lister-of-Lyme-Regis.

"The Centennial Fourth." *Lowell Daily Citizen*. July 5, 1876.

"Chaff." *Farmers' Review*. June 8, 1882.

"Charles H. Day." *New York Clipper*. October 22, 1892.

"A Chat With Barnum." *London Era*. July 29, 1877.

Cheshire, Neil, et al. "Frobisher's Eskimos in England." *Archivaria* 10 (1980): 23-50.

"A Chinese Fair." *New York Clipper*. January 15, 1881.

*The Circassian Girl: Zalumma Agra "Star of the East" Now on Exhibition at Barnum's Museum.* Jas. B. Rodgers Co, 1873, P.T. Barnum Research Collection, Bridgeport History Center Archives.

"The Circus." *Brockport Republic*. June 7, 1883.

"The Circus." *Garnett Republican-Plaindealer*. September 14, 1883.

"The Circus." *Roanoke News*. Aug 2, 1883.

"Circus Folk Mourn 'Best Liked Freak,' Krao, the 'Missing Link,' Buried With Tribute of Tears From Side-Show Associates." *New York Times*. April 19, 1926.

"A Circus on Fire." *New York Clipper*. August 4, 1883.

"Circus Personalities." *New York Clipper*. October 5, 1912.

"The Circus Rows" *Daily City News*. July 2, 1883.

"Circuses," *New York Clipper*. March 17, 1883.

"Circuses." *New York Clipper*. April 28, 1883.

"Circuses." *New York Clipper*. February 4, 1882.

"Circuses." *New York Clipper*. June 16, 1883.

"Circuses." *New York Clipper*. June 4, 1881.

"Circuses." *New York Clipper*. March 4, 1876.

"Circuses." *New York Clipper*. May 12, 1883.

"Circuses." *New York Clipper*. May 19, 1883.

"Circuses: The Tenting Season of '71." *New York Clipper*. April 8, 1871.

"The Circus Sale." *Garnett Republican-Plaindealer*. December 21, 1883.

"City and Suburban News" *New York Times*. February 17, 1884.

"City and Vicinity: Locals in Brief." *Lowell Daily Citizen*. June 24, 1876.

Clarke, Kit. "Among the Showmen: Successful Managers, Tricks of the Profession, Etc." *New York Clipper*. November 25, 1871.

"Clowns and Clowns." *Cincinnati Commercial Gazette*. June 3, 1883.

"Cole's Dime Museum." *St. Joseph Gazette*. January 21, 1885.

"Coming, Entire and Undivided" *Mexico Weekly Ledger*. August 26, 1880.

"Corn Exchange." *Preston Chronicle and Lancashire Advertiser*. December 4, 1847.

"Crimes and Casualties." *Superior Times*. December 8, 1876.

Conway, Susan. *Tai Magic: Arts of the Supernatural in the Shan states and Lan Na*. River Books, 2014.

Coup, William C. *Sawdust and Spangles: Stories & Secrets of the Circus*. H.S. Stone and Co., 1901.

"Curiosities Gone to Sea." *New York Sun*. November 3, 1881.

Cushing, J. N. *A Shan and English Dictionary*. Gregg International Publishers, 1971.

Dahlinger, Jr., Fred. "The American Circus Tent." In *The American Circus*, edited by Susan Weber, Kenneth L. Ames, and Matthew Wittmann, 200-231. Yale University Press, 2012.

Dahlinger, Jr. Fred and Stuart Thayer. *Badger State Showmen: A History of Wisconsin's Circus Heritage*. Grote Publishing.

Dalby, Andrew. "Sir George Scott, 1851-1935, Explorer of Burma's Eastern Borders, in *Explorers of South-East Asia: Six Lives*. Oxford University Press, 1995. 108-157.

Darwin, Charles. *The Descent of Man*. D. Appleton and Co., 1871.

"Dan Rice's Prayer." *Philadelphia Times*. June 20, 1883.

Day, Dave and Margaret Roberts. "A Swimming Family: The Beckwiths." *Swimming Communities in Victorian England*. Springer, 2019.

"Death of a Giantess." *New York Clipper*. June 30, 1883.

"Death of the Tattooed Man," *New Orleans Crescent*, January 30, 1854.

"Deaths in the Profession." *New York Clipper*. November 7, 1903.

Decoursey, Harry. *Life and Adventures of Captain Harry Decoursey: A Book Containing a History of My Life, Accounts of Tattooing, How it is Performed and by Whom*. New York Popular Publishing Co: 1882.

Dennett, Andrea Stulman. *Weird and Wonderful: The Dime Museum in America*. New York University Press, 1997.

Deter-Wolf, Aaron, Benoît Robitaille, Danny Riday, Aurélien Burlot, and Maya Sialuk Jacobsen. "Chalcolithic Tattooing: Historical and Experimental

Evaluation of the Tyrolean Iceman's Body Markings." *European Journal of Archaeology* 27 no. 3 (2024): 267–288.

Deter-Wolf, Aaron, Benoît Robitaille, Lars Krutak, Sébastien Galliot. "The World's Oldest Tattoos." *Journal of Archaeological Science: Reports* 5 (2016): 19-24.

"Dime Museum." *Baltimore Sun*. March 26, 1883.

"The Dime Museum." *New York Clipper*. January 20, 1883.

Dingess, John A. Dingess Manuscript. Unpublished manuscript, 1901. Circus World Museum Library, Wisconsin Historical Society.

Doorbrook, Don. "War is Booming Skin Art, Says Man Who Has Needled 20,000." *Milwaukee Journal*. December 24, 1943.

"Dramatic and Musical Gossip." *Referee*. April 13, 1884.

"Dramatic Offerings." *Boston Daily Globe*. November 17, 1889.

*Drawing With Great Needles: Ancient Tattoo Traditions of North America*, ed. Aaron Deter-Wolf and Carol Diaz-Granados. University of Texas Press, 2013.

"The Dwarves and Giants: Who Some of Them Are, and How They Live." *Evening Star*. October 29, 1881.

Dye, Ira. "The Tattoos of Early American Seafarers, 1796-1818." *Proceedings of the American Philosophical Society*. 133, No. 4 (Dec., 1989): 520-554.

"Eden Musée." *Lincoln Daily Nebraska State Journal*. March 14, 1890.

"Eden Musée." *St. Joseph Herald*. February 24, 1890.

"Edmond's, Late Wombwell's, and Sir James W. Bostock's Monster United Shows, Menagerie, Circus, and Museum… Wanted." *Era*. July 11, 1891.

"Epstean's Dime Museum." *Daily Inter Ocean*. May 26, 1890.

Emergency Passport Applications (Issued Abroad), 1877-1907. National Archives and Records Administration (NARA); Washington D.C. Ancestry.com.

England & Wales, Crime, Prisons & Punishment, 1770-1935/Captivity For Year 1809-1811 & 1812. findmypast.co.uk.

"Evening Echoes." *New Journal*. October 14, 1878.

"Fact and Fancy Focused." *New York Clipper*. February 7, 1880.

"50 Years Ago Today." *Lafayette Journal and Courier*. July 28, 1927.

Finkel, Caroline. *Osman's Dream: The History of the Ottoman Empire*. Basic Books, 2005.

"Firing the Freaks." *Pomona Daily Review*. March 1913.

Fisher, Linda A. and Carrie Bowers. *Agnes Lake Hickok: Queen of the Circus, Wife of a Legend.* . University of Oklahoma Press: 2009.

"Fonograf." *Allgemeine Sport-Zeitung* (Austria). January 2, 1887.

Fox, C. A. O. *Bibliographical Notes on John Rutherford and Barnet Burns.* Christchurch, History and Bibliography. 1950.

"Franklin Theatre." *New York Daily Herald.* October 21, 1849.

Fraser-Lu, Sylvia. *Burmese Crafts: Past and Present.* Oxford University Press, 1994.

"Freaks Always Popular." *Sun.* January 3, 1897.

"Freaks' Bequests." *Daily Saratogan.* April 9, 1885.

Friedman, Renée, Daniel Antoine, Sahra Talamo, Paula J. Reimer, John H. Taylor, Barbara Wills, and Marcello A. Mannino. "Natural Mummies from Predynastic Egypt Reveal the World's Earliest Figural Tattoos." *Journal of Archaeological Science* 92 (2018): 116-125.

"From Our Exchanges." *Perry County Democrat.* May 11, 1881.

"From Saturday's Daily." *Garnett Republican-Plaindealer.* January 8, 1886.

Frost, Linda. *Never One Nation: Freaks, Savages, and Whiteness in US Popular Culture, 1850-1877.* University of Minnesota Press, 2005.

"Fun for the Boys." *The Galveston Daily News.* November 13, 1894.

*Gadsden County, Florida, U.S., Compiled Marriages, 1851-1875,* Ancestry.com.

Garland-Thomson, Rosemarie. *Freakery: Cultural Spectacles of the Extraordinary Body.* New York University Press, 1996.

"G.B. Bunnell's Brooklyn Museum: April 24, 1882." Tibbals Circus Collection, The John and Mable Ringling Museum of Art, Sarasota, Florida.

"G.B. Bunnell's Great Show." *New York Clipper* November 27, 1880.

"G.B. Bunnell's New Museum." *New York Clipper.* October 15, 1881.

George, Alys X. "Anatomy for All: Medical Knowledge on the Fairground in Fin-de-Siècle Vienna." *Central European History* 51 (2018): 535 - 562.

"George Barnet Burns - Death." *Plymouth and Devonport Journal.* January 3, 1861.

"Georgios Konstantinos." *Dagens Nyheder.* July 14, 1873.

"Germany's Largest Steamship." *New York Tribune.* November 20, 1874.

"Gossip of the Corridors" *The Times* (Philadelphia). December 23, 1889.

Granger, Christophe. *Joseph Kabris ou Les Possibilités d'Une Vie: 1780-1822.* Anamosa, 2020.

"The Greek Tattooed Man." *Sun-Journal.* December 22, 1883.

"H. Präuscher's Museum im K. K. Prater." *Morgen-Post* (Vienna, Austria). June 30, 1885.

"H. Präuscher's Museum im K. K. Prater." *Morgen-Post* (Vienna, Austria). August 15, 1885.

Hale, James W. *An Historical Account of the Siamese Twin Brothers, From Actual Observations*. Elliot and Palmer, 1831.

Harris, Neil. *Humbug: The Art of P.T. Barnum*. Little, Brown & Co., 1973.

"Hartford and Vicinity." *Hartford Daily Courant*. March 11, 1880.

Hebra, Ferdinand. "Ein tättowirter Mann: Homo Notis Compunctus." *Atlas der Hautkrankheiten, Lfg. 8. Albinismus, Leucoderma, Lentigo, Chloasma, Argyria, Naevus Verrucosus, Homo Notis Compunctus*. Kaiserl.-Königl. Hof- und Staatsdruckerei, 1872.

Hildebrandt, Nora. *Miss Nora Hildebrandt, The Tattooed Lady*. Merchant's Gargling Oil Liniment, date unknown.

*History of Rudolph Lucasie, a Native of Lenabon, Madagascar... On Exhibition at Barnum's American Museum*. New York, 1860. Circus World Museum Library, Wisconsin Historical Society.

"How He Suffered." *Buffalo Evening News*. April 19, 1881.

"Howe, Lucien." Museum of the Eye Biographies. American Academy of Ophthalmology. accessed September 2, 2022, https://www.aao.org/biographies-detail/lucien-howe-md.

Huang, Yunte. *Inseparable: The Original Siamese Twins and Their Rendezvous with American History*. Liveright Publishing, 2018.

"Human Obesity." *Milwaukee Journal*. August 28, 1883.

"If Barnum Were Alive!" *Boston Globe*. February 17, 1895.

"In All Its Great Entirety: P. T. Barnum's New and Greatest Show on Earth." *Fitchburg Daily Sentinel*. August 17, 1876.

"In New York." *Rock Island Argus*. December 30, 1927.

"Incidents at the Island." *New York Times*. August 8, 1880.

"Incidents at the Island: Lightings Playing Among the Clouds." *New York Times*. August 8, 1880.

Index to Petitions for Naturalization filed in New York City, 1792-1989. Ancestry.com.

"Introductory." *New York Clipper*. December 4, 1880.

Jerome, Jerome K. "The Idler's Club." *Idler*. February 1892.

Joest, Wilhelm. *Tätowiren: Narbenzeichen und Körperbemalen, Ein Beitrag zur Vergleichenden Ethnologie*. Asher, 1887.

Joest, Wilhelm. "Tättowirten von Birma." *Verhandlungen der Berliner Gesellschaft für Anthropologie, Ethnologie und Urgeschichte* 20 (1888): 319-321.

"The Jones Tragedy." *Omaha Daily Bee*. March 2, 1890.

Kabris, Joseph. *Précis Historique et Véritable du Séjour de Joseph Kabris, Natif de Bordeaux, Dans les Isles Mendoça, Situées dans l'Océan Pacifique, Sous le 10e Degré de Latitude Sud, 240e Degré de Longitude*. F. Mari.

"Kansas City Dime Museum." *Kansas City Journal*, September 30, 1883.

Kaposi, Moritz. "Der Tätowirte von Birma." *Wiener Medizinische Wochenschrift* Nr 2 (1872): 39-43.

Kellem, Betsy Golden. "Circassian Beauty in the American Sideshow." *Public Domain Review*. Sept. 16, 2021, https://publicdomainreview.org/essay/circassian-beauties.

Kelley, Tina. "A Museum Visit From an Armchair. *New York Times*. July 1, 2005,

Konstantinus, Djordgi. *The True Life and Adventures of Capt. Costentenus, The Tattooed Greek Prince*. New York Popular Publishing Co, 1881. Harvard Theatre Collection. Houghton Library, Harvard University. Cambridge,. Mass.

Krutak, Lars. "Myth Busting Tattoo (Art) History." Last modified August 22, 2013. https://www.larskrutak.com/myth-busting-tattoo-art-history/.

Kunhardt, Jr., Philip B., Philip B. Kunhardt III, and Peter W. Kunhardt. *P. T. Barnum, America's Greatest Showman*. Alfred A. Knopf, 1995.

Kunzog, John. *One Horse Show: The Life and Times of Dan Rice, Circus Jester and Philanthropist, a Chronicle of Early Circus Days*. 1962.

Kyriakou, G., A. Kyriakou, and Th. Fotas. "Dermatostiksia (Tattooing): An Act of Stigmatization in Ancient Greek Culture." *Actas Dermosifiliogr.* 112 (2021): 907–909.

"Latest News by Telegraph." *New York Clipper*. January 27, 1883.

Leffler, CT, A. Klebanov, W.A. Samara, and A. Grzybowski. "The History of Cataract Surgery: From Couching to Phacoemulsification." *Annals of Translational Medicine*, 8, No. 22, (November 2020): 1551.

Lineberry, Cate and Sonja Anderson. "The Worldwide History of Tattoos: Ancient Ink Exhibited Religious Faith, Relieved Pain, Protected Wearers and Indicated Class." *Smithsonian Magazine*. October 18, 2023, https://www.smithsonianmag.com/history/tattoos-worldwide-history-144038580/.

"Living Chromos." *Public Press*. April 11, 1884, p. 1.

"Living Curiosities." *Era*. December 26, 1885.

"Local Matters." *Bangor Daily Whig & Courier*. July 25, 1876.

"Local Notes." *Middletown Daily Argus*, June 13, 1883.

"Loving a Curiosity." *Boston Globe*. May 1, 1881.

"Ludwig Angerer." *Monoskop*. Last modified May, 25 2022. https://monoskop. org/Ludwig_Angerer.

"Madison Square Garden I." *Ticket Dogs*. http://hockey.ballparks.com/NHL/ NewYorkRangers/1stoldindex.htm.

MacCarthy, Fiona. *Byron: Life and Legend*. Farrar, Straus and Giroux, 2002.

"The Man About Town." *Buffalo Sunday Morning News*. June 10, 1883.

"A Man with a Private Picture Gallery." *Cincinnati Enquirer*. June 6, 1876.

Mander, Raymond and Joe Mitchenson. *The Lost Theatres of London.* Taplinger Publishing Co., 1968.

"Mechanic's Institution." *Hampshire Advertiser.* May 14, 1836.

"Menagerie, Museum and Circus." *Brooklyn Eagle*. Oct. 28, 1876.

"Mexico's Great Sensation, Miss Nora Hildebrandt." *New York Clipper*. March 22, 1884.

"Minstrel, Variety and Circus." *New York Clipper*. July 31, 1886.

"Missing Friend." *The South Australian Police Gazette*. December 17, 1873.

"Missouri." *New York Clipper*. January 3, 1883.

*Mogg's New Picture of London and Visitor's Guide to it Sights.* 1844. https:// www.victorianlondon.org/entertainment/surreyzoologicalgardens.htm.

"Multiple News Items." *Idaho Weekly Avalanche*. January 01, 1876.

"Museum." *The Independent*. April 21, 1890.

"Musicians Wanted Immediately." *New York Clipper*. July 21, 1883.

Mylonakis, Leonidas. "Transnational Piracy in the Eastern Mediterranean, 1821-1897." PhD dissertation. University of California San Diego, 2018.

"Nana Sahib." *Encyclopedia Britannica*. https://www.britannica.com/ biography/Nana-Sahib.

"The Nathans, A Circus Family." *Stuart Thayer's American Circus Anthology*. ed. William Slout, Last modified 2005. http://classic.circushistory.org/ Thayer/Thayer3b.htm.

"Nathans and Co., Circus Yesterday Afternoon and Night." *Norfolk Landmark*. July 24, 1883.

*Nathans and Co. Herald*. CWi 6498 A-B, Circus World Museum Library, Wisconsin Historical Society.

"Nathans & Co., Items." *New York Clipper*. March 3, 1883.

"Needle Pricks." *Boston Post*. March 18, 1894.

"The New Dime Museum." *Evening Star*. December 23, 1882.

"New Dime Museum." *Sunday Herald and Weekly National Intelligencer*. January 21, 1883.

"New Museum." *New York Clipper*. February 25, 1882.

New South Wales, Australia, Convict Indents, 1788–1842. ancestry.com.

New York, U.S., Arriving Passenger and Crew Lists (including Castle Garden and Ellis Island), 1820–1957. Ancestry.com.

"New Zealand." *Leicester Chronicle or Commercial and Leicestershire Mercury*. April 18, 1857.

"Nickelodeon." *Boston Globe*. January 3, 1899.

"Ninth and Arch Museum." *Philadelphia Inquirer*. December 24, 1889.

"A Novel Picture Gallery." *Utica Morning Herald and Daily Gazette*. June 2, 1876.

Norris, Aíne. "The Tenacious Women of Iron Jaw." *Bandwagon* 61, No. 3 (2021): 29.

O'Connell, James. *Life and Adventures of James F. O'Connell, the Tattooed Man, During a Residence of Eleven Years in New Holland and the Caroline Islands*. W. Applegate, Painter, 1845.

Odell, George C. D. *Annals of the New York Stage*. AMS Press, 1970.

"Old-Time Remedy Ruled Off Market," *St. Joseph News-Press*, Oct. 8, 1980.

"An Old Trick of His." *New York Times*. April 4, 1886.

Olson, Amy. "A Brief History of Tattoos." Wellcome Collection, April 13, 2010, https://wellcomecollection.org/stories/a-brief-history-of-tattoos.

O'Nan, Stewart. *The Circus Fire: A True Story of an American Tragedy*. First Anchor Books, 2001.

"Only Big Show Coming: A Mighty Mammoth Monarch and Gigantic Colossus." *Bandwagon*, Jan/Feb 1989: 44-45.

"The Only Tattooed Man Now in This Country." *New York Clipper*. January 14, 1882.

Osterud, Amelia Klem. *The Tattooed Lady: A History*. Taylor Trade, 2014.

Osterud, Amelia Klem. "The True Life and Adventures of Tattooed Performers." In *Tattoo Histories: Transcultural Perspectives on the Narratives, Practices, and Representations of Tattooing*, ed. Sinah Theres Kloß. Routledge, 2020.

Ottenheimer, Martin. *Forbidden Relatives: The American Myth of Cousin Marriage*. University of Illinois Press, 1996.

"The Palace Museum." *St. Louis Globe-Democrat*. April 5, 1886.

"Panic at a Circus." *Boston Daily Advertiser*. June 6, 1883.

"The Panic at the Circus Tuesday Night – Nobody Seriously Injured." *Norfolk Virginian*. July 26, 1883.

*Passport Applications, 1795-1905*. National Archives and Records Administration, Washington D.C.

Peacock, Shane. *The Great Farini: The High-Wire Life of William Hunt*. Viking/Penguin Books, 1995.

"People and Things." *Inter Ocean*. June 3, 1876.

"Phineas T. Barnum, An Interesting Chat with the Proprietor of 'The Greatest Show on Earth'." *Inter Ocean*. July 30, 1878.

"Popular Holidays." *Eddowes' Salopian Journal*. June 6, 1877.

"Präuschers Panoptikum." Wein Geschichte Wiki. https://www.geschichtewiki.wien.gv.at/Pr%C3%A4uschers_Panoptikum.

Preston, Diana and Preston, Michael. *A Pirate of Exquisite Mind: Explorer, Naturalist, and Buccaneer, The Life of William Dampier*. Walker and Co., 2004.

"The Pretended Zulu Princess." *Watertown News*. July 25, 1883.

Price, Pattie. "The Decline and Fall of the Old Shrewsbury Show." *Victorian Shrewsbury: Studies in the History of a County Town*. ed. Barrie Trinder. Shropshire Libraries, 1984.

"Professionals' Bureau." *New York Clipper*. November 3, 1883.

"P. T. Barnum at Gilmore's Garden." Tibbals Circus Collection, The John and Mable Ringling Museum of Art, Sarasota, Florida.

"P. T. Barnum and the Glorious Centennial Fourth of July in Lowell," *Lowell Daily Citizen,* June 24, 1876.

"P. T. Barnum's Greatest Show on Earth." *Bangor Daily Whig and Courier*. July 27, 1876.

"P. T. Barnum's New and Only Greatest Show on Earth." *Evening Herald*. May 14, 1877.

"P. T. Barnum's New and Only Greatest Show on Earth." *Harper's Weekly*. May 26, 1877.

"P. T. Barnum's New and Greatest Show on Earth is Coming on Three Monster Special Trains." *Aurora*. May 19, 1876.

"P. T. Barnum's Own and Only Greatest Show on Earth." *Daily Republican*. Oct. 8, 1879.

"P. T. Barnum's Own and Only Greatest Show on Earth." *Fayette County Herald*. August 15, 1878.

"P. T. Barnum's Show." *New York Clipper*. April 21, 1877.

"Purchasing Power Today of a US Dollar Transaction in the Past." MeasuringWorth. https://www.measuringworth.com/calculators/ppowerus/.

Quirk, John. *The Manx Giant: The Amazing Story of Arthur Caley* (Manx Heritage Foundation, 2009.)

"Eine Redaction als Schaubude." *Neue Freie Presse*. January 29, 1872.

Reiss, Benjamin. *The Showman and the Slave: Race, Death, and Memory in Barnum's America*. Harvard University Press, 2001.

Reiter, Jon. *These Old Blue Arms: The Life and Work of Amund Dietzel*. Solid State Publishing, 2010.

Riesenberg, Saul. "The Tattooed Irishman." *Smithsonian Journal of History* 3, No. 1, (1968): 1-17.

Rivlin, Helene Anne B. "Muḥammad Alī." *Encyclopedia Britannica*. https://www.britannica.com/biography/Muhammad-Ali-pasha-and-viceroy-of-Egypt.

Robbins, Frank A. "The Barnum Show in 1876." *Billboard* 22, No. 12, March 19, 1910. 23.

Robertson, Craig. *The Passport in America: The History of a Document*. Oxford University Press, 2012.

*Route Book of P. T. Barnum's Greatest Show on Earth and The Great London Circus Consolidation 1885*. http://classic.circushistory.org/History/PTB1885.htm.

*Route Book, Season of 1877, P. T. Barnum's New and Greatest Show on Earth*. Circus Historical Society. Last modified 2005. https://classic.circushistory.org/History/PTB1877.htm

*Route Book, Season of 1879, P. T. Barnum's New and Greatest Show on Earth*. Circus Historical Society. Last modified 2005. https://classic.circushistory.org/History/PTB1879.htm.

*Route Book, Season of 1880, P. T. Barnum's Greatest Show on Earth*. Circus Historical Society. Last modified 2005. https://classic.circushistory.org/History/PTB1880.htm.

"Royal Aquarium, England's Palace of Amusement." *Pall Mall Gazette*. March 8, 1882.

"Royal Aquarium." *The Sportsman*. April 1, 1884.

Rutherford, John. *An Account of the Capture of the Ship Agnes, Commanded by Capt. Coffin; The Murder of The Captain and Eight of Her Crew by the Natives of New Zealand in 1816.* C. Malley, Horse Market, 1829.

Rutherford, John. *An Account of the Capture of the Ship Agnes, Commanded by Capt. Coffin; The Murder of The Captain and Eight of Her Crew by the Natives of New Zealand in 1816.* C. Malley, 1829.

*Salmagundi Ledger.* Manuscripts. PT Barnum Research Collection, Bridgeport History Center, https://archives.lib.uconn.edu/node/24215.

Samadelli, Marco, Marcello Melis, Matteo Miccoli, Eduard Egarter Vigl, and Albert R. Zink. "Complete Mapping of the Tattoos of the 5300-year-old Tyrolean Iceman *Journal of Cultural Heritage* 16 (2015): 753-758.

Sands, John. "Sullivan and the Royal Aquarium." *The Gilbert and Sullivan Archive.* Last modified August 30, 2011, *https*://www.gsarchive.net/articles/sull_aquarium/index.html.

Saxon, A. H. *PT Barnum: The Legend and the Man.* Columbia University Press, 1989).

Schaeffer, Katherine and Shradha Dinesh, "32% of Americans Have a Tattoo," *Pew Research Center.* August 15, 2023. https://pewrsr.ch/3QFg5w1.

Schaeffer, Katherine and Shradha Dinesh. "32% of Americans Have a Tattoo." *Pew Research Center.* August 15, 2023. https://pewrsr.ch/3QFg5w1.

Schémann, JF, S. Bakayoko, and S. Coulibaly. "Traditional Couching Is Not an Effective Alternative Procedure for Cataract Surgery in Mali." *Ophthalmic Epidemiology* 7, no. 4 (December 2000): 271-283.

Schoenberger, Nicholas. *Inking Identity: Tattoo Design and the Emergence of an American Industry, 1875-1930.* Thesis, University of Delaware. Summer 2005.

"See Captain Costentenus." *Philadelphia Times.* December 24, 1886.

*Selected Letters of PT Barnum.* edited by A. H. Saxon. Columbia Press, 1983.

"Sektionen for Anatomi og Fysiologi," *Forhandlinger ved de Skandinaviske Naturforskeres* 11 (1873): 497.

"The Sensation of the Day" *Rock Island Argus.* June 9, 1880.

"Shearman, Police to Provincial Secretary – inquiry being made for whereabouts of Barnet Burns, interpreter. Filed with 1847 (Colonial Secretary), 1847.1 to 1847.3–17 November 1873." Reference: CAAR 19936 CH287/CP 139 ICPS 1902/1873. Te Rua Mahara o te Kāwanatanga. Archives New Zealand.

"Sheriff's Sale." *Garnett Republican-Plaindealer.* December 7, 1883.

"Sheriff's Sale." *Garnett Republican-Plaindealer.* December 8, 1883.

"Sheriff's Sale." *Garnett Republican-Plaindealer*. October 12, 1883.

"Short Stops." *Marion County Herald*. September 21, 1883

"Show Stranded." *Evening News*. September 17, 1883.

"Shows and Showmen of Coney Island." *New York Clipper*. July 23, 1881.

Sides, Hampton. "The Polynesian 'Prince' Who Took 18th-Century England by Storm." *Smithsonian Magazine,* September 13, 2021. https://www.smithsonianmag.com/history/polynesian-prince-who-took-18th-century-england-storm-180978618/.

The Simms Initiatives, University of South Carolina Libraries, 2011, https://scholarcommons.sc.edu/digipro/5.

"Shan." *Encyclopedia Britannica*. https://www.britannica.com/topic/Shan.

Sloan, Kim. *A New World: England's First View of America*. The University of North Carolina Press, 2007.

Slout, William. *Olympians of the Sawdust Circle: A Biographical Dictionary of the Nineteenth Century American Circus.* Last modified 2005. https://www.classic.circushistory.org/Olympians/OlympiansA.htm.

Slout, William. *A Royal Coupling: The Historic Marriage of Barnum and Bailey* (Emeritus Enterprise: California, 2000): 139.

"Some Legal Decisions." *Waco Daily Examiner*. May 26, 1882.

"Spectables du 8 Juiilet." *Gil Blas* (Paris). July 9, 1889.

"Sporting Notes." *Sporting Times*. November 26, 1881.

"St. Louis Dime Museum." *St. Louis Post-Dispatch*. September 3, 1884.

"St. Patrick's Evening." *Boston Post*. March 16, 1837.

"State and Vicinity." *Buffalo Evening Telegraph*. June 26, 1883.

"Star State Circus" *Times-Picayune*, October 10, 1852.

"The Stolen Fat Woman." *Nebraska State Journal*. October 5, 1895.

"Street Robbery by a New-Zealand Chieftain." *Lancaster Gazette*. May 24, 1828.

Straus, Eugene and Alex Straus. *Medical Marvels: The 100 Greatest Advances in Medicine*. Prometheus Books, 2006.

Tanabe, Rosie. "Aspasia." *New World Encyclopedia*. Last modified November 8, 2021. https://www.newworldencyclopedia.org/p/index.php?title=Aspasia&oldid=1060004.

Tannenbaum, Nicola. "Tattoos: Invulnerability and Power in Shan Cosmology." *American Ethnologist* 14, no. 4 (1987): 693-711.

"Der Tätowirte Griechenfürst." Berliner Börsenzeitung. October 10, 1882.

"Der Tätowirte." *Baden Bezirks-Blatt* (Austria). April 14, 1888.

"Ein Tätowirter. *Baden Bezirks-Blatt* (Austria), March 13, 1888.

"Ein Tätowirter." *Innsbrucker Nachrichten* (Austria). March 26, 1887.

"Der Tätowirte." *Neue Freie Presse* (Vienna, Austria). April 23, 1887.

 "Ein Tätowirter." *Neues Wiener Tagblatt* (Austria). March 24, 1887.

"Tattooed From Head To Foot." *British Medical Journal* 2, No. 566 (Nov. 4, 1871): 532.

 "The Tattooed Greek Nobleman, to the Editor of the Era." *Era*. December 3, 1881.

"The Tattooed Greek Nobleman, to the Editor of the Era." *Era*. December 10, 1881.

"The Tattooed Greek Nobleman." *Era*. December 3, 1881.

"The Tattooed Greek Nobleman." *Era*. December 17, 1881.

"The Tattooed Man." *Boston Post*. February 16, 1836.

"A Tattooed Man and a Spotted Boy." *Morning Post*. November 22, 1881.

 "The Tattooed Man: Barnum's Great Contribution to History and Ethnology." *St. Louis Globe-Democrat*. August 24, 1877.

"The Tattooed Nobleman: A Full Description of the Wonder." *Bangor Daily Whig & Courier*. July 25, 1876.

"The Tattooed Woman." *New York Times*. March 19, 1882.

"Tattooing." *Daily Union-Leader*. June 17, 1881.

 "Tattooing: An Interesting Review Suggested by the Tichborne Case." *The Inter Ocean*. April 20, 1872.

"Tattooing in New York," *New York Times* January 16, 1876.

"Telegraphic Notes." *Evening Telegraph*. June 23, 1883.

"10 Cents Admits All." *Rocky Mountain News*. March 16, 1890.

Terrell, Jennifer. "Notes and Documents: Joseph Kabris and His Notes on the Marquesas." *Journal of Pacific History*. 17 No. 2 (1982): 101-112.

Thayer, Stuart. *Annals of the American Circus, 1793-1860*. Dauven and Thayer, 2000.

Thayer, Stuart. "Bad Press, Bad Crowds, Circus Historical Society. Last modified 2005. https://classic.circushistory.org/Thayer/Thayer.htm.

Thayer, Stuart. "The Flatfoot Party and the Zoological Institute." Circus Historical Society. Last modified 2005. https://classic.circushistory.org/Thayer/Thayer2c.htm.

Thayer, Stuart. "Prelude to Barnum: The Coup and Castello Circus of 1870." *Bandwagon*, July-August 1970.

Thayer, Stuart. "The Nathans, A Circus Family." *Bandwagon* 29, No. 2 (March-April 1985): 24-28.

Thayer, Stuart and William L. Slout. *Grand Entrée: The Birth of the Greatest Show on Earth 1870-1875*. The Borgo Press: 1998.

"Théatre des Folies-Bergére, L'Homme Tatoué." *L'Album Theatral*. September 22, 1874.

"'Time Cannot Wither...'" *Portland Daily Press*. June 8, 1878.

"The Trade in Tattooing." *Colfax Chronicle*. June 7, 1902.

"Trial," Manchester Courier and Lancashire General Advertiser, Sat. July 28, 1828.

"The Troubles of the Tattooed Greek." *Cincinnati Star*. December 19, 1879.

*Twenty-Eighth Annual Report of the Bureau of Statistics of Labor*. Wright and Potter Printing Co., 1898.

"Two Days." *Poughkeepsie Eagle-News*. May 23, 1881.

"Union-Hall," *Morning Chronicle*, July 23, 1835.

"Unterhaltungen." *Der Deutsche Correspondent*. May 4, 1881.

*U.S., Passport Applications, 1795-1925,* National Archives and Records Administration. Ancestry.com.

"Various Items." *Lowell Daily Citizen*. August 24, 1877.

"Variety, Minstrel, and Circus." *New York Clipper*. February 6, 1892.

Virchow, Rudolf. "Uber den Tattowirten Sulioten Costanti." *Zeitschrift für Ethnologie* 4, (1872): 201-202.

"W. C. Coup's New Monster Shows." *New York Clipper*. April 16, 1881.

Walker, John C. *Health and Wellness in 19th Century America*. Greenwood, 2014.

"Wait for Nothing – The BIG Show is Here!" *Cairo Bulletin*, October 19, 1881.

"Wanted for Nathans & Co.'s Show." *New York Clipper*. June 30, 1883.

"Wanted." *New York Clipper*. February 19, 1876.

Ward, Steve. *Opulence and Ostentation: Building the Circus*. Modern Vaudeville Press, 2023.

"Weeping Willow Tattooed In Side." *Buffalo News*. September 27, 1908.

"Westminster Aquarium." *Era*. November 26, 1881.

"When Barnum Comes." *Galveston News*. October 24, 1880.

"When Barnum Comes." *Weekly Oskaloosa Herald*. July 8, 1880.

"Where Clocks and Watches are Made." *Evening Star*. July 22, 1879.

White, Richard. *Railroaded: The Transcontinentals and the Making of Modern America*. Norton, 2011).

"Will Exhibit at Mt. Carmel." *Mount Carmel Register*. August 9, 1883.

"William E. Sinclair, 1851-1892," *Green-Wood Cemetery Burial and Vital Records: 1840-1937*. https://www.green-wood.com/burial-and-vital-records/.

Williams, L. Pearce. "Hermann von Helmholtz." *Encyclopedia Britannica*. https://www.britannica.com/biography/Hermann-von-Helmholtz.

Wimsatt, Mary Ann. "Native Humor in Simms's Fiction and Drama." *Studies in American Humor* 3, No. 3, (1977): 158-165.

"The Wonderful Leopard Boy." *Nebraska State Journal*. Sept. 25, 1877.

Woodward, Irene. *Facts Related to Irene Woodward, The Tattooed Lady*. New York Popular Publishing Company, 1882.

Woolf, John. *The Wonders: The Extraordinary Performers Who Transformed the Victorian Age*. Pegasus Books, 2019.

"Worth More Alive Than When Stuffed." *Cincinnati Enquirer*. June 8, 1878. *Boston Globe*. February 12, 1877.

Wright, Jr., James R. "How the Public Autopsy of a Slave Joice Heth Launched P.T. Barnum's Career as the Greatest Showman on Earth." *Clinical Anatomy* 31 (7): 956-965.

Yadon, W. Gordon. "Dan Castello." *The Banner Line*. March 15, 1968. Circus World Museum Library, Wisconsin Historical Society.

"Yakub Beg." *Encyclopedia Britannica*. https://www.britannica.com/biography/Yakub-Beg.

Yoe, Shway [Sir George Scott]. *The Burman: His Life and Notions*. McMillan and Co., 1896.

Zimmer, Ben. "Where Did the Supreme Court Get Its Parade of Horribles?" *Boston Globe*. July 1, 2012

# INDEX

# F

# G

# H

# W

# Y

# Z

# OTHER BOOKS BY MODERN VAUDEVILLE PRESS

## *Juggling: Or How to Become a Juggler (annotated edition)*

Rupert Ingalese, annotated by Thom Wall
ISBN – 978-1733971201
99 pages
**MSRP: $15 USD**

The fully annotated edition of Rupert Ingalese's 1921 "how to juggle" manual. This book covers basic juggling technique, tricks with hats and canes, practice methodology, and more. Ingalese's manuscript provides an interesting look at the state of juggling pedagogy in Britain's music hall era. Annotations by juggler and circus researcher Thom Wall bring insight and context to Ingalese's descriptions and instructions.

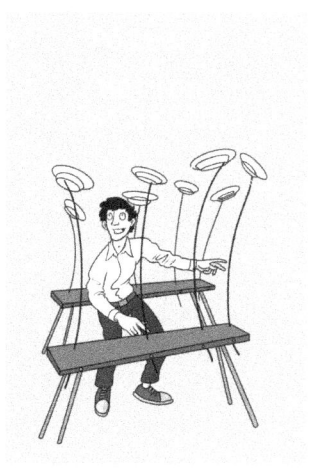

## *Pottery in Motion*

Sam Veale
ISBN – 978-1733971232
71 pages
**MSRP: $15 USD**

British juggler Sam Veale's *Pottery in Motion* is the first of its kind - a straightforward book that provides aspiring plate spinners both the specifics of the props (such as plates, sticks, and rack) and comprehensive instruction on the skill of plate spinning itself. This small but detail-packed guide appeals to individuals looking to learn plate spinning and provides the knowledge to take it to a performance-ready level, just add practice.

# Juggling: From Antiquity to the Middle Ages

Thom Wall
ISBN – 978-0578410845
e-book ISBN – 978-0578410852
129 pages
**MSRP: $25 USD**

As with dance, so with juggling—the moment that the performer finishes the routine, their act ceases to exist beyond the memory of the audience. There is no permanent record of what transpired, so studying the ancient roots of juggling is fraught with difficulty. Using the records that do exist, juggling appears to have emerged around the world in cultures independent of one another in the ancient past. Paintings in Egypt from 2000 BCE show jugglers engaged in performance. Stories from the island nation of Tonga place juggling's creation with their goddess of the underworld—a figure who has guarded a cave since time immemorial. Juggling games and rituals are pervasive in isolated Inuit cultures in northern Canada and Greenland. Though the earliest representation of juggling is 4,000 years old, the practice is surely much older—in the same way that humans were doubtlessly singing and dancing long before the first bone flute was created.

This book is an attempt to catalogue this tangible history of juggling in human culture. It is the story of juggling, represented in art and writing from around the world, across time. Although much has been written about modern jugglers–specific performers, their props, and their routines–little has been said about those who first developed the craft. As juggling enters a golden age in the internet era, *Juggling: From Antiquity to the Middle Ages* offers a look into the past—to the origins of our art form.

## Spanish Edition:

### Malabares - desde la Antigüedad hasta la Edad Media: la historia olvidada de lanzar y cachar

Thom Wall, et. al.
ISBN – 978-1733971263
e-book ISBN – 978-1958604007
179 pages
**MSRP: $25 USD**

*Malabares - desde Antigüedad hasta la Edad Media*, es un divertido viaje por países, por épocas. Desde el Antiguo Egipto y sus ya famosas malabaristas profesionales de la tumba nº 15 de Beni Hasan, a los juegos para niñas de la isla de Tonga y otras zonas del Pacífico Sur; pasando por los edictos del rey Alfonso X de Castilla sobre la regulación de los juglares o los antipodistas aztecas actuando ante el Papa Clemente VII en el siglo XVI. También reserva un espacio al final del libro para, aprovechando su faceta de lingüista, realizar unas reflexiones acerca de la propia definición de la palabra "juggling"[malabarismo] a lo largo del tiempo y sus orígenes. Es, por tanto, un libro ideal no solo para malabaristas o cirqueros, sino para cualquiera con curiosidad sobre la historia, en especial de aquellos hechos que en ocasiones pasan más desapercibidos en los textos cotidianos.

A través de este libro aprendemos sobre leyendas y juegos antiguos, fantaseamos con grandes artistas y actuaciones que nunca podremos ver y que nos hacen dudar sobre esa tan manida sentencia que a veces afirma "esto nunca se ha hecho antes".
- *Malabares en su Tinta*

# Juggling: What It Is and How to Do It

Thom Wall, et. al.
ISBN – 978-1-7339712-5-6
e-book ISBN – 978-1-7339712-8-7
224 pages
**MSRP: $25 USD**

*Juggling: What It Is and How to Do It* teaches learners of all ages how to juggle – one of the world's oldest artforms. With a kind demeanor, humor, and enthusiasm, this authoritative manual explains the process of juggling through four different modalities, bolstered by the latest physical education research.

*Juggling* is an accessible primer that a middle-schooler can hit the ground running with, or that families can enjoy together. The result of six years of work by 2021 International Jugglers' Association *Excellence in Education* award winner and former Cirque du Soleil juggler Thom Wall and featuring guest chapters by some of today's juggling masters, *Juggling* provides great content for even the most serious adult learner.

# Book plus Juggling Kit!
### Includes juggling balls by Alchemy Juggling
**MSRP: $60 USD**

This exclusive kit makes the perfect gift for any aspiring juggler. Includes one copy of *Juggling: What It Is and How to Do It* and three professional-grade beanbags.

Beanbag specs: 90g ea., approx. 2.75" diameter. Machine washable / dryable. Made in USA.

# *Body Talk: Basic Mime*

Mario Diamond
ISBN – 978-1733971218
73 pages
**MSRP: $15 USD**

*Body Talk: Basic Mime* covers the fundamental skills of mime in an easily accessible workbook format. Diamond brings over 40 years of teaching and performance experience to *Body Talk*, which includes rich photography illustrating various mime techniques.

"[*Body Talk: Basic Mime*] should be required reading for any theater participant looking to incorporate elements of mime into their routines." - *Midwest Book Review*

# *French Edition: Corps Expressif: Base du Mime*

Mario Diamond
ISBN – 978-1958604984
68 pages
**MSRP: $15 USD**

Mario a écrit un tour de force sur l'art du mime. Ce livre est éloquent et concis... riche en outils pour les élèves comme pour les professeurs, facile à comprendre et rempli d'exercices pratiques. Ce livre est brodé de segments historiques et anecdotiques qui en font un manuscrit amusant, plein d'observations charmantes et bouffonnes qui font de Mario un artiste phénoménal, prodigue de la caractéristique définitive du mime, la personnalité.

## Circus Games (v1.1)

Compiled by Lucy Little & the American Youth Circus Organization (AYCO)
ISBN – 9781733971225
e-book ISBN – 978-1-958604-01-4
124 pages
**MSRP: $15 USD**

With over 100 games organized for optimal use in cooperative movement based settings, this is a must have for every circus school, teaching artist, and arts education program! Games are organized by age, number of participants, energy level, and social/emotional learning outcome, and also includes special notes for working with a variety of populations that may require adaptation or modifications to each game. Find more info about the project here:
https://www.americancircuseducators.org/gamesproject/

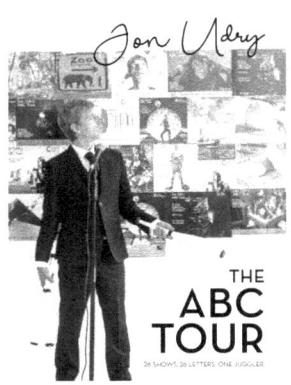

## The ABC Tour

Jon Udry
ISBN – 978-0578410852
**MSRP: $25 USD**

Ever felt like a challenge? For juggler and comedian, Jon Udry, the ABC Tour — 26 letters, 26 shows — seems the perfect way to shake things up. What started as a silly idea he believed would take two to three months to complete, ended up being a mammoth three year project that included some of the toughest, most brutal and most enjoyable performances of his life. From attempting to juggle while wearing roller skates and the unexpected discoveries of performing at a Naturist's Resort, to the challenges that came with working in rainforest conditions covered in ants or in snowy conditions at -10°C, Jon tells the full story from A to Z.

# *Circus Training Journal*

Thom Wall & Rebecca Starr,
Consultant editor: Sarah Baker
ISBN – 978-1-7339712-9-4
9×6" paperback
380 pages
**MSRP: $20 USD**

What's measured is managed! The *Circus Training Journal* is the result of a year of collaboration between Thom Wall and Rebecca Starr, aerial coach. This undated journal, spanning three months of daily training, tracks workouts, nutrition, goal-setting, and more. Heavyweight paper optimized for ballpoint and pencil.

# *Artistes of Colour*

Steve Ward, PhD
ISBN – 978-1-7339712-7-0
e-book ISBN – 978-1-958604-99-1
317 pages
**MSRP: $25 USD**

In a society that places an increasing value in ethnic diversity and cultural identity, the contribution that performers from a variety of ethnic backgrounds made to the development of the circus in the nineteenth century is often dismissed and largely forgotten. Using contemporary records and images, *Artistes of Colour* explores the wealth and depth of talented black and other performers of colour, and their contributions to the success of the nineteenth century circus. Ward draws iconic figures from the margins of history and gives them the recognition they deserve. Long-listed for the American Society for Theatre Research 2022 Book Award.

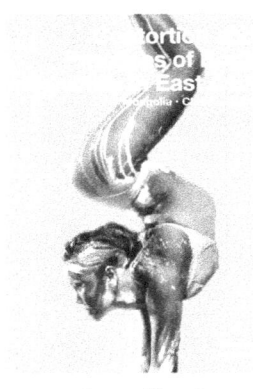

## *Contortion and Practices of Body Flexibility in East Asia - Mongolia, China, Japan*

Mariam Ala-Rashi
ISBN – 978-1-958604-04-5
e-book ISBN – 978-1-958604-06-9
464 pages
**MSRP: $25 USD**

A collection of three monographs: *China's Bending Bodies: Contortionists and Politics in China*; *Mongolian Contortion: An Ethnographic Inquiry*; and *The Kakubei Jishi: The Rise, Fall, and Restoration of a Japanese Folk Performing Art.*

This compendium examines contortion and practices of body flexibility in East Asia. It explores the performance art forms Chinese contortion, Mongolian contortion and the Kakubei Jishi lion dance of the Niigata prefecture in Japan which utilizes body flexibility. It discusses the investigation of the history and genesis of these art forms and how they developed in various political and social dynamics. This work further offers vast knowledge about crucial elements such as the artist's training processes, their training environment, the development of aesthetics, symbolism in costuming and body movements, religious themes, mythology and natural phenomena, and costume designs. This compendium includes data from a wide range of literature, material evidence, oral history, current media reports, and considers recent work in anthropology, archaeology, and political history. It offers the interested reader, the scholar, the contortionist and contortion practitioner a substantial treatise about contortionism and practices of body flexibility.

### *The Contemporary Circus Handbook: A guide to creating, funding, producing, organizing and touring shows for the 21st century*

Eric Bates
ISBN – 978-1-958604-03-8
e-book ISBN – 978-1-958604-18-2
374 pages
**MSRP: $25 USD**

*The Contemporary Circus Handbook* contains interviews with more than 25 professionals, from Gypsy Snider of the celebrated contemporary circus company The Seven Fingers to Lydia Bouchard of La Resistance about their work in the performing arts world. Combining Eric Bates' (Cie Barcode, Cirque du Soleil, et. al.) hard won wisdom as well as tips and insights from his contemporaries, what emerges is an invaluable blueprint of how to progress from the seed of an idea for a show to the full touring timeline. The scope of the book is wide but deeply hands-on, diving into practical details on how to find an agent, start your own company, secure funding and build your niche brand. *The Contemporary Circus Handbook* truly is a unique offering to the circus world, full of insider tips and years of accumulated knowledge from industry insiders.

# *Opulence & Ostentation*

Steve Ward, PhD
ISBN – 978-1-958604-02-1
e-book ISBN – 978-1-958604-05-2
247 pages
**MSRP: $25 USD**

Since the foundation of 'modern' circus in the 18th century, the circus has been presented in defined spaces. Initially, performances were given in the open air and, over a period of time, these spaces first became enclosed and then later roofed. In the 19th century, many permanent stone-built buildings were erected solely for presenting circus. This phenomenon spread from the UK across Europe and beyond, creating a style of circus architecture that has never been repeated. This book examines what caused these buildings to be constructed and their design and architectur, including some still being used for circus performances today. The book also looks at the developments of contemporary circus architecture and raise questions as to the future of the circus building.

# *Cleverer Than God*

CLEVERER
THAN
GOD

Erik Åberg
ISBN – 978-1958604113
116 pages
**MSRP: $25 USD**

ERIK ÅBERG

*Cleverer Than God* is a book that tells the story of Paul Cinquevalli, a juggler who rose from the Circus circuit of the 1880s, to attain celebrity status in the British Music Hall and American vaudeville stages until the outbreak of WWI. Through quotes by Cinquevalli himself, woven together with excerpts from journalists and writers of his era, the book tells his story as poignant fragments, capturing the essence of Cinquevalli's triumphs, defining moments, and heart-rending tragedies.

# The Juggler's Badge Book

Author: Benjamin Domask-Ruh
Editors: Thayer Slichter, Afton Benson
Illustrators: Thayer Slichter and Louis Skaradek
ISBN – 978-1-958604-19-9
**MSRP: $25 USD**

Introducing *The Juggler's Badge Book*, the ultimate companion for aspiring jugglers! Track your progress, unlock achievements, and earn badges as you learn the art of juggling. With its engaging format and rewarding sticker system, *The Juggler's Badge Book* makes learning to juggle an exciting and fulfilling adventure. Whether you're a beginner or a seasoned juggler, let *The Juggler's Badge Book* be your guide to skillful juggling and a collection of well-earned accomplishments. Start achieving your juggling journey today with this activity book from the Youth Juggling Academy, a program of the International Jugglers' Association!

Published in collaboration between the
International Jugglers' Association and Modern Vaudeville Press.

## By Royal Command: Barnum in Europe

Steve Ward, PhD
ISBN – 978-1-958604-26-7
e-book ISBN – 978-1-958604-27-4
240 pages
**MSRP: $25 USD**

On a cold February day in 1844, a small group of travellers disembarked their ship in Liverpool, England. Amongst them was the American showman P. T. Barnum and his protégé Charles S. Stratton, known as General Tom Thumb. This marked the beginning of a three-year long tour of the United Kingdom and continental Europe that would bring both Barnum and Stratton international fame and fortune.

*By Royal Command* charts the progress of this tour, with all its triumphs and disasters, and examines the impact Barnum and Tom Thumb had on social attitudes towards the 'exotic'.

## Behind the Big Top: A Photo Exploration of Circus Flora 2024

Ryan Stanley
ISBN – 978-1-958604-29-8
**MSRP: $25 USD**

Ryan Stanley set out to photograph Circus Flora from start to finish, capturing its unique essence. Meet fantastic performers, crew members, and volunteers who created a sense of community that felt like family. The images in this book showcase the magical moments of the circus along with the behind-the-scenes work that brings it to life.

After dedicating countless hours to this project, Stanley gained a new appreciation for Circus Flora and the Circus Arts. Join him for a behind-the-scenes look at Circus Flora 2024 - Start to Finish.

# An International Circus Affair:
### How a Nanjing Acrobat in San Francisco Changed American Circus Forever

Jeff Raz
ISBN – 978-1-958604-24-3
e-book ISBN – 978-1-958604-25-0
311 pages
**MSRP: $25 USD**

In 1989, the Artistic Director of a San Francisco circus, Judy Finelli, met briefly with Lu Yi, the Director of the Nanjing Acrobatic Troupe, in upstate New York. It was, as Judy now calls it, "a moment that changed circus forever." Lu Yi would move to San Francisco to teach the 2000-year-old art of Chinese acrobatics.

This book looks at the 20 years after Lu Yi's arrival and how his acrobatic training and his students' prowess changed San Francisco and Nanjing, as well as circuses around the world.

www.ingramcontent.com/pod-product-compliance
Lightning Source LLC
Chambersburg PA
CBHW051254120626
46547CB00014B/1942